bangtan
REMIXED

EDITED BY

Patty Ahn, Michelle Cho,

Vernadette Vicuña Gonzalez,

Rani Neutill, Mimi Thi Nguyen,

and Yutian Wong

bangtan REMIXED

A Critical BTS Reader

DUKE UNIVERSITY PRESS   DURHAM AND LONDON   2024

© 2024 DUKE UNIVERSITY PRESS
Printed in the United States of America on acid-free paper ∞
Project Editor: Michael Trudeau
Designed by Matthew Tauch
Typeset in Alegreya Sans by Westchester Publishing Services

Library of Congress Cataloging-in-Publication Data
Names: Ahn, Patty, [date] editor. | Cho, Michelle, [date] editor. | Gonzalez,
Vernadette Vicuña, [date] editor. | Neutill, Rani, [date] editor. | Nguyen,
Mimi Thi, [date] editor. | Wong, Yutian, [date] editor.
Title: Bangtan remixed: a critical BTS reader / edited by Patty Ahn,
Michelle Cho, Vernadette Vicuña Gonzalez, Rani Neutill, Mimi Thi Nguyen,
and Yutian Wong.
Description: Durham: Duke University Press, 2024. | Includes bibliographical
references and index.
Identifiers: LCCN 2023047385 (print)
LCCN 2023047386 (ebook)
ISBN 9781478030621 (paperback)
ISBN 9781478026389 (hardcover)
ISBN 9781478059615 (ebook)
Subjects: LCSH: BTS (Musical group) | Rock musicians—Korea (South) |
Boy bands—Korea (South) | Popular music—Korea (South)—History and
criticism. | Popular culture—Korea (South)—History—21st century. | K-Pop
(Subculture) | BISAC: MUSIC / Genres & Styles / International | MUSIC / Genres
& Styles / Pop Vocal
Classification: LCC ML421.B79 B36 2024 (print) | LCC ML421.B79 (ebook) |
DDC 782.4216/3095195—DC23/ENG/20240429
LC record available at https://lccn.loc.gov/2023047385
LC ebook record available at https://lccn.loc.gov/2023047386

Cover art: Drawing by Ameena Fareeda. Courtesy of the artist.

for the lonely whales
and outcast planets

CONTENTS

NOTE ON TERMINOLOGY
AND ROMANIZATION

Throughout the book, "BTS" is treated as both a singular and plural noun, as is common in fan and media discourse of the phenomenon (e.g., "BTS *is* a South Korean band"; "BTS's songs reflect *their* exploration of a wide range of topics").

ARMY refers to both a singular fan and the collective fandom. Where pluralized as a group of individuals, the use of ARMYs may be preferred by individual authors.

Hangeul words have been romanized in multiple ways. Proper nouns such as names follow no standard romanization system and are presented in the ways they have been spelled on albums or other published work that circulate in print and online (e.g., Seo Taiji, Shin Joong-hyun, Kim Namjoon). In other cases, the Revised Romanization system has been chosen over the McCune-Reischauer Romanization system for the former's ease of use and jettisoning of typographically complicated diacritical marks. In some cases, authors have chosen to include Hangeul text in lieu of romanization.

ACKNOWLEDGMENTS

The coeditors would like to acknowledge Frances Gateward, organizer of BTS: A Global Interdisciplinary Conference II in 2021 at California State University, Northridge, and an early supporter of the book. We are glad for the opportunities to present on *Bangtan Remixed* at BTS: A Global Interdisciplinary Conference III in 2022 in Seoul, and at the 2023 annual meeting of the Association for Asian American Studies in Long Beach, California. In particular, we would like to thank Dr. JeeHeng Lee's generous engagement with our roundtable at the Seoul conference, and Dr. Jiyoung Lee for her words of encouragement. Our work has been enriched by their prompts to take seriously the geopolitics of knowledge production and the barriers that researchers face when they are unable to publish in English. We, like other Anglophone scholars of transnational Asias, bear responsibility to grapple with this unevenness. We also thank our test readers for their feedback on the manuscript, including Jennifer Cheng, Jens Richard Giersdorf, Kellee Hearther, Alice Kim, Pearl Schultz, and Yujai Adrienne Tse.

We thank Ken Wissoker at Duke University Press for his support for this book and Kate Mullen for seeing its details through to the end. We are grateful to the in-house production team, including Michael Trudeau, Susan Albury, David Rainey, and Matthew Tauch, who have attended to copyedits, page proofs, art review, and design. Thank you to our indexer, Diana Witt. We also thank our anonymous reviewers for the press for their insights and enthusiasm for the manuscript. We want to recognize Ameena Fareeda for allowing us to use her work for the cover.

Funding to support the publication was generously provided by the Center for Philippine Studies at the University of Hawai'i at Mānoa and the Abigail Reynolds Hodgen Publication Fund at the University of California, Berkeley.

Collectively, the coeditors would like to thank Inez Amihan Anderson for their inspired cosplay and camera work, and Will Melton, Evan Anderson, and Blake Wong, who each jumped in to buy concert tickets when we were too overwhelmed by the Ticketmaster presale chaos. Mimi's mother, Lien Nguyen, housed a number of overexcited coeditors and fed them delicious meals before the Agust D concerts in Oakland.

Patty Ahn would like to thank Gonji Lee, Nare Park, Jio Im, Haewon Asfaw, Sophia Kim, Ara Kim, Nara Kim, and Kristin Fukushima for many wild text threads filled with GIFs, Twitter snapshots, and interpretations of lyrics. Also, a special shout-out to their collaborator in crime, Grace Lee, with whom they have embarked on an unforgettable journey through ARMY history for more than a year. They are especially indebted to their Spring 2023 undergraduate ARMY research group for their brilliance, diligence, and side-splitting senses of humor. And much love to Vera Miao, Lulu Wang, and Barry Jenkins for an unforgettable night at SoFi Stadium. Forever indebted to their former students, Norman Hsieh and Nicole Moc, for infecting them with the BTS bug back in 2017 with their MV rendition of "Spring Day" for their K-Pop class. Most of all, they want to express utmost gratitude to their unni, fellow K-Pop Stan, and concert sugar mom, Helen Ahn. Being ARMY with Helen has been a healing journey and one of the most special times of their life. It still hurts to close this chapter, but they are so thankful that BTS happened in our lifetime and for all the memories and joy they gave us.

Michelle Cho would like to thank Moonim Baek, Yoon Heo, and Jinhee Ryu—the editors of *Femidology* (2022) and researchers at the Yonsei Institute of Gender Studies—for including her in the transcultural BTS conversation in South Korea; Robert Diaz, Vicky Pappas, and Shanon Fitzpatrick for being concert buddies; Regina Yung Lee and the amazing students in her Transnational Fandoms class for workshopping BTS with her; Jesook Song and Yoonkyung Lee for generative discussions about fandom and generational politics in South Korea; Hae Yeon Choo and Janet Poole for institutional support and encouragement; and her many brilliant, inspiring ARMY students at UofT.

Vernadette Vicuña Gonzalez would like to thank Inez for converting her into ARMY, even if it was all a long game to get her to pay for lifetime concert tickets and a sneaky way to have a cosplay partner, and Evan Anderson for always, always, always enabling. Big love to Jamie Bilog-Mina and Bryson Sato for conjuring the tickets to the gateway BTS concert in Los Angeles and her ARMY students and colleagues (Maria Chun, Angela Tachino) for their mutual appreciation of OT7.

Rani Neutill would like to thank William Melton for his consistent support and fellow love for BTS (it makes being with you so much fun), Mercy Romero for constantly guiding her through the insecurities of writing, Chanhee Heo for her infinite knowledge, and the women of ARMY over 40 and all her ARMY students who indulge and encourage her adoration for BTS.

Mimi Thi Nguyen would like to thank fellow elder punks Yumi Lee and Golnar Nikpour for introducing her to BTS, and Yumi in particular for lending her niche jokes to our niche stickers (including *Abolish Men Except BTS*, and *Bangtan Not Bombs*). She would also like to thank Toby Beauchamp, Cyn Degnan, Thomas Falk, Naomi Paik, and Thera Webb for listening to a lot—*a lot*—of BTS chat.

Yutian Wong would like to thank Kim Schwartz for hallway conversations, Bruce Manning for sustenance, Blake for keen eyes and know-how, and her colleagues in the School of Theatre and Dance at San Francisco State University for breathing life back to the studio after the year of online *temps lié*.

Finally, we thank ARMY of all stripes, for shared commitments and delight. We thank our students, for whom this book is written. Without them, this book would not be. And here at the end, we also thank Kim Namjoon, Kim Seokjin, Min Yoongi, Jung Hoseok, Park Jimin, Kim Taehyung, and Jeon Jungkook. OT7 4EVA <3.

INTRO · On *Bangtan Remixed: A Critical BTS Reader* — Patty Ahn, Michelle Cho, Vernadette Vicuña Gonzalez, Rani Neutill, Mimi Thi Nguyen, and Yutian Wong

"Hey, do you know BTS?" Before they were too famous to travel anonymously, Jin, the oldest member of the world's biggest band, would often pose the question as a greeting to strangers—on the sidewalk, at a cashier's register, during an airport screening, or on the red carpet. While his fellow members were in turn amused, embarrassed, or annoyed after one too many "Hey, do yous . . . ," Jin continued undaunted, though what he truly meant each time is unclear. Was it invitation, self-promotion, or sly commentary on their commodity-image, or all these at once? At the peak of their fame, the query became a running gag for BTS and its fandom, even as "Do you know BTS?" lingers as a question that each member confronts—as idols, artists, citizens, celebrities, ambassadors, humans. For us, "Do you know BTS?" is less about who they are and more what BTS illuminates about ourselves and the world around us.

Conceived in 2010, BTS is a South Korean pop group consisting of seven members: Jin (Kim Seokjin), SUGA (Min Yoongi), j-hope (Jung Hoseok), RM (Kim Namjoon), Jimin (Park Jimin), V (Kim Taehyung), and Jung Kook (Jeon Jungkook).[1] BTS is an acronym for the group's Korean name, "Bangtan Sonyeondan," which roughly translates as "Bulletproof Boy Scouts." The name is somewhat of a bait and switch, regarding the group's complex and self-reflexive relationship to genre or style, as it was often a source of ridicule in their early days. Since their debut, BTS, like other K-Pop groups, has adopted (and just as quickly discarded) a multitude of concepts and personae on stage and screen. They have been bad boys in hip-hop-inspired athletic gear and thick chains or leather jackets and combat boots, but also boys-next-door in preppy sweaters, schoolboy shorts, or overalls. BTS have also graced the stage adorned in pearls, pussy bows, sequins, embroidered robes, and slim-cut suits, while their hair has traveled through all the colors of the rainbow and multiple perms. And though each member's skin appears uniformly flawless in photoshoots, we see their bare faces and personal style (most often sweats or tracksuits) in more casual livestreams and social media posts.

Part of the induction into BTS's fandom, ARMY (Adorable Representative M.C. for Youth), is becoming familiar with the group through the cataloging of each member's specific strengths as rappers, singers, and dancers and their quirks as celebrities and reality television stars. In BTS's Rap Line (the dedicated rappers in an idol group), j-hope is the energetically cheerful (and seemingly boneless) street dancer, SUGA is the lethal "genius" composer and producer, and RM is the group leader and resident intellectual, whose deft and often philosophical lyrics are matched only by his reputation for clumsy destruction. The Vocal Line (the dedicated singers in an idol group) includes the team's official Visual (or most conventionally beautiful) and unofficial prankster, "silver-voiced" Jin; the conservatory-trained modern dancer and countertenor, Jimin; the occasional oddball and baritone crooner, V; and the so-called Golden Maknae (also spelled *mangnae*, or the youngest member of an idol group or line of siblings), Jung Kook, whose perfect pitch and athletic versatility endear him to his *hyeongs* (male elders) and ARMY alike. But there is so much more to track; BTS members constantly slip between using their stage names, nicknames, and birth names and proliferate as personae across media platforms and merchandising.[2] They appear as animated personalities (TinyTANs), intergalactic beings (BT21), and fictional characters in a transmedia narrative (Bangtan Universe), which is all to say that BTS is only seven, but also a multitude.

As performers, BTS members alternate between puppylike playfulness and rockstar intensity. Their musical repertoire includes genres from pop and rock to R&B and hip hop and at times incorporates traditional Korean folk rhythms or instrumentation. They draw from urban dance to borrow elements of popping, locking, breaking, and freestyle and from concert dance vocabularies sometimes fused with vernacular and folk-dance forms. In their live concerts, BTS cycles through a series of costume changes, large-scale set designs, and video projections that propel a musical and visual narrative forward. Each show begins with theatrical spectacle, whether in the form of giant inflatable gold leopards or a Jumbotron close-up of V slowly taking a paperclip out of his mouth to unlock his handcuffs before thirty backup dancers crawl over a jail cell erected on stage. In euphoric call-and-response, ARMY punctuate the music with fanchants that thread through the voices of each member, hugging every chord and beat.[3] And while each evening might begin with BTS adorned in sequins or rhinestones strutting down eye-popping sets, it always ends with the members on a bare stage dressed in concert merch (tees, hoodies, hats, and cross-body bags). In these final moments, BTS conducts ARMY-time, in which fans and their homemade signs and flags are illuminated by light sticks known as ARMY Bombs, held by tens of thousands of fans and synchronized to the music in chromatic waves or made to spell out "BTS" and "ARMY." When it is all over, throngs of people exit the stadium, and the excitement of having just seen BTS lingers in the air while ARMY continues to sing their music.

Since their 2013 debut with Big Hit Entertainment, a small label outside of the "Big Three" management companies of the K-Pop idol industry, BTS has become the most popular music act on the planet, with a passionate and unprecedented fandom.[4] Their list of accolades is by now familiar, from sold-out stadium tours, astronomical YouTube views, Grammy nominations, Billboard hits, and enviable album sales, to South Korean Orders of Cultural Merit, United Nations speeches, and a meeting with US president Joe Biden to talk about anti-Asian hate. BTS's Korean-language tracks address generational economic precarity, emotional risk, and historical injustice, while their 2020 and 2021 English-language pop hits ("Dynamite," "Butter," and "Permission to Dance") offer playful, universal messages catered to the American market. Mapped across their catalog, the beats of their underdog story manifest as a triumphant bildungsroman, unfolding from an idiosyncratic debut to proving their much-heralded artistic chops as songwriters, composers, and producers. "Hard work," "suffering," and "self-sacrifice" are common themes in just about every idol group's origin story. However, these principles are core values given pride of place in BTS's journey of self-development, transforming all of the group's achievements into hard-won victories that signify their commitment to gifting ARMY the best versions of themselves and their talent. BTS and their label BIGHIT MUSIC generate, edit, and release hundreds of hours of behind-the-scenes footage of hard work and camaraderie, ordinary moments, and milestones. In dance practice videos, photoshoot and music video sketches, and documentaries like *Burn the Stage: The Movie* (2018), we see BTS members at work in the studio, collapsed backstage from exhaustion, or bitterly disappointed in themselves on tour. These scenes underwrite claims of authenticity and sacrifice as part of their nearly constant idol performance and their own acknowledgments (in lyrics and interviews) about its tensions.[5]

It is daunting to reckon with BTS. Instead of authoritative pronouncements on what BTS is, *Bangtan Remixed* looks at what BTS makes possible or perceivable, using BTS as a lens for the study of history, aesthetics, economics, culture, sociality, and geopolitics. How do we theorize through BTS to better understand the workings of affect, genre, soft power, masculinity, performance, fandom, language, the global music industry, or a throwaway gesture (a raised eyebrow, a flying kiss, or a wink)? The manifold nature of BTS—as corporate brand, fandom, marketing strategy, industry standard, genre wrecker, global icon, cultural mediator, technological compendium, paradigm, or fantasy—yields necessarily contradictory but also generative tensions. As Michelle Cho observes, their oeuvre comprises a kind of compositional genius that marks the group as extraordinary, even if their work traffics in pop culture cliché.[6] In this way, BTS is a remarkably rich intertextual sensation, one that is so often invoked to explain other phenomena, including how we might grasp the nature of how, as RM puts it, "you be a human."[7] *Bangtan Remixed* takes BTS as a case study that animates many accounts of our contemporary social and political cosmos. These accounts lie in the melancholic affirmations of "Life Goes On," found on their pandemic-era album *BE*, or American music critics' incredulous descriptions of their spectacular success wrapped in racism, or fans' wistful musings on a glance or a caress between members. As a pop band and as a global sensation, BTS produces and provokes expressive works that tell us stories about the present moment and the world.

"Come Back Home": BTS, South Korean Youth Culture, and the Roots of K-Pop

To fully understand BTS's impact on global music cultures, we must situate the group's unprecedented crossover success as an outgrowth of the K-Pop idol system and the powerful youth market it helped to shape in South Korea. BTS, too, despite the compelling narrative of being outsiders to the idol system, are produced in the network media, management, and talent apparatuses that make up the vertically integrated structure of the K-Pop industry. In other words, idols are not born, they are made. From the initial talent audition to intensive, yearslong in-house instruction in dancing, singing, acting, and communication, "trainees," as they are called in English (*yeonseupsaeng* in Korean), compete for selection into a group, with very few enduring until they can debut.[8] Once launched, the ability for a group to survive and achieve commercial success depends on their ability to appeal to the broadest audience *and* carve out a unique identity through the virtuosity of their dancing and singing, and the charms of their individual personas and group dynamics.

While fans and observers might debate whether BTS has outgrown the K-Pop genre, there is no question that the norms of South Korean culture and its media industries have shaped BTS's body of work—the aesthetic codes, performance styles, distribution patterns, and transmedia integration that characterize their creative and marketing concepts. At the same time, BTS redefined many well-established industry conventions, amplifying the group's cultural brand into a cri de coeur of a generation of youth shaped by global forces, including financial crises and the rise of social media platforms and informatized daily life. Moreover, BTS demonstrated that a narrative (and performance) of authenticity and self-reflection resonates more powerfully with international audiences than the sheen of perfection and infallible public images.

When they first entered the arena of commercial pop in 2013, BTS distinguished themselves amid a crowded field of idol hopefuls by underlining their debts to earlier groups. Their first single, "No More Dream," opens with a bass line reminiscent of the song "Warrior's Descendant" (전사의 후예, 1997) by the mega-popular, first-generation idol group H.O.T., or High Five of Teenagers. This first generation of idols emerged in the late 1990s to 2000s, defined by the musical merger of Korean pop with American popular music and urban dance choreography. H.O.T.'s fervent fandom across East Asia led Chinese journalists to coin the term *Hallyu*, or the Korean Wave, likening the powerful pull of Korean teen idols on young fans in Beijing to an ocean tide. They also popularized usage of the term *K-Pop* to refer to the international fan base emerging specifically around South Korea's newest genre of pop music.[9] BTS are preeminent representatives of K-Pop's third generation (which also includes EXO, BLACKPINK, GOT7, Red Velvet, and TWICE), and their call for refusal on the track "N.O," from their second EP, titled *O!RUL8,2?* (*Oh! Are you late, too?*) released in 2013, paraphrased Korean idol pop progenitors Seo Taiji and Boys's infamous screed against the national education system in "교실 이데아/*Gyosil* (Classroom) Idea." With their nod to K-hip-hop pioneer Epik High's 2007 hit "Fly" on their second full-length album, *WINGS*, in 2016, BTS took their lyrical inspirations straight from their *seonbae* (or seniors) to build their name, as they declare in "Attack of Bangtan" ("선배들 등을 밟지 / *stepping on the backs of our seonbae*").[10] And, in 2017, coming off their historic win for Best Social Artist at the Billboard Music Awards, BTS marked the approach of the fourth anniversary of their debut with the release of a new single, "Come Back Home." This track, a remake of a 1990s hip-hop song by Seo Taiji and Boys, commemorated the twenty-fifth anniversary of Seo Taiji's debut. "Come Back Home" also cannily pointed to BTS's own triumphant homecoming after more than six months of nonstop touring and twelve remarkable months of chart-topping, record-breaking ascendance to heights previously not reached abroad by a Korean pop music act. (And, in a boomerang effect, their accolades abroad grew their fan base at home.) Their remake highlighted the group's hybrid hip-hop roots and elevated BTS as the second coming of Seo Taiji—Korean pop's vanguard.

This talent for remixing—for reinvention through repetition—and this mode of intertextuality laced with self-reference, homage, appropriation, and critique is a practice of worlding that continues to characterize the South Korean pop culture landscape as much now as it did at the turn of the millennium. The strong influence of American pop culture is evident throughout the K-Pop genre. Seo Taiji's original "Come Back Home" borrowed heavily from Cypress Hill's 1993 hit "Insane in the Brain." BTS, like Seo Taiji, H.O.T., and other 1990s hitmakers Sechs Kies and Shinhwa, follow from figures like Cho Yong-pil, the Pearl Sisters, and Shin Joong-hyun, South Korean stars of earlier postwar decades who began their careers performing for American troops on US military bases in South Korea, where they also learned to adapt American musical forms for local Korean audiences. These bases hosted large numbers of US service members as part of the US-ROK (Republic of Korea or South Korea) Joint Security Alliance that formed in 1953 and resulted in the continuous deployment of tens of thousands of US military personnel on bases throughout South Korea to deter North Korean (and increasingly in the last decade, Chinese) incursion. As a result, much of South Korean popular music in the postwar era has been heavily influenced by American rock, jazz, folk, country, and, in later decades, hip hop and R&B.[11] Due to the power differential built into the US and ROK's uneven partnership, with the US "defending" a far weaker South Korea, American culture has long been viewed as the epitome of global culture in South Korea. American cultural hegemony shores up American military hegemony, which persists in large part because the Korean War is not yet over. An armistice agreement was signed by North Korean, Chinese, and American military leaders in 1953 (South Korean signatories are notably absent), which put the war on pause until an official peace accord could be negotiated. However, no such settlement has taken place; the conflict remains ongoing, which is why South Korean males are subject to mandatory conscription into the ROK military, and why BTS's group activities went on hiatus in 2022 so that the members could complete their military service.

While some K-Pop fans and commentators claim that South Korean youth culture was born in the 1990s, this isn't quite the case.[12] Young South Koreans were drawn to American pop culture, especially music, through the Armed Forces Korea Network (AFKN)—the US military's broadcast radio and television network—and in the illicit spaces of dimly lit dance halls, live music clubs, and record lounges (*eumak gamsangsil*) where DJs would play requests pulled from massive LP collections.[13] In the '60s and early '70s, domestic acts like Shin Joong-hyun and the Add4 and the Pearl Sisters adapted the sounds of psychedelic rock, as did later groups like Sanullim and numerous other campus bands.[14] But given the domestic and geopolitical conflicts that heavily shaped Cold War–era youth, namely, the Korean and Vietnam wars and the youth-driven protests against authoritarianism from the 1960s through the 1980s, youth-oriented music cultures were generally viewed with suspicion and often suppressed in the decades following the Korean War. After declaring martial law and rewriting the constitution in 1972, the president and former military general Park Chung Hee viewed the influence of American counterculture on politicized youth as a threat to his regime. Throughout the '70s, he targeted rock musicians like Shin Joong-hyun and folk artists like Song ChangSik of Twin Folio and Kim Min-ki, whose song "Morning Dew" became an unofficial anthem in the decade's antiauthoritarian protest culture.[15] (The crackdown effectively halted their careers until their revival in the 1990s, after the country transitioned to democratic elections.)[16] The '80s, under the violent regime of another military general, Chun Doo Hwan, were a syncretic decade in terms of musical influences. Bands like Songgolmae fused the sounds of funk, disco, and rock, and the latter half of the decade saw the rise of hard rock groups like Boohwal and Sinawe, although the latter's hair metal wasn't exactly considered *daejung eumak*, or mainstream music. More successfully, pop artists like Lee Sun-hee serenaded the public with melodramatic ballads that could be enjoyed across generational lines. This aspiration to mass appeal by popular musicians would continue to dominate the commercial music industry until the media market was reshaped by an array of new consumer trends, not least of which was the youth-targeted sound of '90s idol pop.

After nearly four decades of authoritarian rule that followed the Korean War—a civil war between the socialist North Korean state (under Soviet stewardship following the end of thirty-five years of Japanese colonial rule in 1945) and the US-led South Korean state—South Korea underwent massive social reorganization from the late 1980s through the 1990s, embracing democratic reform, self-determination, and consumer choice, lauded as core tenets of a uniquely American brand of liberalism. In 1993, South Korean policymakers launched a national globalization project that would change the way that the state and the public understood the diplomatic and economic role of popular culture, giving rise not only to the K-Pop genre, but also to high profile art and culture events such as the Busan International Film Festival and the Gwangju Biennale. In the meantime, the media labeled '90s youth 신세대/*Sinsedae*, or the "New Generation," characterized by their rebellious attitudes and enthusiasm for technological and consumer trends. Members of the *Sinsedae*, with their seemingly limitless adaptability, were the unruly offspring of South Korea's consumer modernity. Uninflected by the political tumult of student- and worker-led antigovernment activism of previous decades, '90s South Korean youth culture was explicitly commercialized, successfully commodified, and subsequently exported. It was in this moment that the rest of the world began to know Korean idol pop as K-Pop.

Idol Pop between Empires

While the form and global consumerist logic of K-Pop grew directly out of the postwar influence of American military, political, economic, and cultural forces in South Korea, the organizational structure of the idol system itself can be traced to a broader imperial triangulation between the US and Japan.[17] As the region's largest economic player that rebuilt its postwar economy most quickly with American aid, Japan maintained a regional hegemony across Asia, shaping many norms and conventions of business, cultural production, and social life. South Korea and Japan "normalized" diplomatic relations in 1965, under strong US pressure, after which the South Korean government and industry welcomed the transfer of Japanese industrial knowledge.

The assumption that K-Pop is merely American music, and specifically Black American music, repackaged for Korean and regional Asian audiences, sidesteps other critical regional influences and matrices of power that have impacted K-Pop's development. The roots of the idol system go back to the Japanese uptake of American media and cultural influence amid Japan's postwar redevelopment. According to anthropologist Hiroshi Aoyagi, commodified adolescence emerged as a societal ideal and popular music and entertainment genre in late-1960s Japan.[18] For Aoyagi, the youthful performer of the *aidoru* (idol) industry was a direct analog for the American teen idol of earlier eras, like the young Frank Sinatra or midcentury Mouseketeers Annette Funicello and Frankie Avalon.[19] The teen idol phenomenon has thus been an important marketing tool for an aspirational ideal of wholesome, optimistic adolescence for mainstream national audiences in both the US and Japan, the world's two largest and most crowded pop music markets. Idol pop's emergence as a commercial genre in Japan is said to have been inspired by the local popularity of an obscure 1963 French teen caper film, *Cherchez L'idole*, featuring cameos by French pop stars performing their hits within the fictional narrative.[20] This led to the formation of a new genre of popular entertainment, in which the blurring boundary between pop star, actor, celebrity persona, and "lifestyle model" catapulted adolescent stars onto the national stage. This form of youth celebrity flourished in the 1980s, Japan's peak years of high growth economics and capitalist optimism.

Japan's idol industry also produced pop music with tie-ins to broadcast media, especially radio and television; indeed, the term *aidoru*, a Japanese transliteration of the word *idol*, comes from the commercial media culture of postwar Japan, where musical entertainers began to be recruited, trained, and promoted for the purpose of cultivating a dedicated fan following.[21] From the early days of the Japanese idol industry, teen idols were promoted as television acts. For example, 1971, the year that scholars of Japanese pop culture designate "the first year of the idol era," saw the first televised idol talent competition show, *Birth of a Star*, thirty years prior to US television's paradigm-shifting *American Idol*. Dominating music charts, television screens, magazine covers, and advertising campaigns, young idol performers were multiplatform artists within a Japanese marketing system that magnetized fans' attachments to celebrities through tie-ins across media franchises and physical merchandise. Korean idol management companies adapted this "media mix" strategy in the late 1990s.[22] In particular, SM Entertainment, led by Lee Soo Man, adopted many of the practices and features of Japanese *jimusho* (performer management companies), inspired by the monopolistic success of Johnny's and Associates, the Japanese company that has dominated the arena of male idol groups since 1967. This is the highly centralized industry that BTS was up against as outsider idols, signed to the upstart management company Big Hit Entertainment.

Japan's industrialized idol production system has greatly impacted the development of the K-Pop industry, particularly in the following areas: the transmedia formats and domains for idol performers and their promotion; the centralized management and systematized training, production, and promotion model of the entertainment agency as a highly technical business enterprise, replete with trade secrets; and, finally, in the combination of familiarity through localization and novelty—often judged as facility with Western musical forms, choreography, fashion, and attitude or "swag." This emphasis on novelty would push to the reaches of posthuman, gender- and genre-bending fluidity and hybridization in the digital age, with initiatives to integrate AI, virtual avatars, and game practices as K-Pop's newest frontiers, which Dal Yong Jin details in this collection.[23]

We contextualize BTS's emergence and ascendance to mainstream visibility in the United States and Japan in this broader postwar history to show the entanglements between geopolitics, culture, and everyday life. BTS offers a lens that makes visible the continuities and possible disruptions in this history, despite the impression that they give of being utterly unprecedented and sui generis. Their popularity and fandom are consistent with new inter- and intra-regional dynamics, especially in the shift to two-way traffic between American mass culture and media and what have formerly been understood as peripheral and culture-bound media industries.

K-Pop's Consolidation and Diversification

Changing global media flows and Hallyu's presence outside of the Asian region offer a larger backdrop for BTS's success, but a more detailed overview of the development and transformation of the Korean popular music industry as a sector of the Korean wave brings BTS's contributions into sharper relief. Following on the commercialization and transnationalization of South Korean youth culture as a market in the 1990s, K-Pop developed as a formal industry by incorporating elements of Japanese and US music production modes. South Korean record producers adapted this image-driven model of idol production for the local market, codifying a "trainee system," in which idols are recruited and developed by elite management companies to garner a commercially loyal fanbase.

K-Pop's largest companies prior to BIGHIT's 2021 reorganization as HYBE—SM Entertainment (SME), YG Entertainment (YGE), and JYP Entertainment (JYPE)—became known as Korea's Big Three and led the development of this system. Each devised a trainee system organized around a specific market niche, narrowing the range of styles and artists each produced in order to hone their formula. SME cultivated a reputation for its "polished" image and Euro-pop sound, putting potential idols through a grueling seven- to ten-year training period to ensure "perfect" execution. Meanwhile, YGE and JYPE established themselves as rap- and R&B-focused labels, respectively. YGE, which aimed to project an image of rebellion and creative freedom, implemented a trainee system that allowed time for the development of its artists. Unlike in the US, where "authenticity" and "individualism" are prized artistic values, Korean entertainment houses explicitly promote their carefully orchestrated systems as key selling points.[24] While American media criticize K-Pop for being overly "manufactured," K-Pop's founding fathers have claimed that this controlled approach allowed them to edge out far more resourced Western competitors from taking hold of South Korea's media market while establishing a regional media empire in Asia.

This centralized business model drew from Japanese *jimusho*, but conformed to the vertically integrated organizational structure of *chaebol*, family-owned conglomerates in South Korea that drove the nation's post–Korean War economic "miracle."[25] *Chaebol* use the disciplinary ideology of Confucian familism—with the corporate head as the metaphorical father—to develop strategic export industries.[26] Korean entertainment houses have mobilized a similar rhetoric and familial structure through their trainee system in which idol hopefuls submit to an excruciating disciplinary process as a matter of indebtedness and patronage. This structure has even become a key feature of idol celebrity texts, emphasized in the narrative tropes of idol origin stories, particularly in television formats like the idol competition shows through which many groups are constituted and promoted. In this manner, neoliberal values underwrite a centralized corporate management structure that continues to thrive on the precariousness and exploitation of its labor force, especially its idol hopefuls.

SME, YGE, and JYPE consolidated their power in part by cultivating long-standing business partnerships with local television networks. Throughout its history, South Korean commercial pop has been uniquely beholden to those networks, for publicity and informal distribution. State investment in the growth of local television outlets and production studios yielded a multichannel landscape where variety shows and music programs reigned supreme, acting as the country's main music charting system until the Gaon Music Chart was launched by the Korea Music Content Association under the Ministry of Culture, Sports, and Tourism in 2010.[27] Most music television consisted of live performance shows, a tradition that still prevails today in the local broadcast industry; no less than five weekly live music performance shows air each week, on which commercial pop artists are expected to tirelessly promote each new single and album release. These live television stages provide a crucial platform within a tightly integrated apparatus.[28] Every idol debut or comeback release is accompanied by an aggressive cycle of media appearances and performances on nationally televised networks, which not only increases the visibility of artists in a densely saturated music market, but makes their fights for chart position an important site of investment and debate for fans and the news cycle.

While K-Pop relies on a predictable and systematized formula, the industry has only grown and survived through relentless experimentation and the diversification of concepts and revenue streams across multiple platforms and markets. Since the early 2000s, the industry has pivoted toward an international-facing business model. SM Entertainment began globalizing its trainee system after its first idol group, H.O.T., saw unexpected success in the Chinese-language market in the late 1990s. The company soon after debuted a female R&B singer named BoA in both Japan and Korea, marking the first time a Korean idol was recruited and trained with the intention of reaching local *and* overseas audiences. SME integrated this approach into its idol group formula when it debuted Dong Bang Shin Ki (DBSK, also known as TVXQ! or Tohoshinki), originally a five-member boy band featuring South Korean members who performed and recorded albums in both Korean and Japanese. SME not only developed a strategy for breaking into Japan, which remains K-Pop's most important secondary market, but also effectively created the blueprint for how Korean entertainment companies could expand their global influence.

Idol concepts are now almost always devised with an eye toward reaching multiple markets, especially outside of Asia. Group acts have been key to this strategic shift. SME again pioneered strategies like the formation of megagroups that could be broken into subunits tailored for specific national markets, and the inclusion of non-Korean members to broaden their appeal. As a result, the size of K-Pop groups has grown considerably across the board, not only expanding their potential for drawing transnational fans but also heightening the visual spectacle of live and on-screen performance. By 2011, the industry had fully integrated YouTube as a centerpiece of its globalization plan, including inroads in North America. By 2012, the fateful meeting of K-Pop and YouTube resulted in the biggest viral video hit to date, "Gangnam Style," by the comedic pop music performer Psy, then represented by YGE. Large-scale synchronized dance routines became a key ingredient for creating spreadable media and K-Pop's larger promotion strategy. This shift to a social media–driven strategy was the result of a strategic partnership forged with K-Pop's Big Three by Silicon Valley, which saw South Korea's web-driven media culture as a major piece of their expansion plans. Google and YouTube led the charge when it began pursuing SME in 2008. Twitter followed by launching a localized version of its platform in Korea in 2011 that allowed Korean users to type in Korean script or Hangeul. Although it took several years for Korean entertainment companies to build a comprehensive social media strategy, their eventual integration of US-based platforms dramatically globalized fan engagement with artists and each other. Whereas SME had long been the vanguard of K-Pop's technological savvy, BTS's innovative use of Twitter, in particular, made Big Hit Entertainment a new player within the industry's oligopoly.

From the late 2000s into the 2010s, when BTS debuted, the K-Pop industry was a crowded field of competing groups racing to initiate novel configurations of multimember, single-sex music and performance groups (we know them in the West as boy bands and girl groups). The figure of the "beast idol" (jimseungdol) emerged in the 2010s as an image that played with the way that young male performers' status as visual spectacle was inherently gender-bending—feminizing the performer while also acknowledging the androgyny of male adolescence (see S. Heijin Lee's contribution in this volume, chapter 22). This gender fluidity already characterized idealized masculinity in various domains of East Asian media targeting a young female audience, namely "girls" comics (shōjo manga in Japan; sunjeong manhwa in Korea). The primary visual characteristic of the beast idol was the dualism of youthful, androgynous facial features and hypermasculine, "hard" musculature. In this field of male idol group concepts, BTS's hip-hop image mediated regional tastes, appealing at first more to non-Asian fans, in contrast to Asian audiences, whose preferences at the time were met by fellow third generation, modular, multilingual group EXO (split into subunits EXO-K [Korean] and EXO-M [Mandarin]) managed by SME.[29] A growing emphasis on rap in idol-pop, which had functioned previously to offer sonic variety and verse interludes for less vocally adept group members, distinguished BTS in their early years as an iconoclastic hip-hop idol group.[30]

BTS is often cited by fans and critics as a much-needed antidote to K-Pop's highly "manufactured" system. Their image as super-earnest acolytes of hip-hop history and aesthetics, coming from a scrappy, small company on the verge of bankruptcy, both confirmed and departed from the industry by the time of the group's debut. While moving across the industry's genre and gender landscapes, BTS nonetheless displayed a fierce commitment to a youth cultural ethos beyond commercial motives. Along with their embrace of social critique, BTS and Big Hit Entertainment built on fan-artist communication modes that had previously been tightly managed and orchestrated by company-run and moderated fancafes (proprietary web forums) and official fan meetings. While their social media strategy was borne out of the need for free promotion, their choice to open up fan-artist engagement on transnational and multilingual platforms like Twitter and YouTube proved prescient, as the K-Pop industry took their cues from BTS's practices. To take just one example, their @bts_twt Twitter account was established in 2012, before the group's debut, while their rivals in the industry EXO, managed by then industry leader SME, lacked a Twitter presence until 2017. This five-year lag—an eternity by the standards of social media trends and the digital news cycle—shows how little regard the K-Pop establishment had for BTS until they were legitimized in North America with their Billboard Music Awards, and how thoroughly the group pushed the industry away from the sedimented practices of limited and company-controlled fan engagement.

Race and K-Pop: Diaspora and Localization

BTS's group concept and unifying message are rooted in their interpretation of hip hop. In their early years, BTS endured resistance and even ridicule in some quarters of Korean pop criticism and the independent music arena, since hip hop's antiestablishment ethos and idol pop's commercial mandates seemed mutually exclusive. But, in anchoring their work as homage to pathbreaking popular artists from earlier eras, BTS also underlined the debt that South Korean popular music has to Black American musical forms, as Nykeah Parham and Jheanelle Brown detail in their chapters for this collection (chapters 2 and 11, respectively).[31] While K-Pop's influences have diversified over the last two decades beyond the initial transposition of R&B, rap, and new jack swing, the influence of Black American music on the industry's forerunners like Seo Taiji and Boys, H.O.T., Sechs Kies, g.o.d., S.E.S., Fin.K.L., 1TYM, and Shinhwa is unmistakable. In the case of BTS, their studious references to their musical roots in American hip hop accord with the genre's history as a cultural idiom of social critique from below. These elements make up the core of BTS's star text, which encompasses a classic, coming-of-age narrative that runs through their body of work.[32]

BTS's engagement with Black American popular music also brought them criticism from some fans and observers for what are perceived to be acts of cultural theft. In the context of North American K-Pop fandoms, fans have been the first ones to call out K-Pop artists who don cornrows or dreadlocks, or perform in blackface while claiming ignorance of the racist connotations of such gestures. Often, fans direct their ire at the management companies, whose styling and marketing decisions result in these distressing images. Fans then become industry monitors, protecting the performers who are thought to be innocent of negative intent and merely in need of education, and calling for changes in the industry's top-down structures.[33] However, it is important not to conflate Korean and American pop culture industries and fan-industry relations. Instead, we should return to the history of race and racism in South Korea and in Korean American communities, which do confirm the global scope of anti-Blackness, but which are also a result of complex power dynamics and influences, among them American pop-cultural hegemony and the colonialism of the English language.

During the nineteenth and twentieth centuries, modernizing East Asia directly adapted concepts of race from Euro-American scientific racism, which, combined with Korean Confucianism's existing colorist and caste hierarchies, resulted in South Korea's dominant ideology of ethnonationalism.[34] Nadia Y. Kim explains that this notion of hierarchized hereditary traits was reinforced by Korean immigrants' experiences in the United States, where they were targets of anti-Asian racism, while also students of the anti-Blackness of American society.[35] While Korean society at large and many Korean Americans have internalized anti-Black racism, the history of these beliefs is refracted through a painful and violent experience of colonization, first by the Japanese—who were thought to be "closer" to white Europeans in the global racial hierarchy because they were also colonizers—and then through American military occupation. The United States incorporated South Korea into the Cold War as a strategic ally and protectorate, and many South Koreans still associate modernity with American ideas and cultural influence. Persisting alongside a self-denigrating notion of South Korea's belated (and still incomplete) modernity is also a defensive ethnonationalist chauvinism that developed under Japanese colonial occupation, when every domain of Korea's culture, language, and identity was threatened by official assimilation policies intended to transform Koreans into ideal colonial subjects. South Korean ethnonationalism, in other words, the "pure blood" claim that Korea is a monoculture, already reflects the transnational impacts of scientific racism and eugenic thought.

Thus, the function of race in South Korea is both traditional and foreign. Racism and racialization in Asia are multilayered, with social Darwinist concepts of ethnoracial hierarchy affirming racist judgments of winners and losers in a regional contest of national development.[36] Given this unique conjuncture of relational and intersectional forms of race-thinking, K-Pop artists who seek to adopt the sonic and visual styles of Black American popular culture primarily relate to the Americanness of these cultural forms and the artists who developed them. As Kim explains, "Much of Korean society . . . is simultaneously and begrudgingly attuned to Black Americans' significant power over Koreans as agents of the American occupational forces."[37] In this way, the pursuit of access to the eyes and ears of American fans by a group like BTS still plays as an underdog story, compared to Black American musical artists and celebrities who are more often idolized by Korean artists, especially those who engage with musical forms like hip hop and R&B.

BTS's approach to Black culture often contrasts, however, with common attitudes found in the Korean American diaspora and the South Korean public, which has historically looked to white America for cues on how to be successfully modern and capitalist, including the anti-Blackness of the model minority stereotype held among whites and Asians alike. However, in K-Pop celebrity cultures, groups like BTS have made concerted efforts to center Black American culture as American culture writ large. Criticisms of the K-Pop industry on the part of fans are generally warranted, and are a way for fans to register both their agency and their investments in their favorite groups. Yet when cultural appropriation debates turn to arguments about how K-Pop or Korea aren't "ready" for the global spotlight, or sufficiently modernized to be consumed in North America, what gets reactivated are theories of progressive development rooted in colonial perspectives and hierarchies of civilization. As K-Pop travels more widely, this history helps us avoid reductive claims about racism in K-Pop and better understand how BTS and K-Pop's popularity are transforming conventional ideas about race and culture.

ARMY: The Adorable and Representative Eighth Member of BTS

The first major media tour in the United States for BTS took place after they won the Billboard Music Award for Best Social Artist in 2017. During their guest spot on daytime television host Ellen Degeneres's eponymous show, Degeneres commented on the large crowd of ARMYs who greeted BTS on arrival at LAX, and teased them about "hooking up" with fans (she assumed that the members would understand American slang). BTS, however, refused to pathologize their fandom as crazed fangirls or to sexualize them as manipulable groupies. ARMY's love for BTS—repeatedly noted in English-language media stories focused on the mystifying enthusiasm of their American fans—was often compared to Beatlemania, a signal case for moral panics over the vital energies of fans subsequently characterized as feminine hysteria. But the idol system out of which BTS emerged displays a careful deference toward fans—prioritizing fans' responses and affective investment in their favorite groups—that is absent from most American fan cultures. In the face of US media's misogyny toward boy band fandom, BTS's attitude was both refreshing *and* indicative of their status as cultural outsiders.

The deference to fans, common in the sphere of Asian idol pop, became much more visible with the changed context of BTS's popularity and reception in the American pop music and media market. Although the group is conventional in many ways—assembled using a trainee system and developed using a transmedia strategy incorporating a core metanarrative of underdog status—BTS targeted worldwide audiences by foregrounding their singularity in a global media landscape. With the odds stacked against them in the face of the Big Three's dominance, and as themselves youth facing down the demands for conformity and institutionalized hierarchy in schools, workplaces, and neoliberal Korean society at large, BTS's struggle resonated translocally, radiating far beyond the customary sites of K-Pop reception. Further, the group deviated from the most conservative aspects of the Korean idol pop industry, unleashing social media's forces of digital intimacy (instantaneous connection, liveness, and fan-networking), and linking their own experiences of precarity in the idol industry to those of their fans and generational peers. The group's success despite their refusal to accept the industry status quo, particularly the collusion between the Big Three and the domestic broadcast apparatus, led to increased scrutiny of the industry by fans across the globe and resignified K-Pop fan culture as a site of participatory intervention with progressive political stakes.

These currents were amplified during the COVID-19 pandemic, during which the K-Pop industry quickly pivoted from large-scale, global tours to remote live performances facilitated by mass digital streaming technologies. As South Korea gained praise as a model state for its virus-containment measures, its government initiated an industrial development campaign to limit human contact yet boost service sectors. The awkward name for this technological sector is *untact*, a gesture toward the paradox of intimacy without physical contact, as in telehealth, online shopping, or robot baristas.[38] Untact became the K-Pop industry's key assignment during pandemic lockdown, and BTS and Big Hit Entertainment (which restructured and rebranded as HYBE during the pandemic, in March 2021) were no exception. The group held two remote concerts that each drew hundreds of thousands of fans for a fully produced online event, captured for a livestreaming platform.

While falling short of the in-person concert experience, these remote concerts made possible the temporal convergence of a truly global fandom (with the caveat that uneven internet infrastructure maintains digital divides in many regions).[39]

In contrast to the technocapitalist priorities of untact initiatives, ARMY's activities during the pandemic era took an unanticipated turn toward collective action, often bringing fandom into the domains of either mutual aid or political organizing. Just as BTS have exceeded the genre conventions and expected influence of commercial idol pop in Asia, ARMY around the world have channeled their fandom energies beyond the limited sphere of ardent consumption, embracing new roles in antiracist activism, democratic political organizing, and other forms of collective action in the name of both progressive politics and ARMY affinity as described in the chapters by Karlina Octaviany, Alptekin Keskin and Mutlu Binark, and Allison Anne Gray Atis, Noel Sajid I. Murad, and Hannah Ruth L. Sison.

In June 2022, on the ninth anniversary of BTS's debut on the global stage, all seven members gathered around a table to enjoy a "family" dinner on VLIVE, a livestreaming app launched and operated by South Korean internet giant NAVER. RM, the team's leader, bemoaned how much the group's meteoric rise had taken a toll on their physical and mental well-being. The group, which had expected to take a hiatus after their 2020 *Map of the Soul* tour, instead encountered a period of unprecedented fame during the pandemic, catalyzed largely by the release of three chart-topping English-language singles and the innovative use of web platforms that facilitated social connection during a time of prolonged isolation. Staying with their critical take on the crushing pressures of the K-Pop industry for young artists, RM and other members remarked on how much they had lost a sense of self under such duress. They proceeded to make a formal announcement that they would be taking a break from group activities in order to focus on their personal growth and pursue solo projects, to ask who they are beyond BTS.

While ARMYs took to Twitter and Instagram to mourn the end of the group's historic run, many also began to reflect on their own participation in a system that had seemingly broken the hearts and spirits of seven boys who had come to feel like family. We, as ARMY and coeditors, see this as precisely the moment to reflect on what BTS has meant to us personally and for global culture broadly. We see this reader as a necessary pause, a long, deep breath with which we might ask, "What is K-Pop, and who are ARMY, without BTS?"

"Love Maze": Overview

This book is indebted to the work of Jiyoung Lee's BTS, *Art Revolution*, JeeHeng Lee's *BTS and ARMY Culture*, and Youngdae Kim's *BTS: The Review; A Comprehensive Look at the Music of* BTS. Following Gilles Deleuze, philosopher Jiyoung Lee theorizes the relationship between BTS and ARMY as well as BTS's work itself as a rhizome to characterize the necessity of decentered methodologies for interrogating BTS as a cultural phenomenon. Cultural studies scholar Jee-Heng Lee documents the multiplicity of ARMY culture and ethnomusicologist and music critic Youngdae Kim details the contexts and aesthetics of BTS's extensive discography. Together, these works have opened up space for an interdisciplinary reader focused on critical perspectives on BTS in relation to art, geopolitics, and community.[40]

Bangtan Remixed takes its cue from the practice of separating the component parts of an original composition and adapting, altering, and rearranging those materials into a new object, whether a track, a poem, a painting, or a video. In other words, a remix comprises a singular and specific event from which we might observe or gauge movement or change from an original. BTS remixes all the time, repackaging whole albums with previously unheard B-sides or Japanese-language vocals, staging and re-creating canonical European artworks for the "Blood Sweat & Tears" music video, adapting Murray Stein's *Jung's Map of the Soul* to riff on psychoanalytic concepts of persona, shadow, and ego, and releasing seasonal remixes of their English-language hits "Butter" or "Dynamite." Fans also remix multiple media to create new works, including GIFs, video edits, bootleg DVD rips, fan cams, stickers, song covers, and prints featuring lyrics or original art based on photographs or performance stills. Such acts often allow fan-creators to establish both a principle or foundation for an original composition, while also facilitating its further transmission. Our reader unfolds in a similar fashion, as each individual chapter remixes and riffs on a lyric, a music video, a concept, or a fleeting moment, to provide insight into what BTS constellates through their multitudinous product and presence.

The study of BTS is necessarily interdisciplinary because the band itself emerges from histories that require grappling with a myriad of aesthetic genres, institutional practices, cultural geographies, and domains of knowledge. Our authors are artists, scholars, journalists, activists, and fans (and some combination of these all at once), working from a wide range of disciplinary perspectives, methodological approaches, and personal commitments.

Despite the important presence of contributors from other parts of the world, we note that this volume comprises works entirely composed in English, and is skewed toward North American perspectives, which reflects the continuing asymmetries that exist in structures of academia and fandom. Indeed, BTS's initial struggle to be taken seriously in Western markets mirrors some of the obstacles and biases (around language or industry connections) that have likewise created absences in this reader. We hope that these shortcomings are taken as provocations and invitations for others to add to the existing body of work about BTS.

For our part, this collection is driven by questions about how BTS as a band and as a phenomenon address certain norms about "success," gender, labor, and desire, among other things, that shape their trajectory. Many of our contributors examine how the multiple texts and media platforms that BTS uses shift personal and collective sensoria; in their chapters and art, they consider how BTS is a multisited phenomenon, situated simultaneously within South Korea and global flows of culture and capital.[41]

The second half of BTS's nearly forty-minute performance at the 2019 Melon Music Awards (MMA), which begins with a lone figure onstage draped in a Greek tunic blowing a large, curved horn, is a case study of BTS as master re-mixer.[42] In turns, each member of BTS is featured in a solo dance performance before RM walks downstage to the prelude of "Dionysus," where he grabs and drives Dionysus's thyrsus into the ground. Two giant inflatable leopards flank the stage as a line of female attendants strew flowers on the floor and a regiment of soldiers and horses form a procession to the theater of Dionysus where BTS—embodying the Greek gods and goddesses—hold court. The act comes to a climax as BTS members repeat the chorus of the song, while dancing faster and faster until returning to their seats, this time on top of a table, to look out onto an ocean of light illuminating a euphoric crowd.

Invoking the ecstasy of losing oneself in music and dance, BTS's references to rituals, rites, and mysteries are hard to miss. This stage performance calls forth the Greek god of theater who represents not just chaos, rebirth, and debauchery, but the artifice and duality inherent to the actor's body. SUGA's line, "Born as an idol, then reborn as an artist," signals how this duality lies at the heart of performance. This staging of BTS as both subject and object of Dionysiac rituals places the members at the imagined historical moment in which rites and rituals are transformed into institutionally recognized forms of music, dance, and theater. If ritual is that which is culturally valued as the originary practice of authenticity, and the classical is aesthetically valued as the originary practice of sanctioned authenticity, the "popular" encompasses too many categories—the folk, the masses, the resistive, and the appealing. At the 2019 MMA award show, they return to the center of Western art, theater, music, and dance history, which has long been assigned as the point of reference dictating all hierarchies of cultural production, and reframe this troubling legacy on their own terms. In this modern-day incarnation of a Greek amphitheater (a stadium) and ritual competition (MMA), BTS would go on to sweep all four *daesangs* (grand prizes) of the night, in perhaps the biggest art flex on the planet. Holding Dionysus's thyrsus, RM stands center stage with BTS as the embodiment of the ritual, the popular, and the classical brought together without concern for aesthetic hierarchies between these references and their rearrangements.

We linger on this singular performance as exemplary of BTS's own practice of remixing aesthetic genres and incorporating distinctive genealogies of performance. Along with "Blood Sweat & Tears" and "Black Swan," "Dionysus" is part of a triptych of songs, music videos, and live performances that places BTS at the center of theater, art, and dance histories. Part 1, "'You Can Call Me Artist, You Can Call Me IDOL!,'" considers the place of BTS's work within the aesthetics and genealogies of performance. The chapters in this section map the interrelationships between the aesthetic vocabularies from which BTS's music, choreography, and scenography draw sense and sensation.

Part 2, "'Mikrokosmos,'" turns to the wider universe of BTS and the multiple transmedia platforms that HYBE, BIGHIT MUSIC, BTS, and ARMY create and share together. The chapters in this section highlight the technologies of intimacy and parasociality spurred by BTS. From music videos, reality television shows, video games, graphic novels, brand endorsements, fan fictions, fan edits, memes, GIFs, and so much more, BTS generates "seven billion different worlds / shining with seven billion lights."[43] These "seven billion lights" are scattered widely, and to that end, part 3, "'Not Today,'" explores the geopolitical landscape of BTS as a planetary phenomenon traversing both well-worn and new paths for migrants, militaries, and monies. As performers, tourists, ambassadors, and "seven normal boys," BTS illuminates circuits of capital and campaigns of care, each enfolding global histories of race and gender in changing constellations.

In the interlude, "'Magic Shop,'" we include fanart (included in the plates section) that engages the multidimensional nature of BTS's presence—as commodity, muse, or something else—in the lives of ARMY. Navigating what it means to love a commodity-image, fans stretch their imaginative powers and transform these original materials through their labors. Without ARMY, as BTS says, who would they be? Consequently, part 4, "'You Never Walk Alone,'" further considers the fruits of their star performances found in proliferate fan labors and personal reflections. The chapters in this section illuminate how BTS—or attachments to BTS—facilitate sites of love, desire, friendship, safety, lust, communion, and hope.

Ultimately, our focus is less on BTS as a singular phenomenon than on the encounter with and the desire for what BTS might be said to stand for or against. We might click an aspirational "follow" on the luxury brands modeled by the members; compose feverish fan fiction to explore our deepest longings; fill our social media feeds with art and nature to solicit reflection, what ARMY dubs "Namjooning";[44] offer love and support to strangers, which might readily be translated as mutual aid, as we imagine BTS does or seems to do; or rest in a time of uncertainty and build social forms that allow life to go on. *Come here, I'm your paradise, hello, my alien, we are each other's mystery, at that moment the tuna asked me, Hey, what is your dream? A good house, a good car, will these things bring happiness? Why are they killing us before we can even try? I'm now in front of the door to the world, I know what I am, I know what I want, set everything on fire, bow wow wow.*[45]

Notes

1   BTS members' stage names are listed from oldest to youngest, with birth names in parentheses.

2   Some BTS members also have separate monikers for their solo projects: SUGA has produced work as Agust D, and RM is an evolution of Rap Monster and Rap Mon.

3   Fanchants are a regular feature of live K-Pop performances. See the glossary.

4   The Big Three consist of SM Entertainment, YG Entertainment, and JYP Entertainment, companies that, until BTS's rise, dominated the field of Korean idol pop, which has been defined by its integrated corporate production model of talent scouting, training, in-house content production and distribution, live performance schedule, new release cycles with broadcast-centered promotion, and ancillary merchandise sales. While BTS's management company, HYBE, has risen to the status of industry leader, the historical importance and industry influence of the Big Three remain discursively and materially significant.

5   Jin has spoken frankly about how the performance of access is still a performance, commenting during a VLIVE—a livestream that purports to offer a slice of life window into the members' daily routines—"I don't need to be honest here, actually."

6   Cho, "Nostalgia for Nostalgia."

7   RM, "Yun," featuring Erykah Badu, *Indigo* (2022).

8   Shin and Kim, "Organizing K-Pop."

9   See Jung-Min Mina Lee, "Finding the K in K-Pop," on the term *K-Pop* origi-
        nating outside of Korea.

10   BTS's later album *MAP OF THE SOUL: 7* references not only Carl Jung but
        also Epik High's 2003 album *Map of the Human Soul*.

11   Shin and Kim, "Birth, Death, and Resurrection."

12   Noah Yoo's review of Seo Taiji and Boys' self-titled 1992 album errone-
        ously claims that Seo's work constituted "Korea's first homegrown youth
        music." As influential as Seo Taiji and Boys were to the development of
        the idol pop industry, there was youth culture in Korea before the 1990s.
        Noah Yoo, review of *Seo Taiji and Boys*, July 5, 2020, *Pitchfork*, https://
        pitchfork.com/reviews/albums/seo-taiji-and-boys-seo-taiji-and-boys/.

13   Shin and Kim, "Birth, Death, and Resurrection," 279.

14   See Shin and Kim, "Birth, Death, and Resurrection," 287–93, for an
        account of the rise of campus bands, and A. Park, "Modern Folksong,"
        for a fuller account of the role that the genre of *p'ok'eusong* (the Korean
        transliteration of "folksong") played in 1970s South Korean youth coun-
        terculture movements.

15   See "Song Chang-sik: A Life Immersed in Music," *Korea JoongAng Daily*,
        February 22, 2015, https://koreajoongangdaily.joins.com/2015/02/22
        /etc/Song-Changsik-A-life-immersed-in-music/3001101.html. See also
        Hwang, "Kim Min-ki."

16   Kim and Shin, "The Birth of 'Rok.'"

17   The end of the Japanese empire in 1945 reorganized, yet also preserved,
        existing power structures in the region. As Lisa Yoneyama explains, with
        Japan's war defeat in 1945, "nations that formerly were subjected to
        Japanese domination in the subsequent cold war fell under the economic
        and military aegis of the United States." Yoneyama, *Hiroshima Traces*, 7.

18   Aoyagi, *Islands of Eight Million Smiles*.

19   Aoyagi, *Islands of Eight Million Smiles*, 4.

20   Aoyagi, *Islands of Eight Million Smiles*, 5.

21   Aoyagi, *Islands of Eight Million Smiles*. See also Galbraith, "'Idols' in Japan,
        Asia and the World."

22   For information about the history and industry context of "media mix,"
        see Steinberg's *Anime's Media Mix*.

23   Since the late-twentieth-century golden age of national idols, Japan has
        seen the development of an extensive idol subculture linked to content
        industries like manga and anime. A controversial twenty-first-century
        outgrowth of the convergence of media forms is the "virtual idol," or
        humanoid, animated figure voiced by vocaloid processing software,
        the most famous of which is Hatsune Miku. In K-Pop, the convergence

of digital and live idol performance is a recent phenomenon, targeting audiences among gamers and VR enthusiasts through the virtual K-Pop group K/DA's performance at the World Competition of League of Legends in 2018—a promotion strategy for the K/DA skins introduced to the game. SME's group aespa has tried to further the mainstreaming of virtual idols with its core concept as a group consisting of live members and their AI avatars.

24 The respective founders of Korea's Big Three are perhaps the biggest stars produced out of these systems. G. Park, "Manufacturing Creativity."

25 Shin and Kim, "Organizing K-Pop." *Chaebol* are a localized form of Japanese family-owned conglomerates or *zaibatsu*, which dominated the Japanese economy until the *zaibatsu* system was broken up during the Allied occupation of Japan after World War II.

26 Moon, "Begetting the Nation."

27 The Gaon Chart has been renamed the Circle Chart: https://circlechart.kr.

28 For an extended overview of the codependency between K-Pop and the television industry, see S. Kim, *K-Pop Live*, and Jung-yup Lee, "Broadcasting, Media, and Popular Music."

29 A subunit is a smaller group formed of members in a larger group. Subunits allow for members to explore other genres, languages, and concepts than in the larger group.

30 Groups like Block B, whose central concept and most popular members were rappers with existing reputations in the underground hip-hop scene, offered BTS an example to emulate. Arguably not an idol group, MFBTY, the collaboration between K-hip-hop artists Yoon Mirae, Tiger JK, and Bizzy, also debuted in the same year as BTS, offering a bridge between idol pop and the language of hip hop's social critique. At the same time, however, hip hop was being incorporated into the Korean commercial media landscape of televised competition programs with the premiere of the cable music station Mnet's rap competition show, *Show Me the Money*, in 2012.

31 For an informative account of this history, see Anderson, *Soul in Seoul*.

32 BTS is especially prolific, with five Korean and four Japanese studio albums, six EPs, four world tours, six reality TV series—three broadcasts on Korean cable outlets Mnet (*Rookie King, American Hustle Life*) and JTBC (*IN THE SOOP*), and three web series produced and distributed by NAVER VLIVE, a now defunct celebrity livestreaming app recently acquired by HYBE and merged with its proprietary fan-artist chat platform Weverse (BTS *Gayo, Run BTS!*, and BTS *BON VOYAGE* seasons 1–4), and thousands of short video clips, vlogs, and social media posts on their BANGTANTV YouTube channel, Twitter, TikTok, and Weverse.

33 Fan debates that have arisen since the resurgence of Black Lives Matter (BLM) activism and antiracist, police abolition protests after the murder

of George Floyd in the summer of 2020 have directly linked the anti-Blackness of global K-Pop fandoms with the anti-Blackness of US franchise fandoms, including Star Wars and the Marvel Cinematic Universe. For further discussion of fan debates about BTS's relationship to Black American culture and issues of anti-Blackness in K-Pop fandom, see Cho, "BTS for BLM."

34   Tikhonov, "Discourses of Race and Racism in Modern Korea."

35   See N. Kim, *Imperial Citizens*.

36   Writing on similar remappings of race and colonialism in Thailand under the influence of contemporary inter-Asian media flows, anthropologist Dredge Byungch'u Kang-Nguyên explains that the desirability of racialized features like light skin reflect not a desire to look Caucasian but, rather, a desire to pass as "white Asian," Kang-Nguyên's term for a "new racialization of Asianness associated with light skin, economic development, and modern lifestyles." Kang-Nguyên, "The Softening of Butches," 20.

37   N. Kim, "The United States Arrives," 275.

38   The World Economic Forum reported on "untact" in 2020: Rosamond Hutt, "'Untact': South Korea's Plan for a Contact-Free Society," World Economic Forum, August 11, 2020, https://www.weforum.org/agenda /2020/08/south-korea-contactless-coronavirus-economy.

39   "BTS: 100 Million Fans Watch Virtual *Map of the Soul ON:E* Concert," BBC, October 11, 2020, https://www.bbc.co.uk/newsround/54497760. Ikran Dahir reports in Buzzfeed News, "'I have no religion,' RM said, 'but I thank God that we live in 2020. I'm so glad we have this technology.'" Dahir, "BTS's Virtual Concerts Connected People on a Global Scale Not Seen before the Pandemic," October 15, 2020, https://www.buzzfeednews .com/article/ikrd/bts-map-of-the-soul-one-concert-experience.

40   Jiyoung Lee, BTS, *Art Revolution*; JeeHeng Lee, BTS *and ARMY Culture*; Y. Kim, BTS: *The Review*.

41   See Lowe, *The Intimacies of Four Continents*; Grewal and Kaplan, *Scattered Hegemonies*.

42   BTS, "PERSONA+Boy In Luv+Boy With Luv+Mikrokosmos+Dionysus," November 30, 2019, YouTube video, 34:00, https://www.youtube.com /watch?v=BVqLzxNMTXM; BTS, "Full Performance (view from 4th flr) / Kath Parungao," November 30, 2019, YouTube video, 38:42, https:// www.youtube.com/watch?v=5x6rITXDans; BTS, "Intro: Persona (Boy In Luv)+(Boy with Luv)+Dionysus @2019 MMA," December 25, 2019, YouTube video, 12:27, https://www.youtube.com/watch?v=k-ov1fNVdas; "[BANGTAN BOMB], 'Dionysus' Special Stage (BTS focus) @ 2019 MMA," November 30, 2019, YouTube video, 7:07, https://www.youtube.com /watch?v=lQswxVHDo8U.

43   Lyrics from "Mikrokosmos," from the 2019 album MAP OF THE SOUL: PER-SONA, translated by Genius English Translations, April 12, 2019, https://

genius.com/Genius-english-translations-bts-mikrokosmos-english
-translation-lyrics.

44 RM coined "Namjooning" to describe his activities while on vacation
    in 2019. Sandy Lyons, "BTS's RM Explains 'Namjooning,' Here's How the
    Word Came to Be," March 30, 2021, Koreaboo, https://www.koreaboo
    .com/news/bts-rm-namjooning-definition-history-origin/.

45 Lyrics from the BTS catalog, including "Pied Piper," "Friends," "Super
    Tuna," "No More Dream," "N.O," "Dope," "Dionysus, "IDOL," and "Fire."

Works Cited

Anderson, Crystal S. *Soul in Seoul: African American Popular Music and K-Pop*. Jackson:
    University Press of Mississippi, 2020.

Aoyagi, Hiroshi. *Islands of Eight Million Smiles: Idol Performance and Symbolic Pro-
    duction in Contemporary Japan*. Cambridge, MA: Harvard University Asia
    Center, Harvard University Press, 2005.

Cho, Michelle. "BTS for BLM: K-Pop, Race, and Transcultural Fandom." *Celebrity Stud-
    ies* (2022): 1–10. https://doi.org/10.1080/19392397.2022.2063974.

Cho, Michelle. "Nostalgia for Nostalgia: BTS on American TV." *Los Angeles Review
    of Books*, March 16, 2021. https://www.lareviewofbooks.org/article
    /nostalgia-for-nostalgia-bts-on-american-tv/.

Galbraith, Patrick W. "'Idols' in Japan, Asia and the World." In *Routledge Handbook of
    Celebrity Studies*, edited by Anthony Elliott, 202–14. New York: Routledge,
    2018.

Grewal, Inderpal, and Caren Kaplan, eds. *Scattered Hegemonies: Postmodernity and
    Transnational Feminist Practices*. Minneapolis: University of Minnesota
    Press, 1994.

Hwang, Okon. "Kim Min-ki and the Making of a Legend." In *Made in Korea: Studies in
    Popular Music*, edited by Hyunjoon Shin and Seung-Ah Lee, 133–41. New
    York: Routledge, 2016.

Kang-Nguyên, Dredge Byungch'u. "The Softening of Butches: The Adoption of
    Korean 'Soft' Masculinity among Thai Toms." In *Pop Empires: Transnational
    and Diasporic Flows of India and Korea*, edited by S. Heijin Lee, Monika
    Mehta, and Robert Ji-Song Ku, 19–36. Honolulu: University of Hawai'i
    Press, 2019.

Kim, Nadia Y. *Imperial Citizens: Koreans and Race from Seoul to LA*. Stanford, CA: Stan-
    ford University Press, 2008.

Kim, Nadia Y. "The United States Arrives: Racialization and Racism in Post-1945
    South Korea." In *Race and Racism in Modern East Asia: Interactions, Nation-
    alism, Gender and Lineage*, edited by Rotem Kowner and Walter Demel,
    274–95. Leiden, Netherlands: Brill, 2015.

Kim, Pil Ho, and Hyunjoon Shin. "The Birth of 'Rok': Cultural Imperialism, Nation-
    alism, and the Glocalization of Rock Music in South Korea, 1964–1975."
    positions: East Asia Cultures Critique 18, no. 1 (2010): 199–230.

Kim, Suk-Young, *K-Pop Live: Fans, Idols, and Multimedia Performance*. Stanford, CA:
    Stanford University Press, 2018.

Kim, Youngdae. BTS: *The Review; A Comprehensive Look at the Music of* BTS. Translated
    by H. J. Chung. Seoul: RH Korea, 2019.

Lee, JeeHeng. BTS *and* ARMY *Culture*. Translated by Hon Oul and Park Solbee. Seoul:
    Communication Books, 2019.

Lee, Jiyoung. BTS, *Art Revolution*. Translated by Stella Kim, Myungji Chae, Chloe Jiye
    Won, and Shinwoo Lee. Seoul: parrhesia, 2019.

Lee, Jung-Min Mina. "Finding the K in K-Pop Musically: A Stylistic History." In *The
    Cambridge Companion to K-Pop*, edited by Suk-Young Kim, 51–72. Cam-
    bridge: Cambridge University Press, 2023.

Lee, Jung-yup. "Broadcasting, Media, and Popular Music: Institution, Technologies,
    and Power." In *Made in Korea: Studies in Popular Music*, edited by Hyunjoon
    Shin and Seung-Ah Lee, 143–54. New York: Routledge, 2016.

Lowe, Lisa. *The Intimacies of Four Continents*. Durham, NC: Duke University Press,
    2015.

Moon, Seungsook. "Begetting the Nation: The Androcentric Discourse of National
    History and Tradition in South Korea." In *Dangerous Women: Gender and
    Korean Nationalism*, edited by Elaine H. Kim and Chungmoo Choi, 33–66.
    New York: Routledge, 1998.

Park, Aekyung. "Modern Folksong and People's Song (*Minjung Kayo*)." In *Made in
    Korea: Studies in Popular Music*, edited by Hyunjoon Shin and Seung-Ah
    Lee, 83–93. New York: Routledge, 2016.

Park, Gil-sung. "Manufacturing Creativity: Production, Performance, and Dissemi-
    nation of K-Pop." *Korea Journal* 53, no. 4 (Winter 2013): 14–33.

Shin, Hyunjoon, and Pil Ho Kim. "Birth, Death, and Resurrection of Group Sound
    Rock." In *The Korean Popular Culture Reader*, edited by Kyung Hyun Kim and
    Youngmin Choe, 275–95. Durham, NC: Duke University Press, 2013.

Shin, Solee I., and Lanu Kim. "Organizing K-Pop: Emergence and Market Making
    of Large Korean Entertainment Houses, 1980–2010." *East Asia* 30, no. 4
    (2013): 255–72.

Steinberg, Marc. *Anime's Media Mix: Franchising Toys and Characters in Japan*. Minne-
    apolis: University of Minnesota Press, 2012.

Tikhonov, Vladimir. "Discourses of Race and Racism in Modern Korea, 1890s–1945."
    In *Race and Racism in Modern East Asia: Interactions, Nationalism, Gender and
    Lineage*, edited by Rotem Kowner and Walter Demel, 242–73. Leiden,
    Netherlands: Brill, 2015.

Yoneyama, Lisa. *Hiroshima Traces: Time, Space, and the Dialectics of Memory*. Berkeley:
    University of California Press, 1999.

"You Can Call Me Artist, You Can Call Me IDOL!"

CONTEXTS, GENEALOGIES, AND
AESTHETICS OF PERFORMANCE

Within their discography of nineteen albums (studio albums, compilation albums, and singles), "IDOL" is one of BTS's signature works. As the lead single for their 2018 *LOVE YOURSELF 結 'ANSWER'* album, its catchy hook and intense soundscape are vintage BTS. In the official music video, the song's mix of musical influences—electronic dance music, South African house music, and traditional Korean rhythms—accompanies the circular rolling arm and leg movement of the South African *gwara-gwara*, the fast-stepping motion of the Nigerian *shaku shaku*, and the playful shaking of Korean lion dancing. Poised for a global audience, the song, music video, and live performances of "IDOL" reference the African cultural traditions that K-Pop's grounding in Black popular music and dance is indebted to, while also claiming a cosmopolitan Korean identity in the musical syncretism of hip hop, Afrobeats, and traditional Korean culture. The lyrics of "IDOL" tell a story about how the band members have come a long way to loving who they are despite constant criticism about their identity and legitimacy as artists. Denigrated for being sellouts by their contemporaries in the South Korean underground hip-hop scene for pursuing musical careers in the idol industry, the Rap Line (RM, SUGA, and j-hope) has addressed such accusations in works such as their Cyphers PTS. 1–4, a song cycle in the tradition of the hip-hop diss track that directly addresses their haters. In "Cypher, PT.3: KILLER," SUGA spits (in Korean) what one ARMY calls his "iconic bisexual verse":[1] "Like you all know my voice turns people on / whether it be men or women / my flexible tongue technique sends them to Hong Kong."[2] In "IDOL," five years after their debut, after going "around the long way," they embrace the artistic choice to be who they are—to "do my thang" by writing music, singing, rapping, and dancing regardless of being labeled as artists or idols.[3]

Just short of a decade after their debut—considered to be long-lived for K-Pop idol groups—BTS's repertory spans a diverse range of music and dance genres and influences found within individual songs, across their albums, and in the arrangements created for live performances (comebacks, concerts, award shows, and guest appearances on music, variety, and talk shows). The chapters in this section attend to the sonic, choreographic, and visual aesthetics found in the music, choreography, and music videos that make up the body of their work.

The first two chapters in this section describe how two main musical and dance aesthetics have shaped BTS's repertoire and how the group continues to innovate across multiple genres. Wonseok Lee's "Tradition, Transition, and Trends: Contextualizing BTS's *Gugak*-Inspired Performance of 'IDOL'" looks at the state's role in K-Pop's integration of traditional Korean music and dance. Using BTS's performance of "IDOL" at the 2018 Melon Music Awards, Lee demonstrates how incorporating elements of Korean traditional music and dance cultures is a significant part of the band's global success story and reflects broader trends of cultural promotion within the K-Pop industry. In "Hustlin' until Dope: How BTS's Rap Line Cultivated Their Hip-Hop Identities," Nykeah Parham highlights the US hip-hop genealogy from which BTS emerged. Originally debuted as a hip-hop group, BTS had roots in rap and hip hop that stood in stark contrast at the time to the flash of the K-Pop idol world. Parham provides a close reading of how RM's, SUGA's, and j-hope's education and investment in hip-hop culture, as the primary songwriters of the group, are central to BTS's musical identity within the K-Pop industry.

BTS members are deeply invested in visual aesthetics, a key element that is spotlighted in their storytelling. As K-Pop idols, their visual appeal, cultivated in costuming, makeup, and choreography for music videos, photo stories, and live performances, plays just as central a role as their discography. In "'Life Goes On': Social and Musical Space in BTS's Midpandemic Album

BE," Stefania Piccialli analyzes the band's 2020 album, released at the height of the COVID-19 pandemic, during which the band's activities—especially their MAP OF THE SOUL TOUR—were canceled or postponed. In this meditation on the spatiality of isolation and loneliness, she considers the aesthetic of the album's promotion and packaging as well as its musical and lyrical messages as a deliberate embrace across what felt like insurmountable distance. BTS's aesthetics also draw on and extend genealogies of visual art and dance that are sometimes recognizable and evident, and sometimes obscure but no less foundational. In her chapter, "Blood, Sweat, and Tears: BTS, Bruegel, and the Baroque," Marci Kwon reads the music video for "Blood Sweat & Tears" through the lens of European art history, examining how the canon of Renaissance and Baroque art provides a visual language to invoke the band members' exploration of art and life. She argues that as artists themselves, BTS turns to aesthetic histories to reflect on the categories of the real or authentic that are often brought to bear upon the group. And in "Martha and the Swans: BTS, 'Black Swan,' and Cold War Dance History," Yutian Wong situates stage performances of BTS's "Black Swan" as the end result of the culture wars that took place in theaters across East and Southeast Asia in the 1950s. Wong reflects on the dance rivalry between the United States and the Soviet Union, using the performance conventions, choreographic structures, movement motifs, and costume choices of "Black Swan" to trace the condition of a K-Pop idol as a product of Cold War culture wars.

Notes

1   Yumi Lee, personal communication, October 15, 2022.
2   Quotes are from the lyrics of "IDOL" as translated by Genius English Translations, August 19, 2014, https://genius.com/Genius-english-translations
        -bts-bts-cypher-pt-3-killer-ft-supreme-boi-english-translation-lyrics.
3   Quotes are from the lyrics of "IDOL" as translated by Doolset Lyrics, August 24, 2018, https://doolsetbangtan.wordpress.com/2018/08/24/idol/.

01 · Tradition, Transition, and Trends: Contextualizing BTS's *Gugak*-Inspired Performance of "IDOL" — Wonseok Lee

K-Pop is often regarded as dance-oriented music inspired by African American musical genres. Because of this assumption—and despite the growth of K-Pop scholarship across a variety of disciplines—academic works that focus on musical characteristics of K-Pop beyond pop, R&B, and hip hop are relatively rare. Of course, it is hard to deny that many K-Pop musicians and producers are significantly influenced by African American musical and cultural forms, such as hip hop.[1] However, K-Pop artists embrace diverse styles and genres and BTS is a case in point. Although the group's 2013 debut "No More Dream" was hip-hop oriented, the breadth of BTS's music and performance repertoire is not confined to a single style or genre. In particular, BTS has given *gugak* (traditional Korean music)-inspired performances since the late 2010s, demonstrating how K-Pop can exist beyond the distinction between Korean tradition and Westernized popular music.

BTS's 2018 release "IDOL" incorporated both visual and sonic elements of traditional Korean culture. Traditional Korean expressions in its lyrics, such as *eolssu jota*, 얼쑤 좋다 and *jihwaja jota*, 지화자 좋다 (musical exclamations heard in *pansori*, a traditional Korean musical drama consisting of two performers, a singer, and a drummer), and *deonggideok kungdeoreoreo*, 덩기덕 쿵더러러 (an onomatopoeic word representing a traditional Korean drumbeat), have been picked up and sung by numerous ARMY across the world when the group performs this song. In addition, BTS has used Korean historic sites—such as the Gyeonghoeru Pavilion at Gyeongbokgung (the main royal palace of the Joseon dynasty, built in 1395) and Sungnyemun (or Namdaemun, the first

National Treasure of South Korea)—as backdrops for internationally televised performances on the *Tonight Show Starring Jimmy Fallon*, BANGTANTV, and *Global Citizen Live*.

Besides BTS, several K-Pop groups have also incorporated *gugak* elements since the middle of the 2010s.[2] Why have K-Pop groups actively utilized visual and sonic elements of traditional Korean culture? There are many reasons, one of which is the South Korean government's involvement in the K-Pop industry. The government has not only become a main force in promoting K-Pop and K-Pop's musical diversity, but also functioned to fill the gap between traditional Korean culture and global K-Pop fans through the deployment of K-Pop idol groups to introduce traditional Korean culture. From among many examples of K-Pop groups' *gugak*-inspired performances, BTS's "IDOL" performance at the Melon Music Awards (MMA) in 2018 is a case study in how contemporary K-Pop incorporates elements of traditional Korean culture and creates a new musical aesthetic. The exemplary demonstration of "IDOL" illuminates how the musical boundaries of K-Pop performers, specifically BTS, are not confined to any particular style but are expanding to accept *gugak* elements, and government policies contribute to making elements of traditional Korean culture not only more acceptable but also desired in the K-Pop industry. BTS's *gugak*-inspired performances may not be directly dictated by the government, but government policy plays a role in the integration of *gugak*-fusion in BTS's performance.

As a New Patron State: Cultural Policy Transformations

The South Korean government's policy on popular culture changed dramatically from regulation to promotion, beginning in the 1990s.[3] The first civilian government, the Kim Young-Sam administration (1993–98), established the Globalization Promotion Committee in January 1995 that brought about changes in many aspects of Korean society, including mass media and popular culture.[4] The Kim Dae-Jung administration (1998–2003) established the Basic Law for Promoting Cultural Industries to invigorate the globalization of South Korea's cultural sector. Given these changes in cultural policy in both the Kim Young-Sam and Kim Dae-Jung administrations, it is no coincidence that K-Pop began receiving attention from people across the world, starting in the late 1990s.

Creative industries scholar Hye-Kyung Lee explains that South Korea's cultural policy is unique because it has institutionally embraced globalization and neoliberalism as part of its national agenda. Lee states, "Korea's approach is very different as it aspires to 'actively manage' globalization and turn it into a 'national(ist) project' centered on increasing the nation's cultural export and brand power."[5] Lee also defines contemporary Korea as "a 'new patron state' that has developed a distinctive cultural policy, in which democratic, neoliberal and globalist agendas have been actively articulated within the statist policy framework."[6] Indeed, the cultural policies of the contemporary Korean government cannot be understood through a binary view, such as the state vs. markets, the state vs. civil society, and national vs. global. They are all interwoven in South Korea's cultural policy framework.

Since the 1990s, it is commonplace to see bipartisan consensus for promoting Korean popular culture. The liberal Roh Moo-Hyun administration (2003–8), for example, designated the culture industry as one of the country's primary industries. The subsequent conservative Lee Myung-Bak administration (2008–13) also supported the cultural sector by establishing government agencies in order to promote Korean popular culture globally. Specifically, the Lee administration not only reified the national brand introduced by the Roh administration but also expanded the Korean Wave (or *Hallyu*) by labeling all cultural content with the prefix K, such as "K-fine art, K-musicals, K-literature, and K-food."[7]

In 2009, the Lee administration established the Korea Creative Content Agency (KOCCA) that is affiliated with the Ministry of Culture, Sports, and Tourism. One of the agency's main goals is to support local musicians through several promotional programs, such as K-Rookies, MUSE ON, K-Pop Night Out, K-Music Week, On The K Series, and so forth. Among them, the annual music convention, called MU:CON, which encompasses a showcase, conference, festival pitching, and choice interview, is notable as MU:CON has been a bridge between local musicians and well-known figures in the global music industry since 2011. Through MU:CON, KOCCA provides local musicians with an opportunity to perform in front of an audience of music industry professionals, such as Fernando Garibay (producer of American pop artist Lady Gaga), James Minor (head of the music section at the American culture festival SXSW), Danton Supple (studio engineer for Coldplay), and Kate Dick (booker of the Glastonbury Festival in the UK). Under the auspices of KOCCA, selected local musicians from MU:CON have performed at global music festivals—including Glastonbury, SXSW, MIDEM in France, Canada Music Week, and Reeperbahn Festival in Germany—under the banner "K-Pop Night Out," which later became "Korea Spotlight." It is important to note that all of KOCCA's efforts aim to promote Korean popular music and maintain the global popularity of K-Pop, yet KOCCA does not confine its promotion to any specific style of Korean music. The agency supports both K-Pop idol groups and independent musicians. In other words, global audiences are exposed to different styles of Korean musicians on the same stage under the title "Korea Spotlight." For example, a prominent K-Pop boy group from YG Entertainment, iKON, performed on the same stage with the *gugak*-oriented postrock band Jambinai at SXSW 2019. In fact, KOCCA supports more independent musicians than idol groups. For example, in the Reeperbahn Festival 2021, DRIPPIN was the only K-Pop idol group out of nine participants in the Korea Spotlight. The other groups were IDIOTAPE, Kim Sawol, Chimmi, Bryn, Bosudong Cooler, Wedance, Thama, and hyangni. For the Korea Spotlight 2022 in the Reeperbahn Festival in Germany, all of the government-sponsored musicians, such as Nerd Connection, Dajung, CHE, and 250 (pronounced Eah-Oh-Gong), were neither dance-oriented nor idol groups. As such, the government contributes not only to expanding the musical boundaries of Korean popular music as it is understood by overseas audiences but also to shrinking the gap between traditional and popular music.

Another cultural policy initiative that aims to integrate traditional and popular music is the K-Community Festival, run by the Korean Foundation for International Cultural Exchange (KOFICE), which is affiliated with the Ministry of Culture, Sports, and Tourism. This festival, initiated in 2019, has received growing attention from global K-Pop fans, as KOFICE employs K-Pop idol groups to promote traditional Korean culture. For example, several K-Pop idol groups—including MONSTA X, BTOB, Weki Meki, Loona, WEi, and Oh My Girl—have offered presentations introducing aspects of traditional Korean culture, including *minyo* (Korean folk song), *buchaechum* (fan dance), *hallyangmu* (Korean folk dance), *seoye* (Korean calligraphy), *hanbok* (traditional clothing), *sogochum* (small drum dance), and so on. KOFICE also runs a "K-Community Challenge" not only to stimulate global K-Pop fans' interest in traditional Korean culture but also to make the fans themselves into online promoters of traditional Korean culture. To participate in the Challenge, fans are required to choose one of four artforms—*minyo*, *buchaechum*, *Taekwonmu* (also known as Taekwondo Dance, a performance incorporating dance and Korean martial arts), or *hanbok*—and to make a cover video to be uploaded with specific hashtags, such as #kcommunity_challenge, #kcommunity_festival, and #its_ktraditional_time. KOFICE advertises that "the winners will be invited to perform at K-Community Festival in Korea."[8] Given global K-Pop fans' participation in initiatives like this, it is safe to say that the government actively contributes to making traditional Korean culture accessible and familiar to K-Pop fans.[9]

The Iconic Performance of BTS's "IDOL" at the Melon Music Awards (MMA) 2018

Since the mid-2010s, it has become more common to see K-Pop idol groups incorporating traditional elements into their music and performance. BTS's "IDOL" is an iconic example of this phenomenon. Specifically, their performance of "IDOL" at MMA 2018 exemplifies K-Pop's incorporation of *gugak* elements and presents the new aesthetics of K-Pop. The original album version of the song is known for its usage of diverse cultural elements, such as *Gqom* (a subgenre of Kwaito, a South African style of house music), *gwara-gwara* (South African dance), *chuimsae* (traditional Korean musical verbal expressions), and *hanbok*. For their performance of "IDOL" at MMA 2018, BTS emphasized the traditional Korean elements more explicitly by performing with two traditional Korean music performance groups, Gwanggaeto Samulnori and World Fusion Sinawi.[10] These groups are known for their attempts to popularize *gugak* by combining traditional Korean music with foreign elements: Gwanggaeto Samulnori combines *samulnori* (a percussion ensemble performed by four instruments) with hip-hop forms, including deejaying and b-boying, and World Fusion Sinawi absorbs foreign elements for their music. The version of "IDOL" presented at MMA is distinct from BTS's other performances incorporating Korean tradition. While other performances mainly employ only visual elements of Korean tradition, "IDOL" at MMA actively engages with *gugak* fusion groups and incorporates both sonic and visual elements of traditional Korean culture, such as the usage of traditional Korean instruments and background images of traditional Korean landscape painting for this performance.

The introduction—performed by group members j-hope, Jimin, and Jung Kook—is particularly noteworthy in this regard. With the stage lights turned completely off, a screen shows images of red and blue waves that recall the flag of South Korea known as *Taegukgi* pulsing in time with the strong bass drum sound. The performance venue fills with the audience's chanting. A stage rises, arranged like a vertical grid, with fourteen *samgomu* (three-drum dance) performers filling each square except one, and performing traditional dance movements. In the middle square, surrounded by the dancers, j-hope, wearing *hanbok*, begins the performance, mixing elements of hip-hop popping with modern dance to the accompaniment of traditional percussion instruments including *jing* (gong) and *kkwaenggwari* (tambourine-sized flat gong). At the end of his segment, j-hope picks up a red fan and seemingly flings it across the stage to Jimin, who "catches" the fan and begins his part.

Skillfully employing the red fan and performing with other dancers holding white fans, Jimin creates new aesthetic values of *buchaechum* from each dance move. Whereas the traditional fan dance is performed at a slow tempo, typically in 12/8 meter, Jimin's performance is in 4/4 meter at a lively 127 beats per minute. Notably, all the performers in this segment are male, with each employing a single fan, whereas the traditional fan dance is usually performed by female performers with two fans apiece. Even so, Jimin's performance expresses traditional characteristics of *buchaechum*. For example, traditional performers usually evoke flowers by using fans; the first formation created by Jimin and the other dancers also represents a blooming flower. In this formation, Jimin holding the red fan looks like a pistil surrounded by white petals. The formation looks like a swaying flower as performers wave their fans. In that sense, Jimin's performance corresponds to the basic idea of traditional fan dance, which is "how to harmonize the dancers' bodies with the fans to make beautiful figures in space."[11] After his performance, Jimin received an award from the Kim Baek Bong Fan Dance Conservation Society for his reinterpretation of the form and "contribution in raising the status and aesthetic value of the Korean fan dance globally."[12] At the end of his segment, Jimin passes the *hansam* (long sleeve extensions) to Jung Kook, who continues the introduction.

The *hansam* is one of the main elements in *talchum* (mask dance), a theatrical musical genre that encompasses music, dance, and narrative.[13] Referring specifically to *Bongsan talchum* (a mask dance-drama originally from Bongsan, Hwanghae Province, North Korea), Jung Kook's style differs from the ways in which he has previously performed as a member of BTS.[14] Jung Kook uses centrifugal force to swing his arms in a circle, which is often seen in traditional *Bongsan talchum*. Making his right leg look like the number seven and raising his right hand, Jung Kook jumps and turns right. He pulls his arm behind his head and whips it in a certain direction. What he performs in his segment is mainly from the *single sawi*, the last basic movement of *Bongsan talchum*. By throwing a *tal* (mask) to the next stage at the end of his segment, Jung Kook directs the camera to the main stage action, concluding the introduction.

On the main stage, as a door decorated with the *tal* representing the *Chwibali* (one of the main characters in *Bongsan talchum*) opens, *samulnori* joins the introduction of "IDOL," along with performers executing a lion dance (or *Bukcheong sajanoreum*); both of these are also part of *Bongsan talchum* (see

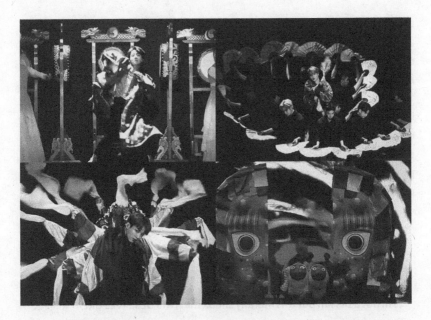

1.1 · Introductory dance sequence of "IDOL" performance at MMA 2018. Screengrab by author. https://youtu.be/LfgXdDaryBE.

figure 1.1). Twirling *sangmo* (a kind of a hat with feathers or paper streamers attached to the top) and performing a *jaban* flip (turning over while continuing to jump and land to make a circle in a counterclockwise direction), the two lead performers signal that the introduction is reaching its climax.

The musical accompaniment for "IDOL" also shored up the excitement and exhilaration of the introduction. At the end of the introduction section, other traditional Korean instruments, such as *taepyeongso* (a reed instrument), were added to the melodic line of the introduction. What is notable is that the main riff of "IDOL" is also played by traditional instruments, which make the riff consonant with other *gugak* elements of the performance. In this way, the melodic line of *daegeum* (a woodwind instrument) and the main riff of "IDOL" create a distinct soundscape along with the rhythmic part performed by *kkwaenggwari*, *jing*, and bass drum.

After the introduction, the members of BTS, all wearing *hanbok*, regroup on the main stage to perform a visually and musically *gugak*-oriented version of "IDOL." The background images on the stage represent traditional Korean colors, called *obangsaek* (five colors: black, white, blue, red, and yellow), Korean landscape paintings, and *dancheong* (colored patterns on wooden buildings). Musically, this version of "IDOL" is rearranged to reinforce *gugak* elements. In addition to the iconic introduction part, traditional instruments, such as *jing*, are constantly played throughout the song. Performers of traditional Korean music who were present in the introduction rejoin the song's last chorus as BTS builds it to a climax.

BTS's "IDOL" at MMA exemplifies how contemporary K-Pop can appeal to international audiences by reinterpreting traditional Korean elements. It also reveals BTS's influential role as national ambassadors of Korean culture. Many people applauded the way BTS utilized traditional Korean culture and reinterpreted it in its MMA performance. The YouTube comments section of the performance's footage abounds with praise:

> The best stage performance in kpop history. They showed their culture so well while maintaining that idol touch that they have. This is forever [and] will be a masterpiece. (Justine Tuasic)

> I'm not a bts fan but this literally shook me. THIS DESERVES GREAT RESPECT. (vamshi)

> still remember how my heart ran a mile per minute when hoseok started to dance followed by jimin and Jungkook!!!! The idol performance in traditional hanbok, absolutely phenomenal! I often question myself how will bts ever beat this one but again they're bts, impossible is not in their dictionary! (rhea gurung)

> omg, I get goosebumps, this stage is really amazing, from the choreography to the arrangement, the way BTS shows the Korean culture makes me really like it, one day I'll come South Korea. (Lemlem Park)

> The way how they present their nation, culture and their music . . . goosbumps [sic]. (Konysbayeva Diana)

> I'm not even Korean but this performance makes me feel proud of Korea's culture! (Araceli Seráfico)[15]

These comments on BTS's "IDOL" at MMA demonstrate the possibilities for *gugak*-oriented K-Pop's appeal to both domestic and global audiences. Several Korean viewers wrote that BTS's "IDOL" at MMA makes them proud of being Korean and of Korean culture. Amazed by the performance, global audiences also explicitly mention that the *gugak*-oriented "IDOL" makes them more interested in Korea, K-Pop, and Korean tradition. Some viewers also talk about the meaning of BTS's adaptation of *gugak* for both local and international audiences. For example, MayLily on YouTube evaluates this performance by saying, "Koreans (and all Asians in general) should be proud [of] how BTS has done what no other Asian group has ever done—transcending cultural and language barriers to bring their music [to] the masses (without a single song fully in English), and still honoring their cultural heritage."[16] The different languages in the comment section, including Korean, English, Japanese, Spanish, Russian, Vietnamese, Arabic, and Thai, show that this feedback is not confined to only one region.

The government's use of cultural content as a means of soft power not only serves to enhance national branding but also influences the cultural content itself. As examined, the exposure of global K-Pop fans to a wide variety of Korean musicians and Korean tradition has been facilitated by the government's supportive programs. Because the government has intensively promoted diverse types of local musicians, including *gugak*-fusion bands, to the global market since the early 2010s, and actively utilized K-Pop idol groups to promote traditional Korean culture, it follows that international audiences are likely to have seen *gugak*-inspired performances since the mid-2010s. In this way, the government contributes to making an environment where K-Pop artists can actively adopt *gugak* elements into their music. This indicates the expanding musical boundaries of K-Pop in the global audiences' understanding. BTS's *gugak*-inspired performances, for example, show ARMY around the world that their music and performances are not confined to a certain style. From hip hop to *gugak*-oriented performances, BTS's musical boundaries have expanded, as have those of K-Pop as a whole.

BTS's notable success with their *gugak*-inspired performances, including "IDOL" at MMA 2018, demonstrates the convergence of the state's goal of diversifying K-Pop and the K-Pop industry's desire to integrate into the global music scene. Given their popularity and influence, I expect that BTS's *gugak*-oriented performances will inspire future trends and influence the musical diversification of K-Pop.

Notes

1   Crystal Anderson states, "While K-Pop is influenced by several foreign music cultures, its hybridity is largely informed by African American popular music." Anderson, *Soul in Seoul*, 17.

2   For example, 2NE1's "I Am the Best" (2011), B.A.P.'s "No Mercy" (2012), G-Dragon's "Niliria" (2013), Topp Dogg's "Arario" (2014), Big Bang's "Bae Bae" (2015), VIXX's "Shangri-La" (2017), Mino's "Fiancé" (2018), BLACKPINK's "How You Like That" (2020), Oneus's "LUNA" (2021), A.C.E.'s "Jindo Arirang" (2021), Stray Kids' "Thunderous" (2021), Kingdom's "Ascension" (2022), and BLACKPINK's "Pink Venom" (2022). I want to clarify that there has been an effort to incorporate elements of traditional Korean culture among Korean popular musicians, such as Shin Joong-hyun, Chong Tae-Chun, Cho Yong-Pil, Kim Soo-Chul, among others, since the middle of the twentieth century. Also, Seo Taiji utilized *gugak* elements for his song "Hayeoga" (1993). Nevertheless, it was rare to observe incorporation of traditional elements when it comes to K-Pop "idol" groups before the late 2010s.

3   S. Kim, "Controlling or Supporting?," 185.

4   According to Fuhr, structural reforms of Korean society include "education, the legal system and economy, politics, mass media, national and local administration, environment, and culture." Fuhr, *Globalization and Popular Music in South Korea*, 133. Shim also states, "In 1994, the Presidential Advisory Board on Science and Technology submitted a report to the president suggesting that the government promote media production as the national strategic industry by taking note of overall revenue . . . from the Hollywood blockbuster, *Jurassic Park*, which was worth the foreign sales of 1.5 million Hyundai cars." Shim, "Hybridity and the Rise of Korean Popular Culture in Asia," 32. See also J. Kim, "[Future of Korean Film Industry]."

5   H. Lee, *Cultural Policy in South Korea*, 9.

6   H. Lee, *Cultural Policy in South Korea*, 4.

7   H. Lee, *Cultural Policy in South Korea*, 127.

8   K-Community Festival, "[2022 K-Community Challenge] Challenge HOW TO Guide," August 1, 2022, YouTube video, 1:40, https://youtu.be/5iiRKfFSUhY.

9   Dayal, a K-Pop cover dance crew from Ukraine, participated in the Challenge by performing *buchaechum*. See Dayal Dance Crew, "[K-Community Challenge] 2022 Buchaechum_Ukraine_Dayal," September 10, 2022, YouTube video, 2:41, https://youtu.be/N9yQZQHUcd4.

10   baejuhwi, "We, World Fusion Sinawi and Gwanggaeto Samulnori, perform together with BTS at MMA 2018," Instagram, December 1, 2018, https://www.instagram.com/p/Bq2LvOVAS5s/.

11   Nam and Gim, *An Introduction to Korean Traditional Performing Arts*, 101.

12   BTS_twt, "오늘 여러가지," Twitter, February 26, 2019, 12:35 p.m., https://twitter.com/BTS_twt/status/1100449341200773121/photo/2.

13   According to Byoung-ok Lee, "Korean mask dance deals with stories which were satirical in nature, such as accusations of social immortality,

the corrupt aristocracy, [the] triangular relationship between husband, wife, and concubine, and vulgar apostate Buddhist monks, all expressed in a humorous manner." B. Lee, "The Concept of Korean Folk Dance," 130.

14 *Talchum* was designated by the Korean government as one of the National Intangible Cultural Properties and, today, thirteen repertories are preserved and disseminated throughout Korea. *Bongsan talchum* is a version of *talchum* from the Hwanghae province that began about two hundred years ago. It was performed on the night of Dano (fifth day of the fifth lunar month) and Haji (summer solstice). See B. Lee, "The Concept of Korean Folk Dance," 130; Jeon, *Korean Mask Dance Dramas*, 44.

15 Melon, "믿고보는 [MMA] *소름주의* 방탄소년단 (BTS)—IDOL Full.ver," October 22, 2019, YouTube video, 6:31, https://youtu.be/LfgXdDaryBE.

16 Melon, "믿고보는 [MMA] *소름주의* 방탄소년단 (BTS)—IDOL Full.ver."

Works Cited

Anderson, Crystal S. *Soul in Seoul: African American Popular Music and K-Pop*. Jackson: University Press of Mississippi, 2020.

Fuhr, Michael. *Globalization and Popular Music in South Korea: Sounding Out K-Pop*. New York: Routledge, 2015.

Jeon, Kyung-wook. *Korean Mask Dance Dramas: Their History and Structural Principles*. Translated by Eur Do-seon. Gyeonggi-do, Korea: Youlhwadang, 2005.

Kim, Jaehong. "[Future of Korean Film Industry: A Film Is Equivalent to an Established Company."] *Kyunghayng*, April 30, 2004. https://n.news.naver.com /mnews/article/033/0000003819?sid=114 (in Korean).

Kim, Soojin. "Controlling or Supporting? A History of Cultural Policies on Popular Music." In *Made in Korea: Studies in Popular Music*, edited by Hyunjoon Shin and Seung-Ah Lee, 181–90. New York: Routledge, 2016.

Lee, Byoung-ok. "The Concept of Korean Folk Dance." In *Dance of Korea*, edited by Anthony T. Rauche, Yu Si-hyeon, and Chang Yoon-hee, 123–51. Seoul: National Gugak Center, 2014.

Lee, Hye-Kyung. *Cultural Policy in South Korea: Making a New Patron State*. New York: Routledge, 2019.

Nam, Sang-suk, and Hae-suk Gim. *An Introduction to Korean Traditional Performing Arts*. Seoul: Minsokwon, 2009.

Shim, Doobo. "Hybridity and the Rise of Korean Popular Culture in Asia." *Media, Culture and Society* 28, no. 1 (January 2006): 25–44. https://doi.org/10.1177 /0163443706059278.

02 · Hustlin' until Dope: How BTS's Rap Line Cultivated Their Hip-Hop Identities

— Nykeah Parham

In his 2019 review of BTS's then six-year-old discography, Youngdae Kim, a Korean music critic and Korean hip-hop historian, posits that BTS "didn't simply borrow hip hop; they are one of the few idols that embraced the genre as their identity."[1] There is much to be unpacked from Kim's declaration about the group's musical oeuvre. The evolution of BTS's career certainly demonstrates a deepening engagement with and understanding of hip-hop culture, particularly through the cyphers or mixtapes featuring members of the group's Rap Line (RM, SUGA, and j-hope).[2] However, this chapter elaborates on Kim's pronouncement to track how BTS "hustled" their way to credibility as hip-hop artists—connecting the seemingly interminable physical and cultural work demanded of industry idols with the self-reflexive labor it took to be considered genuine contributors to the genre.

Prior to BTS's debut in 2013, hip hop held a tenuous place in South Korea's idol industry. While K-Pop idol groups commonly used hip hop as part of a rotation of musical and visual concepts, they rarely made it their main musical style. This can be attributed in part to the long-standing stigma hip hop has carried in South Korea because of its association with antiauthoritarianism and Black American gang culture. Even as we have seen an increasing number of designated rappers in idol groups, hip hop still typically serves as one among a number of genres featured within a group's discography or even within a single song rather than an organizing feature of its entire musical persona. In this context, BTS took a risk by calling themselves a hip-hop idol group when they debuted in 2013 and was unsurprisingly met with mixed responses from Korean audiences.

BTS faced criticism from Korea's underground hip-hop community in particular. Underground Korean rappers have widely rejected K-Pop idols as "puppets" of the big talent management agencies.[3] In a now infamous round-table discussion on Korean hip hop, Korean rapper B-Free openly criticized RM and SUGA for selling out to become idols who are unable to "resist the temptation of money."[4] Both RM and SUGA were active rappers in Korea's underground hip-hop scene before they were recruited to be idol trainees.[5] Credibility within hip-hop culture is tied to a certain type of authenticity, which is conferred upon artists by each other based on perceptions of an artist's genuine motivation and grounding in hip-hop culture. At the time of BTS's debut in 2013, hip hop was still seen as a marketing tool used by the idol industry rather than a genuine form of artistic expression. Hip-hop authenticity was understood to be antithetical to the idol world.

BTS's first three mini albums—2 COOL 4 SKOOL (2013), O!RUL8,2? (2013), and SKOOL LUV AFFAIR (2014)—were rooted in American hip hop. The music featured on the group's "School Trilogy" was driven by the fast beats and heavy bass reminiscent of 1990s hip hop, particularly gangsta rap, with lyrics full of youthful angst and social critique often expressed through AAVE (African American Vernacular English). Their debut song, "No More Dream" (2013), introduced BTS as a group who not only penned their own music, but also delivered a clear social message that aligned with the values of social critique and rebellion enshrined in American hip-hop culture. The song is dedicated "to all the youngsters without dreams," features a strong bass line that defines the track, and allows for the members to rap and sing while playing with the rhythmic patterns in the beat. The song itself is satire, critiquing youth's lack of genuine ambition for personal dreams possibly due to the pressures of parents and the larger Korean society (i.e., to pursue college education and a desk job at a big company, or medical or law careers). In its opening verse, SUGA literally laughs about not having "big dreams" but dreams of wealth, whereas RM reminisces on childhood dreams that have been forgotten due to a particular push to the "study room" by parents. BTS's debut song represented a major departure from most other K-Pop, which almost exclusively focused on romantic themes and lyrics. Despite the originality of BTS's music, the release of "No More Dream" garnered mixed reactions. For many observers, the purported authenticity of the social message was difficult to reconcile with the seeming inauthenticity of the visual style. BTS's debut image traded in commercial rap tropes globally circulated through music videos: members sported gold chains, oversized "baggy" clothes, and Afro-textured hair.[6] Thus, while the lyrics were seen as "real" in speaking to youth, the baggy clothes, gold chains, and paisley bandanas were judged as insincere imitations of an outdated hip-hop concept. Their earliest singles either fell in ranking on the Korean music charts or failed to chart at all.[7]

When BTS arrived in Los Angeles in 2014 to film their reality series *American Hustle Life* (AHL), the members were styled in a wardrobe reminiscent of their look in the "No More Dream" music video. The show aimed to document the members' journey to be "born again as a true hip-hop artist," through rigorous training in hip-hop history, dance, songwriting, and Black American culture.[8] Even though many of the show's scenarios are awkwardly staged and cringeworthy, the show nonetheless exposes BTS to a "Hip Hop 101" curriculum that became foundational for their development as artists. In an early episode, hip-hop legend and rapper Coolio, who served as one of their mentors, posed a series of questions to BTS on hip-hop history, such as the origins of hip hop, the first rap single to go platinum, certain icons in the hip-hop industry, and so on.[9] The show also familiarized members with guidelines for how to respect Black American culture and understand the context behind AAVE vocabulary. For instance, Coolio scolded V for using "turn up" in conversation without knowing its meaning. The show gave BTS an unflinching introduction to the intersections of rap and American race politics, imparting critical lessons about the social and cultural genealogy of the genre that helped the group become more reflexive about their interactions with its history and culture. Later, RM recalled that Warren G not only reoriented RM's understanding of *who* could do hip hop, since it was "open to anyone" regardless of racial background, but also that hip hop was not about "shooting guns, doing drugs, [or] robbery," dismantling stereotypes built on the criminalization of Black men in particular.[10]

Ironically, *American Hustle Life*—despite being heavily staged and scripted—gave BTS credibility in Korea's hip-hop scene. As a group with only one fluent English speaker and no *gyopo* members (ethnic Koreans born and raised outside of Korea) from the United States, BTS did not have strong ties to American culture built into the group's identity and thus was not perceived as having an "authentic" connection to "real" (read: American) hip hop. However, the stamp of approval they received from their mentors Coolio and Warren G regarding their artistry as hip-hop artists gave them cultural currency. In an episode focused on songwriting, hip-hop legend and SUGA's icon, Warren G, shared about his upbringing and gave BTS members a lyric-writing assignment in which they had to tell their life stories over his song "Regulate." RM expressed apprehension about the possible inauthenticity of adding his own lyrics to a song originally about Warren G's past struggles and gang-related activity. However, BTS learned from their mentors that "simple copying will be dismissed; artful borrowing and paying respect are highly regarded."[11] Warren G assured them that the "hustle" of hip hop was grounded in the truth of one's experience: "Once you tell your story over it, then it becomes you."[12] This stamp of approval from Black American hip-hop legends told South Korea's hip-hop scene not only that the group had paid their dues to the originators of hip hop but that they were also authentic in their pursuit of hip hop regardless of their idol status.

BTS's first full-length album, *DARK & WILD* (2014), demonstrated the first major shift in the group's image following the education they received on *AHL*. Moving away from the visual tropes seen in the "School Trilogy," they shifted focus to the message in their music. The song "힙합성애자 / Hip Hop Lover" (2014), for instance, served as the group's ode to hip hop's genealogy. Written by members of BTS's Rap Line and Big Hit's in-house producer Pdogg, the song references rap icons such as Nas, KRS-One, and Eminem as BTS proclaims why the BTS members were "down" for hip hop. Moreover, the album features the third cypher of the discography—"BTS Cypher PT.3: KILLER (Feat. Supreme Boi)," which displays their commitment to the cypher form as a point of reference to their hip-hop identities and their dedication to the craft of lyricism, wordplay, and rap delivery.[13]

"This a Cypher I'm a Rider": Self-Identity in the Cypher

BTS features cyphers across the discography as a way of asserting their roots of hip-hop culture. A cypher is a type of song fundamental to hip-hop performance. Initially rooted in improvisation, freestyle rap, and the call-and-response structure of Black American musicality evident in the beginnings of hip hop, cyphers feature battling rappers or dancers encircled by an audience. The cypher is meant to exhibit talent and engage in friendly competition: "If you have the guts to step into the [cypher] and tell your story and, above all, demonstrate your uniqueness, you might be accepted into the community."[14] It also carries the notions of fighting back, representing, collaborating, and sometimes "aggressively claiming your own voice, your own right to speak."[15] To craft and perform a cypher is "to borrow and to lend . . . exacting care for each word and carefully [considering] all the sounds, meanings, and interpretations."[16] While cyphers are traditionally improvised freestyles from a group of rappers, dancers, or deejays, the form has evolved to include prepared lyrics and formal song structures such as choruses, sometimes as diss tracks or posse tracks meant to showcase the relationship of a group of artists. This is the style that BTS uses.[17]

Diss tracks, another element of hip-hop culture and a form of Black American cultural performance born out of a comedic competition called the Dozens, utilize rap delivery, musical skill, and quality lyricism to publicly embarrass and figuratively fight back against those who have been negatively critical. Acting as a diss track, "BTS Cypher PT.3: KILLER (Feat. Supreme Boi)" addresses BTS's haters, figuratively murdering the detractors, not only by calling them out but also through the virtuosity of the group's rap skills. Part 3 features Supreme Boi, an underground rapper who had been in the original BTS lineup as a trainee but ultimately transitioned into a solo artist and in-house producer for Big Hit Entertainment. His voice is blended with the others, with no stand-alone part typical of featured artists, as if to signal through his seamless inclusion that BTS has left neither him nor their hip-hop roots behind.

The song begins with quick repetitive sounds resembling the tense background music of an arcade-style combat video game like *Street Fighter*. A woodwind instrument then floats in over muffled bass and snare drums that reproduce the feeling of being crowded in a circle. The rhythms build up to a cadence reminiscent of the seconds leading up to a double Dutch performance or the footwork of a boxer about to land a first punch. RM begins with direct language, stating that he will "kill," he is "real," he is better than a "lazy" so-called rapper, and he is in his "beast mode." The track shows that the members are not afraid to engage in a lyrical battle, particularly while rapping on a full album rather than an EP. Others have had their say in the public sphere; here, BTS replies through the music, where the members do not necessarily have to show respect when they have not been respected. They are fully established, settled, and ready to fight.

First up is RM, then known as Rap Monster, who creates lyrical carnage as he raps speedily through the bars, a skill highly sought after in hip hop. RM's verse effortlessly blends Korean and English, using rhyme and bilingual wordplay to mock the detractors who characterize hip hop as an "easy genre."[18] RM, showcasing his knowledge of how cyphers thrive on sound rhyme and layered meanings, plays with Korean pronunciation to open up multiple translations. For instance, he cleverly distorts his pronunciation of the phrase "넌 하수구 / *neon hasugu*," which roughly translates into English as "You're a sewer," to add a secondary layer of meaning. By pronouncing "하수구/*hasugu*" as "하수고/*hasugo*," he simultaneously calls his haters "losers" or "someone lacking skills."[19] With his critics characterized either as a sewer or a loser, RM comes out as the winner. He uses this type of wordplay again when he pokes fun at artists who claim to be rappers but do not actually have the skill (yet have the nerve to critique him). He uses 돌팔이/dolpari to describe someone faking expertise, literally a faker in the rap game. His verse exposes rappers without sincerity or skill and are fakers claiming authenticity in hip hop. His virtuosity as a bilingual rapper not only generates multiple meanings that cut deeper but also showcases a layering effect of beat and cadence on his rhythmic delivery. In his verse of the cypher, he proves his skill and calls out all who "raps the same" as every other rapper.[20]

After the chorus comes j-hope's verse, where he adds a playfulness to the cypher that is framed by heavy masculine bravado and more anger through rhyme schemes that continue over multiple lines. Rather than beginning with speed, his lyrical delivery rides the groove of the beat to get the audience to pay close attention. Later, he pairs his delivery with quick onomatopoeia showcasing his famously cheeky personality: "Oh, I'm on top of the beat beat, wiggle wiggling jingle jiggling / roll rolling, beagle beagling / And my power that blazes, blazing / The god who owns rules the ring, ring, now, now, the king who'll list his name up there."[21] In Korean and English, these lines end in an -ing, -jit, -him, and another -ing, where all the sounds carry a long e and rhyme. Here he is like a "beagle," full of playfulness and cheer. Yet, he also delivers hard-hitting lines with a smile, arguing that he should not be discounted since he has a rap that feeds his country. He uses less English in his verse than RM, centering the Korean language as a rejoinder to debates over what "good" Korean rap ought to sound like. Not only does j-hope show that he is aware of Korean hip hop's debate regarding the use of English and being seen as a copy of American hip-hop artists, but he also makes a statement of his own skill as opposed to rappers with their "sloppy English," who do not understand how English can be used to enhance lyrics and are instead relying on English to make them seem better than they are.[22] Although they might have been perceived as distant from authentic American hip hop because they have no gyopo member and only one English fluent member, this verse on this cypher solidified the end of attempting to prove their authenticity and talent in hip hop to others. By the end of his verse, j-hope is the one "standing above" these haters with no issues.

Rounding out the last verse is SUGA who begins by boasting about his "music that breathes alive in every corner of the world."[23] His verse uses a "represent" approach, drawing on a hip-hop practice that invokes place and space to signify street-savvy credibility and demands respect for one's origins. Hip hop's injunction to "represent" grounds artists and their cultural expression to specific places and posses that mark their local allegiances and identities.[24]

When SUGA "represents" BTS and Daegu in his first few lines, he does so to let the haters and other listeners know that they are to respect his 'hood and ultimately respect him and his posse (BTS and ARMY). SUGA contends that he is an excellent representative of BTS, his hometown Daegu, and Korean rappers. He declares that people, regardless of how they feel about him, not only know his reputation but also whisper it from his hometown all the way to the most fabulous place in Seoul and all around the world. He traces his origins even further back in history, conjuring Korean folk imagery to depict himself as a shaman with a gift for dodging verbal attacks and proving his enemies unworthy. At the end of his verse, he uses *saturi*, the regional dialect of his hometown, to address his haters as 행님/*haengnim*, an honorific used by males to address older men in Daegu and the broader Gyeongsang region. His show of respect for his elders immediately proves to be sardonic as he tells them how they have "aged immaturely" and are truly "babies" who are not at his level.[25] Those who were "arrogant" enough to critique him, instead of being good *hyeongs*, or older brothers who would mentor him, are lazy while he works and travels all around the world. Now and in the future, SUGA (and his posse) have become hip-hop idols despite all the trash talk.

BTS's hip-hop sensibility is anchored in its Rap Line. All three members had earned a level of credibility within their respective artistic communities before being recruited into the group—RM and SUGA as underground rappers and j-hope as a street dancer. Their use of cyphers throughout their discography shows how the BTS Rap Line remains true to their hip-hop roots by honing their rapping and production skills, while expressing their anger at being disregarded despite their obvious competence and love for the music, genre, and culture. These songs, among others in their discography, created space to establish BTS's legitimacy as hip-hop artists and to prove that they have not left hip hop behind or traded their message for idol popularity.

Mixtapes: The Heart and Soul

RM, SUGA, and j-hope have released a number of solo tracks apart from the group and are among a small handful of idol-rappers who specifically refer to their solo efforts as "mixtapes." Creating a mixtape is a deliberate call-back to a hip-hop practice from the 1980s and 1990s, when aspiring deejays and hip-hop artists would self-create (cassette) tape mixes of their music to introduce themselves to the public. They often sampled past artists' lyrics, baselines, or instrumentals and combined their skills as amateur producers, emcees, or deejays to distribute their tapes (for free or very cheap) to gain listeners or as demos for record labels. This practice also served as a way to connect intimately with an audience without alienating potential fans who could not afford the purchase.

BTS's Rap Line's use of the mixtape as a curation of solo work and identity was born out of a desire to be taken seriously as hip-hop artists. By 2015, BTS as a group had begun to grow in popularity and fame. The two breakout singles from their third mini album, *The most beautiful moment in life pt.1* (2015)— "I NEED U" and "Dope/쩔어"—garnered much international attention. "Dope/쩔어" became their first music video to reach 100 million views on YouTube, making BTS the first idol group from outside the "Big Three" of K-Pop entertainment companies (SM Entertainment, JYP Entertainment, and YG Entertainment) to achieve this feat.[26] BTS's Rap Line, alongside other idol rappers like iKON's Bobby, VIXX's Ravi, and Block B's ZICO, created mixtapes to continue associating themselves with the Korean and global hip-hop scenes. But they also used their mixtapes to establish who they were, apart from BTS, and distinguished their artist personas as rappers. Each mixtape not only allowed a deeper exploration of their individual hip-hop styles, but also illustrated the depth of their genre knowledge. All three rappers produced tracks that draw on old school hip-hop styles and the practice of sampling, fusing them with traditional Korean musical styles and cultural themes to craft their own approach to hip hop and showcase their individual identities.

RM was the first Rap Line member to release a mixtape, which he titled *RM* (2015), a clear expression of his desire to present himself as an individual. In it, RM provides an inward analysis of his life's struggles and concludes with a declaration of belief in himself. RM continued this theme of introspection in his second solo effort, *mono* (2018), which RM considers a playlist. *mono* offers fans an intimate glimpse into his mind through a rap style reminiscent of RM's idol, legendary rapper Nas, who was a major influence on his first mixtape.[27] In his second mixtape, RM uses Nas's one-mic approach to the song "moonchild" to create a personal, conversational atmosphere. Nas's "One Mic" (2002) song and music video features Nas repeating that all he needs is "one mic" to identify and expose the issues in the world that he notices, similar to a soapbox. "One Mic" centers the use of his platform as a rapper, with one mic amplifying his voice to discuss his social consciousness and hopes the world not only understands him and his feelings, but also moves to action to change reality.[28] In "moonchild," RM similarly raps over a slower rhythm and invites the listener to share in his thoughts as the song and his voice grow in speed, power, and volume. His lyrical style is like a "street corner prophet," an older term referring to rappers who would perform on street corners and comment on situations in the community. Even though he is alone—hence *mono*—his repetitive "come on y'all" at the beginning of the verses and every chorus invites listeners into the song. Different from traditional music videos, "moonchild" is a lyric video where the lyrics become the protagonist and focus of the music video. Similar to Nas's "One Mic," RM sits alone in a room, without facing the camera, after appearing in the frame sometime after the song has begun, specifically once the Korean lyrics begin. The styling of the lyric video signals to the viewers that RM is not the focus, but his thoughts are. The lyrics appear in various computerized fonts centered in the video and also as clippings of RM's own handwriting. Sometimes, the written lyrics appear around his body and at times literally flow from his heart, visually expressing his use of "y'all" and "우리," which carries the weight of "we" in Korean.[29] The bilingual lyrics speak to his identity as a polyglot, and position RM as a voice that sheds light on loneliness. This song is meant to comfort those who are struggling like him with feeling alone (being singular or *mono*) while they all "dance in the pain." For RM, the mixtape became an opportunity to craft a voice as an artist and rapper that stretches the story of the intimate and personal to a broader scale.

When j-hope released HOPE WORLD (2018), many fans eagerly anticipated how it would add to the Rap Line's mixtape repertoire. HOPE WORLD is a declaration of who j-hope wants to be as an artist and public figure: a representation of hope for fans and the hope of BTS. From the bright colors and plump calligraphy of the album art to the velour jumpsuits and bucket hats j-hope wears in the mixtape's music videos, each aesthetic element creates a nostalgia for the late 1980s and early 1990s, the golden age of hip hop. HOPE WORLD features boom-bap rap, one of the calmer rap styles popular in the 1980s and 1990s. Its slower pace is more conducive to storytelling and the listener's comprehension of the rapper's message, which typically addressed social problems or personal struggles and offered solutions. The mixtape's dreamy soundscape and overall message reflect j-hope's rap approach as a storyteller. The track "P.O.P (Piece Of Peace)" carries the message of encouragement and empathy to his fans who are anxiously preparing to step into new chapters of their lives (e.g., job seekers facing unemployment and other stress). Although much of the song is in Korean, j-hope chooses an almost equal use of Korean and English in the repeated chorus, which offers himself as a "Piece of Peace," "strength," and a "light to someone."[30] His chorus carries simple phrases that do not require lengthy translation that might muddy the clarity of his message.

SUGA's mixtapes use hardcore rap style, the most aggressive sound and style of hip hop, to proclaim his identity as Agust D, his solo rap alter ego. Similarly, to its origins in the 1980s with Run DMC and later gangsta rap from N.W.A., SUGA's solo music features little to no singing or dance grooves, relying on a grungier and more monotonous beat as the backtrack for his dense lyrical expression of anger and confrontation. He also utilizes the practice of sampling, common to hardcore rap, to include and introduce his listeners to Korean folk music. For example, in "대취타 (Daechwita)" on D-2 (2020), SUGA samples the *daechwita*, the traditional Korean musical accompaniment for the king's royal procession, to announce his success. The song opens with the sounds of Korean wind and percussion instruments reverberating beneath a chanting voice that signals the start of the musical procession. We hear the jangle of a *kkwaenggwari* (a small handheld cymbal) build anticipation before a heavy electronic bass beat, and SUGA simultaneously erupts onto the soundtrack. SUGA's confrontational lyrical delivery mixed with the cacophonous sounds of the *daechwita* creates a headbanger that demands to be played loudly. Throughout the song, SUGA links himself to Korean history and his personal experience as he does in BTS's cyphers: his lyrics declare that he is a "rags-to-riches" king and does not need to flex.[31] He did not come from money, but now he is a king in his musical element. His past is what fueled his ambition and practice, so he will "eat them all" to keep moving forward. By sampling a traditional piece, SUGA (re)introduces his cultural history to the public by combining it with his hip-hop style. He still maintains his "represent" approach throughout, representing himself, his hometown Daegu, BTS, and hip hop.

Becoming Dope

From the beginning of their careers, BTS understood the notion of hustling. They began as a group of underdogs, written off as a joke or an aberration in the K-Pop industry and as copycats or sellouts in the Korean hip-hop world. To change this image and claim legitimacy as hip-hop artists, the group studied the genre they identified with and found a way to connect it with their own backgrounds and struggles. Humbled by and drawing from their personal struggles and their hip-hop training on *American Hustle Life*, BTS took to heart the message to "Be who you are, straight from your heart."[32] Today, the BTS Rap Line continues to utilize its hip-hop sensibilities to express frustrations and share social critiques. From the cyphers to the mixtapes, hip hop is essential to the group's musical and cultural understandings and continues to flow through their music. Rather than using hip hop as one concept among many, BTS came to craft and express their hip-hop identities through the use of cyphers, mixtapes, and other hip-hop styles across their group and individual discography. Where once their association with hip hop had marginalized them as artists, they found a way to creatively hustle and pursue a path that expressed their love for hip hop and their deep connection to it.

Notes

1   Y. Kim, BTS: *The Review*, 50. As coauthor of 한국 힙합: 열정의 발자취 (*Korean Hip Hop: Footsteps of Passion*, 2008), Kim established his bona fides to comment on the evolution of Korean popular music, especially Korean hip hop.

2   The term *Rap Line* is used to describe the group members who have set positions as rappers. They usually rap instead of singing (even if they have the ability) in songs and performances.

3   Anderson, *Soul in Seoul*, 122.

4   Bwiyomi, "(ENG) B-Free Disses BTS 방탄소년단 디스하는 비프리," November 24, 2013, YouTube video, 15:27, https://www.youtube.com/watch?v=evfNBEeChek.

5   Similarly, j-hope was a street dancer who was then recruited to JYP Entertainment before becoming a trainee at Big Hit Entertainment.

6   In *2 COOL 4 SKOOL*'s promotional pictures, RM (then known as Rap Monster) dons an Afro-perm.

7   "국내 대표 음악 차트 가온차트! [Korean National Leading Music Chart Gaon Chart!]."

8   This was mentioned in episode introductions of *American Hustle Life* on Mnet.

9   DAILYBANGTANNIES, "BTS American Hustle Life Ep. 1 (ENG SUB)."

10   B. Kim, "랩몬스터 | '욕하기 위해서라도 믹스테잎을 꼭 들어주시면 좋겠다' [Rap Monster | I hope you listen to the mixtape despite cursing]"; Jones, "Respect Must Be Earned."

11   Watkins and Gaines, "Cyphers."

12   DAILYBANGTANNIES, "BTS American Hustle Life Ep. 4 (ENG SUB)."

13   The first two cyphers fall under BTS's initial styling that was criticized as imitative and old school.

14   Chang, "It's a Hip-Hop World."

15   Chang, "It's a Hip-Hop World."

16   Watkins and Gaines, "Cyphers."

17   Also called "posse cuts."

18   "BTS Cypher PT.3: KILLER (Feat. Supreme Boi)." The bilingual wordplay interpretation in this section is drawn from the translator's notes on the site *Doolset Lyrics*, a fan-made blog that serves as the source of all the English lyrics translations discussed in this chapter.

19   "BTS Cypher PT.3: KILLER (Feat. Supreme Boi)."

20   "BTS Cypher PT.3: KILLER (FEAT. SUPREME BOI)."

21   "BTS Cypher PT.3: KILLER (FEAT. SUPREME BOI)."

22   Kalka, "Taking Pride in Korean Hip Hop."

23   "BTS Cypher PT.3: KILLER (FEAT. SUPREME BOI)."

24   Forman, "'Represent.'"

25   "BTS Cypher PT.3: KILLER (Feat. Supreme Boi)."

26   J. K., "BTS's 'Dope' Becomes Their 1st MV to Hit 100 Million Views."

27   McIntyre, "BTS Member RM Announces Surprise Project 'Mono.'"

28   Nas, "Nas—One Mic."

29   "moonchild."

30   "P.O.P (Piece Of Peace) PT.1."

31   "대취타 (Daechwita)."

32   DAILYBANGTANNIES, "BTS American Hustle Life Ep. 7 Part 4 (ENG SUB)."

Works Cited

Anderson, Crystal S. *Soul in Seoul: African American Popular Music and K-Pop*. Jackson: University Press of Mississippi, 2020.

"BTS Cypher PT.3: KILLER (Feat. Supreme Boi)." *Doolset Lyrics*, March 11, 2019. https://doolsetbangtan.wordpress.com/2019/03/11/bts-cypher-pt-3-killer/.

Chang, Jeff. "It's a Hip-Hop World." *Foreign Policy*, October 12, 2009. https://foreignpolicy.com/2009/10/12/its-a-hip hop-world/.

"대취타 (Daechwita)." *Doolset Lyrics*, May 22, 2020. https://doolsetbangtan.wordpress.com/2020/05/22/daechwita/.

DAILYBANGTANNIES. "BTS American Hustle Life Ep. 1 (ENG SUB)." December 4, 2021. YouTube video, 22:23. https://youtu.be/bck4PVIShxM.

DAILYBANGTANNIES. "BTS American Hustle Life Ep. 4 (ENG SUB)." December 5, 2021. YouTube video, 46:09. https://youtu.be/i7nYVPxpvbg.

DAILYBANGTANNIES. "BTS American Hustle Life Ep. 7 Part 4 (ENG SUB)." December 5, 2021. YouTube video, 10:58. https://youtu.be/mPqLQE3vhAE.

Forman, Murray. "'Represent': Race, Space and Place in Rap Music." *Popular Music* 19, no. 1 (2000): 65–90. http://www.jstor.org/stable/853712.

J. K. "BTS's 'Dope' Becomes Their 1st MV to Hit 100 Million Views." *Soompi*, October 24, 2016. https://www.soompi.com/article/909623wpp/btss-dope-becomes-1st-mv-hit-100-million-views.

Jones, Monique. "Respect Must Be Earned: BTS' Journey towards Gaining Its Stripes in Black America." *Reappropriate*, December 7, 2017. https://reappropriate

.co/2017/12/respect-must-be-earned-bts-journey-towards-gaining-its
-stripes-in-black-america/.

Kalka, Emma. "Taking Pride in Korean Hip Hop: Honey Family's Digiri Hopes More
Artists Rap in Korean." *Korea Herald*, December 1, 2013. https://www
.koreaherald.com/view.php?ud=20131201000202.

Kim, Bong Hyun. "랩몬스터 | '욕하기 위해서라도 믹스테잎을 꼭 들어주시면 좋겠다' [Rap
Monster | I hope you listen to the mixtape despite cursing]." *HipHop
Playa*, March 24, 2015. https://hiphopplaya.com/g2/bbs/board.php?bo
_table=interview&wr_id=782.

Kim, Yongdae. BTS: *The Review; A Comprehensive Look at the Music of* BTS. Translated
by H. J. Chung. Seoul: RH Korea, 2019.

"국내 대표 음악 차트 가온차트! [Korean National Leading Music Chart Gaon Chart!],"
June 2013. Archived August 28, 2016, at Archive.org. https://web.archive
.org/web/20160828194450/http://gaonchart.co.kr/main/section/chart
/online.gaon?PageNo=2&nationGbn=T&serviceGbn=ALL&targetTime
=25&hitYear=2013&termGbn=week.

McIntyre, Hugh. "BTS Member RM Announces Surprise Project 'Mono' Slated to
Drop in Just a Few Days." *Forbes*, October 20, 2018. https://www.forbes
.com/sites/hughmcintyre/2018/10/20/bts-member-rm-announces
-surprise-project-mono-slated-to-drop-in-just-a-few-days/.

"moonchild." *Doolset Lyrics*, October 24, 2018. https://doolsetbangtan.wordpress
.com/2018/10/24/moonchild/.

Nas. "Nas—One Mic (Official HD Video)." October 25, 2009. YouTube video, 4:22.
https://youtube/JCOURZ-yx4E.

"P.O.P (Piece Of Peace) PT.1." *Doolset Lyrics*, November 3, 2018. https://doolsetbangtan
.wordpress.com/2018/11/03/p-o-p-piece-of-peace-pt-1/.

Watkins, Paul, and Rebecca Gaines. "Cyphers: Hip-Hop and Improvisation." *Critical
Studies in Improvisation / Études Critiques en Improvisation* 10, no. 1 (2014).
https://doi.org/10.21083/csieci.v10i1.3518.

03 · "Life Goes On": Social and Musical Space in BTS's Midpandemic Album *BE*

_ Stefania Piccialli

When the pandemic hit, I had just finished my master's degree in gender and media, and instead of starting the next phase of my life, I spent a year stuck inside my house. At the time, lockdowns in Italy were particularly severe due to the devastating impact of COVID-19 on the nation. In 2020 alone, Italy recorded the highest ever number of dead since the end of World War II.[1] People were completely locked in their homes for a little more than two months during the nationwide lockdown and intermittently for the rest of the year due to pandemic containment measures.[2] In order to connect, people sang to each other from their balconies, illustrating the hunger for human interaction and the role of music in creating intimacy in the face of isolation. I spent most of my time in my room, which I tried to make cozy, for I was bound to occupy the space for an unknown period of time. I remember feeling enthusiastic about the promotional photos for BTS's comeback, featuring each of the members alone in fantastically furnished rooms. I could see myself, in my own tiny space, reflected in those pictures. BTS's take on our period of isolation was filled with their infamous creativity and, when BE was released in late 2020, I found refuge and escape in the album as if it were a hug from a friend, whom I could only reach online.

The 2020 COVID-19 pandemic changed how we perceive space, as we were forced to isolate and experience life at a distance. While social theorists have long considered space to be a social construct produced by societal norms, power dynamics, habits, and relationships, this reorientation of space beyond its simplistic, everyday connotations became the task for so many of us during this time, including BTS themselves. BE, their ninth studio album, released in

2020, reflected this shift in the experience of space in both its concept and music. The album can be viewed as a space of its own, with the potential for both BTS members and ARMY to coexist, connect, heal, and reflect on their inner lives during difficult times. In this chapter, I examine BE's production, content, and promotion, bringing BE into conversation with theories of space that emphasize its necessarily social dimensions. Doing so uncovers how this album centers social, auditory, and physical spaces and their placemaking promises to create a shared venue for artists and listeners.

The album BE was an unexpected glitch in BTS's plans.[3] At the beginning of 2020, the group was poised to start the MAP OF THE SOUL TOUR. Their plans were stymied by the global response to COVID-19, which included quarantine measures, lockdowns, and social distancing. For professionals in the music and creative industries worldwide, the pandemic resulted in loss of revenue and jobs from closed concert venues.[4] However, audiences continued to support their favorite artists in the digital realm. In a study on social convergence under COVID-19 mitigation strategies that included spatial and social distancing, neuroscience and music scholars concluded that real-time virtual performances constituted a space for social connection and positive emotional responses.[5] They reported that audiences attending concerts in online spaces experienced the same feelings of community as people attending live performances. Under these circumstances, listeners viewed music as a "surrogate for an empathic friend, providing solace and understanding when one is working through negative emotions."[6] The study's authors, Dana Swarbrick, Beate Seibt, Noemi Grinspun, and Jonna K. Vuoskoski, maintain that even solitary music listening can be a social experience, conveying a sense of the presence of another person. This sense of connection can take the form of identifying or empathizing with the performer or composer or experiencing the music itself as a virtual being. In promotions for BE, BTS members talked about the album as an expression of their frustrations and a conduit to deliver a message of healing and comfort to ARMY.[7] BE, they hoped, could be experienced as a space where ARMY could connect both with BTS and with each other through music, to find solace from loneliness and the stresses of the pandemic.

An album such as BE can be considered a space in itself. In The Production of Space, philosopher Henri Lefebvre argues that social relations produce space and, conversely, that social ties are informed by the spaces in which they develop.[8] He posits that meanings related to space are ultimately political—they are created and understood through relationships between humans with their unique cultures, economies, and power dynamics. In this sense, space is not a neutral quality but the direct consequence of different communities interacting among themselves in a specific moment in time. This conceptualization of space suggests that listening to music, whether in solitude or with others, connects the listener to the artist or fellow human beings, creating a shared social experience based on the emotional response that art can produce in the face of common adversity.

Between March and October 2020, while making BE, BTS released a series of YouTube videos and VLIVE streams in which they talked about the creative process for the album.[9] They shared ideas and details about the album with ARMY and described how they had created a product that was the result of the ties between the members, between the label and artists, and between the band and fans. RM described the group's intention of including ARMY in the production process, "like a good restaurant sharing their secret recipe with each other." He also affirmed, "Even when we can't meet in person we created this album in a way that when our album comes out, they [fans] can watch our vlogs and whatnot later and think, this topic came up then so that's why they put this in to make them feel that it's an album that we created together with the fans," and, that as a result, he hopes "many people feel more connected to the album."[10] These references to connection with ARMY in these brainstorming and production videos invite fans to engage with BE as a space of collaboration and camaraderie.

BE reflects a shift in how BTS presented the process through which their albums are produced. Previously, the band participated in the composition of the songs without assigning specific roles related to the production and visual aspects of the album. However, during a YouTube vlog, RM stated, "We have reached a conclusion that we should try a new thing. We started preparations for a new album. We will share the process [of the album preparations with fans] . . . although nothing has been fixed including the time of its release."[11] In interviews and during their livestreams, BTS emphasized their individual involvement in the entire workflow for BE. Each member carried out a specific task as a project manager in various production areas, setting the album and its production up as an outlet for creativity and emotion. Jimin explained, "As our team's production of a new album has been assigned independently to ourselves, we named the project managers [for each category], and I was put in charge of music."[12] Taking on specific and individual production roles, as well as sharing more of the behind-the-scenes creative process with ARMY for the very first time, BTS characterized the album as an artistic outlet for them to share their impressions of the pandemic, both as a collective effort and through their own individual exploration of roles they had not performed before.

The promotional pictures for the album, staged as representations of personal spaces of solitude and as invitations for the audience to share quarantine with BTS, generated stories of space. Gesturing to the physical isolation and psychic interiority that defined many people's experiences of quarantine during the pandemic, each member was photographed in a single room designed to represent his individual interests. On HYBE's official promotional website for BE, the members elaborated on their choices for each promotional room. RM's room reflected his aesthetic philosophy, full of artworks, bonsai, and earthy tones. Jin's room, decorated with sparkling gemstones and luxury furniture, made him look "completely at home," hinting at a connection between his choice to display opulent gems and his attitude toward life in the pandemic, which he later described as free, true to himself, and a reflection of a "do-whatever-I-want personality."[13] SUGA explains that his "outfit is in the blue tone of the room" in his "own stylistic interpretation." The mirror under his feet gestures to how the room is his space to reflect. j-hope is photographed in a room with vivid blues, reds, and yellows, wearing a comfortable robe, baggy shorts, and cozy slippers to represent what he wears at home. Jimin fills his room with multicolored, delicate flowers. V's room is decorated with a photo he took that represents the way he sees the world and himself within the limited space of his bedroom. Jung Kook's room is covered in speakers, which he sees as the object that best represents him, as a "conduit for the comfort and joy that a song delivers."[14] Each room is self-contained and singular, and each room is missing a fourth wall—as though inviting each of us to join them there. These rooms, designed as individual places of comfort, nonetheless connect BTS members to their audience, emphasizing the role of social relations within space.

BTS's conception of the room-as-invitation in the promotions for BE culminated in the launch of an interactive room curated by BTS, a visually simple and cartoonlike location that fans could access on HYBE's official website (see figure 3.1). Fans could decorate the room with a variety of objects that each member had drawn, all representing their favorite decorating styles, self-care items, and pets (e.g., moon jars, BTS and ARMY Polaroids, fluffy carpets, perfume, a piano, and the legendary puppy, Bangtani), and each member explains his choices in hidden videos for ARMY to discover. Users are also invited to make this digital space their own, by adding items they prefer to the ones drawn by the members, and to share their version of the room with BTS

3.1 · A screenshot of the webpage of the room "Curated for ARMY" by BTS members, where each member has created elements that can be used to decorate the room. March 25, 2023. https://ibighit.com/bts/eng/discography /detail/be.html.

on social media. Both the individualized promotional rooms and the interactive one dedicated to ARMY represent an invitation to a virtual fantasy space shared with the members, where the promotional rooms reflect the members' public personas and the interactive ARMY room offers an opportunity for both BTS and their listeners to assign meanings to these spaces according to each individual's diverse experiences. Both kinds of rooms provide an opportunity for the audience to consider how to make a space their own and to feel comforted and safe in the face of the pandemic.

The relational aspect of *BE* is ever present in its music, marketing, and production and their digital manifestations during the pandemic reflect both Lefebvre's vision of social space and Manuel Castells's idea of the space of flows. Castells translated the social attributes of space to the digital realm, coining the term *space of flows* to represent embodied and virtual locations apart from the physical places we inhabit. The space of flows is made up of electronic infrastructure and telecommunication systems, but it is also built through the connection of humans across distant places.[15] These networks are not neutral and universally accessible: the digital divide often replicates existing social inequalities, and for some the infrastructure is not available at all for real-time interaction.[16] Through the privilege of access to the internet and technological devices, people can connect to each other by exchanging flows of time-sensitive content, words and images, creating a networked community that interacts in real time (or close to it) all over the globe. Media scholar Arjun Appadurai posits that electronic infrastructure has the capacity to make media (as in images, music, and information) flow across borders, in a fluid network that in its many ramifications can connect distant locales.[17] The space of flows works similarly, linking through electronic flows, media, and, most of all, people.

The pandemic pushed many of us toward the digital realm where physical distances of whatever magnitude might be purportedly bridged in cyberspace. People from opposite parts of the globe could connect to BE and its messages and promotional materials through their devices, accessing the same flows of information despite lockdowns and geographical distance. In this way, listeners could experience the content that BTS had created and, if they so wished, build community and networks through the expression and exchange of feelings about BE, potentially finding solace in the face of the pandemic.

The packaging of the album also reflects the spatial concepts that informed BE. The physical album for BE Deluxe Edition is a white, featureless block; however, when opened it reveals a black frame (where the CD is stored) and photos (fragments of city streets, clear skies, nature, a window glittery with light, a wooden table, mirrors) that can be inserted into that frame (see figure 3.2). These pictures come from the VLIVE streams that BTS did during the lockdown period in South Korea, in which they were creating art and keeping ARMY company virtually. By referencing different spaces inside and outside the home, the packaging of the album reflects the lyrics of "Life Goes On" ("Like an arrow in the blue sky / . . . On my pillow, on my table") and evokes the different creative and social spaces of the album, united in one cohesive project. Using the available materials of the album, listeners are invited to personalize BE and make it their own.

The various components of BE converge in one space, where music, production, and promotion reflect the stated intention to provide solace, comfort, or a space for self-expression. In the acknowledgments and thank you letters the members wrote for their families, BIGHIT staff, and ARMY, they express their intention of producing BE as a potentially unbounded space of communion. RM writes, "Thinking of the many stars that are watching us [ARMY], resolutely, we stand up once again. This album is the outcome of that.

3.2 · The packaging of BTS's album *BE* Deluxe Edition, showing the black album frame personalized with one of the postcards. Photograph by Stefania Piccialli.

We couldn't stay withered forever, and it was also because we refused to."[18] Just as stars coexist with each as a distinct entity in a shared universe, *BE* is offered as a common space that allows different people to be connected through the experience of the album. Jin explains, "This album consists mainly of songs that could give you some comfort. I hope you'll be able to get some healing through listening to these songs," while SUGA similarly offered, "In a time full of frustration for everyone around the world, we worked on this album in hope that we could be a source of strength for our ARMY, even just a little bit. . . . I will always be your strength, whenever you need it. When you're facing difficult times, I hope you can lean on this music."[19] The members present *BE* as a curative place, an instrument to overcome the loneliness of the pandemic, promising the album as a virtual space of gathering and healing for both BTS and ARMY.

Access to this space of healing is most of all offered through the album's sound. Josh Kun's observation of the power of music to shape experiences has a distinctly spatial quality: "I can put on a song and live it, hear it, get inside its notes and chords, get inside its narratives and follow its journeys and paths. Dropping the needle or pressing the play button was the equivalent of walking into a building, entering into an architecture of sound, a space that can be seen and experienced only if it is heard."[20] *BE*'s song list pulls together a story about space in the midst of the pandemic. From "Dis-Ease," to "Fly to My Room," "Telepathy," "Blue & Grey," "Dynamite," and "Life Goes On," BE builds its own architecture through sound.

"Fly to My Room" engages with the image of space most explicitly: "Everyday / It's so suffocating that I'm going crazy / Somebody, please turn the clock back / The whole year got stolen / I'm still in bed, / feeling bloated in the stomach / It's killin' me slowly nah."[21] The song paints a very clear picture of the lockdown experience, tying it to the specific moment of the pandemic. The lyrics represent the space of the room as limiting and oppressive. In addition, having a year stolen from our lives is not only disorienting and disheartening, but it also indicates the spatial shift of the pandemic. Time is perceived in relation to space, and when movement was denied for public health and protection, spatial dimensions took over the perception of time, making it seemingly stop. Not all is lost, though, as the narrative turns around in the next parts of the song: "This room is too small, / yeah, to contain my dream / My bed, I land on it / This is the safest place / Happiness, sadness, whatever emotion it is, / this place just takes it in / Sometimes, even when this room becomes a trash can of emotions, / it holds me."[22] Here the narrative is reversed and the previously stifling room becomes a safe space, a container of emotions and a portal toward the exploration of the self.

In earlier BTS albums *MAP OF THE SOUL: PERSONA* and *MAP OF THE SOUL: 7*, and their songs "EGO," "Mikrokosmos," "Outro: Shadow," "Intro: Persona," "Black Swan," or "HOME," the inner self, the home, outer space, and other metaphors were employed as repositories of feelings and thoughts about selfhood. However, they did not center space as a theme that was connected to society/self and physical place so tightly. The emphasis on the alignment (or disconnection) between inner being and physical space in the album allows listeners to think of *BE* as an artistic response to the pandemic that fosters connection with and among ARMY and generates a possible place of care for the self and for others.

Made up of different spaces, disparate and yet linked, and aimed at articulating and yet countering the feelings of despair of the pandemic, BE presents itself as a microcosm of care in trying times. In fact, during the COVID-19 pandemic, inequalities and discrimination produced by capitalist, ableist, heteropatriarchal, and white supremacist social relations worsened racist attacks aimed at Asian communities around the world, engendered a rise in domestic violence against women, anti-LGBTQ bigotry, and in the disproportionate deaths of essential workers and of those already marginalized in society (racial minorities, immigrants, the poor).[23] At the same time, such social inequalities decreased equitable access to healthcare services.[24] In *BE*'s content, production, and promotion, however, BTS created a space with ARMY where the complexity of human emotions could be elaborated and where self-expression thrived. In opposition to the distancing demanded by the pandemic, like the citizens of Italy who sang from balcony to balcony, a vocal touch of another human's hand, *BE* explicitly aspired to bring people together and provide a space where messages of hope and optimism resisted the despair of the pandemic.

Notes

1   ISTAT, "Impatto dell'epidemia COVID-19 sulla mortalità totale della popolazione residente anno 2020," March 5, 2021, https://www.istat.it/it/files//2021/03/Report_ISS_Istat_2020_5_marzo.pdf.
2   Il Tempo.it, "COVID, 2020 anno del Dpcm."
3   Yonhap, "BTS Begins New Journey for First Self-Produced Album."
4   UNESCO, "UNESCO Launches a Report on the Impacts Suffered by the Creative Industry during the Pandemic," February 10, 2022, https://www.unesco.org/en/articles/unesco-launches-report-impacts-suffered-creative-industry-during-pandemic.
5   Swarbrick et al., "Corona Concerts."
6   Swarbrick et al., "Corona Concerts," 2.
7   HYBE LABELS, "BTS (방탄소년단) Global Press Conference 'BE' (+ENG)," November 21, 2020, YouTube video, 39:58, https://youtu.be/T31mfmw8bS8.
8   Lefebvre, *The Production of Space*, 80–85.
9   VLIVE was a video streaming platform where South Korean idols could stream and interact with the fans in real time. It merged with Weverse in late 2022 and was subsequently shut down.
10   HYBE LABELS, "BTS (방탄소년단) Global Press Conference 'BE' (+ENG)."
11   Yonhap, "BTS Begins New Journey for First Self-Produced Album."
12   Yonhap, "BTS Begins New Journey for First Self-Produced Album."
13   Myungseok Kang, "Jin 'It Feels Like My Memories of ARMY Were All a Dream,'" Weverse, November 26, 2020, https://magazine.weverse.io/article/view?num=60&lang=en.
14   *BE* promotional website, 2020, https://ibighit.com/bts/kor/discography/detail/be.html.
15   Castells, "Grassrooting the Space of Flows"; Castells, *The Rise of the Network Society*.
16   Ragnedda and Muschert, *The Digital Divide*.

17   Appadurai, "Disjuncture and Difference."

18   @minimoniT_T, "@BTS_twt's RM 'Thanks to' ENGLISH TRANSLATIONS"
        (quoting Kim Namjoon), Twitter, November 22, 2020, 6:53 a.m., https://
        twitter.com/minimoniT_T/status/1329754740712902660.

19   Quotes from all members are from @iilejeons, "#BTS_BE 'Thanks To'
        English Translation," Twitter, November 22, 2020, 9:56 a.m., https://
        twitter.com/iilejeons/status/1330525595789234177.

20   Kun, *Audiotopia*, 3.

21   "Fly to My Room," *Doolset Lyrics*, November 20, 2020, https://
        doolsetbangtan.wordpress.com/2020/11/20/fly-to-my-room/.

22   "Fly to My Room."

23   Human Rights Watch, "COVID-19 Fueling Anti-Asian Racism and
        Xenophobia Worldwide. National Action Plans Needed to Counter
        Intolerance," May 12, 2020, https://www.hrw.org/news/2020/05/12/covid
        -19-fueling-anti-asian-racism-and-xenophobia-worldwide; Mlambo-
        Ngcuka, "Violence against Women and Girls"; Graeme Reid, "Global
        Trends in LGBT Rights during the COVID-19 Pandemic," Human Rights
        Watch, February 24, 2021, https://www.hrw.org/news/2021/02/24/global
        -trends-lgbt-rights-during-covid-19-pandemic; Rogers et al., "Racial
        Disparities in COVID-19 Mortality among Essential Workers in the United
        States."

24   Akobirshoev et al., "Delayed Medical Care and Unmet Care Needs."

Works Cited

Akobirshoev, Ilhom, Michael Vetter, Lisa I. Iezzoni, Sowmya R. Rao, and Monika Mi-
        tra. "Delayed Medical Care and Unmet Care Needs Due to the COVID-19
        Pandemic among Adults with Disabilities in the US." *Health Affairs* 41,
        no. 10 (2022): 1505–12.

Appadurai, Arjun. "Disjuncture and Difference in the Global Cultural Economy."
        Theory, Culture and Society 7, nos. 2–3 (1990): 295–310.

Castells, Manuel. "Grassrooting the Space of Flows." *Urban Geography* 20, no. 4
        (1999): 294–302.

Castells, Manuel. *The Rise of the Network Society*. Vol. 1 of *The Information Age, Econ-
        omy, Society, and Culture*. Cambridge, MA: Blackwell, 1996.

Il Tempo.it. "COVID, 2020 anno del Dpcm: Tutti i decreti del presidente." Decem-
        ber 29, 2020. https://www.iltempo.it/adnkronos/2020/12/29/news/covid
        -2020-anno-del-dpcm-tutti-i-decreti-del-presidente-25704039/.

Kun, Josh. *Audiotopia: Music, Race, and America*. Berkeley: University of California
        Press, 2005.

Lefebvre, Henri. *The Production of Space*. Translated by Donald Nicholson-Smith.
        Oxford: Blackwell, 1991.

Mlambo-Ngcuka, Phumzile. "Violence against Women and Girls: The Shadow
        Pandemic." UN Women, April 6, 2020. https://www.unwomen.org/en
        /news/stories/2020/4/statement-ed-phumzile-violence-against-women
        -during-pandemic.

Ragnedda, Massimo, and Glenn W. Muschert. *The Digital Divide: The Internet and
        Social Inequality in International Perspective*. London: Routledge, 2015.

Rogers, Tiana N., Charles R. Rogers, Elizabeth VanSant-Webb, Lily Y. Gu, Bin Yan,
        and Fares Qeadan. "Racial Disparities in COVID-19 Mortality among
        Essential Workers in the United States." *World Medical Health Policy* 12,
        no. 3 (2020): 311–27.

Swarbrick, Dana, Beate Seibt, Noemi Grinspun, and Jonna K. Vuoskoski. "Corona
        Concerts: The Effect of Virtual Concert Characteristics on Social Connec-
        tion and Kama Muta." *Frontiers in Psychology* 12 (2021): 1–21.

Yonhap. "BTS Begins New Journey for First Self-Produced Album." *Korea
        Herald*, May 4, 2020. http://www.koreaherald.com/view.php?ud
        =20200504000453.

04 · Blood, Sweat, and Tears: BTS, Bruegel, and the Baroque — Marci Kwon

We begin in an art gallery. BTS members saunter through the space with the insouciant air of high school students on a mandatory museum field trip, more interested in each other than the works of art. SUGA weaves through the pedestals on a BMX bike while Jimin fiddles with a slingshot and RM shows Jung Kook a page in his book. V caresses a sculpture as he strikes a pose for j-hope, who surveys the scene through a pair of gilt opera glasses as if to parody the decorous viewing expected in such places.

Behind them, Jin is pulled toward a painting. *The Fall of the Rebel Angels* (1562) by Flemish artist Pieter Bruegel the Elder shows Lucifer and his denizens tumbling from the heavens in a tangle of feathered appendages and insectoid limbs. It is difficult to discern demon from angel in this writhing mass. Jin seems a world away from the band's youthful antics as he contemplates this nightmarish battle between good and evil. What is he thinking as he gazes upon Bruegel's nightmare? What is he feeling? His expression is unreadable. We cut to the back of his head (see figure 4.1).

The music video has turned Jin into a *rückenfigur*, the back-turned figure of Romantic painting. In Caspar David Friedrich's famed *Wanderer above the Sea of Fog* (1818; see figure 4.2), the *rückenfigur* invites the viewer to see through his eyes. Secure on his rocky outcropping, secure in himself, Friedrich's wanderer inhabits a position of mastery above the panoramic swirl of fog and mist.[1] Jin's position is different. The camera pulls back to place him within the frame of Bruegel's composition; his cherry-blossom hair and broad shoulders merge with the picture.[2] Two portals, black and white, transform the painting's archetypal struggle between evil and good into a decision Jin must make, a path he must choose.

4.1

Cut to BTS members in a lavish parlor filled with paintings and chandeliers (0:47). As Jimin's breathy voice intones the opening lines of "Blood Sweat & Tears," the video bursts into a kinetic riot of sensual choreography punctuated by psychedelic flashes that evoke Bruegel's thicket of bodies. Later, an impish V leaps into another Bruegel painting, *Landscape with the Fall of Icarus* (c. 1560). It becomes clear: "Blood Sweat & Tears" takes place within the world of Bruegel's paintings.

"Blood Sweat & Tears" was the lead single off BTS's 2016 album *WINGS*. Released while the members were nineteen to twenty-four years old, *WINGS* signaled the band's entry into young adulthood and their departure from the romantic adolescence of their previous cycle of albums, known collectively as *Hwayangyeonhwa* (HYYH), or *The Most Beautiful Moment in Life* (2015–16). *WINGS* portrays growing up as awakening to the world's complexity, a world of lies and stigma (titles of solo songs on the album), a world of anger, sorrow, and desire. The video for "Blood Sweat & Tears" allegorizes this transition from adolescence to adulthood as a plunge into the earthly perils and delights of art.[3] The music video (MV) references luminaries of Western culture such as Michelangelo, Hermann Hesse, Paul Klee, and of course Bruegel, whose work comes to represent the alluring and dangerous spoils of adulthood. Both *The Fall of the Rebel Angels* and *Landscape with the Fall of Icarus* depict fatal plunges from the heights of hubris. Just as Lucifer is cast from Heaven for daring to defy God, Icarus plunges into the sea after soaring too high on wax wings. That these pictures hang alongside one another in the Royal Museums of Fine Arts of Belgium (whose Beaux-Arts entry hall recalls the setting of the MV's prologue) invites a reading of BTS from within the canon of Western art.

4.2 · Caspar David Friedrich, *Wanderer above the Sea of Fog*, 1818. Oil on canvas, 94.8 × 74.8 cm (37.3 × 29.4 in.), Hamburger Kunsthalle, Hamburg.

Accordingly, this chapter explores "Blood Sweat & Tears" as a Baroque proposition. *Baroque* is a capacious term that can describe a historical period, a philosophical orientation, or an aesthetic of excess and extravagance.[4] Within art history, the Baroque names the dynamic compositions, dramatic chiaroscuro, and frank sensuality of European art and architecture of the long seventeenth century.[5] The Baroque was "an art of gilt and pathos," whose exuberant artifice (gilt is a veneer of applied gold rather than pure precious metal) was designed to elicit intense emotion in the viewer.[6] In its Dionysian excess, exuberant sensuality, and unapologetic theatricality, "Blood Sweat & Tears" is a work of Baroque art.

What does a work of art reveal about an artist? How does an artist's life enter into a work of art? Art historians and K-Pop fandoms share an abiding interest in these foundational interpretive questions. "Blood Sweat & Tears" illuminates BTS's use of the Western art historical canon to reconfigure expected relationships among artist, audience, work, and world.[7]

✳ ✳ ✳

In 2019, *Time* magazine asked Bang Si-Hyuk about the "common perception" that K-Pop is "manufactured by committee." He responded:

First, I believe in the West there is this deeply embedded fantasy of the rock star—a rock star acts true to their soul and everyone must accept it as part of their individuality, and only through that does good music come. . . . Another layer is that in the U.S., an artist will work in the underground scene for many years before signing with a major label. In Korea, that time is spent as a trainee. I think it's debatable which system produces the better artist. In addition, I believe the statement that an artist must sing their own songs to have good results cannot possibly be true. A singer is foremost a performer, and a good performance can convince audiences.[8]

Bang PD proposes that Korea and "the West" use different criteria to define and evaluate art. In the West, art is a "true" expression of an artist's soul. This definition privileges individual authorship ("an artist must sing their own songs to have good results") over performance and audience impact. A true artist does not care about commercial success, and their authenticity is confirmed by their formation in "the underground scene" rather than the culture industry. This definition is also value judgment: "Only through that does good art come."[9]

The irony is that BTS does meet these criteria: SUGA and RM famously began in Korea's underground hip-hop scene, and the band participates in writing and producing their music. Yet as Bang PD points out, this definition of "good art" necessarily implies freedom from commercial interests, a purity of purpose that Western aesthetics calls "disinterestedness."[10] Because they were assembled by a company to sing pop music, BTS cannot fulfill this requirement. The band's exclusion from the category of artist is augmented by the Orientalist assumption that they are a "manufactured" product. This "common perception" invokes two tropes of Asian racialization: the Yellow Peril discourse of Asian bodies as machinic, interchangeable, and perfectly adapted to capitalism, and the related stereotype of Oriental inscrutability, which Xine Yao describes as "Oriental ontological hollowness."[11] Within this cultural imaginary, "orientals" are products or tools rather than people. They cannot make art because they have no interiority to express.

The Baroque issued a challenge to artistic purity from the heart of the Western canon. Baroque art was the art of Catholic splendor and monarchical opulence, as well as an instrument of colonization exported to the "New" World as a tool of shock and awe.[12] Despite these violent origins, artists in the Americas adapted the Baroque for their own ends. Édouard Glissant describes the Baroque's flamboyant aesthetic as a "reaction against so-called natural order, naturally fixed as an obvious fact."[13] By foregrounding the Baroque's implicit critique of rationalism, New World artists "rerouted" the movement against its originators.[14]

"Blood Sweat & Tears" likewise reroutes its many references to the Western canon. Although the video's citations evince deep art historical knowledge, it is strikingly unconcerned with creating the illusion that BTS is performing in front of original works of art. While the MV preserves the relative scale of each work, for example, it makes no attempt to match the precise layout and wall colors of the Brussels museum that houses Bruegel's paintings. At moments the video even seems to take a perverse glee in its panoply of reproductions, using framed photographs of sculptures to decorate the prologue's sculpture hall, and staging the band's Last Supper scene amid projections of pink brush-strokes that recall an immersive art experience. "Blood Sweat & Tears" treats works of art like screens: mobile, scalable surfaces unencumbered by the ex-pectation of originality. The video is a precedent to BTS's 2018 single "IDOL," in which the band addresses their relationship to the term *artist*: "You can call me artist / You can call me idol / Or you can call me anything else."[15] Here BTS announces that they understand the derogatory connotations of the word *idol* as manufactured product, an object of false worship, and the opposite of a true artist. To these impoverished categories, BTS declares: "I don't care."

Although "Blood Sweat & Tears" is skeptical of art's many pieties, it also rev-els in its power. In the MV, art represents all that escapes conventional mo-rality and instrumental use: emotion, sensuality, beauty. Art is the tempter. Answering its call offers a chance of flight but also risks a fatal fall. Jung Kook spends his solo scenes suspended from a swing in a room dense with paint-ings. Above him is a reproduction of Giulio Quaglio the Younger's magnificent Baroque ceiling for the Ljubljana Cathedral (1703–6). Quaglio uses trompe l'oeil architecture and foreshortened figures to create the illusion of an aper-ture to the heavens, an opening through which the faithful may ascend into the firmament. As Jung Kook's celestial falsetto breaks through the song's driving rhythm at 3:43, he levitates toward the ceiling as if to breach the plane between the "real" space of the parlor (itself a set) and the fictive world of Quaglio's painting (see figure 4.3).

This blurring of artifice and reality is another hallmark of the Baroque. Baroque theater combined dance, fine art, and technologically innovative stagecraft to "collaps[e] the visual boundaries of the proscenium frame with an overwhelming appeal to the embodied pathos of the spectator,"

4.3

as Joseph Cermatori has observed.[16] Jung Kook is this embodied pathos. He is the viewer who willingly enters art's crafted world and cares not whether it is "fictive" or "true." He is, in other words, a K-Pop stan. Bathed in golden light and suspended in a state of mystic ecstasy, Jung Kook is poised to take his place among the Quaglio's panoply of floating figures.

"Blood Sweat & Tears" offers a trenchant commentary on this Baroque merging of art and life. Another Bruegel painting, *Landscape with the Fall of Icarus* (c. 1560; see figure 4.4) first appears as a framed painting on the wall of Jung Kook's solo scenes. It appears again as the backdrop for V's dramatic plunge from a neoclassical balcony (see figure 4.5). At this scale, Bruegel's picture is strikingly grainy, as if a low-resolution JPEG has been blown up to the size of life. V leaps *into* the world of the painting, although it is unclear whether he takes flight or plunges into the water. This green sea recalls the absinthe prepared earlier by RM, the source of the jade smoke that fills the chamber where Jimin and SUGA sit before the French doors of V's balcony. It is as if Bruegel's ocean has escaped its frame to permeate the very atmosphere of the MV as a hallucinogenic haze. Perched on the balcony railing, V embodies the Baroque permeability of work and world, screen and life.

Bruegel's painting offers a corollary figure in the fisherman at bottom right. Unlike the plower and shepherd in the foreground, who famously turn away from Icarus's death, the fisherman's body bridges land and water. Holding a filament-thin fishing pole he seems almost to reach into the sea itself, an illusion augmented by a felicitous crack in the paint where the rod seems to sink below the work's surface. Icarus drowns at the edges of his vision. The fisherman neither looks at the boy's death throes nor looks away. Rather, the fisherman grasps at that which he will never catch. If, as Alexander

4.4 · Pieter Bruegel the Elder, *Landscape with the Fall of Icarus*, c. 1560. Oil on canvas, 73.5 × 112 cm (28.9 × 44 in.), Royal Museums of Fine Arts of Belgium, Brussels.

4.5

Nemerov has suggested, the plower's turn away from violence can be anachronistically read as a model of midcentury American artistic autonomy, the fisherman offers a cognate figure for the digital age.[17] He embodies the illusion of action and, perhaps, even the desire to act, while the violence before him remains on the periphery of sight and perpetually out of reach.

The stakes of Bruegel's fisherman come into view in relation to one of the most iconic moments in "Blood Sweat & Tears": Jimin's jacket slip. As he sings "다 가져가, 가" ["Take them all away"] (3:06), Jimin throws his torso back with such force that his royal blue blazer slips from his shoulder.[18] This moment elicits yells from BTS during the "Blood Sweat & Tears" reaction video. In K-Pop reaction videos, idols are filmed watching their videos for the first time. The reaction video positions the idol as both artist (in the video) and fan (watching the video)—allowing fans to watch idols watch themselves. The space between idol and fan blurs as this mise en abyme of spectatorship places them together outside of the MV's fiction, as if they existed on the same plane of reality. RM teases that the moment likely required a great deal of practice, but Jimin protests that the move was unplanned. Did the jacket slip from his shoulder because of his passionate dancing, or was it merely planned to look that way? As BTS members try to figure it out, they briefly become their fans: in awe of Jimin, and desperate to know if he did it on purpose. Yet they remain within the world of the screen. This, too, is a Baroque proposition. Although the Baroque dangles the tantalizing prospect of an ecstatic unity of art and life, in the end its exuberant artifice embodies what Glissant calls "the illusory nature of the world of appearances."[19]

Jimin's jacket slip frustrates the desire to know the truth of someone else's intentions, their emotions, to excavate their interior being.[20] And this frustration takes on additional valences in relation to the previously discussed trope of oriental inscrutability. Xine Yao observes that the common response to such racism is "the usual move of arguing for the humanity of minoritized subjects by enlisting literature to affirm that they feel too."[21] In keeping the truth of this moment to himself, Jimin refuses this demand, and the related demand that art reflect an artist's "true" interior, their true self, their true humanity. This moment holds knowing itself in suspension. We fans will never truly know if Jimin flicked his jacket off on purpose, just as we will never truly know Jimin. Our feelings as we watch BTS, as we encounter art, are real. Although we might project them onto the artist, the work, the world, ultimately they belong to us and us alone.

* * *

Back in the art gallery, Jin approaches a crouching angel. The oversized figure recalls Paul De Vigne's *Glorification de l'art* (c. 1880), a winged allegory that looms over the museum that holds the video's Bruegels. Jin caresses the angel's face and places a gentle kiss on its lips (5:24) and the sculpture begins to weep neon tears and bleed neon blood. Jimin removes his black blindfold to reveal rivulets of absinthe-green staining his face. The elemental fluids of the song's title turn out to be substances of artifice and imagination rather than biological proof of humanity. This is the wisdom of the Baroque. One need

4.6

not follow the prescribed criteria of what is real—real life, real human—to quicken the pulse and make tears fall.

At the end of "Blood Sweat & Tears," Bruegel's painting has been replaced by a mirror enclosed in an elaborate gilt frame and crowned with a decidedly Baroque sentiment drawn from Nietzsche's *Thus Spoke Zarathustra*: "*Man muss noch Chaos in sich haben, um einen tanzenden Stern gebären zu können*" ("One must still have chaos in oneself to be able to give birth to a dancing star.")[22] Jin walks toward the mirror and once again becomes the *rückenfigur* (5:46). The mirror does not reflect his face, or anything else for that matter, but remains a black void, a blank screen. In the final seconds of the video, Jin finally sees his reflection in Nietzsche's mirror. He looks at the white flower and its purple reflection. He turns his gaze to his own image as cracks appear across his face (see figure 4.6). What lies beneath this gorgeous visage? Does his placid expression conceal a glimmer of Nietzsche's chaos? Or will his face break apart, like that of Michaelangelo's *Piéta* at 5:50, and reveal nothing underneath? The only certainty is our desire to know.

Notes

1   Within art history, Friedrich's *rückenfigur* has come to stand for "a model of early nineteenth-century bourgeois subjectivity concomitant with the rise of modern spectatorial practices." O'Rourke, "Staring into the Abyss of Time," 33.

2   I am grateful to the Bangtan Remixed Editorial Collective for suggesting this reading.

3   For the sake of readability, the remainder of this text will refer to this music video with the song title "Blood Sweat & Tears," the abbreviation "MV," or "the video." HYBE LABELS, "BTS (방탄소년단) '피 땀 눈물 (Blood Sweat

& Tears)' Official MV," October 9, 2019, YouTube video, 6:03, https://www
.youtube.com/watch?v=hmE9f-TEutc.

4   Zamora and Kaup, "Introduction: Baroque, New World Baroque,
Neobaroque."

5   This stylistic account of the Baroque derives from Wölfflin's *Principles
of Art History*. Although numerous art historians have productively
challenged and critiqued Wölfflin's formalist account, the term *Baroque*
remains shorthand for this period of European cultural production.

6   Gallego, "Spain," 14–17.

7   The remainder of this text will omit the scare quotes from "Baroque,"
"art," and "artist." Throughout, I use these terms as cultural constructs
rather than transcendental essences.

8   Bruner, "The Mastermind behind BTS Opens Up about Making a K-Pop
Juggernaut."

9   This reading is indebted to Yutian Wong's brilliant discussion of BTS's
refusal of modern dance's "binary categories of mimicry vs. innovation,"
included in chapter 5 in the present volume.

10   Following the work of Sylvia Wynter, Kandice Chuh observes that the
philosophical discourse of aesthetics became a way to distinguish "Man"
from his other: "The aesthetic's history as an axis along which the kinds
of persons idealized as the modern liberal subject have been distinguished from those incapable of achieving such subjectivity speaks to
the long-lived ways that it has operated as a limit test in the articulation
of liberal humanism and underwrites its analytic and poetic power." Aesthetics is therefore central to the construction of race, gender, sexuality,
and other markers of colonial difference. Chuh, *The Difference Aesthetics
Makes*, 18. See also Wynter, "On Disenchanting Discourse."

11   Yao, *Disaffected*, 176. On "Yellow Peril" and economic modernity, see Lye,
America's Asia.

12   Zamora and Kaup, "Introduction: Baroque, New World Baroque, Neobaroque," 2–3.

13   Glissant, *The Poetics of Relation*, 77.

14   Glissant, *The Poetics of Relation*, 77.

15   Quotes are from the lyrics of "IDOL," *Doolset Lyrics*, August 24, 2018,
https://doolsetbangtan.wordpress.com/2018/08/24/idol/.

16   Cermatori, *Baroque Modernity*, 10.

17   Nemerov, "The Flight of Form," 796. See also Auden, *The Age of Anxiety*.

18   Quotes are from the lyrics of "Blood Sweat & Tears," *Doolset Lyrics*,
June 20, 2018, https://doolsetbangtan.wordpress.com/2018/06/20/blood
-sweat-tears/.

19   Édouard Glissant, editorial in *UNESCO Courier*, 3.

20   Vivian L. Huang would describe this as a "performance of inscrutability."
See Huang, *Surface Relations*.

21   Yao, *Disaffected*, 3.

22   Nietzsche was also a foundational theorist of the Baroque. Nietzsche, "On the Baroque," 44–45.

Works Cited

Auden, W. H. *The Age of Anxiety: A Baroque Eclogue*. Princeton, NJ: Princeton University Press, 2011.

Bruner, Raisa. "The Mastermind behind BTS Opens Up about Making a K-Pop Juggernaut." *Time*, October 8, 2019. https://time.com/5681494/bts-bang-si-hyuk-interview/.

Cermatori, Joseph. *Baroque Modernity: An Aesthetics of Theater*. Baltimore: Johns Hopkins University Press, 2021.

Chuh, Kandice. *The Difference Aesthetics Makes: On the Humanities "After Man."* Durham, NC: Duke University Press, 2019.

Gallego, Julian. "Spain: An Art of Gilt and Pathos." *UNESCO Courier* 40, no. 9 (1987): 14–17.

Glissant, Édouard. Editorial in *UNESCO Courier* 40, no. 9 (1987): 3.

Glissant, Édouard. *The Poetics of Relation*. Translated by Betsy Wing. Ann Arbor: University of Michigan Press, 2010.

Huang, Vivian L. *Surface Relations: Queer Forms of Asian American Inscrutability*. Durham, NC: Duke University Press, 2022.

Lye, Colleen. *America's Asia: Racial Form and American Literature, 1893–1945*. Princeton, NJ: Princeton University Press, 2005.

Nemerov, Alexander. "The Flight of Form: Auden, Bruegel, and the Turn to Abstraction in the 1940s." *Critical Inquiry* 31, no. 4 (Summer 2005): 780–810.

Nietzsche, Friedrich. "'On the Baroque' (1878)." Translated by Monika Kaup. In *Baroque New Worlds: Representation, Transculturation, Counterconquest*, edited by Lois Parkinson Zamora and Monika Kaup, 44–48. Durham, NC: Duke University Press, 2010.

O'Rourke, Stephanie. "Staring into the Abyss of Time." *Representations* 148, no. 1 (2019): 30–56.

Wölfflin, Heinrich. *Principles of Art History: The Problem of the Development of Style in Later Art*. Translated by M. D. Hottinger. New York: Dover, 1950.

Wynter, Sylvia. "On Disenchanting Discourse: 'Minority' Literary Criticism and Beyond." *Cultural Critique* 7, no. 2 (Autumn 1987): 207–44.

Yao, Xine. *Disaffected: The Cultural Politics of Unfeeling in Nineteenth-Century America*. Durham, NC: Duke University Press, 2021.

Zamora, Lois Parkinson, and Monika Kaup. "Introduction: Baroque, New World Baroque, Neobaroque: Categories and Concepts." In *Baroque New Worlds: Representation, Transculturation, Counterconquest*, edited by Lois Parkinson Zamora and Monika Kaup, 1–35. Durham, NC: Duke University Press, 2010.

05 · Martha and the Swans: BTS, "Black Swan," and Cold War Dance History — Yutian Wong

During the 2022 FESTA dinner party celebrating the ninth anniversary of their debut, BTS revealed that their 2020 MAP OF THE SOUL: 7 album would have been their last group album before enlistment had their 2020 world tour not been canceled due to the COVID-19 pandemic. While they did not broach the topic of mandatory military service during the FESTA, the issue has loomed over the fate of BTS (as it has for other male K-Pop groups) since individual members began approaching the age for enlistment. Though the South Korean parliament passed an amendment to the Military Service Act in December 2020, allowing K-Pop artists with significant global reputations to defer military service until the age of thirty, enlistment is inevitable. The announcement during the 2022 FESTA dinner party begs a reading of their MAP OF THE SOUL: 7 song and video "Black Swan" as an actual swan song to BTS from BTS. Through citation of the unfettered existentialism of modern dance and disciplined tragedy of classical ballet, the song can also be read as commemorating the end of youth, marked by military conscription and the still unresolved conflict of the Cold War.

Continued US military presence and cultural influence on the Korean peninsula is a constant reminder that Asia served as a staging ground not just for "hot wars" of martial dominance but also for ideologically driven debates over cultural relevance on the global stage. The selective adoption of references to modern dance and ballet aesthetics in "Black Swan" can be viewed as the result of cultural diplomacy practiced by the US and the Soviet Union in Asia during the Cold War, during which each sought to foist Western ideologies vis-à-vis Western dance aesthetics on Asian bodies. Analyzing "Black Swan" through the lens of Cold War dance history illuminates how BTS's repertory reinterprets these concert dance traditions and claims ownership of the universalizing discourses of dance modernism imposed on Asia since the 1950s. Such a reading casts light on the fact that the Cold War has never ended, as the conflict lingers in the invocations of death and aging in "Black Swan."

On Modernism and Martha

In 1955, American modern dance choreographer Martha Graham and her company of dancers embarked on the first of a series of Cold War goodwill tours to South Korea, Japan, the Philippines, Indonesia, and other countries in East and Southeast Asia deemed by the US government to be "regions of concern."[1] Graham's tours were part of a larger project of sending American artists abroad to Africa, Asia, and Europe to improve America's public image and advance American-style democracy under the guise of cultural exchange. While on tour, the Graham company occasionally performed in the same venues as the stars from the USSR's famous Bolshoi Ballet. Framed by journalists and dance critics as a "dance war" between the US's abstract modernism and the Soviet Union's classicism, this ideological battle was fought onstage through the bare flexed feet and sharp jagged arms of modern dance and the satin-clad pointed toes and round elegant port de bras of classical ballet.

The Martha Graham Dance Company was carefully selected to appear apolitical even as Graham herself met with officials to promote American interests and values. By the 1950s, Graham had already been heralded by American dance critics as one of the four pioneers of modern dance and chosen through the United States Information Agency (USIA) sponsorship as its avatar in Asia. These tours affirmed the place of Graham technique and repertory within the genealogy of Western concert dance history as the logical outcome of innovation after (European) ballet. The abstract modernism of Graham's choreography was narrated as a break from tradition, allowing artistic progress to stand in as social/political progress, and sold to Asian dance artists as a universal aesthetic. Perceived as free from the demands of historical precedent, fixed meaning, and previous training, abstract modernism recycled the American frontier mythology of expansionist opportunity and continual self-reinvention. Applied to dance, manifest destiny served as a metaphor for liberating choreography, as Graham technique promised a vibrant and virile future enabled by genius and hard work. In contrast, classical ballet and its socialist realist adaptations in the Soviet Union were viewed as practices steeped in centuries of established tradition and disciplined protocol.

Aligned with modernist art as a masculine endeavor, modern dance was intellectual, inventive, daring, and open, whereas ballet was beautiful, feminine, mannered, and exclusionary. The modern dancer could one day become the auteur of one's subjecthood, whereas the ballet dancer could only ever be an object of desire and unattainable perfection.

Auteurship is intimately tied with Western and, particularly, American notions of rugged individualism and artistic worthiness as a form of cultural gatekeeping. Modern dance and classical ballet are historically construed as forms that are conceptually at odds with one another, even when both forms take up the position of high art within hierarchies of cultural production. Ballet is elitist as a classical form that has come to stand in as a universalized measure of physicalized perfection, and modern dance is elitist in its obscurity, opacity, and refusal to please the viewer. If "Black Swan" as a song must inhabit the space of popular music as sound designed to please, it is through dance and dance references that "Black Swan" (music videos and stage performances) also embodies modernist aspirations of the refusal to please. This refusal to please is not usually afforded to Asian artists and does not fit within binary categories of mimicry vs. innovation that at times haunt discourses about contemporary Asian performance.[2] Asian dancers are often viewed as tradition-bound performers who can only innovate by incorporating Western forms; but, by adopting Western forms, they risk accusations of being mere copyists. There is a fine line between mimicry as copying, which is derided as "not art," and innovation as inventing, which is elevated as "Art." The perception of the difference between the two is rooted in colonial relations of power. Western artists who borrow from Asian forms are expanding their repertoire, whereas Asian artists who borrow can't borrow *too much*; otherwise they are accused of copying or pandering.[3]

The irony of Martha Graham's own appropriation of Asian dance aesthetics is part of the long history of European and American choreographers lifting elements of Asian (and other) performance traditions.[4] Graham's uncontextualized "borrowing" was subsumed into abstract modernism as a form of invisible orientalism, and presented back to Asian artists as a model for artistic experimentation.[5] As part of her USIA tours, Graham's company not only performed, but Graham herself sought to teach young dance students in Asia with the express purpose of creating a generation of dancers who would make use of her technique to create their own work. Thus, Asian dance artists were given "permission to dance" by merging traditional practices with a universalized (American) modernism as the ideal path toward artistic legibility on the global stage.

Concern over auteurship, mastery, and mimicry has been integral to the public image of BTS members as artists who have struggled in both their personal and professional lives. The oft-repeated origin story about RM, SUGA, and j-hope's fight to be taken seriously as rappers, RM's concerns over how he will be remembered outside of BTS, and j-hope's repeated declarations of wanting to show his true self in his 2022 solo album, *Jack In The Box*, serve an important function in promoting two competing narratives about BTS: one, BTS as artists have expanded the boundaries of K-Pop music; or two, they have superseded the boundaries of music that can be produced from within the K-Pop industry such that they are no longer making K-Pop music. Both narratives are premised on a struggle for artistic autonomy and a desire to self-actualize artistic impulses. The story of BTS's success is fueled by narratives of self-doubt about what K-Pop idols as performing artists can or should be expected to aspire to. Can they achieve the Western modernist formation of what a "real artist" is from within an industry that demands adherence to the exacting standards of physical perfection and bodily discipline usually found in ballet?

Black Swans

Citations of modern dance and ballet in the body of work that is BTS's "Black Swan" take up the tensions of BTS's place within the global ordering of artistic production that was set in motion in the 1950s. Whereas non-Western forms serve as utilitarian supplements to dance education in the Global North, modern dance and ballet as a type of lingua franca are taught in dance conservatories (such as the one in which Jimin studied) all over the Global South, and even the modernization of traditional and folk dance forms has often meant the adoption of Western choreographic structures and body types for presentation on the proscenium stage. These Cold War tensions appear repeatedly throughout performances of "Black Swan." The art film version is the first of two official music videos of "Black Swan" and opens with the oft-repeated quote attributed to Martha Graham: "a dancer dies twice—once when they stop dancing, and this first death is the more painful." Graham's musings on aging and the dancing body set the mood in the music videos, and those familiar with Graham's mythology would recognize in the quote stories about her spiral into self-loathing and depression, when her aging body was replaced by younger dancers in roles she had created for herself.

As if mirroring Graham's eventual absence from her own choreography, the members of BTS are not in the art film version of "Black Swan." In their place are modern dancers from the MN Dance Company, based in Slovenia. Filmed at an abandoned shopping mall near Los Angeles, the choreography by Michal Rynia and Nastja Bremec Rynia is standard fare for contemporary European concert dance. Breathy release technique is coupled with wide sweeping leg and arm gestures, deep lunges, and dynamic lifts. An ensemble of six dancers (male and female) and one male soloist stands in for the seven members of BTS. Filmed in a desaturated palette, the melancholy aura of the music and choreography sets the mood for subsequent productions of "Black Swan" and asks the question, can BTS's music stand alone without the physical presence of BTS? More pointedly, can the group's celebrity survive the inevitable disruption of their military enlistment?

Without the voyeuristic close-up shots lingering on the faces of individual dancers that are typical of K-Pop music videos, the choreography by Rynia and Rynia is filmed to be seen in the entirety of its choreographic design. The absence of BTS is further enforced by the male soloist's torso isolations and distorted arm movements, referencing swans and swanly things associated with ballet and ballet dancers. In ballet, swans are tragic figures, the legacy of nineteenth-century French Romantic—era ballets in which women dressed in white tutus portrayed supernatural creatures (ghosts, sylphs, wilis) who die or have died from heartbreak. This melodramatic portrayal made its way to Russia when French ballet master Marius Petipa expanded upon the structure of Romantic ballets to create Russian classical ballet. While Petipa's *Swan Lake* (1895) might be the most common reference to the swan, it was Fokine's choreography for his 1905 *The Dying Swan*, performed by Anna Pavlova, that has informed all subsequent interpretations of how the swans in *Swan Lake* are performed. Pavlova is so closely tied to *The Dying Swan* that dancers and swans are often imagined as interchangeable figures. By the mid-twentieth century, ballet had consolidated a century's worth of gothic romance as a swan, connoting death from unfulfilled passions and desires.

If the lyrics for "IDOL" (2018) take an "I don't care, I'm proud of it" approach to the question of BTS's place within hierarchies of popular culture, the members' absence from the first iteration of "Black Swan" shifts attention away from the bodies of BTS and their celebrity to the question of their repertoire within hierarchies of cultural production. The sonic arrangement of the music used for the art film differs from the album version, using syncopated but discordant sounding strings to create an ominous soundscape. As if affirming that their music can exist outside the category of popular music, the modern classical sound of the musical arrangement coupled with the abstract choreography moves the music video into the realm of screendance. Often conceptual in nature, screendance (also known as dancefilm, dance for the camera, or cinedance) is viewed as a stand-alone art form combining cinematography and choreography to push the artistic boundaries of dance.

The art film of "Black Swan" operates as a foil for subsequent performances of "Black Swan," which more closely meet the expectations for spectacle featuring the members of BTS. For instance, the version performed on *The Late Late Show with James Cordon* (January 28, 2020) begins in semidarkness, such that one can just make out their silhouettes. Dressed in closer fitting versions of the all-black suits worn by the MN Dance Company, BTS forms a seven-member ensemble of swans who appear to be dancing on a mist-covered lake in an otherworldly grotto of bare trees and waterfalls. Lit in eerie blue light, the set design is the most literal interpretation of Act II in *Swan Lake*, when the male lead (Prince Siegfrid) is out hunting and comes upon the female lead (Odette/White Swan) and the corps de ballet (a bevy of female swans) near a lake. While the performance cites *Swan Lake*, it does not cite the details of the ballet's narrative but rather the structural elements of classical ballet.

Classical ballets tie narrative to a formulaic structure. The pas de deux (partnered duet) signals the romance between the main characters, the ballet blanc (ensemble choreography performed by the corps de ballet) marks the encounter between men and the supernatural, and divisions between acts I–II and III–IV utilize the contrast between interior daytime scenes and exterior nighttime scenes to differentiate between the rational and irrational. This choreographic structure propels a narrative in which mortal men leave the comforts of home and proper society to fall in love with the ghosts and memories of doomed or cursed women. As idols, the members of BTS are not (just) mortal men, but supernatural creatures inhabiting the real and unreal. Their celebrity is built upon public personae that depend on the fantasy that the shimmering pop star and the pizza-eating boy-next-door are the same person.

During *The Late Late Show*, dancing in bare feet, BTS perform choreography that echoes modernist elements of both form and affect usually associated with modern dance. Unlike the art film, however, this stage performance features the physical virtuosity of the group's ability to sing live while executing complex choreography—a cornerstone of BTS's mastery and charisma as live performers. Choreographed by Sergio Reis, the movement vocabulary features slowed-down elements of hip hop. The choreography juxtaposes sharp and fast isolations, halting steps, and slow languid movements. The staging also differs from the official choreography that accompanies BTS's other songs. Instead of using front-facing presentational symmetry, the seven members are arranged facing different directions in a loose diamond formation. Hunched with contracted torsos, the broken lines make the bodies look disjointed and vulnerable, and precise unison is interspersed with moments in which the members face away from the audience to reach out to each other. The dance ends on a quiet note as the lights dim, and the seven members return to their same positions at the beginning of the choreography. After such a somber performance, the sound of the audience cheering and screaming, and host James Corden's jovial exclamations of glee, make for a dissonant experience as the members drop their "Black Swan" personae to greet the crowd.

This collision between celebrity, American late-night talk show, modern dance, classical ballet, and popular music defies each individual category. The performance makes use of all available cultural referents across media and genre to demonstrate not just mastery but ownership over form and content to tease out, utilize, and recombine the same referents in each iteration of the performance. While the version performed at *The Late Late Show* overlays hip-hop-inflected choreography with modern dance aesthetics, the solo performed by Jimin to the orchestral version of "Black Swan" for the online ON:E *Concert* (October 2020) dispenses with hip hop altogether and utilizes a more lyrical modern dance vocabulary. Jimin is not the swan from *Swan Lake*; he is instead Fokine's dying swan. Fokine whittled down the swan's vocabulary to a series of bourrées and flapping arm movements to depict a swan's struggle to stay afloat above the surface of water before succumbing to an elegant end.[6] In his solo, Jimin dances acrobatically against a projection of rippling blue light punctuated with streams of bubbles rising like a last gasp underwater, as if he is moving toward a graceful death.

The 2020 Melon Music Awards (MMA) version of "Black Swan" featured six members of BTS (SUGA was missing due to an injury) as dancers, performing to an instrumental track of "Black Swan" in a pool of water on stage. The members begin the performance as white swans paired together in a series of duets before transforming into black swans. This version included a large ensemble of backup dancers who function as a corps de ballet for BTS and serve as living/moving architecture to hide BTS, creating moments of surprise when different pairings of the members (dressed in white) emerge from within the ensemble. Jung Kook and Jimin's pas de deux, in which Jung Kook lifts Jimin into a classical fish pose, is followed by a series of duets between Jin and RM and then j-hope and V. The partnering between the members of BTS has precedence in Matthew Bourne's all-male version of *Swan Lake* (1995), where the Prince encounters a group of all-male swans and dances a pas de deux with a menacingly seductive White Swan.

When Bourne's *Swan Lake* premiered in London's West End, it was celebrated as the "gay *Swan Lake*," disrupting the compulsory heteronormativity of ballet technique and repertory.[7] Despite the promise of staging queer desire, the production was criticized as ultimately homophobic, because Bourne maintained the narrative convention of unrequited love. The duets in the 2020 MMA performance refer to a formalized choreographic structure of a grand pas de deux within classical ballet but also allude to the practice of homoerotic fan service expected in K-Pop stage performances. The staging of the romance in the form of the grand pas de deux between the Prince and the Black Swan in Act III of *Swan Lake* is deliberately abstract. Dancers step out of character to execute bravura steps (turns, leaps, or turning leaps) for the sake of demonstrating physical virtuosity. This purely acrobatic section of the ballet is accepted as a depiction of a love story, even though the codified vocabulary does not drive the narrative forward. While previous versions of "Black Swan" do not feature a climactic end, the choreography for the 2020 MMA performance ends in a dramatic reveal in which the ensemble assembles, disassembles, and reassembles around BTS to form the silhouette of the side view of a swan.

The live stage performance of "Black Swan," at the 2021–22 *PERMISSION TO DANCE ON STAGE* concerts in Los Angeles, Seoul, and Las Vegas, included a large chorus of dancers whose white feathered arms are reminiscent of the feathered pants worn by Bourne's male swans. Choreographed to be viewed from above at a distance, the staging employed Busby Berkeley–like spectacle as the chorus formed and reformed into a single pair of wings to flank individual members of BTS, who each took turns emerging from the center of the ensemble to become the head of a swan possessing a giant pair of wings. The richly textured suits incorporated velvet, satin, silk, tulle, and mesh, accented with ruffles, bell bottoms, skirts, and silver body chains. This material reference to ballet costumes was amplified in Las Vegas when Jung Kook's loose cropped jacket and its infamously wayward button was replaced with a more fitted jacket cut to look like the bodice of a classical tutu. As the most dramatically theatrical portion of the concerts, "Black Swan" momentarily transformed a sports stadium into an opera house.

The reference to the opera house is not isolated. The second official music video of "Black Swan" (March 4, 2020) was filmed at the Los Angeles Theater.

In contrast to the abandoned shopping mall featured in the art film, the interior of the Los Angeles Theater is an opulent space modeled after the Hall of Mirrors at Versailles. Filming "Black Swan" in a theater that resembles Louis XIV's residence invokes the origins of ballet history. Louis XIV founded the Académie Royale de Danse in 1661 to standardize ballet vocabulary, professionalize dance training, and institutionalize the deployment of ballet as court etiquette and political propaganda. In his bid to consolidate power and establish an absolute monarchy, Louis XIV asserted his divine right to rule by performing in court ballets as the Greek god Apollo, associated with youthful masculinity, art, music, poetry, and the sun. Louis XIV took on the mantle of the Sun King, a divine leader who could bring light and life to France. Court ballets were strategically used to maintain social order by keeping the French aristocracy under control and displaying the wealth and power of the French monarchy. Not unlike the way the USIA spread American modern dance throughout the world, French court ballet was disseminated throughout Europe, and Russian czars adopted ballet in the attempt to modernize (Europeanize/Westernize) the Russian court. The gilded grandeur of the Los Angeles Theater, with its French Baroque–inspired architecture, reinforces the tie between "Black Swan" and the history of ballet's roots as a form that was entirely concerned with social hierarchy and cultural diplomacy.

By the time BTS performed "Black Swan" at SoFi Stadium in Los Angeles, almost two years had passed since the album's release and the COVID-19 pandemic shut down public performances around the world. The issue of BTS's looming military enlistment had become part of a global discussion among ARMY (the official name of the BTS fandom). Much of the discussion revolved around whether the members of BTS should be exempt due to their contributions to South Korea in the form of revenue, their global popularity, or their official role as cultural ambassadors. None of these reasons addressed the fact that the Cold War has not ended and, until it does, military conscription will continue to exist.

HYBE INSIGHT

The assertion of BTS's place within hierarchies of art is best exemplified by the "Moving Body" exhibit at HYBE INSIGHT in Seoul. In a space organized as a museum, a four-minute video of "Black Swan / Fake Love" loops on a screen that is approximately 25 feet by 10 feet. The size and resolution of the screen allows

the viewer to see the edges of the black floor tiles so it looks like BTS are dancing on a proscenium stage covered with a vinyl dance floor, and the viewer is
on stage with them. Unlike watching BTS on a phone, or computer screen, or
on a Jumbotron in a stadium, the performers are life-sized. The human scale
of the dancing bodies makes it feel as if the members are present even if one
is fully aware of the two-dimensional screen. In the quiet of a museum, one's
view of the choreography is unobscured, and the spectator can move around
the space to watch the dance from different angles as the video loops contin-
uously. Because the sound score is barely audible, one must watch the video
quietly to hear the music. The atmospherically percussive music provides just
enough rhythm to offset the constant drone of an electronic humming and
provides the sonic architecture that gives the choreography an ongoing med-
itative quality. The combination of minimalist black-and-white projections,
dramatic spotlights, ambient music, and silky black costumes situates BTS's
dancing as modern dance / contemporary dance / concert dance. Removed
from the aesthetic markers of a music video, BTS's "artiness" as dancing bodies
is doubled by serving as subject matter of what is essentially a video art installation. It is here, preserved on the wall of a museum, that the viewer comes
full circle to see the legacy of Cold War dance history that ultimately requires
the physical (but not visual) absence of dancing bodies to exceed the colonial
insistence on the primacy of modernism.

Bookended by the art film video in which we hear BTS, but do not see
them, and the "Moving Body" exhibit in which we see BTS, but do not hear
them, the different versions of "Black Swan" expose how modernism can be
reinterpreted in terms that do not fully ascribe to Western fetishization of
sole authorship. "Black Swan" is instead a series of collective projects that
navigate all available forms in different measures. Just as the hegemony of
continued US military presence on the Korean peninsula results in the creation of cultural hierarchies, "Black Swan" exists as an introspective art installation meant to be seen up close in person, a raucous mass spectacle to be
seen from a distance, and everything in between. BTS takes an artistic stance
from the space of popular culture to prove they are artists like Graham. In
their citation, we find a swan song to youth and a reading of Cold War dance
history alongside the haunting and ongoing fact of military conscription. Each
performance defies the binary of the Cold War to demonstrate the many different iterations through which BTS as Asian artists navigate the legacy of the
Cold War dance war. But at the end of the day, they, like other Korean men,
must enlist because the Cold War is not over.

Notes

1. While the South Korean leg of Martha's tour was canceled during the 1955–56 goodwill tour to Asia, the Graham technique would become the de facto modern dance technique spread throughout Asia and thus would make its way to South Korea. For histories of US State Department–sponsored cultural diplomacy during the Cold War, see Croft, *Dancers as Diplomats*; Franko, *Martha Graham in Love and War*; Phillips, *Martha Graham's Cold War*; and Prevots, *Dance for Export*.
2. See Savigliano's "Worlding Dance and Dancing Out There in the World" and Chatterjea's "On the Value of Mistranslations and Contaminations."
3. See Wong, *Choreographing Asian America*.
4. For a history of Ruth St. Denis and Martha Graham's use of Indian dance, see Srinivasan, *Sweating Saris*.
5. See Wong, *Choreographing Asian America*, for a discussion on invisible orientalism in twentieth-century American modern and postmodern dance history.
6. Bourrées are a series of small steps performed *en pointe* (on point, or on the tips of one's toes) with one foot crossed over the other.
7. Traditionally, only girls and women train to dance *en pointe*. The technique was developed in the service of nineteenth-century Romantic ballets in which female dancers portrayed supernatural creatures floating through space.

Works Cited

Chatterjea, Ananya. "On the Value of Mistranslations and Contaminations: The Category of 'Contemporary Choreography' in Asian Dance." *Dance Research Journal* 45, no. 1 (2013): 7–21.

Croft, Clare. *Dancers as Diplomats: American Choreography in Cultural Exchange*. Oxford: Oxford University Press, 2015.

Franko, Mark. *Martha Graham in Love and War: The Life in the Work*. Oxford: Oxford University Press, 2012.

Phillips, Victoria. *Martha Graham's Cold War: The Dance of American Diplomacy*. Oxford: Oxford University Press, 2020.

Prevots, Naima. *Dance for Export: Cultural Diplomacy and the Cold War*. Middletown, CT: Wesleyan University Press, 1999.

Savigliano, Marta Elena. "Worlding Dance and Dancing Out There in the World." In *Worlding Dance*, edited by Susan Leigh Foster, 163–90. Basingstoke, UK: Palgrave Macmillan, 2009.

Srinivasan, Priya. *Sweating Saris: Indian Dance as Transnational Labor*. Philadelphia: Temple University Press, 2011.

Wong, Yutian. *Choreographing Asian America*. Middletown, CT: Wesleyan University Press, 2010.

"Mikrokosmos"

THE UNIVERSE OF BTS

During the 2019 BTS *World Tour Love Yourself: Speak Yourself*, BTS concluded each concert with "Mikrokosmos," a song from the *MAP OF THE SOUL: PERSONA* album released that same year. The lyrics speak of a multitude of celestial bodies in a shared sky: "Oh let us light up the night / we shine in our own ways"—also an apt description of the tens of thousands of ARMY Bomb light sticks that illuminate their concert venues like distant stars across the galaxies. "Mikrokosmos" is a song for ARMY, referring both to the "microcosm" of each individual and the "cosmos" of a larger universe, or as BTS croons, "Perhaps the reason this night's features is again so beautiful / Is not because of these stars or lights, but *us*."[1]

This beautiful, bountiful "us" broadly encompasses a universe—or as observed in the chapters in this section, the multiple transmedia platforms that BIGHIT (now HYBE), BTS, and ARMY create and share. Media convergence and corporate conglomeration have made transmedia content pervasive in popular culture. As content, BTS is legion, proliferating across digital and physical spaces not just as singles, albums, music videos, reality-based television series, documentaries, digital short-form "behind the scenes" videos, and recorded performances (award shows, concerts, and more), which is already a lot. BTS members also appear as characters in licensed merchandise, video games, webtoons, and illustrated books. They provide celebrity endorsements for consumer goods (clothing labels, massage chairs, water purifiers, chewing gum, and automobiles), and national campaigns for Korean tourism and World Expo hosting bids. As activists supporting international goals (from climate action and gender equality to vaccination and mental health), BTS advocates for organizations such as the United Nations and its humanitarian agency UNICEF. A distinctive feature of BTS transmedia content is the story world of the Bangtan Universe, an ever-expanding multimodal narrative of intertextual references that threads across different media. And finally, BTS appears as the subject of flourishing (and at times chaotically so) ARMY-generated media in art, fiction, memes, fan edits, shitposts, and GIFs. In other words, BTS sits at the heart of a thousand constellations, made of singular stars within an ever-expanding universe.

Offering a historical overview of the K-Pop industry's early adoption of digital technologies, this section opens with Dal Yong Jin's "The Platformization of K-Pop: From Weverse to NFTs." Jin outlines how emergent media platforms drove shifts in the marketing and distribution of music, the facilitation of interactions between K-Pop idols and fans on social media, and the innovation of new forms of digital performance and art. In "Under the Same Sky: Synchronicity in BTS Media, Online and Offline," Despina Kakoudaki examines the cyber-physical connection enabled by these same technologies. Invoking fans' ability to sync official BTS light sticks with music and with other ARMY during a concert livestream, she maps the way copresence creates feelings of intimacy that are fluid, effortless, and coherent in shared time within the physical realms of in-person events, the digital realms of online spaces, and the physical/digital realms of remote venues.

Inter- and extratextual media platforms define much of the realm of fandom and franchising. In "Bridging the Senses: Medium and Materiality from Music Videos to Graphic Lyrics," Andrew Ty analyzes a set of illustrated books based on BTS songs and music videos. Ty highlights how the physical objects of the Graphic Lyric books invite readers to manually handle the texts to engage with tactility. In "Sweet Chili and Cajun: Tasting the Power of Language with the BTS McDonald's Meal," Melody Lynch-Kimery observes that the 2021 BTS Meal was the first time McDonald's promoted a meal worldwide using a language other than English on food packaging. Lynch-Kimery tracks the meal's release and reception in different countries and linguistic landscapes to understand how the marketing campaign reinforced and disrupted linguistic capital across cultural and economic contexts. In her contribution, "Fragmentary Redemptions: ARMY, RPF, and the AU at the Heart of the Bangtan Universe," Regina Yung Lee provides a close reading of the video "Euphoria" to demonstrate how the story world of the Bangtan Universe borrows heavily from two subgenres of fan fiction—real person fiction (RPF) and alternative universe (AU)—to engage ARMY's affectionate receptions of the story world. Framing this interaction with the narrative and materials of the Bangtan Universe as a critical and participatory activity, Lee considers how it is a reparative practice of imagining and longing for a more just world.

Given the commonplace reduction of Blackness to an aesthetic in K-Pop and the racism found in its fandoms, many Black K-Pop fans struggle with questions and conflicted emotions around BTS's relationship to Blackness and Black music. In her chapter, "'Black Guy Reacts to BTS for the First Time': Provocations from a Black ARMY," Jheanelle Brown examines another form of fan-created transmedia—the reaction video. Recognizing that BTS does not lean on performative Blackness through gesture, AAVE (African American Vernacular English), or dress, while at the same time being critically aware of BTS's debt to Black music, Brown explores how reaction videos made by cis-hetero Black men might provide a space for validation, solace, and dialogue about race, authenticity, and aesthetics. In "'Your Story Becomes Our Universe': Fan Edits, Shitposts, and the BTS Database," Jaclyn Zhou asks how BTS games such as BTS *Universe Story*—and the communities that play them—shape ongoing conversations in K-Pop fandom and scholarship about fan labor, the ownership of digital assets, the relationship between idols and their images, and the limits of intimacy between fans and idols. Finally, Mimi Thi Nguyen turns to fan-made animated GIFs fixating on the singular moment of Jung Kook's button coming undone during a performance on the 2022 BTS: *PERMISSION TO DANCE ON STAGE* tour. Turning to the erotic possibilities of this looping instance of uncalculated flesh, in "Jung Kook's Button, or the GIF That Keeps on Giving," she examines the communal desire captured in this repetitious striptease to highlight the pleasure of the obsessive return and anticipation of the GIF.

Note

1   Lyrics translated by doyoubangtan, BTS *Translations*, September 24, 2021, https://doyoubangtan.wordpress.com/2021/09/24/mikrokosmos/.

06 · The Platformization of K-Pop: From Weverse to NFTs — Dal Yong Jin

With the rapid growth of digital technologies, K-Pop has been the center of the Korean cultural industries in the early twenty-first century. K-Pop has become globally popular as several famous idol groups, including EXO, TWICE, BTS, and BLACKPINK, enjoy global fandom phenomena.[1] These idol groups' presence in bòth Western and non-Western cultural markets has been made possible due to various elements; however, the increasing role of digital technologies, including social media platforms like YouTube, certainly contributes to the contemporary fandom of K-Pop.

The convergence of digital technologies and popular culture, including K-Pop, is not new, as the Internet has already influenced popular music. However, seemingly one of the most distinctive popular cultures in the Korean Wave tradition, K-Pop has arguably been more deeply connected to digital technologies than any other cultural form. From social media like Facebook to streaming platforms, including YouTube and Spotify, K-Pop has extensively utilized digital platforms for its global reach and popularity. In very recent years, the K-Pop world has also attempted to employ cutting-edge digital technologies, such as artificial intelligence (AI) and nonfungible tokens (NFTs), to transform its business norms, which means that local entertainment houses continue to attempt to converge cultural content and AI or NFTs to develop new growth engines.

The convergence of popular culture—in this case, K-Pop—and digital technologies has consequently become a norm in the local music industry.[2] Global K-Pop fans quickly access a variety of social media platforms, including Weverse, Lysn, and Viki, to enjoy their favorite music while utilizing social media to form a K-Pop fandom. K-Pop highly depends on social media platforms rather than conventional media outlets for its global circulation. Social media have played an essential role in accelerating global youth's participatory consumption of K-Pop. The fans' grassroots and interactive online activities have consequently contributed to the development of social platforms.[3]

This chapter discusses the convergence of popular culture, in this case, BTS, as a representative of K-Pop, and digital technologies, including social media platforms, AI, and NFTs, to map out the shifting trends in the K-Pop world. By employing platformization, referring to "the penetration of infrastructural extensions of digital platforms into the web and app ecosystems, fundamentally affecting the operations of the cultural industries," as a theoretical framework in cultural production, it interrogates the ways in which digital technologies drive the continuity and change of K-Pop.[4] Finally, it critically discusses the shifting media ecology in tandem with K-Pop—again, particularly BTS—to determine power relations between digital platforms, K-Pop musicians, and K-Pop fans.

Convergence of K-Pop and Social Media Platforms

Over the past decade or so, the K-Pop industry has primarily adapted to utilize varied digital technologies. Unlike the 1990s, the music industry witnessed a fundamental shift, developing digital music instead of depending upon selling CDs and cassette tapes. Starting in the mid-2000s, the music industry experienced a more significant change due to the increasing influence of social media and streaming services, including YouTube and Spotify.

As an early adopter of digital technologies, the K-Pop world has been a test bed of new digital technologies. A handful of mega entertainment houses, including SM Entertainment, JYP Entertainment, and YG Entertainment, have extensively utilized social media to appeal to global youth. HYBE has also created its social network, Weverse, and the platform lets BTS fans interact with artists anytime through their smartphones. These developing trends certainly imply that the K-Pop industry has changed and will be rapidly shifting due to the increasing role of digital technologies, both national and global. For example, BTS and BLACKPINK offered online concerts, known as *BANG BANG CON The Live* (2020) and YG *Palm Stage—2021 BLACKPINK: THE SHOW* (2021), respectively, during the COVID-19 era, as they were highly embedded in digital platforms. Social media platforms have become, as Kim Ju Oak writes, "a salient site for enhancing BTS' celebrity power through establishing digital networks with global pop consumers. BTS, [more than any other K-Pop idols], has actively used social media accounts in order to upload posts, videos, and pictures directly. The group's timeless virtual presence has been effective in connecting with its physically distanced fans."[5] As the rightful winner of a social media influence award at the Billboard Music Awards, their performance has been viral, "with TV and the web co-creating an extensive field of social interactions. Fans mediated the broadcast's liveness through tweets and posts, remediating liveness by amplifying their experiences through this meta-discourse."[6]

K-Pop has certainly utilized social media platforms to develop its global fandom as consumers in their teens and twenties enjoy popular music online. Social media platforms like YouTube are driving engines in the contemporary music industry, and musicians and fans interact online as well as offline due to the snowballing role of social media in global fandom activities. K-Pop idol groups and solo artists have been able to build global fandoms thanks to their strategic use of social media to interact with their fans abroad. Given its tech-friendly nature, it is no surprise that the production, circulation, and consumption of K-Pop remained strong during the COVID-19 era.[7] From social media to streaming services, digital platforms are the primary engines for the growth of K-Pop. Korean entertainment houses have recently advanced their use of innovative digital technologies, including AI and NFTs, to diversify their revenue sources while creating new forms of cultural production.

K-Pop and Artificial Intelligence

One of the major distinctive dimensions in the K-Pop industry has been the convergence of K-Pop and AI. Several local entertainment agencies develop new idol groups through AI technologies, as can be seen in SM Entertainment's aespa and Riot Games' K/DA—virtual K-Pop girl groups. ETERNITY (also spelled IITERNITI), a female idol group that debuted in 2021, also represents AI-created virtual musicians. Based on their success, a few entertainment houses have advanced their adaptation of AI to create new forms of music to attract Korean youth while expanding their global reach.

Among these, SM Entertainment partnered with SK Telecom to introduce AI technology into K-Pop.[8] SM Entertainment showcased the new girl group aespa, which debuted with the unprecedented concept of including virtual avatars. The band comprises four human members—Karina, Winter, Giselle, and Ningning—and their avatars, the quartet's digital selves created through AI. According to SM Entertainment, the name *aespa* comes from the English words *avatar*, *experience*, and *aspect*, with the name meaning "to be able to meet another self through an avatar and experience a new world." Lee Sooman, former chairman of SM Entertainment, stated at the first World Cultural Industry Forum (WCIF) held in October 2020, "We are in the era of the next industrial revolution. As technology advances in the future, more changes will occur in human lifestyles, and as we have said, the future world will be celebrities and robots." He continued to say:

> aespa will project a future world centered on celebrities and avatars and will be born into a group of completely new and innovative concepts. . . . I think it would be good to create a world view with innovative and powerful storytelling from the planning stage, and how to create and convey a story and how to enter the world view in the future content. I think that is the game. . . . When aespa is released to the world, their music and lyrics will experience new entertainment through all IP (intellectual property rights), visuals, performances, including video content including music videos, as well as fascinating stories.[9]

The debut of aespa has been creating new waves in the K-Pop music sphere. The music video of its debut track, "Black Mamba," surpassed 240 million views on YouTube as of May 15, 2023. aespa is not the only virtual girl group supported by AI. Prior to aespa, there were other AI-powered acts like K/DA, consisting of four female characters from the popular online game *League of Legends*, which debuted with the single "POP/STARS" in 2018.[10] The AI-created idol groups continue to grow. In March 2021, girl group ETERNITY made its debut with the song "I'm Real." YG Entertainment has also been working with NAVER—a mega digital platform in South Korea—to create a new global music service platform by pooling NAVER's technologies, including AI, resources, and global influence, since 2017. Through this collaboration, NAVER also planned to embark on procedures to build a so-called meta database for the music it owns.[11] As such, these local music powerhouses aim to create virtual musicians via AI and consequently develop new songs and dances through collaborations among AIs.[12]

Music entertainment houses immerse themselves in producing AI-powered virtual singers due to several significant advantages. They believe virtual singers enjoy eternal youth and can work around the clock. They are free from scandals too. Most of all, virtual singers enable K-Pop entertainment houses to create a new revenue stream and expand their intellectual property as these new virtual singers are more widely available to youth who want to engage with their favorite idol groups in various forms.[13]

AI-supported K-Pop has brought up a handful of sociocultural dilemmas, however. Some people are concerned about potential negative outcomes; "virtual singers can fall prey to deepfake porn, digitally altered pornographic videos and images that replace the face of the subjects with someone else's." In the case of aespa, "the human members share the same identities as their virtual avatars, so if their digital selves fall victim to digital sex crimes," the human members are likely to be affected.[14] Another potential issue is copyright. Since it is still in its initial stage, it is not a big issue; however, when the human members terminate their contract, it will be a huge issue. Virtual singers can continue to work, but not humans.[15] Virtual singers are almost the same as humans; therefore, there are concerns about privacy violations, hate speech, and sexual harassment. No law regulates virtual singers and NFTs.[16] AI-supported K-Pop will create both new opportunities and potential disasters. The K-Pop world, including the government, the producers, and musicians, as well as fans, needs to be more considerate about the human singers and their rights.

The cultural value chain is being transformed, and the AI-supported new cultural systems will continue to expand their market penetration, which creates a new media environment. The current status of AI is fundamentally shifting the cultural industries, and AI has profoundly reshaped the production of popular culture, including K-Pop.[17] Digital platforms supported by AI will take a significant role in the production of popular culture in the future. For cultural industry firms, adopting AI technology in their creative work is no longer an option.

K-Pop toward NFTs

As one of the latest movements in the K-Pop world related to digital technologies, several entertainment agencies, such as HYBE, JYP Entertainment, and FNC Entertainment, have jumped on the NFT bandwagon, which needs to be carefully analyzed. HYBE announced its plan to set up a joint venture with the local crypto exchange platform Upbit to enter the nonfungible token (NFT) business in November 2021.[18] It planned to create NFT photocards that can be traded on Weverse, HYBE's global fan-to-artist communication app. HYBE's BTS NFTs may include moving images, voices of artists, and more, and global fans can exchange digital photocards in virtual spaces.[19] This original plan has not been easily achieved due to several barriers, including BTS's temporal hiatus due to their military service, but this does not mean that HYBE has given up its plan.

HYBE has both globally famous artists and a communication app, which greatly affects the operation of the K-Pop industry as a form of platformization, that is, a restructuring of the culture industries around digital platforms.[20] The majority of ARMY has access to it to enjoy BTS music. Unlike other big entertainment houses, it is a tremendous advantage for HYBE, as the platformization of culture can be achieved relatively quickly and responsively. Furthermore, HYBE created its game company HYBE IM in 2021 when it acquired Superb. One of the first few games is BTS *Island: In the SEOM*; BTS members themselves participated in developing this game. It was published as a casual simulation and puzzle game in June 2022. HYBE seems to be attempting to reduce its reliance on BTS, while diversifying its portfolio into new business areas, including games, the metaverse, and nonfungible tokens.[21]

Of course, cryptocurrency markets are subject to speculation.[22] The need for NFTs is also a speculative one. However, artists and musicians seem to champion NFTs as "a viable model of digital ownership," because "nonfungible digital assets are unique goods that don't have interchangeable value."[23] Artists and creators can upload digital assets like video clips, tweets, and music on the Ethereum blockchain. No two NFTs are identical since each piece contains unique digital properties. This scarcity theoretically benefits the creator and the buyer of the artifact. From fans' perspectives, buying and trading NFTs can provide creative support. They feel community-like support through their activities.[24]

Korean K-Pop giants are seriously bracing for the arrival of NFTs to extend their revenue potential by turning their existing intellectual property into digital assets. HYBE, JYP Entertainment, SM Entertainment, and YG Entertainment have competed to tap into the new tech. In July 2021, JYP partnered with Dunamu to set up a K-Pop-based NFT platform. SM Entertainment already announced its launch to build a cryptocurrency and blockchain platform in 2019.[25]

HYBE's move toward NFTs has triggered backlash as fans see the move as contradictory to BTS's previous sustainability efforts. HYBE's attempts are still in nascent stages, as a few hurdles are to be clarified. Seemingly beneficial to both musicians and fans, transactions of items on the Ethereum blockchain are incredibly energy intensive; "one transaction uses more power than the average US household does in a day," which is why BTS fans are fiercely against HYBE's plan.[26] BTS fans have since criticized HYBE for its plans to launch NFTs, with many citing the potential negative impact the digital asset has on the environment. ARMYs also noted how the company's NFT plans could be seen as contradictory to the boy band's speech at the UN, where they explained climate change as an important problem. BTS has continued to send various messages through both their lyrics and campaigns, which talk about the ideas of self-love, hard work, and social awareness, especially of a handful of socio-cultural issues, including climate change; however, HYBE's plan defies these talking points.[27]

As pop culture critic Kim Heon-sik points out, "BTS fans are also over-all feeling a sense of fatigue since the boy band is being 'overused' recently. They're feeling that BTS is being overly consumed too easily through so much content, especially if the content is not up to par."[28] When BTS announced their willingness to take a break from group activities in June 2022, some BTS members expressed that they could not be what they were as artists. RM stated that after BTS's last few singles, including "Permission to Dance" (2021), he "didn't know what kind of group we were anymore," adding later the band's members were "exhausted."[29] HYBE, instead of reevaluating its business models, has continued to overuse BTS, resulting in the hiatus of BTS at least for a while.

Consequently, BTS fans have trended the hashtags #BoycottHybeNFT and #ARMYsAgainstNFT to voice their displeasure over the company's plans. Some fans have canceled orders of merchandise from HYBE over the news about the NFTs, not to protest BTS but rather HYBE's business decisions.[30] BTS fans' online activities in response to different events and incidents, including the resurgence of the Black Lives Matter movement in 2020 and Jimin's T-shirt incident that occurred in 2018 (when Jimin wore a shirt featuring a slogan celebrating Korea's liberation from Japanese colonial rule in August 1945 that featured the atomic bomb's mushroom cloud—which triggered complaints from many Japanese), were active and well organized as they wanted to promote BTS's messages while protecting BTS in their fandom movement.[31] NFTs have rapidly become part of popular culture, and HYBE, alongside the K-Pop industry more generally, has advanced this particular marketization strategy. It is premature to predict the current status and future directions; however, it is certain that the platformization of cultural production in the realm of K-Pop will continue to grow. This is mainly because of some benefits that it brings about:

> The fundamental benefit of an NFT is that it helps creatives prove the authenticity of their digital works, thus making it possible to trade them. . . . It eliminates gatekeeping of the traditional art market that usually comes in the form of curators, galleries and art dealers who decide what artists

are worth the attention and the money. The NFT art market dismisses any middlemen between an artist and buyers, so it's the collectors who decide. Moreover, the NFT art market has the infrastructure anyone can access. There are already a number of marketplaces that let creatives mint their NFTs, connect with the audience and trade the art. . . . NFTs make it possible even for aspiring creatives to profit from their art and get recognition.[32]

In the digital platform era, several platforms supported by AI and big data will not only continue to grow but will likely explode in popularity, regardless of a variety of serious setbacks, like competitions with humans, ethical issues surrounding intellectual property, and representations. As other cultural genres, including gaming and sports, have already started to actualize NFTs as parts of their new business strategies to extend fans and revenues, the K-Pop world practices the platformization of popular culture in tandem with various digital technologies, including AI and NFTs.

Conclusion

The convergence of K-Pop and digital technologies, particularly digital platforms, has become one of the major dimensions in the local music industry. Unlike other cultural forms, K-Pop has been a symbol of innovation in various ways, as it, as an industry and a fan culture, is more than tech-savvy. As digital platforms have rapidly increased their roles in cultural production, local music agencies utilize several cutting-edge technologies, from social media to AI and NFTs, to develop new revenue sources while advancing new youth culture. By setting platformization as a tool and target, the K-Pop industry has fundamentally changed its media ecology. Digital technologies, including AI and NFTs, in the realm of popular culture consequently create new forms of interaction between cultural creators, fans, and platforms.

However, the K-Pop industry has appropriated K-Pop's participatory fan culture, as the K-Pop industry and digital platforms commodify fan culture. On the one hand, the K-Pop industry has strategically explored social media platforms to promote its music and expand its global presence. On the other hand, global social media platforms have accelerated the commodification of K-Pop's participatory culture as the platform providers increase their monetization strategies of both K-Pop content and fan activities.[33] As Yoon Kyong explains, "By dedicating their time and labor to promoting not only their K-Pop idols but also their own reaction videos and dance cover videos, the fans have incorporated their media practices deeply into the attention economy and thus engaged in the commodification of culture," which is potentially detrimental to the K-Pop industry and audience.[34]

Interestingly, the increasing utilization of digital technologies, including NFTS, has pushed the hardship of cultural producers and performers into the limelight.[35] The ongoing development and application of AI and NFTS in cultural production both rehumanize and dehumanize people's understanding of creativity, although they attempt to develop new business models. Contemplating digital technologies' involvement in creativity provides people with opportunities to look beyond the economic paradigm and consider key traits of human creativity and the creation process, some of which are successfully emulated by digital technologies. Digital technologies, including AI, dissociate creativity from human agency, and its cost-cutting effect can challenge human creators in many areas; however, certainly, humans are still major actors in various stages of cultural production. Eventually, it is culture rather than economy that people want to enjoy.[36]

Overall, the use of digital technologies, including AI, in cultural production has brought up a handful of significant sociocultural matters. Furthermore, the increasing dominance of digital technologies in the K-Pop industry may trigger the subordination of cultural creators and consumers to these cutting-edge digital technologies. What cultural creators and consumers have to develop at this particular juncture are balanced approaches to digital platforms and AI-driven cultural production.

Notes

1   J. Kim, "BTS as Method"; S. Kim, *K-Pop Live*; Lynch, "Fans as Transcultural Gatekeepers"; McLaren and Jin, "'You Can't Help but Love Them'"; Yoon, *Diasporic Hallyu*.
2   Jenkins, *Convergence Culture*.
3   Yoon, *Diasporic Hallyu*, 183–90.
4   Nieborg and Poell, "The Platformization of Cultural Production," 4276.
5   J. Kim, "BTS as Method," 1065.
6   Cho, "3 Ways That BTS and Its Fans Are Redefining Liveness."
7   Kwak, "K-Pop in 2021."
8   Murphy, "Past the Sheen and into the Underbelly."
9   S. Lee, "The Future of the World Entertainment Industry and Culture Universe."
10   Jin and Yoon, "Convergence of Gaming and Media."

11   Shon, "NAVER, YG Entertainment Begin Work."

12   Yeo, "SKT Partners SM Entertainment on AI-Based Technology."

13   Dong, "Will AI-Powered Groups Take Over K-Pop?"

14   Dong, "Will AI-Powered Groups Take Over K-Pop?"

15   H. Lee, "Rethinking Creativity."

16   Byun, "Fast-Growing Metaverse Creates Legal Risks."

17   Elliott, *The Culture of AI*; Jin, *Artificial Intelligence in Cultural Production*.

18   Jung, "Upbit Operator Picks."

19   Park, "BTS Enters NFT Market."

20   Nieborg and Poell, "The Platformization of Cultural Production."

21   Cha, "HYBE to Develop Game Biz Further to Cut Reliance on BTS."

22   Grobys and Junttila, "Speculation and Lottery-Like Demand in Crypto-currency Markets"; Zaucha and Agur, "Newly Minted."

23   Nguyen, "NFTs, the Digital Bits of Anything That Sells for Millions of Dollars."

24   Nguyen, "NFTs, the Digital Bits of Anything That Sells for Millions of Dollars."

25   Park, "BTS Enters NFT Market."

26   Nguyen, "NFTs, the Digital Bits of Anything That Sells for Millions of Dollars."

27   McLaren and Jin, "'You Can't Help but Love Them.'"

28   Kim Heon-sik, cited in Yang, "ARMY Calls for Boycott of HYBE over 'Homoerotic' Web Novel, NFTs."

29   McCurry, "BTS to Take a Break as K-Pop Band Members Announce 'Hiatus' to Pursue Solo Work."

30   Yang, "ARMY Calls for Boycott of HYBE over 'Homoerotic' Web Novel, NFTs"; Ziwei, "BTS Fans Threaten to Boycott HYBE over Plans to Launch NFT Content."

31   Jin, "The BTS Sphere."

32   Drobitko, "Can Artists Still Benefit from NFTs?"

33   Yoon, "K-Pop Pedagogy in the Digital Platform Era."

34   Yoon, "K-Pop Pedagogy in the Digital Platform Era," 187.

35   H. Lee, "Rethinking Creativity."

36   H. Lee, "Rethinking Creativity."

Works Cited

Byun, Hye-Jin. "Fast-Growing Metaverse Creates Legal Risks: Law Firm." *Korea Herald*, November 26, 2021. http://www.koreaherald.com/view.php?ud =20211126000610.

Cha, Jun Ho. "HYBE to Develop Game Biz Further to Cut Reliance on BTS." *Korea Economic Daily*, April 12, 2002. https://www.kedglobal.com/entertainment /newsView/ked202204120017.

Cho, Michelle. "3 Ways That BTS and Its Fans Are Redefining Liveness." *Flow*, May 29, 2018. http://www.flowjournal.org/2018/05/bts-and-its-fans/.

Dong, Sun-hwa. "Will AI-Powered Groups Take Over K-Pop?" *Korea Times*, June 8, 2021. https://www.koreatimes.co.kr/www/art/2021/06/398_310095.html.

Drobitko, Andrey. "Can Artists Still Benefit from NFTs?" *Forbes*, June 29, 2022. https://www.forbes.com/sites/forbesbusinesscouncil/2022/06/29/can-artists-still-benefit-from-nfts/?sh=7396401648da.

Elliott, Anthony. *The Culture of AI: Everyday Life and the Digital Revolution*. London: Routledge, 2018.

Grobys, Klaus, and Juha Pekka Junttila. "Speculation and Lottery-Like Demand in Cryptocurrency Markets." *Journal of International Financial Markets, Institutions and Money* 71, no. 2 (2021): 1–15.

Jenkins, Henry. *Convergence Culture: Where Old and New Media Collide*. New York: New York University Press, 2006.

Jin, Dal Yong. *Artificial Intelligence in Cultural Production: Critical Perspectives on Digital Platforms*. London: Routledge, 2021.

Jin, Dal Yong. "The BTS Sphere: Adorable Representative M.C. for Youth's Transnational Cyber-nationalism on Social Media." *Communication and the Public* 6, nos. 1–4 (2021): 33–47.

Jin, Yae Won, and Tae-jin Yoon. "Convergence of Gaming and Media: Music and eSports." In *Global Esports: Transformation of Cultural Perceptions of Competitive Gaming*, edited by Dal Yong Jin, 184–201. New York: Bloomsbury, 2021.

Jung, Min-kyung. "Upbit Operator Picks NFT Venture with BTS' HYBE as Most Anticipated Project." *Korea Herald*, September 22, 2022. https://www.koreaherald.com/view.php?ud=20220922000629.

Kim, Ju Oak. "BTS as Method: A Counter-Hegemonic Culture in the Network Society." *Media, Culture and Society* 43, no. 6 (2021): 1061–77.

Kim, Suk-Young. *K-Pop Live: Fans, Idols, and Multimedia Performance*. Stanford, CA: Stanford University Press, 2018.

Kwak, Yeon Soo. "K-Pop in 2021: Social Media-Friendly Musicians Survive Pandemic." *Korea Times*, January 3, 2021. https://www.koreatimes.co.kr/www/art/2021/01/398_301592.html.

Lee, Hye-Kyung. "Rethinking Creativity: Creative Industries, AI and Everyday Creativity." *Media, Culture and Society* 44, no. 3 (2022): 601–12.

Lee, Soo Man. "The Future of the World Entertainment Industry and Culture Universe since COVID-19." First World Cultural Industry Forum, Daegu, Korea, October 28, 2020.

Lynch, Kimery S. "Fans as Transcultural Gatekeepers: The Hierarchy of BTS' Anglophone Reddit Fandom and the Digital East-West Media Flow." *New Media and Society* 24, no. 1 (2021): 105–21.

McCurry, Justin. "BTS to Take a Break as K-Pop Band Members Announce 'Hiatus' to Pursue Solo Work." *Guardian*, June 14, 2022. https://www.theguardian.com/music/2022/jun/15/k-pop-band-bts-to-take-a-break-as-members-pursue-solo-work.

McLaren, Courtney, and Dal Yong Jin. "'You Can't Help but Love Them': BTS, Transcultural Fandom, and Affective Identities." *Korea Journal* 60, no. 1 (2020): 100–127.

Murphy, Sam. "Past the Sheen and into the Underbelly: A Deep Dive into the K-Pop Industry." *Music Network*, July 15, 2019. https://themusicnetwork.com/deep-dive-k-pop-industry/.

Nguyen, Terry. "NFTs, the Digital Bits of Anything That Sells for Millions of Dollars, Explained." *Vox*, March 11, 2021. https://www.vox.com/the-goods/22313936/non-fungible-tokens-crypto-explained.

Nieborg, David B., and Thomas Poell. "The Platformization of Cultural Production: Theorizing the Contingent Cultural Commodity." *New Media and Society* 20, no. 11 (2018): 4275–92.

Park, Kate. "BTS Enters NFT Market in Joint Venture with Upbit." *TechCrunch*, November 4, 2021. https://techcrunch.com/2021/11/04/bts-enters-nft-market-in-joint-venture-with-upbit.

Shon, Ji Young. "NAVER, YG Entertainment Begin Work on New Global Music Service Platform." *Korea Herald*, October 18, 2017. http://www.koreaherald.com/view.php?ud=20171018000684.

Yang, Haley. "ARMY Calls for Boycott of HYBE over 'Homoerotic' Web Novel, NFTs." *Korea JoongAng Daily*, November 11, 2021. https://koreajoongangdaily.joins.com/2021/11/11/entertainment/kpop/HYBE-boycott-HYBE-NFT-BTS-NFT/20211111145350421.html.

Yeo, Jun-suk. "SKT Partners SM Entertainment on AI-Based Technology for K-Pop Content." *Korea Herald*, January 11, 2019. http://www.koreaherald.com/view.php?ud=20190111000628.

Yoon, Kyong. *Diasporic Hallyu: The Korean Wave in Korean Canadian Youth Culture*. New York: Palgrave Macmillan, 2022.

Yoon, Kyong. "K-Pop Pedagogy in the Digital Platform Era." *International Journal of Media and Cultural Politics* 17, no. 2 (2021): 183–90.

Zaucha, Trever, and Colin Agur. "Newly Minted: Nonfungible Tokens and the Commodification of Fandom." *New Media and Society* (2022): 1–22.

Ziwei. Puah. "BTS Fans Threaten to Boycott HYBE over Plans to Launch NFT Content." *NME*, November 5, 2021. https://www.nme.com/news/music/bts-fans-threaten-boycott-hybe-over-plans-launch-nft-content-environment-3088083.

07 · Under the Same Sky: Synchronicity in BTS Media, Online and Offline — Despina Kakoudaki

After the cancellation of their world tour during the COVID-19 pandemic, BTS performed and broadcast a series of concerts online, and their team developed new techniques to connect with audiences. For example, in April 2020, the team livestreamed *BANG BANG CON* on Weverse and YouTube, a free online festival of eight BTS concerts from 2014 to 2018. During this "Bangtan Concert in Your Room," fans could link their official light stick, the ARMY Bomb, to the Weverse app, so that it would pulse and change color in sync with the music on screen.[1] If this cyber-physical application brought the concert into the fans' personal space, the next concerts, *BANG BANG CON The Live* (June 14, 2020) and *BTS MAP OF THE SOUL ON:E* (October 10–11, 2020), transported fans into the concert venue. In the latter, a massive screen mosaic appeared behind BTS on stage showing live footage of fans watching the concert, the audio included sound recordings of fans cheering and singing along, and image mixing combined physical and virtual imagery to form a hybrid spatial dimension (see figure 7.1).

These technological innovations created the impression of "being there" for online viewers, but they also added a live audience of sorts for BTS members themselves, who were visibly touched by seeing ARMY after so long. On a VLIVE broadcast later that month, Jimin described his surprise: "I didn't know that we could see each other real-time like that at the concert. . . . You suddenly appeared in the LED screen." Jimin interprets his reaction as a realization of the personal impact of the pandemic: "I tried to accept the reality, telling myself that it's okay. But when I saw your eyes during the concert, I realized it was not okay. . . . The moment I saw you, the tears just poured down."[2]

7.1 · *BTS MAP OF THE SOUL ON:E* onstage screen mosaic with fan footage.

The emotional connection revealed in Jimin's comments is more striking in the context of the massive global viewership of these online events.
Over 1.33 million paid viewers from 195 regions watched each night of the BTS
2021 MUSTER SOWOOZOO concerts (June 13–14, 2021), livestreamed from an
infinity-shaped stage in Seoul Olympic Stadium. How does one create intimacy at such a scale and distance? Fans appeared on LCD mosaics on stage,
and on screens set up in rows between the walkways, where seats might have
been, and their recorded cheers were added to the audio (see figure 7.2).[3]

The technological feats that power these images and sounds and stream the
high-definition event are fueled by the desire for immediacy that drives the
fan/artist relationship. And the concert thematized this quest, starting with
a filmed introduction of BTS driving an RV through a desolate planet looking
for ARMY, and ending with BTS asking fans to shine the flashlights of their
cellphones out their windows to "create a galaxy together." Although as a fan
I know that BTS members are brand ambassadors for the Samsung Galaxy
cellphones that they were holding on stage, the product connection did not
distance me from the poignancy of this mid-pandemic project or the sentimentality of Jung Kook's next comment: "We'll always be headed toward each
other. Never forget that."

7.2 · *BTS 2021 MUSTER SOWOOZOO.* BTS onstage with a backdrop of fan footage during their online concert.

Fans, Platforms, and Mediation: Everyone Everywhere at the Same Time

In the media ecology that surrounds BTS, the distancing tendencies of global, dispersed, or asynchronous contexts are countered by a primary desire for localization, connectivity, synchronicity, and copresence. In this intimate universe nothing feels more synchronous than the massive, global response of fans to a specific event, whether this is a new album release, media appearances, or posts from BTS on social media. At such moments, the fandom seems to be acting as one, with engagement maps on Twitter and other platforms showing the immediate response of everyone, everywhere, at the same time. This effect is both a natural reaction and a cultivated fan behavior. For scheduled performances, music releases, and award shows, fans coordinate their reactions, organizing special hashtags to trend on social media and amplifying the effect of BTS's presence on a venue. Fansites, such as US BTS ARMY, often provide instructions or guidelines for purchasing tickets or voting for awards, even translating content for the benefit of international fans, and it is not uncommon for regional fan groups to develop common aims for new music releases.[4] One of the fandom's favorite visualizations of these activity surges uses a map of the world that lights up to show global levels of engagement. Powered by tools such as Trendsmap, which uses animation to show the Twitter traffic of topics, keywords, and hashtags over time, these visual records are celebrated as a snapshot, a self-portrait of the fandom. For Nicole Santero, a researcher publishing such visualizations online, the maps remind fans that they "are a part of something incredible."[5]

Contemporary media users treat online and social media environments with increasing comfort and familiarity, and older media platforms reinvent themselves to capitalize on the availability of faster internet speeds and higher broadband capacities in more regions. As Suk-Young Kim has argued in the context of K-Pop, these technological and cultural changes converge into a thematics of "liveness" that dispels distance and realigns the relationship between performers and audience.[6] The online maps offer yet another example of this paradoxical choreography of mediation and presence in contemporary social media. The two used to be imagined as opposites in classic media theories: presence meant colocation in physical space, proximity, tangibility, live-ness; mediation meant distance in space or time, screens, recordings, projections, the dependence on technologies that capture or reproduce an event, and the associated risk of interference and manipulation. The barrier imagined between direct experience and mediated experience was never this simple, of course, and it feels even more antiquated now. Especially after the outbreak of COVID-19 forced many in-person interactions into online spaces and remote venues, it is even clearer how much of our experience of copresence is in fact mediated, and how much of mediation is in fact intimate.

Seen through a techno-pessimist lens, the glowing map reduces individual action into a data point, a mere number, as the energy of the individual behind the screen is abstracted, made impersonal. Contemporary worries and chilling discoveries about fake news, conspiracy theories, the manipulation of identities and online communities, and interference with global elections flow from this awareness that mediated presence is depersonalized and thus potentially inauthentic and unreliable. This is the opposite of the narrative interpretations made by fans themselves. For them, the glowing image or trending hashtag is a register or proof of collective action. The map renders visible and concrete both their individual presence somewhere in the world and their participation in the fandom as an entity of vastly larger scale. Fans insist that what look like numbers are actually people.

The successes of BTS across the world, from blockbuster albums and multiplatinum hits, to sold-out tours and record-breaking online concerts, are often celebrated at the level of numbers and metrics, with information constantly tracked by dedicated Twitter accounts such as @btschartdata. But the resistance of certain music markets to this success is also often couched as speculation about the accuracy of numbers and about chart manipulation.[7] The ability of K-Pop fans to harness the power of social media also came to mainstream attention during the summer of 2020, when fans deployed hashtags, fan cams, and fundraising drives in support of the Black Lives Matter movement.[8] The scale of response itself was unrecognizable. One report noted that the volume of focused fan activity felt like the operation of a single body or of automated entities like bots. "But, of course, they're not bots," the report concluded. "They're a body of people, and people are far more complex than a hashtag."[9] BTS fans indeed insist on the power of metrics that rely on human desire and human presence, tracing the organic growth of the ARMY community that sells out albums, stadiums, merchandise, and basically any product BTS touches, sponsored or not, in opposition to metrics that are safeguarded by industry practices, such as radio play for BTS songs. The contrast that fans identify is not between people and bots but between people and antiquated, nationalistic, hegemonic media practices.

What fans experience as a sense of community is partly this extraordinary synchronicity of everyone doing the same thing, at the same time, everywhere around the world. The temporal dimension registers direct experience: fans respond to an event in real time through individual action. The spatial dimension, the glowing map of the world, is an aftereffect of many layers of mediating technologies: the platform that records fans' responses, the Twitter algorithms that track levels of activity, the markers or hashtags that make the activity trackable, the apps that capture this information, the data visualization programs that translate it in new forms, and so on. The map is a mediated artifact that seems to concretize or embody an impossible virtual closeness, a purple wave that goes around the world, a fandom that is one entity or one single emotion or impulse.

The sense of intimacy is thus possible precisely because it is mediated. It is only through these aggregated and technology-dependent forms of copresence that the fandom can see the abstraction of itself as one body. There is no single physical venue that would allow copresence in space for so many, so copresence in time, on media platforms and on the visualization map, creates the only form of copresence possible at this scale. But the pattern on the screen is also not felt as an abstraction that sublimates real people into the "mass ornament" of their collective action.[10] Instead, the map is a materialization of action and desire into an amplified tangible form. The focus on amplification and collective action is also what drives the volunteer fundraising collective

One In An ARMY, which organizes monthly microdonation drives to support charities and nonprofit organizations around the world.[11] The desire for oneness is thus powerful, political, often sentimental, but also self-aware. When cast in meme terms, fans make fun of themselves by joking that the whole fandom sometimes "shares one brain cell."

These complex networks of emotions and associations manifest differently depending on the technological platform they occupy. In her analysis of how social media users value "liveness and sharedness," Michelle Cho identifies a range of transformative practices that "multiply and expand forms of mediated liveness."[12] From unscripted, behind the scenes, or "reality show" material released by the artists, to fan-produced YouTube reaction videos and shared clips and fan cams, these expanded texts share a specific platform, YouTube in her case study, and develop a visual, behavioral, and intertextual vocabulary for registering a sense of community in this highly mediated space. The desire for copresence and authenticity emerges differently on Twitter, a platform that favors quick action and response, and facilitates the wide dissemination of information. As used by fans, Twitter also functions as a traffic director of sorts, alerting users to media and texts on other platforms. Part of the temporal effect that I am tracing here, the desire to experience things together at the same time, is visible because of the temporal dimension of the platform, its prioritization of interactions in time.

Managing Distance: Same Place, Same Time

The promise or desire for closeness is of course central to fandom experiences in general. But BTS's global fans start a priori from a sense of distance: they may be based outside South Korea, they may not speak Korean, they may not share cultural references or historical legacies. Their attachment to BTS and their music is a victory over these forms of distance. This characteristic of the ARMY fandom as a global entity intensifies the methods and narratives that fans develop to create closeness—in fact, it is the main reason technological mediation is either made transparent (not really there) or is seen as an active facilitator in the fandom, as a method for bridging distance. But the fandom also exhibits an exaggerated self-consciousness about distance, as if there is always some other, more direct level of access or closeness elsewhere. Even if I spoke Korean fluently, or lived in Seoul, or shared more cultural affinity with BTS's work, they would still be superstars that I can only "know" through their work and public appearances.

A spatial visualization of this sentimental understanding of distance may look like a series of concentric circles, with BTS at its center. Fans often idealize any condition that would bring them closer to BTS, going to a concert or fan meeting, visiting a restaurant BTS has been to, studying the song lyrics, practicing the choreography to a song, reading books referenced in songs or recommended by BTS members, learning Korean or visiting South Korea, and so on. Some of this proximity is spatial, some is emotional or cultural, seeking to experience part of what BTS experienced, or see the same art object or landscape view. Following RM / Kim Namjoon's frequent posts about visits to museums, art galleries, and parks, a whole concept called "Namjooning" emerged to describe these forms of contemplation, with measurable impact for cultural organizations worldwide.[13] Similarly, the fandom's own time zone starts from Korean Standard Time, the fans' preferred mode for publicizing events on global media platforms, and then revolves around where BTS is located at that moment. The fandom is so adept at closing the figurative gap between themselves and BTS that any form of proximity, however small, abstract, mediated, or imagined, feels magnified. Just having BTS in one's own hemisphere, continent, or time zone, for example, is experienced as a transformation. Some of it is simply practical. When BTS performs in venues in the United States, for example, fans in the Americas marvel at the comfort of not having to wake up at 3:00 or 4:00 a.m. to catch a South Korean broadcast. Just the fact that BTS may post a photo or comment when one is awake feels like the band is suddenly closer, and gives fans the sense of being on time, being there for once, a relief from the perennial feeling of "what did I miss" every morning.

Concerts are a prime example of arriving at the epicenter of this imaginary world, of finally being with BTS and ARMY in the same place at the same time. The sentimental response to this proximity is often couched in terms of reciprocity: BTS arrives at a place to see their fans. The fans go to the same place to see BTS. "We wanted to see you," "It's so good to see you," the members say from the stage, and the fans see their own feeling mirrored back to them. "We are breathing the same air" was a phrase that Canadian ARMY trended when they found out BTS had landed in Canada during their *Love Yourself World Tour* in September 2018. "We are breathing the same air," RM noted from the stage in Hamilton, Ontario, on September 20, 2018, showing that he was aware of the feelings and hashtags, and uniting the online and offline worlds yet again.

Despite this outpouring of emotion about the value of direct presence, a BTS concert is by no means an unmediated event. On stage and in the arena or stadium as a whole, the production team constructs a spectacle of intensive multimedia interactivity. The members of BTS, their singing and dancing, formations, costumes, and choreography, the background dancers and musicians, and the mood and meanings of their songs are all further amplified through coordinating animations in the massive screens behind and around them, complex props, stage elevators, movable platforms, inflatable structures, vehicles, projections on the floor, light effects throughout the stage, and a light show that includes the ARMY Bombs in the venue and beyond. The whole stadium is treated as one space, a spectacle of oneness that is projected back to fans through aerial shots and drone footage on screen. The concert in fact has a multitude of extra audiences. Concerts in Los Angeles in 2021 and Las Vegas in 2022 played to the live audience in the main venue, a second audience watching on big screens at a nearby theater or concert space, the online audience watching a live broadcast on Weverse or Kiswe, a remote in-person audience watching a live or delayed broadcast at a participating movie theater in other regions, and then, later, the audience that watches a rebroadcast online or on DVD or Blu-ray. From the point of view of the BTS production team, the concert is designed to satisfy the image, sound, quality, and narrative needs of these diverse audiences and formats.

As a fan, I have attended BTS concerts in all these configurations. In relatively direct contact with BTS in a stadium concert, my perspective is limited by the location of my seat, and I am still looking at screens in order to appreciate the overall design and to see details and close-ups of the members' faces. I am in the same space at the same time as BTS but the actual physical distance between me and the stage is still significant and, if my seat is in the upper sections, I only see BTS as small vague human shapes unless I look at the screens. My perspective is also so skewed by all my screen-based experiences of their work, that I have to remind myself that these figures, these bodies, are the actual people, BTS. And then I marvel for different reasons that we are all experiencing the same heat or rain or cold, that I have been merely standing or dancing by my seat while they have been singing and running all over the stage, and that they are powerful, intense, magnetic. Their talent as performers is even more evident in this space, where they are smaller but also bigger than their images on screen, minuscule in the vastness of the stadium but irresistible in their capacity to capture the affective power of this whole crowd. Looking around I feel the visual impact of having so many people at the same place at the same time, with the ARMY Bombs accentuating the space into a fantasy world of lights as it gets darker. My photos are fabulous even if some are blurry. And the sound is overwhelming, a Dionysian atmosphere of ARMY together, the singing along and excited screaming of thousands.

When the concert ends, I still go online to find other people's photos and footage, to see angles from better seats, and to admire the captured snippets of improvisation and mischief that BTS is so good at and that localize each concert as a unique event. These clips are about to become definitive memories or memes of the experience of that day, and even though I was there I did not directly see most of them myself. The full concert experience, in other words, is not located just in the live venue but combines materials seen live, filmed, broadcast, and uploaded online. By the time BTS appears on VLIVE for the customary postconcert chat, we are all united again online, fans watching at home from everywhere joined by those of us still in cars and buses after the concert, braving traffic to get back to our hotels.

BTS is metaphorically "closer" to me when I watch the concert on Weverse or Kiswe. This is a familiar experience, watching BTS on screen, but, in this context, I can toggle the multiview camera perspectives facilitated by these platforms to watch four or five camera feeds simultaneously and catch both the details and the overall choreography. I also potentially have the advantage of subtitles, so that I can understand the members' comments between sets. Watching at a participating movie theater is even better since the size of the screen and the surrounding sound allow me to be fully immersed. I have the best seats in the house. But I am only watching one selective feed from the broadcast, and the experience feels a little more formal, lacking the side attractions of seeing and hearing others' enjoyment and watching whatever randomness may be taking place on other parts of the stage.

Which one of these formats and venues is the best concert experience? And which one counts most as copresence? Fans answer this question not on the basis of sound and image quality, but through the emotional longing to be "part of that purple ocean" that BTS and ARMY create together. Admittedly, these are radically different experiences, rather than one being a recording of the other, and many fans compound them, as I did, by watching a concert in multiple formats. But, in addition to the holy grail of "being there" in person, a second fundamental tendency that affects this experience is again synchronicity, the drive to watch the concert as close to when it's happening as possible. This focus is evident both in fans' desire to not miss out on a developing narrative about BTS-related events and media and the tendency of BTS and their team to value and prioritize live performance. Even when a concert may be rebroadcast or available for viewing-on-demand online, the focus on timeliness inspires fans to adjust their work and sleep schedules in order to attend the event on time, at the same time. The key word here is "attend," not watch. Despite the concert's expansion across the many media, platforms, and venues I outlined before, despite the capacity to archive and replay the event in an asynchronous way, the chief propelling force is temporal copresence.

When BTS does something, in other words, fans attend, they show up, they are present, in person or online, but in time. Fans may use the asynchronous, nonlocalized, always-on capacities of contemporary media to catch up, rewatch, or strengthen their attachment to the BTS archive, but they put a secondary value to this vital accessibility of content and a primary value to the timeliness of the experience. The fandom's foundational desire for copresence appears to revolve around being at the same place at the same time, but, more accurately, it should be described as the desire to be there at the same time, no matter the place. Desire is related to time. Technological mediation takes care of the place.

Under the Same Sky: Fandom and Emotion

Perhaps the way in which space and time switch roles is inevitable in a global context. It's easier to understand the scale of the moment, the now, than the scale of massive numbers and vast distances. And when it comes to fans' experience of BTS's music, closeness is also produced emotionally, regardless of the physical limits. Who cares about distance in the intimate space of one's room, one's laptop or phone, one's mind, or one's earbuds? BTS songs and ancillary productions often address the fan/artist relationship directly, from songs such as "2! 3!," "Pied Piper," and "Magic Shop" that meditate on the nature and emotional impact of this attachment to the animated versions of BTS as TinyTAN tumbling out of a fan's cell phone or TV screen to cheer her up, help her make egg tarts in her bakery, or lullaby her to sleep after a hard day.[14] The desire to connect forms a coherent narrative strategy across texts and formats in this ever-expanding multimedia ecosystem.

The phrase *under the same sky* refers to this play of closeness and distance in BTS-related media. The phrase appears in many texts and communications, in song lyrics, speeches, interviews, and tweets by the members of BTS, and has also been appropriated repeatedly by fans to describe a specific experience. On Twitter, it trends periodically when fans create posts with images of themselves in specific places, or images of natural landscapes and cityscapes, or just images of the sky. The sentimentality of the phrasing is always about affirming a relationship that both acknowledges and defies distance.

One of its first iterations comes in a song that BTS performed as early as 2011, before their official debut, "팔도강산" ("Paldogangsan"), in which RM comments on a battle between different Korean dialects: "Why keep fighting, in the end, it's all the same Korean / Look up, we are all looking at the same sky."[15] The lyrics reemerge as an affective rather than political statement a few years later in "For You" (2015): "Even if you are far, we are looking at the same sky. / No matter what happens, as long as you're here, nothing seems scary."[16] In both cases, the phrasing affirms connection despite distance, and over the years it has acquired a wistfulness about mutuality. For example, RM posted a note to ARMY on Weverse on March 30, 2021, writing, "Whenever I feel uneasy, I feel that I am living with a similar heart as you under the same sky! Let's gain strength while looking at the sky and I am happy that we are together."[17] Fans reciprocated by posting pictures of the sky and natural landscapes with hashtags such as #SkyForNamjoon. These trends pop up at times that may be seen as affirming or trying for BTS or reference an experience in the fan's own life or a particular issue in the world in general. BTS acknowledged these emotional images on stage during the BTS 2021 MUSTER SOWOOZOO concert later that year.

As a resident metaphor of the fan/artist intimacy narrative that has evolved around BTS, the sky produces and feeds a desire for direct presence everywhere. Fans use BTS as a guide, as we see with the "Namjooning" trend, as a signpost or curator for traveling, discovering cultural events, visiting museums, galleries, amusement parks, the beach, and nature in general. They also use the same process for introspection, as they localize their own experiences in terms of the ARMY fandom, describing daily life in fandom-specific terms, engaging in forms of self-awareness inspired by the fandom, and adding their life experiences into the BTS ARMY archive. In the overall terms about space and time I have engaged here, this is like saying one is always with BTS, in all places all the time, a sentiment that the band encourages in songs like "You Never Walk Alone," in lyrics such as "We were only seven, but we have you all now," and in personal accounts, as in Jimin's powerful comment, "Remember there is a person here in Korea, in the city of Seoul, who understands you."[18]

Notes

1   According to Big Hit Entertainment, the almost twenty-four-hour festival reached 50.59 million views, with a peak of 2.24 million concurrent viewers, and 500,000 ARMY Bombs from 162 regions connected to the app.

BANG BANG CON The Live had 756,600 paid viewers from 107 regions; and *BTS MAP OF THE SOUL ON:E* had 993,000 paid viewers from 191 regions.

2   Jimin, "I'm Here," VLIVE, October 20, 2020, archived on Weverse, https://weverse.io/bts/live/3-104695841.

3   Kiswe, "How BTS Managed to Connect with Fans Virtually at 2021 Muster Sowoozoo."

4   Established in 2014, US BTS ARMY was the first US-based fanbase of BTS. See https://www.usbtsarmy.com.

5   Such maps were created by Nicole Santero as @ResearchBTS and posted on Twitter and Instagram. For an interview with Santero, see "The (Remote) Interview: Nicole Santero," interview by Diane Russell, UNLV News Center, August 3, 2020, https://www.unlv.edu/news/article/remote-interview-nicole-santero.

6   Kim, *K-Pop Live*.

7   Kwaak, "Inside the Business of BTS."

8   Yim, "Surprised at Seeing K-Pop Fans Stand Up for Black Lives Matter? You Shouldn't Be."

9   Andrews, "BTS Donates $1 Million to Black Lives Matter."

10 For the concept of the mass ornament, see Kracauer, *The Mass Ornament*.

11 See more on their website, https://www.oneinanarmy.org/.

12 Cho, "Three Ways That BTS and Its Fans Are Redefining Liveness."

13 Harrington, "BTS's RM Has Sent K-Pop Fans Flooding to Art Museums."

14 The lyrics focus on reciprocity and describe the band members' desire to comfort and support fans through their songs. The lyrics of "2!3!" include the refrain "It's okay, When I say one two three, forget it / Erase all the sad memories, Hold my hand and smile." In "Magic Shop," the song builds a door in the fan's mind to reach a place of comfort, and BTS members themselves find comfort there. For lyric translations, see the *Doolset Lyrics* blog, https://doolsetbangtan.wordpress.com/. TinyTAN are cartoon versions of BTS that are used for merchandise and in short films and clips. See TinyTAN Animations, "Magic Door," featuring the song "Mic Drop" (BangtanTV, YouTube video, 2:41, https://www.youtube.com/watch?v=Yf9Nlq5wrf8), and "Dream ON," which uses "Zero O'Clock" (BangtanTV, YouTube video, 3:14, https://www.youtube.com/watch?v=K7BMF00zFS0).

15 Translation by popgasa, *Popgasa Kpop Lyrics*, https://popgasa.com/2013/09/11/bts-satoori-rap-팔도강산/.

16 Translation by Nanami, *BTS-Trans / Bangtan Subs*, https://www.bangtansubs.com/for-you.

17 RM on Weverse, March 30, 2021, archived at https://weverse.io/bts/profile/a7c80e82107be5cb10b52d3575744c8a. Translation by @bora_twts, Twitter, March 30, 2021, 12:38 p.m., https://twitter.com/bora_twts/status/1376936839932690436.

18   "BTS Commencement Speech, Dear Class of 2020," BangtanTV, June 7, 2020, YouTube video, 12:32, https://www.youtube.com/watch?v =AU6uF5sFtwA.

Works Cited

Andrews, Travis M. "BTS Donates $1 Million to Black Lives Matter after K-Pop Fans Flood Hashtags to Support Movement." *Washington Post*, June 7, 2020. https://www.washingtonpost.com/technology/2020/06/07/bts-donation -k-pop-fans-black-lives-matter/.

Cho, Michelle. "Three Ways That BTS and Its Fans Are Redefining Liveness." *Flow* 24, no. 8 (May 29, 2018). https://www.flowjournal.org/2018/05/bts-and-its -fans/.

Harrington, Delia. "BTS's RM Has Sent K-Pop Fans Flooding to Art Museums Thanks to His Instagram." *ARTnews*, June 28, 2022. https://www.artnews.com/list /art-news/news/btss-rm-has-sent-k-pop-fans-flooding-to-art-museums -thanks-to-his-instagram-1234632793/bts-rm-art-influence/.

Kim, Suk-Young. *K-Pop Live: Fans, Idols, and Multimedia Performance*. Stanford, CA: Stanford University Press, 2018.

Kiswe. "How BTS Managed to Connect with Fans Virtually at 2021 Muster Sowoo- zoo." Editorial, June 15, 2021. https://www.kiswe.com/news/how-bts -managed-to-connect-with-fans-virtually-at-2021-muster-sowoozoo.

Kracauer, Siegfried. *The Mass Ornament: Weimar Essays*. Translated by Thomas Y. Levin. Cambridge, MA: Harvard University Press, 1995.

Kwaak, Jeyup S. "Inside the Business of BTS—and the Challenges Ahead." *Billboard Magazine*, August 26, 2021. https://www.billboard.com/music/features /bts-billboard-cover-story-2021-interview-9618967/.

Yim, Hyun-su. "Surprised at Seeing K-Pop Fans Stand Up for Black Lives Matter? You Shouldn't Be." *Washington Post*, June 11, 2020. https://www.washington post.com/opinions/2020/06/11/surprised-seeing-k-pop-fans-stand-up -black-lives-matter-you-shouldnt-be.

08 · Bridging the Senses: Medium and Materiality from Music Videos to Graphic Lyrics _Andrew Ty

In June 2020, Big Hit Entertainment released a collection of hardcover books graphically illustrating the lyrics of five BTS songs released between 2015 and 2017. Collectively referred to as the Graphic Lyrics series, each volume features a visual interpretation of a select song by a different artist. Each book offers a narrative extension of the Bangtan Universe (BU, for short), a fictional world created by Big Hit, which centers around the lives of seven young men navigating the emotional fallout from physical abuse, illness, and other traumatic events. Told through officially branded music videos, short films, album notes, webtoons, and other audiovisual texts, the BU offers fans a textually rich and emotionally immersive transmedia story world through which BTS's music and personae could be experienced. While most official BU content is delivered in the form of web-based materials, Graphic Lyrics volumes expand the Bangtan Universe through a physical form of visual storytelling—picture books enriching the presentation of BTS's story world by appealing to a reader's sense of touch and sight.

Although the lyrics featured in each volume are printed primarily in Hangeul (except when they are originally in English), the form and aesthetic logic of each book communicate much more about the meaning of each song than the words alone. Reminiscent of pop-up books, Graphic Lyrics volumes use inventive visual layouts and textures to invite readers to rely on nonlinguistic literacies to draw meaning from BTS's music, providing both Korean and non-Korean speakers a rich interactive experience. For instance, volume 2, *Save ME*, uses full-page images printed on translucent paper so that scenes are overlaid upon each other, creating a visualization of how events linger in the spaces where they have happened. Most of the pages in volume 5, *Butterfly*, are cut horizontally, so that readers can turn either the top or bottom part of the page and combine its imagery with the illustrations on adjacent pages. This design literally splits the storyline but still lets readers follow its narrative tracks as they are reintegrated at the end. Volume 4, RUN, uses a horizontal format to spatialize its representation of the journey of two characters' friendship across time. Wider than it is tall, RUN drives a reading direction that reproduces the metaphorical and literal trajectories taken by the characters on the page. Unlike a traditional English-language literary text, which requires readers to move through each word and sentence in the order that they appear on the page, each Graphic Lyrics volume forces us to move our gaze in a variety of directions, inviting us into a multisensory interaction with illustrations and words. While all forms of textual reading can be described as embodied, Graphic Lyrics volumes offer a potentially more reflexive mode of tactile interaction by making us simultaneously aware of the physicality of the book and our own bodies in the process.

In this chapter, I examine the haptic, graphic, and textual representations of BTS's music in three of the five Graphic Lyrics volumes—RUN, *Save ME*, and *Butterfly*, all named after the songs represented in each book. I focus on these texts in particular because they converse with the imagery and storylines communicated through official music videos released for each song. Specifically, the visual and tactile experiences of reading these three Graphic Lyrics volumes connect to another embodied and multisensory encounter: the audiovisual experience of watching the music videos. With the Graphic Lyrics volumes adding touch to "the fundamentally audiovisual and multimodal nature of music video," the stories associated with the songs are now experienced through a third sense.[1] The result is a fuller multimedia experience of BTS songs and stories that invite an activation of aesthetic sensibilities as an approach to multimedia texts.[2]

Graphic Lyrics and the Bangtan Universe

BTS represents a vast intertextual universe through which audiences can form multiple points of personal and emotional connection with both the group's music and the persona of each member. While the lyrical and musical composition of each song offers a primary point of meaning production for listeners, their experiences are also mediated by a vast volume of paratextual content released around the music, such as music videos, dance rehearsal clips, promotional teasers, and short films. Moreover, the seemingly endless stream of reality show content, behind-the-scenes footage, and live web broadcasts produced by Big Hit offers fans a sense of interpersonal connection with the unique personalities, daily habits, and larger dynamics of the group, inviting fans to project parasocial meanings onto their interpretation and experience of BTS's music.

Although not different from other K-Pop idol groups in this regard, the interpretive world built around BTS by Big Hit Entertainment stands apart in both volume and narrative complexity. Any fan will tell you that BTS's music is profoundly allegorical—each song and album tells a story about their growth as artists and people, and much of the paratextual content released by the company has expanded and enriched this narrative. Big Hit tracks the evolution of the group's music and personae according to distinctive eras within their discography. The group's first major conceptual transformation took place with the release of three mini-albums between 2015 and 2016 titled *The most beautiful moment in life*, or 화양연화/*Hwayangyeonhwa*. Often referred to by fans as the "HYYH Trilogy," this collection of albums pivoted them toward a more inward-facing reflection on the social isolation and longing that come with masculine adolescence, a shift from the outward-facing critiques of the social pressures faced by Korean youth, characterized by their debut-era messaging. BTS displayed a resolute image of youthful defiance against authority in the "School Trilogy" that started their career, but the coming-of-age story that followed needed a more sophisticated and nuanced presentation. As the unofficial birth of the Bangtan Universe, HYYH allowed the group to bring an imaginative storytelling element to these new introspective personae, enriching their engagement with fans.

When Big Hit formally branded BTS's fictional story world as the "Bangtan Universe" in 2017, they retroactively traced its narrative origins to the music video released for "I NEED U," the lead single from *The most beautiful moment in life pt.1* (2015), the first installment of the HYYH Trilogy. For the first time, BTS released a music video that featured no singing and dancing but instead set up several dramatic situations. While the seven members were seen interacting with each other, other scenes established distinct narrative situations for individual members, such as Namjoon working at a gas station, where a motorist pays him by dropping money from the car window to the ground, Taehyung stabbing his physically abusive father with a broken bottle, or Jimin looking bereft next to an overflowing bathtub. By creating a parallel narrative universe starring fictionalized characters with the BTS members' actual birth names, BTS was able to explore difficult subjects and issues such as class division, domestic violence, and depression. The stories in the Bangtan Universe may not be directly autobiographical, but the themes they raise are based on real-world issues.

The BU storyline was further expanded through five more videos released during the HYYH era: "화양연화/Hwayangyeonhwa on stage: prologue"—a short film that played onscreen during the HYYH concert tour (2015), and the music videos for "RUN" (2015), the Japanese-language versions of "I NEED U" (2015) and "RUN" (2016), and "EPILOGUE: YOUNG FOREVER" (2016). The Japanese videos used only brief shots from the BU, opting to show more song-and-dance performances, but the Korean ones further developed the BU through their own dramatic vignettes that include Jimin and Hoseok talking in what looks like a hospital room, with an IV drip set up beside a bed. By the end of 2020, the BU evolved into a sprawling, elusive story world told through a repertoire of media forms earmarked by the company as "official BU content," including webtoons, album inserts, a promotional poster, and bits of narrative text released as tweets and small booklets, not all of which has necessarily served to advance the development of story or character. In this way, the BU revealed itself to be an ever-expanding world more than a coherent arc, thus lending itself to robust interpretive engagement by fans and artists.

Graphic Lyrics volumes offer another expansion of the BU. Labeled as "inspired by BU" rather than "official BU content," the series graphically reinterprets the storyline rather than simply extending it. More specifically, it presents a graphic treatment of BU-related songs released mostly during the HYYH era. On the one hand, *A Supplementary Story: You Never Walk Alone* (vol. 1) and *House of Cards* (vol. 3) interpret their respective songs using the HYYH *The Notes: Book 1*—a story guide to the HYYH-era Bangtan Universe, published in 2019 by Big Hit. *Save ME* (vol. 2), *RUN* (vol. 4), and *Butterfly* (vol. 5), on the other hand, offer reinterpretations of the music video as well as lyrics of each song. Except for *A Supplementary Story: You Never Walk Alone* (vol. 1), the Graphic Lyrics volumes work on 2015–16 HYYH-era content. This may be because this phase of the BU seems the most substantial, in terms of both the multimedia world-building that launched the BU and the discussions it initiated across ARMY fandom. The BU content of this era is an optimal blend of official and fan-made content, and the Graphic Lyrics volumes can be considered midway between the two: official releases open to loose reinterpretations that deviate from the canon.

One possible indicator of this looseness may be seen in how the Graphic Lyrics volumes are numbered, which do not follow the release-date order of the songs depicted across the series. For instance, volume 1, *A Supplementary Story: You Never Walk Alone*, features a song that was released in 2017, a year after the third and final installment of the HYYH series was released, while volume 4, *RUN*, and volume 5, *Butterfly*, feature tracks released on the second HYYH album in 2015. This apparently arbitrary ordering makes each book appear independent of the others. My discussions here follow the order of the release date of the song, rather than their order in the Graphic Lyrics series.

RUN: Walking Bodies, Crossing Spaces

RUN (vol. 4), illustrated by Choi Ji Wook, offers a graphic interpretation of "RUN," the lead single from the second album in BTS's HYYH Trilogy. The lyrics of the song represent a number of themes that characterize BTS's music during this era with lines in the chorus about continuing to run, even if one falls or gets hurt.[3] While the musical composition of "RUN" sonically captures the themes and emotions contained in its lyrics, the music video (MV) visually dramatizes the lyrical, sonic, emotional, and thematic meanings of the song. Departing from the usual dance-driven music videos seen in K-Pop and other BTS videos, "RUN" follows a loose story structure, depicting BTS members in the role of fictional BU characters rather than musical performers. Dressed in jeans, T-shirts, and jackets, the members look like ordinary young men, instead of the pop stars they are. The song hangs its insistent "run run run" lyrical hook on a dark minor-key sound and an upbeat danceable rhythm, mirrored by the MV's alternating scenes of the group engaging in boisterous fun and scenes of members suffering in isolation. During the song's chorus, we see shots of all seven members sprinting across the screen in collective force, visually and narratively representing a desperate desire to escape their situation.

RUN, the fourth volume of the Graphic Lyrics series, focuses on the lives of two unnamed characters who are styled to resemble the characters played by RM and V in the MV. The first half of the volume depicts the story of BU "Namjoon," who must navigate the anguish of unfulfilled class fantasies. The second half of the volume depicts the story of BU "Taehyung," who is haunted by the scars of his abusive father. In the Graphic Lyrics volume, there are few indications of their relationship and more a general sense of how each one's specific circumstances result in troubled lives. Though it remains unclear in the book how they know each other, the artist shows them together to illustrate the comfort they have found in each other's company. Interestingly, in *RUN*, no one runs. Both characters simply walk. The slower pace of action maintained in RUN distinguishes it from the up-tempo rhythms that propel both the song and its MV. Instead, it focuses on those MV scenes in which the characters are alone. Where the MV shows the members knowing each other well, including key moments featuring Namjoon and Taehyung together, the Graphic Lyrics volume is more starkly abstract in plot and character. Instead of the backstory seen and implied in the MV, the book opts to enrich the story through material form and design, which invites certain ways of reading depending on how the pages are constructed.

Choi uses a horizontal layout to embellish the theme depicted in the MV of running through and from the enveloping pain of an adolescent psyche. Taking advantage of the elongated design of the book, Choi paints a sequence of panoramic scenes that stretch across the left- and right-hand side of the book binding (see figure 8.1). The book maintains a dynamic tension between the distance its widescreen pages evoke and the solitude of two characters who spend much of it separate from the other, only coming together at the end. Recalling the MV's scenes of solitary members, two characters walk alone, drawn in rather forlorn postures. RUN depicts Namjoon's journey as a movement through urban space. Positioned as a street-level view, the flatness presents spaces he crosses from end to end, where comforts are rare, at least until the end. Taehyung's journey is depicted through more abstract representations of emotions and memories arranged as a broken collage on the page. Choi orients their characters' eyeline and direction of movement toward the right side of the page in order to guide the flow of the story and reader's progression through the book in a lateral movement across the page. Spatial continuity is implied in invisible spaces that readers must imagine. Having to turn individual pages, each reader can nevertheless imagine a continuous space being crossed by the characters that readers follow with their eyes, connecting one page to the next. The blend of sight and imagination in going through RUN's wide horizontal layout is further augmented by the inclusion of two-page foldouts that extend the frame of visible space and action beyond the boundaries of one page. The foldouts compel the reader to broaden the scope of their gaze (upon the pages they are looking at and in the spaces they imagine).

While the reader does not need to be familiar with the "RUN" MV in order to make sense of the story contained in its Graphic Lyrics volume, the richness of the reader's experience is enhanced by one's memory and personal association with the song and the music video. Where the MV shows Namjoon and Taehyung together, fleeing from police who saw the latter spraying graffiti, the book keeps them apart, walking for purposes and to destinations

8.1 · The horizontal design emphasis of Graphic Lyrics series vol. 4, *RUN*. Photograph by Andrew Ty.

that remain unclear until the end. When the two meet at the end, readers who recall the MV may feel like the book has finally caught up with the MV's depiction of their friendship.

Save ME: Opaque Bodies, See-Through Spaces

The "Save ME" MV was not part of the BU story. Unlike narratively driven MVs, such as "I NEED U" or "RUN," the "Save ME" MV was shot in one take as a performance video of BTS members singing and dancing in an open field. This nondescript setting foregrounds the musical performance, with the camera focusing on certain members during quieter parts and pulling back to capture the group during the more dynamic moments of the song. Without a story, "Save ME" only enters the BU as an "Inspired by BU" Graphic Lyrics book.

Illustrator Lee Kang Hun visualizes the song's plaintive title in two characters suffering the lingering effects of past trauma in the present. Pictorially coded by BU props and settings recognizable from BU music videos, the two figures in the book are made to resemble Hoseok and Jimin, the characters played by BTS members j-hope and Jimin. Some BU objects in the visual background of "Save ME" in its Graphic Lyrics form include Snickers bars, a carousel, a bathtub, and a hospital room, props that do not appear in the "Save ME" MV, but which are linked to the characters of Hoseok and Jimin from the BU. The *Save ME* volume shares similarities with the *RUN* volume. Both books use images of two figures suffering in solitude for much of the book, with the two characters joyfully meeting at the end. A shared setting in each (*RUN*'s bus stop, *Save ME*'s bedroom) signifies integration of the separate characters and stories through visual symmetry. These shared settings are also where the book shifts its perspective from one character to another.

These broadly similar events are presented differently in both books, given the distinctions in the formal and material composition of each book. *Save ME* visualizes the lingering pain of past trauma in present-day lives. This theme and situation are literally materialized using translucent sheets that add layers of detail to the illustrations, details that disappear as readers flip pages and move on (see figure 8.2). When turning the translucent pages of *Save ME*, readers may flip them repeatedly back-and-forth to see differences in the details and experience the persistence of trauma by reenacting it through repetition. These translucent sheets allow the printed lyrics *save me* to be read in reverse like a mirror image, referencing 2018's "FAKE LOVE" MV.

The *Save ME* book uses several translucent pages at key moments in its story, not only to produce but also to enact thematic meaning. In scenes where the characters traverse dimly lit settings (a neglected theme park or a flowering arboretum overgrown with foliage), two translucent pages are layered to depict these dark places and reveal the lonely child in each character. When the adult characters dance, first individually and then together, readers need to flip three translucent pages. By the book's conclusion, the repeated gesture of flipping pages transforms that relived trauma into a repetition associated with release, through an image of the dancing bodies of two characters who have found each other. Such visual and tactile patterns integrate sight and touch to generate a kind of reading rhythm that uses both senses.

If the Graphic Lyrics series attempt to communicate music in nonaural forms, it is interesting to see the formal and material transformation that *Save ME* and its preoccupation with dance undergoes. What differentiates the narrative trajectory of the *RUN* and *Save ME* volumes is how the latter takes an emphasis on dance from its MV. The virtuosity in choreographing a dance performance, filmed in a single-take MV, is narrativized in the book as a story of healing that takes place as its characters dance together. The use of the translucent sheets conveys a seriality of movement, and the material of

8.2 · The translucent pages of Graphic Lyrics series vol. 2, *Save ME.*
Photograph by Andrew Ty.

the sheets itself creates distortions that make it seem like the characters are moving as the pages are bent and flipped. The volume as a physical book cannot show nonstop dancing like the MV. Still, whenever Jimin and Hoseok are pictured dancing, it evokes a similar sense of release through dance, whether these characters do so alone or, in the end, together.

Butterfly Effects, Split Pages, Split Stories

The closest MV equivalent for *Butterfly*'s book is "HYYH on stage: prologue," a twelve-minute video that contains snippets of Claude Debussy's "Clair de Lune," a few lines from the BTS song "Ma City," and instrumental excerpts from "Outro: House of Cards" and "Outro: Love Is Not Over." (Melodic snatches from "Butterfly" also appear in other MVs, most notably "RUN.") Like the insect in its title, the song "Butterfly" lives in an audiovisual intertextuality marked by flitting and fleeting melodies.

Unlike the RUN and *Save ME* Graphic Lyrics volumes, *Butterfly* features all seven BU characters together at the beginning of the book. Despite illustrator Lee Kyutae using images most closely resembling those in its audiovisual

8.3 · The split page design of Graphic Lyrics series vol. 5, *Butterfly*. Photograph by Andrew Ty.

origins in "HYYH on stage: prologue," the material construction of this Graphic Lyrics volume undercuts its visualization of the members as a collective unit by having most of its pages physically cut (see figure 8.3). The book's construction means that each split page can be flipped separately, alternating between top and bottom, creating different combinations that mix the top and bottom of each page. While some pages show one image split physically, the book more often presents two separate images on one page. This visual layout splits the narrative between scenes of the group together and scenes of one character alone.

The pages are not cut into equal divisions. The upper portion takes up two-thirds of a page and depicts scenes of group conviviality, while the bottom third usually depicts a lone figure. The opening split image is of a solitary figure outdoors, holding a video camera, the MV prop by which Seokjin, the BU character played by BTS member Jin, can be identified; the second image is an open hand against a clear sky, presumably from Jin's point of view. These paired images—camera and hand—highlight visuality and tactility. The bottom third of the page sets up a visual rhythm with images of Seokjin lying in bed in a fetal position, seated on a bed while staring straight ahead, or standing before a window with half-drawn curtains. This three-image pattern—lying down, seated and staring, and standing looking out—occurs twice, each instance separated from the other by a single image. The first single image is an empty view of the exterior setting, where all seven characters are enjoying the outdoors, and from where Seokjin was using his video camera; the second is the interior space of the bedroom, also empty. The book then reverts to an intact single page with Seokjin taking videos of his six friends all together again. The characters and the story are made whole, just as the book's pages are also made materially whole.

There is one more split in this book: a musical one. Printed song lyrics in the Graphic Lyrics volumes evoke songs not directly heard by readers but only recalled. In *Butterfly*, lyrics appear only on the split-page layouts, always on the left-hand side where illustrations are minimal. With lyrics on the left and images on the right, music is isolated horizontally from image, just as Seokjin is isolated vertically from his friends. As split pages become whole again, the art on the right-hand side spills to the left; song lyrics now appear on both sides of the book. The integration of pages and characters matches the integration of image, music, and texture, and the corresponding senses of sight, sound, and touch. Lyrics appearing across both sides of the pages present a song recalled and reconstructed by visibility and tactility.

Music across Media

Reading these books feeds into memories of the songs and their MVs, bridging the aural, the audiovisual, and the tactile. These BTS songs in all their forms become intermedial and multisensory; experiencing them this way blends the immediate and the remembered. To examine the interplay of elements in the aesthetic experience of reading the Graphic Lyrics books is to ask how the text happens. Such questions of textual phenomenology necessarily begin with a concrete engagement with specific texts. The continuing question, however, is to ask how to "generalize these specifics as larger structures of experience."[4] MVs are common ways of enriching the sensory impact of songs using innovative audiovisuals. BTS Graphic Lyrics do this too, innovating an older medium of the physical book to renew the experience of pop music, and adding touch to pleasures mostly experienced audiovisually. The result refines aesthetic sensibilities for engaging intermedial content, enriching our experiences of the work. By adding a tertiary mediation of meaning in the format of a picture book, what results is a multisensory engagement with BTS's music that engages sight, sound, and touch. The songs become intermedial and intertextual artifacts that then invite "a complex multi-sensory perceptual engagement by means of a cultivated sensibility."[5] Experiencing the songs across different media encourages an "aesthetics of perception."[6] These books activate not only sonic memories and meanings attached to hearing the songs, but also residual visual imagery from music videos. The Graphic Lyrics volumes for these three songs add another type of visualization, shifting from onscreen moving images of music videos to still images made to move by the reader's handling of the pages. Additionally, as the songs play in memory—in the mind's ear, as it were—senses of hearing, sight, and touch are intermedially bridged in the perceptual experience of reading these Graphic Lyrics volumes. This approach to art seems more amenable to lingering in rich descriptions of an aesthetic experience, rather than deploying artistic judgment and critical evaluation. This is how the song assumes different forms: audio recording, video, picture book. Each one exists as a discrete artifact, but the reading process as a perceptual experience combines them, creating rich intermedial and multisensory song texts that invite an equally rich engagement.

Notes

1   Korsgaard, *Music Video after* MTV.

2   Berleant, "Aesthetic Sensibility."

3   The song's chorus includes the lines "다시 Run Run Run 넘어져도 괜찮아 / 또 Run Run Run 좀 다쳐도 괜찮아," which are translated as "Again, I run run run, even if I fall down, it's alright / Again, I run run run, even if I get a little hurt, it's alright" ("RUN," BTS-TRANS/BANGTANSUBS, May 22, 2022, www.bangtansubs.com/run).

4   Bukatman, "Vivian Sobchack in Conversation with Scott Bukatman."

5   Berleant, "Aesthetic Sensibility."

6   Nanay, *Aesthetics as Philosophy of Perception.*

Works Cited

Berleant, Arnold. "Aesthetic Sensibility." *Ambiances: International Journal of Sensory Environment, Architecture and Urban Space,* March 30, 2015. https://doi.org/10.4000/ambiances.526.

Bukatman, Scott. "Vivian Sobchack in Conversation with Scott Bukatman." *Journal of e-Media Studies* 2, no. 1 (2009). https://dx.doi.org/10.1349/PS1.1938-6060.A.338.

Choi Ji Wook. RUN. BTS Graphic Lyrics, vol. 4. Seoul: Big Hit IP, 2020.

Koo Ja Seon. *A Supplementary Story: You Never Walk Alone*. BTS Graphic Lyrics, vol. 1. Seoul: Big Hit IP, 2020.

Korsgaard, Mathias Bonde. *Music Video after MTV: Audiovisual Studies, New Media, and Popular Music*. Oxfordshire, UK: Routledge, 2017.

Lee Kang Hun. *Save ME*. BTS Graphic Lyrics, vol. 2. Seoul: Big Hit IP, 2020.

Lee Kyu Tae. *Butterfly*. BTS Graphic Lyrics, vol. 5. Seoul: Big Hit IP, 2020.

Nanay, Bence. *Aesthetics as Philosophy of Perception*. Oxford: Oxford University Press, 2016.

Park, Joseph. *House of Cards*. BTS Graphic Lyrics, vol. 3. Seoul: Big Hit IP, 2020.

09 · Sweet Chili and Cajun: Tasting the Power of Language with the BTS McDonald's Meal — Melody Lynch-Kimery

What does the power of a language taste like, look like, or sound like? Does the power of language look like eBay listings for used McDonald's dipping sauces, decorated with Hangeul (the Korean alphabet), still selling for three times the cost of the original meal? Or does it look and sound like the chaos inside a McDonald's restaurant in Indonesia, shut down due to overcrowding by delivery drivers racing to fill orders of Korean-inspired recipes of Sweet Chili and Cajun sauces?

The world has grown accustomed to McDonald's being seared on its consciousness, from restaurants on every corner to ads in train stations to the center of Olympic villages. The ubiquitous presence of McDonald's as a global standard is also paralleled by and packaged with the power that the English language wields. Considered the lingua franca of commerce, English functions as the language of capitalism. McDonald's global success is intrinsically linked with language as it colonizes food markets, with a menu grounded in American food and packaging emblazoned in English no matter what the location. In the United States, East Asian languages are frequently sidelined, deemed strange, exotic, or viewed as lacking financial value. Packaging labeled in Mandarin, circulating in the US, for example, often carries the racialized stigma of being "Made in China" and thereby marking a low-quality product.

In 2021, McDonald's launched the BTS Meal, which represented the first time in the company's history that the franchise promoted a food product on a global scale using a common language other than English. For one month

9.1 · BTS Meal with nugget box, sauces, cup, and bag. Photograph by Melody Lynch-Kimery.

from May to June, McDonald's sold a ten-piece McNugget meal packaged in most countries in purple (the official color of BTS) bags, boxes, and cups with the Hangeul for *borahae* (보라해, a BTS neologism for "I purple you," a term of team endearment for ARMY) (see figure 9.1). The highlight of the meal was the two nugget dipping sauces, Sweet Chili and Cajun, packaged in Hangeul. These sauces are not traditionally Korean in origin but were marketed as "hand-picked by BTS and inspired by popular recipes from McDonald's South Korea."[1]

Marketing for the BTS Meal differed from previous celebrity endorsements that featured Western athletes and musicians or campaigns aimed at cultivating non-Western consumers. For decades, McDonald's has offered localized menu options for specific regions, such as McAloo Tikki in India or the Shrimp "Ebi" burger in Japan. The BTS Meal represented the first time Asian celebrities and an Asian language (Korean) were used in a global marketing campaign. For one month (May to June), the chaos and excitement surrounding the release of the BTS Meal demonstrated how the ascendancy of the Korean language on McDonald's food packaging and the collective experience of consuming the meal can disrupt traditional hierarchies of linguistic landscapes.

When the BTS Meal was released, I found myself driving for twenty miles, careening down the rural backroads of Indiana, a rural state located in the middle of the United States, and speeding through cornfields past gun shops and political billboards, to purchase a BTS Meal. Despite my urgency, it was not lost on me that I was driving through the "American Heartland," a region often characterized as white, conservative, and monolingually English-speaking, to be sold a McDonald's meal wrapped in packaging featuring Hangeul, by an employee wearing a shirt with Hangeul lettering, in an American fast-food restaurant adorned with signs featuring the name of a South Korean band. My fascination with the power exemplified by the meal was solidified when I asked the employee working at the drive-thru window what the Hangeul on their shirt said. The employee replied, "They told us we had to wear these shirts today for this meal. I don't know what it says, so I looked it up. It's like Korean letters."[2] Here in the American Heartland, the BTS Meal had exposed non-Korean speakers to Hangeul, changing the language in their environment.

Having been raised in the diverse linguistic landscapes of Southeast Asia and East Asia, where multiple languages are frequently on display in public spaces, for me, this moment was a small but welcome glimpse of future progress toward transnational and multilingual appreciation in monolingual spaces within the United States. I was also reminded of my past, recalling my move from Japan to a rural Midwestern community in the United States. As a preteen living in Japan, I was immersed in the world of J-Pop, so I was eager to share music and culture with new American friends. My peers reacted with confusion and disgust to my J-Pop idol magazines, exclaiming things like "Eww, they look like girls" and "I can't read any of this!" They followed up with racist imitations of Asian languages and remarks about how unattractive Asian men are. These encounters keenly focused my attention on any shift, no matter how slight, in how Asian languages and cultures are valued in the US, particularly in isolated rural areas where many people are not regularly exposed to languages other than English. I learned very quickly back then that English was the language of power and access and the standard of success. The availability of the BTS Meal in a small Midwestern town represented a cultural change, as I watched the children of my former middle-school classmates now clamor for East Asian pop music and promotions.

How to Feed an ARMY

In April 2021, McDonald's announced their collaboration with BTS and a social media frenzy erupted, especially on McDonald's Twitter, as fans expressed excitement in multiple languages, often mixed with Korean. Primed to cater to ARMY on a global scale, the meal was presumably based on BTS's favorite McDonald's order when they were trainees in Seoul, and met a variety of religious and cultural restrictions. The BTS Meal itself consisted of ten-piece chicken McNuggets, medium French fries, medium Coca-Cola, and the two dipping sauces, Sweet Chili and Cajun. The two dipping sauces were marketed as "inspired by popular McDonald's South Korea recipes."[3] From Cyprus to El Salvador, in fifty different countries, the dipping sauce packets featured Hangeul lettering that phonetically spelled *Sweet Chili* and *Cajun*, 스위트칠리 and 케이준, and again, in most markets, the packaging would also feature the Hangeul for *borahae* (보라해). During the campaign, McDonald's employees worldwide were also expected to wear a promotional shirt bearing the Hangeul consonants for BTS/McDonald's. Additionally, BTS x McDonald's Merch Collection was sold online through the Weverse store and featured the Hangeul for *Sweet Chili* and *Cajun* on items such as tote bags, bathrobes, and T-shirts.

McDonald's promoted the BTS Meal through continuous interactions on Twitter with ARMY. The restaurant added a small number "7" to their Twitter handle (a widespread practice by ARMY to represent the seven members of BTS), and they exchanged banter using common BTS/K-Pop phrases such as *bias* (a term designating one's favorite member) and OT7 (an abbreviation of "One True 7," a refusal to choose a bias among equally loved members). The corporation appeared up to the challenge of delivering an experience tailored for the global BTS fandom. What McDonald's may not have expected, however, was the scope and variety of the launch experience and the underlying value ARMY would bring to the meal itself.

Hungry for Hangeul

In McDonald's restaurants across Malaysia, long lines of people gathered as purple balloons swayed over large posters of BTS members posing with fries and Cokes. Restaurants created a separate line marked "BTS Meal Only" and gave away BTS-themed merchandise to the first customers in line.[4] Due to differences in time zones, Malaysia was the first country in which the BTS Meal was available. The release was successful as fans posted to social media, celebrating the meal's sauces and the purple packaging inscribed with Hangeul. The rest of the world—or ARMY, at least—quivered with excitement as they awaited their turn to buy the meal.

Hours later, excitement turned to dismay as social media in the United States showed a vastly different picture. While BTS Meals across the globe were priced similarly to regular value meals (seven to ten dollars in the United States), what consumers received in different countries was not uniform. Videos on TikTok and Twitter captured expressions of surprise and disappointment as US ARMYs were handed greasy, standard McDonald's packaging. If lucky, a fan received both sauces. Twitter user @BTS_Jen complained, "How is this even the same? I ordered the #BTSMeal, and I got no BTS!" and posted side-by-side images of a BTS Meal bought in the United States against one purchased in Southeast Asia.[5] US-based fans also posted videos of themselves attempting to navigate the terrain of McDonald's promotions. There was footage of an excited family driving forty minutes to a McDonald's only to be told that they had been given the wrong information, and the purple packaging with Hangeul was not offered. After receiving a box of chicken nuggets that included a confounding slice of cheese and a container of ranch sauce for dipping, fans tried explaining to confused employees what the BTS Meal was supposed to contain. Some fans posted images of their own artistic handiwork, handwriting Hangeul on regular McDonald's packaging to mimic what they should have received. At the end of the first day of the promotion, a post from McDonald's FAQ went viral stating, "I'm sorry, but BTS packaging is different across the globe, and the U.S. does not have the BTS cup or McNuggets Box."[6]

ARMY in the United States realized that even though they are members of a global fandom, their access to global goods may be restricted by the West's racist inability to comprehend demand for East Asian goods. McDonald's failure to fully distribute the complete BTS Meal in the United States echoes other instances in which BTS's popularity has been underestimated and even constrained in the West, from their snubs at the Grammy Awards to intense scrutiny by the Billboard Charts. Following the BTS Meal debacle, ARMY worked harder to demand recognition for BTS. After registering their disappointment through social media, criticism by US BTS fans was picked up by news outlets and trended as #BTSMEALFAIL and #BTSMEALSCAM. One US fan lamented on Reddit, "I don't understand how they could have gotten this so wrong. It's not like this would have flown under the radar. It's their [McDonald's] home country and the biggest market. I enjoyed the sauces, but my enthusiasm has definitely soured."[7] In these moments, ARMY in the US actively constructed linguistic capital or language value for Hangeul by communicating their frustration and demand through videos, tweets, Reddit threads, and Facebook posts, and otherwise contacting the McDonald's corporation directly.

Fans also demonstrated the economic value of the Korean language. Sellers on e-commerce marketplaces such as eBay and Mercari quickly began listing used cups, paper bags, and sauces for as high as one thousand dollars (USD). ARMY in other countries reached out on social media to ARMY in the US, offering to share or mail products. Other fans in the US purchased the incomplete BTS Meal, despite their disappointment, in order to disrupt hierarchies of language and culture. One tweet read, "A little disappointed that I didn't get the purple BTS packaging that other countries are getting, but just thinking of the overall impact of having Hangeul on an English franchise's product and the exposure that @BTS_TWT is getting from this collab. So proud of them."[8] Another user noted, "But I am nothing if not resilient so. . . . I got to stream Butter [sp] while in the drive-thru, plus I was letting an American company know that a BTS partnership is profitable."[9] The poorly executed launch in the US signaled to consumers that McDonald's considered the collaboration to be of interest only to Asian countries, and badly misjudged the popularity of BTS (and by extension Korean language and culture) outside of it. Fans took the chance to remind McDonald's of its failure, even as they worked to transform the sound and sight of language during the meal's release.

Annyeonghaseyo: You Know Why We're Here!

Despite the lackluster launch in the United States, the linguistic environment of McDonald's in different countries was disrupted nonetheless. Linguistic environments or landscapes can operate as a "public arena where language battles are taking place and where the choice of languages can establish the domination of space."[10] Unlike a concert or BTS event, McDonald's is a highly public space in which any consumer might encounter the Korean language during the BTS Meal promotion, through fan activities, decorations, or the meal itself. This indirect contact also builds value for the language by introducing Korean to people who may not have either seen it written or heard it spoken.

From the most elaborate restaurant decorations, such as life-size cardboard cutouts of the members propped up beneath balloon arches in the Philippines, to the more minimal promotions, such as employees wearing the required shirt with Hangeul in the United States, all of these small changes in which Hangeul is used as a power brand disrupted an environment that normally privileges English-centric marketing across the globe.

A recurring TikTok trend featured fans rolling up to the drive-thru, yelling a welcome greeting in Korean, then stating, "You know why we're here," all while blasting a BTS song. Groups of fans shouting the BTS fanchant outside the restaurant, hosting meal-unboxing events and photo sessions, and explaining the sauces to employees disrupted the regular routine of McDonald's. Even without humans in the linguistic landscape, the presence of BTS photographs, special advertisements, and Hangeul on employee T-shirts, and the dipping sauces painted a rich layer of language. The availability of Hangeul merchandise in the Weverse store and the creative methods in which fans preserved and recycled their packaging (creating purple cardboard shoes and hats, laminating their paper bags) extended the disruption of language. Fans physically carried the language outside of McDonald's, spreading and building even more linguistic capital in their respective locales.

English was not the only language that was shifted or decentered. The normal practice in many international McDonald's franchises is to have English listed on packaging alongside each country's "official" language of use. For example, in parts of Latin America, "Quarter Pounder with Cheese" is printed near the top of the box and "Cuarto de Libra Con Queso" appears below it in a larger font. With a massive BTS following in Latin America, it was not surprising to see Hangeul printed prominently on the sauce packets. In Colombia, the sweet chili dipping sauce packet read *Dulce Chilli*, *Sweet Chilli*, and 스위트칠리 (*seuwiteu chili*).[11] The Hangeul was larger than both "Dulce Chilli" and "Sweet Chilli," thus emphasizing the Korean text. Outside the United States, a very public example of the meal's popularity occurred in Indonesia. On June 11, 2021, global media outlets reported the police closure of several McDonald's restaurants in Indonesia due to safety concerns, as delivery drivers sought to fulfill orders for the BTS Meal during a surge in COVID-19 cases.[12] Only available through delivery, the demand for the meal was overwhelming. The internet was flooded with images of restaurants packed shoulder to shoulder, with delivery drivers being commanded to leave by the police as McDonald's employees looked on helplessly, surrounded by purple cups and dipping sauces strewn on the floor. The financial competition between drivers trying to deliver products featuring the Korean language serves as a physical representation of what sociologist Pierre Bourdieu terms a linguistic market, or a place where exchanging a particular language may result in access to better financial opportunities.[13] Globally, English holds a high market exchange rate, sought after for better life opportunities such as education or employment, but in this brief moment, Korean stepped into the linguistic spotlight.

The Meal Unboxed

In addition to examining the symbolic linguistic power of the BTS Meal, it is also crucial to unwrap its contents in a cultural context. While a by-product of the meal may be the increased visibility for the Korean language and culture, McDonald's still dictated and controlled a localized version of food, language, and culture. Intriguingly, the sauces were an Americanized version of a Koreanized version of American food, exported back out to the world as a product never before released in the US. McDonald's promoted the allure of tasting sauces "inspired by flavors of McDonald's South Korea," which are not actually part of traditional South Korean cuisine, but are instead readily available flavors in South Korean McDonald's. Selling a piece of the Korean experience by using their own products as a proxy, McDonald's has ingrained these flavors as a norm in contemporary Korean culture so much so that they could be sold as a recognizable staple. In 1998, McDonald's had previously aimed to market their version of an East Asian sauce during a promotion for the animated Disney film *Mulan*.[14] Originally offered for a brief time in the United States, McDonald's "Szechuan Sauce" was intended to mimic traditional Szechwan sauce. In 2022, this sauce returned by popular demand to the US and, for a few days, to China and Australia. However, the sauce was criticized in China as "foreigners describing a Chinese taste."[15] This was the form of exoticism expected from a US-based corporation, producing and promoting its version of a traditional sauce as authentic "Asian culture." While McDonald's took direction from Korea as a contemporary locus of marketability and power, creating an exclusive feeling of access to "exotic" flavors available outside the US, in the end McDonald's tightly orchestrated the entire meal experience (if not its execution). A more critical question to ask then is whether McDonald's has become so enmeshed in the global psyche that they can dictate just how and which flavors are imbued with cultural significance.

Fans did push back against this fast-food version of Korean culture with their own commentary about the taste of the meal, sometimes offering humorous corrections. Posts on social media in the US mentioned the need to add gochujang (traditional Korean chili paste) to the available sauces or to use it as a separate sauce, in order to be more "authentic." Some users shared images of their table spread at McDonald's, with the BTS Meal sitting alongside a large tub of gochujang and a pair of scissors in a nod to Korean dining practices. Even though fans bought the meal, they also felt empowered to share their critiques of its cultural accuracy. Furthermore, they understood exactly what this moment of representation meant on both local and global scales. The visual representation of Hangeul in the meal incited pride, for instance, for those with Korean heritage. Twitter user @jxhnxsxng shared, "My Korean mother (who immigrated to Canada) mentioned how she never would've thought she would ever see Hangeul/Korean on McDonald's packaging in Canada, mentioning @BTS_twt impact [sic] I never would've imagined it either (being born and raised in Canada)."[16] Food blogger Dennis Lee observes, "It's an interesting feeling, realizing that I don't have to go to an entirely different grocery store just to see Korean written on the packaging. It's right here, at McDonald's, printed on every order."[17] Perhaps, as a response to the question that opened this chapter, "What does the power of language taste like?" Lee has an answer: "Nowadays, being Korean is cool as shit, and the whole world knows it."

Future Orders

After the dust settled from the launch of the BTS Meal, it became clear that the promotion was still profitable despite the failure to fully anticipate demand. The corporation successfully converted a globally emergent language into economic capital around the world, and profits almost doubled compared to the previous year, before the pandemic. In the United States alone, in-store sales increased by 21.5 percent.[18] Even though the company provided the bare minimum to customers in the United States, the BTS Meal was still highly successful. Joseph Sung-Yul Park and Lionel Wee argue that "the true value of linguistic capital lies in its capacity for conversion into different types of capital, including economic capital," and the BTS Meal did not disappoint.[19] The profitability of the meal proved that a new language could occupy a position of linguistic domination through which major Western corporations might beat a new path to increased sales.

But the linguistic landscapes constructed by the BTS Meal also raise other questions. Is the value of language essentially lost if McDonald's maintains control of the entire method and style of transmitting the language? Could it be that the corporation is so ingrained in global society that it can dictate cultural norms internationally? Or was this moment in which McDonald's could make record-breaking profit only possible by exoticizing and commodifying an Asian language and culture?

There are no simple answers, but for a few months, the BTS Meal normalized multiple ways of speaking, being, and believing. In the shadow of the COVID-19 pandemic, people united, celebrated, and expressed passion over a humble fast-food meal. For a moment, language had a chance to breathe, bend, and blend, allowing the world to taste things in a new way.

Notes

1 McDonald's (@McDonald's), "Coming This May: The BTS Meal," Twitter, April 19, 2021, 9:00 a.m., https://twitter.com/McDonalds/status /1384129736570327045.

2 Author's personal recollection, McDonald's drive-thru worker, Indiana, May 27, 2022.

3 Ethan Shanfeld, "The BTS Meal, with Sauces Inspired by South Korean Recipes, Coming to McDonald's in May," *Chicago Tribune*, April 20, 2021, archived September 28, 2022, at Archive.org, https://web.archive.org /web/20220928025405/https://www.chicagotribune.com/entertainment /ct-ent-bts-mcdonalds-meal-may-20210420-zpld75gvkfeolasjwu7oc jaqri-story.html.

4 @soorin_tan, "The BTS Meal at Malaysia," Twitter, May 26, 2021, 10:13 p.m., https://twitter.com/soorin_tan/status/1397556500613066755.

5 @BTS_Jenn_, "like, HOW IS THIS EVEN THE SAME?," Twitter, May 26, 2021, 4:42 p.m., https://twitter.com/bts_jenn_/status/1397654323006525441.

6 @rosemarypogyo, "As a manager at McDonald's in the U.S.," Twitter, May 26, 2021, 1:17 p.m., https://www.trendsmap.com/twitter/tweet /1397602747269140480.

7 FreakFlagHigh, [LIVE THREAD] BTS x McDonald's Meal—270521, Reddit, May 26, 2021, https://www.reddit.com/r/bts7/comments/nlkytq /comment/gzkn33y/.

8 @gem_jam, "a little disappointed," Twitter, May 21, 2021, 3:33 p.m., https://twitter.com/gem_jam/status/1397637042662690825.

9 Natalie_M_K, comment on FreakFlagHigh, [LIVE THREAD] BTS x Mc-Donald's Meal, May 26, 2021, 5:16 p.m., https://www.reddit.com/r/bts7 /comments/nlkytq/comment/gzk9wu3/.

10 See Corter, "Linguistic Landscapes in a Multilingual World," 197; Shohamy, *Language Policy*.

11 "Here's What McDonald's BTS Meal Looks Like in Different Countries," *BollywoodLife*, June 2, 2021, https://www.bollywoodlife.com/hollywood /entertainment-news-bts-news-latest-bts-update-kpop-news-korean -entertainment-news-heres-what-mcdonalds-bts-meal-looks-like-in -different-countries-1839110/.

12 Shashank Bengali, "McDonald's in Indonesia Are Forced to Close after a 'BTS Meal' Frenzy That Violated Covid Measures," *New York Times*, June 11, 2021, https://www.nytimes.com/2021/06/11/world/asia/mcdonalds-bts -meal-indonesia.html.

13 Bourdieu, "The Economics of Linguistic Exchanges," 651–56.

14 Zhou, "McDonald's Finally Brings Its 'Authentic' Szechuan Sauce to China. They're Not Lovin' It," *South China Morning Post*, March 30, 2018, https://www.scmp.com/news/china/article/2139643/mcdonalds-finally -brings-its-authentic-szechuan-sauce-china-theyre-not.

15 Zhou, "McDonald's Finally Brings Its 'Authentic' Szechuan Sauce to China."

16 @jxhnxsxng, "My Korean mother," Twitter, June 5, 2021, 8:21 p.m., https://twitter.com/jxhnxsxng/status/1401333442961461249.

17 Dennis Lee, "Is the New McDonald's BTS Meal Collab 'Dynamite'?" *Takeout*, September 30, 2022, https://thetakeout.com/review-mcdonalds -new-bts-meal-collaboration-1846974860.

18 E. Cha, "BTS Meal Helps Boost McDonald's Worldwide Sales by 41 Percent in 2nd Quarter of 2021," *Soompi*, July 21, 2021, https://www .soompi.com/article/1481325wpp/bts-meal-helps-boost-mcdonalds -worldwide-sales-by-41-percent-in-2nd-quarter-of-2021.

19 Park and Wee, *Markets of English*, 142.

Works Cited

Bourdieu, Pierre. "The Economics of Linguistic Exchanges." *Social Science Information* 16, no. 6 (1977): 645–68. https://doi.org/10.1177/053901847701600601.

Gorter, Durk. "Linguistic Landscapes in a Multilingual World." *Annual Review of Applied Linguistics* 33 (March 2013): 190–212. https://doi.org/10.1017 /S0267190513000020.

Park, Joseph Sung-Yul, and Lionel Wee. *Markets of English: Linguistic Capital and Language Policy in a Globalizing World*. New York: Routledge, 2012.

Shohamy, Elana. *Language Policy: Hidden Agendas and New Approaches*. London: Routledge, 2005.

10 · Fragmentary Redemptions: ARMY, RPF, and the AU at the Heart of the Bangtan Universe — Regina Yung Lee

"그 손을 내밀어줘 save me save me / I need your love before I fall, fall," sings V in the chorus of BTS's 2016 song "Save ME."[1] But who saves them from the fall, and how? I argue that the answer is ARMY, BTS's ardent fan base, through an active, critical reception praxis that pieces together media fragments into an entire narrative, an affective participatory story world—the Bangtan Universe, or BU. A key fragment of this parallel fictional universe, the music video for the song "Euphoria," acknowledges ARMY's crucial role in this collective cocreation.

Released across several years, the BU has emerged through music videos, short films, a webcomic, album liner notes, social media posts, photocards, live performances, and concert video interludes (VCRs), beginning with two music videos and a related short film release for the group's 2015–16 화양연화 / 花樣年華 / *The most beautiful moment in life* album series (HYYH), which consisted of two EPS—*The most beautiful moment in life pt. 1* and *pt. 2*—and the compilation album *The most beautiful moment in life: YOUNG FOREVER*. Briefly, the BU traces the stories of seven young men, inseparable during high school, and how their youthful closeness is both created and destroyed by interlacing oppressions, collectively represented as the "world of adults." The BU's first arc, partially contained in the HYYH music videos, records the members' enmeshed tragedies: Taehyung (V) arrested for his abusive father's murder, Hoseok (j-hope) and Jimin (Jimin) institutionalized, Namjoon (RM) imprisoned, Yoongi (SUGA) embittered, Jung Kook (Jung Kook) dead.[2] In the wake of these catastrophes, eldest member Seokjin (Jin) receives a supernatural chance to relive a single fraught day, repair their broken relationships, and save their lives. But within the BU, with its structural inequities focused on society's relentless consumption of disposable youth, there is no way for them all to survive. HYYH unrolls across the music videos (MVs), the webtoon, and *The Notes*,[3] as Seokjin desperately loops and reloops these events, proliferating a small multiverse while seeking an increasingly improbable collective redemption, with Taehyung's climactic, deliberate plunge from a tall platform to the sea below, resetting the action each time. But the "Euphoria" music video, released in 2018 to open a new album trilogy, returns to the BU with a completed alternate universe (AU) in which Seokjin finally figures out how to solve the rest of the members' problems: by taking Taehyung's place at the top of the platform.

The BU's narrative fragmentation is echoed by its distribution methods, which rely on something fan scholar Henry Jenkins calls "transmedia storytelling," where the fragments of the story are distributed across multiple media (concert footage, social media, liner notes, music videos, webtoons, *The Notes*), and each fragment has the power to alter the reception, understanding, and meaning of the others.[4] Its transmedia storytelling makes the BU porous; as Jenkins puts it, "Any given product is a point of entry into the franchise as a whole."[5] Film philosopher Jiyoung Lee's concept of the network image, based on her study of Gilles Deleuze's film theory in combination with BTS's work, describes the interaction between repeated images—that of the BTS members themselves—traceable across the BU. Lee calls these network images "fragments of emotion," and they are key, I argue, to how ARMY demonstrate the possibility for a reparative or even salvific vision of the BU.[6] Bringing these ideas to bear, Carol Vernallis's description of the music video romance, which represents an entire relationship through brief fragments, offers a critical vocabulary for the overriding emotional tenor of the BU videos.[7] In the case of HYYH, these fragments combine to produce an existential despair. But the BU's fragmentation itself invites synthesis and, potentially, recombination, channeling a powerful collective longing for a better life together by its most ardent viewers. In watching the BU, retracing the members' virtual steps, and reconstructing fragments from across various media, ARMY produces an intensely personal rendition of each storyline, relationship, and member.

Through its many looping timelines, the BU draws heavily on the alternate universe, a genre of fan fiction that changes one or several central aspects of a canonical plotline to transform the entirety of a narrative universe. The AU's hallmarks include both the transformation of narrative through alterations in plot and location and the intensification of crucial relationships within those transformations; in their dissertation on the Coffee Shop AU, Katharine McCain defines the AU as "a substantial re-imagining of the source where characters are placed into entirely new worlds and face radically different conflicts."[8] These hallmarks power the BU, as each of Seokjin's loops through the plot demonstrate that strength of the dyadic relationships between the characters, as well as the different ways they cannot save each other. Specifically, the BU relies on the AU genre's intense focus on relationships and unique characterization to keep its characters consistent from one timeline to the next, as Seokjin continually relives the multiple versions of that fraught day. The BU uses the AU's implicit but undergirding relational focus to maintain the bonds between the members as characters, even as the worlds around them shift, change, and transform. In HYYH, however, there is no timeline that results in a future where all seven members survive. It is ARMY who steps into this gap, deploying the genre's inherent malleability to engineer possibilities for reconciliation or escape.

Fans have long been invited to fill the calculated lacunae of public celebrity images. Real person fiction (RPF), a real-world version of the AU, is one of the ways this happens. As its name suggests, RPF denotes fan-created narratives that combine celebrity bodies and public lives with fan interpretations of both, alongside fan-made interpolations of internal thoughts, private emotional responses, and intimate mundane details, which can either reify or transform reception of celebrities' public interactions. These can take shape as long-form narratives, recut videos of public interactions, GIFsets, and more. Given the invasive appropriations of personhood that can result from such media-based manipulations, RPF remains a divisive fan genre, with a checkered history in North American and Anglophone media. Examples include the One Direction RPF that spilled over into fans' harassment of band members and their partners, and UK journalist Caitlin Moran's request that the actors of BBC's *Sherlock* read erotic fan fiction written about their characters aloud.[9]

In celebrity fandoms, RPF and the AU go hand in hand, placing celebrity bodies and public interactions in different contexts to further explore, intensify, or—in the case of the BU—restore their relationships. This dynamic emerges from a longer history of parasocial celebrity interactions. Forms of RPF also have a history as an effective marketing tool in East Asian media contexts, despite the genre's complex representational politics and ethics and celebrities' sometimes uneasy relationship with the outcomes. However, multiple fan scholars argue for considering RPF a mundane fandom activity, including it as one of many mediations of celebrity bodies through heavily narrativized star texts, alongside other forms such as real-time documentaries or fictionalized films.[10] But in the BU, the "real person" under discussion is already also a character, explicitly narrativized and malleable. In casting the BTS members as characters in the Bangtan Universe, HYBE/BigHit brings the BTS members' celebrity personas into a complex universe that borrows heavily from the tropes surrounding RPF.[11] One example of this dynamic in action appears in the cast list for the BU. The characters in the BU carry the members' given names (e.g., Seokjin, Taehyung), but the cast list gives the members' stage names (e.g., Jin, V), placing characters, members, and celebrity images onto a single continuum. The slippage between these names brings out a constitutive but sometimes sidelined part of RPF: the Alternate Universe genre, or the AU.

In the BU, RPF's interplay between public celebrity persona and the AU's detailed, recognizable characterization and deep relationships pulls interested viewers to synthesize the fractured flow of multimedia texts into recognizable timelines. This dynamic effectively renders the watching ARMY the organizing principle of the BU. Analyzing the Bangtan Universe through the hallmarks of these fan-created genres clarifies the BU's major concerns with time and fragmentation and the necessity of ARMY to interpretation of the BU. In using aspects of RPF and AU this way, the Bangtan Universe doesn't just invite fans in using techniques they already know. It acknowledges fans' constitutive role in its own creation—and, potentially, its resolution as well. These aspects of the Bangtan Universe not only enhance sales and increase views by heightening engagement, they also demonstrate the importance of social critique to its message. It is this longing that might break the desperate loops, uniting the BU characters again through ARMY's deeply invested gaze. The literal interpolation of the viewer into the BU transfigures what RPF can be, mean, and do by harnessing the desire for reparative relationality that powers the AU genre.

The BU's time loops do not lead toward a future where all seven members can successfully reunite; Seokjin cannot save his friends or himself.[12] Instead, the BU clearly indexes their structural oppression by a society that doesn't value them. Modern constructions of youth often come with ideologies of fragile possibility, which falter or bloom in the transition between childhood innocence and the Icarian fall into adulthood. The BU captures that tenuous bloom, as well as its devastation, in the opening scene of the music video for "RUN," from *The most beautiful moment in life pt. 2*, which juxtaposes rusted metal and decaying paper with Taehyung's backward fall through time, condensed into a single ice cube. The camera follows Namjoon's hands in the opening, with only diegetic sound, but pulls back and stops as he walks offscreen.

The HYYH logo appears, ironically superimposed on the detritus of modern life: the camera contradicts the title (*The most beautiful moment in life*) by lingering on displays of cultural and industrial transience (the decrepit papers) and senescence (the sagging chairs and rusted siding) (see figure 10.1).[13] This juxtaposition is the opening salvo to the powerful social critique leveraged in HYYH against the medical, parental, judicial, class-based, and academic inequities that result in the characters' collective disillusionment, separation, and eventual ends.

This theme of youth consumed by societal decay is especially clear in the BU music videos' internal chronologies: time is literally the essence of their critique. Seokjin's loops through the BU make bigger, societal, structural problems leap into immediate relief by reducing them to human scale. Seokjin's desperation with each failed attempt to save his friends is a miniature version of the crises experienced by those living at the margins of capitalist excess, in a system designed to consume them. This is the state of crisis ordinariness Lauren Berlant calls "slow death."[14] Taken together, the BU presents, then critiques, constructions of youthfulness (specifically but not only youthful masculinity) as disposable, aimless, and lawless. Seokjin's loops thus form a concentrated tragedy that represents structural issues like class-based oppression and toxic masculinities as inescapable. The friends' collective happiness before they were separated by "the world of adults" (for example, the joyous scene at the abandoned pool in "I NEED U"), so at odds with societal norms of stoic masculinity and productive time use, becomes the focal point of Seokjin's frantic restoration. Inside of the BU, the friends' plights serve as a kind of wordless plea, not only for solidarity or identification, but also for salvation.

Seokjin asks in 花樣年華 The Most Beautiful Moment in Life: The Notes 1, in a journal entry dated "13 June Year 22," "Had we worked so long and so hard for no reason? Were we destined to fall apart like this?"[15] It is ARMY who steps in to answer. ARMY's methods involve manipulating the emotion-laden network image, which is only possible because of transmedia storytelling's openness and shifts in meaning across platforms. Recombination and transformation are the outcomes. This fragmentation leads not just to proliferating AUs but also to forms of RPF, through the emotional heft of repeated network images, which all change meaning and purpose as the time loops of HYYH recur but retain their sense of despair. The crucial HYYH network images—Taehyung's fall from the tower, Hoseok's collapse on a bridge, Jimin's loneliness in the cafeteria, Yoongi's stupor in the burning room, Jung Kook's despair before he jumps from the top of a building, Seokjin and Namjoon's meeting at the gas station—reappear as part of the AU in "Euphoria," as the video represents these BU fragments through one more diegetic variation. This new

10.1 · Screen capture of *The most beautiful moment in life pt.2* logo over the prologue to "RUN." Note the deliberate contrast between the logo, the muted light and color, and the industrial detritus.

recombination cements the AU as a propulsive structuring mechanism within the BU.

In watching the BU, a fan might create the only whole version of it that exists. ARMY's work piecing together multiple storylines, from fragments scattered across platforms, is repeatedly echoed in the BU through the viewfinder, the polaroid, and the video camera, all tools Seokjin deploys to try and capture an evanescent moment, to fix it in place forever. Not incidentally, Seokjin himself is framed to one side in the closeup: eyes down and attention elsewhere, a contrast to the camera's centralized proxy lens. He almost disappears into the background—an echo of his wavering presence across the BU (see figure 10.2).[16]

Seokjin's feverish archival efforts are unsuccessful. But ARMY steps into the gap, widening Seokjin's viewfinder to gaze at all seven of the members and privilege their relationships with each other as the most important part of the BU. The collective fan activity of weaving together symbolic fragments is one of the most important ways that the BU opens the relationship between star and fan to refashioning. This collective reweaving and its acknowledgment are the crux of the short film for "Euphoria."

"Euphoria" opens with a silent minute spent revisiting Taehyung's climactic jump, repeating his leap off the platform at the montage's peak—then a lingering shot of the blood on his hands from his father's death transitions to Seokjin's hands holding the six white petals, indicating a reset. The opening triads of Claude Debussy's "Clair de Lune," a song intimately related to time, ring across the scene.[17] In contrast to the music video for "RUN," which layers

10.2 · Seokjin holding a video camera filming the other members from the top of the platform in the music video for "Euphoria." Recording is a recurrent image in the BU, seen in the revelatory polaroids Seokjin takes throughout HYYH, as well as the viewfinder gesture performed by both Seokjin and Taehyung in the video for "Spring Day" (2017).

the song "Butterfly" only over its opening scene and end credits, "Euphoria" relies on "Clair de Lune" to structure significant amounts of its video. "Clair de Lune" is an exemplar of the arabesque, the aural capture of an evanescent moment. It is specifically known for its "shimmering" effect, created as the performer varies the tempo or speed of play, regulating it precisely across the entire piece. Time is therefore central to "Clair de Lune's" performance: no time can be taken that is not later restored. These intricate layers of aural, visual, and symbolic meanings are references to the AU and the RPF in action, all directed at and framed through ARMY.

By recutting its fragments into a new narrative, the long introduction to "Euphoria" shows that timing (momentum, variation) is crucial to the BU. The use of rubato ("robbed" or borrowed time) in "Clair de Lune" centers the variability of time: every acceleration must have equivalent compensation, so each rubato must be returned by the end of the piece. We see how this interacts with the AU in cuts, as two versions of Jimin's attempt to escape his institutionalization interweave over the second section of "Clair de Lune" (tempo rubato, from the E-flat octave in the left hand). Alone, Jimin slows, then stops before the door just as the music gains speed and urgency. Jimin's momentum transfers from his body, which slows to a stop, to the piano, whose sound tries to carry him forward but fails. But in the intercut alternate version, Jimin and the other members keep their momentum, running out the opened door, as the first arpeggiated chord of the harmonic resolution to that section of "Clair de Lune" ripples across the scene. The last chord, a clear transition from one section to the next, sounds as the door completes its outward swing onto a field of white. This transition not only indicates the necessity of the group to each member's survival; it also clearly brackets the careful attention to time that constructs the AU out of (mostly) preexisting parts, transposing them to produce a new story iteration.

The first lines of "Euphoria" drop soon after, a hollow EDM tune with crunchy, compressed bass under Jung Kook's voice. This instrumentation echoes that of "Butterfly" at the beginning of "RUN"—also Jung Kook's voice, backed by a hollowed-out instrumental score, and another deployment of aural indicators for an AU. The tape recorder click and video game sound could reference a new game, another run-through, or a powering up—all relevant ways to envision an AU. Instead of Jung Kook alone, about to dive off the roof, the camera lingers on the members as they reiterate their friendships, much like the outdoor swimming pool scene from the "Prologue" short film from HYYH. This is the idyllic companionship Seokjin has futilely fought to reestablish; in the "Euphoria" AU, its appearances (previously in Jimin's escape, here on Jung Kook's rooftop, and most crucially at the seashore) indicate that these relationships are indeed the goal or purpose of the narratives.

Then, ARMY is explicitly invited into the world of "Euphoria" itself. And this makes the moments of carefree companionship into forms of RPF, as the BTS members in character act out their own and ARMY's linked longings for meaningful happiness together, in an idyllic space away from the abusive demands of the "world of adults." As the video heads through another montage toward that climactic leap at the seashore, something odd happens: reality breaks, not within the narrative, but toward the viewer. The video's entire color scheme washes out to the same blue and white as the sky and the sea, with the discolored concrete forming an ugly interruption of human civilization. (This is also a network image but an inversion of the scene in "I NEED U," in which the other friends run past Jung Kook, who is walking alone on the concrete wall.) Jung Kook runs into the scene with the other six members already seated on the wall, except Jimin, who stands. Colorwise, the members are far closer to the sea than the concrete, suggesting their relative freedom from societal demands in this moment. Then, slowly, all seven friends look at the camera, turning their heads to gaze at the viewer (see figure 10.3).

The music stops: fade to black. ARMY looked; and now, in character, the members look back, recognizing ARMY's role in bringing them to this point. In using RPF's embodied meanings to structure this AU, corporate deployment of these tactics does not diminish HYYH's critique of capitalism through tragedy unfolding at a human scale, nor deny ARMY's collective longing for continuing

10.3 · The members turn to look at the viewer, as the last notes of "Euphoria" fade, replaced by the sound of pounding surf. Given that the hidden track "Sea," from *LOVE YOURSELF 承 "HER"!*, presents the sea as a metaphor for hope, this moment can be analyzed as an in-world recognition of ARMY's attention.

on together with BTS. That break in the fourth wall is acknowledgment and invitation without resolution.

This returned gaze recognizes ARMY's coconstitutive role in the creation and extension of its storylines, as well as the fans' attentive interpolation into the BU's transmedia lacuna. This fourth wall break is the central discontinuity within the video, indicated through its placement near the halfway mark, the sound (the music literally stops), the rhythm (which fades back into the surf), and the members' gazes. And then the music rushes back in—but the song that returns is "Clair de Lune," in its final variation, with the plaintive dominant 7th introduced in the left hand. We know the rest: Taehyung's disquieted gaze tracing Seokjin's upward climb, Seokjin's tilting horizon, Debussy's last sweet arpeggio ringing out alongside Seokjin's final tremulous smile. "Euphoria" only returns after this second fade, playing over the credits until we reach one last question, and the final black-and-white flash of Jung Kook caught in the ominous light of an oncoming truck.

The "Euphoria" MV argues that in the BU, the members are unable to overcome their fragmentation; it is ARMY who comes through the fourth wall to save them. If, as Seokjin fears in 花樣年華 *The Most Beautiful Moment in Life: The Notes 1*, they are all "destined to fall apart," it is ARMY's constitutive gaze and constant, affectionate attention that keeps putting them all back together.[18] The AU genre marker of world-based transformation with consistent relational character-building comes alongside the RPF-based wavering lines between member, character, and celebrity concept to create these longed-for reunions.

The BU's deployment of RPF and AU hallmarks is an intricate, sophisticated technique for cocreating worlds populated by characters, whose persistent interrelations, laced together through their fans' longing gazes, form a kind of happiness. This interpolation has proved an effective marketing technique, as the BU's fragments produce additive and addictive urges to interpret and collect.[19] It also requires centering a nuanced fan response that connects marketing prompts and creative transformation. This forms its own odd discontinuity: a consumerist industry model acknowledging the rapacity of the capitalist ties that bind them. But it also opens a space for collective understanding of youth's fragility and its destruction by outside forces—a point of genuine connection, shared by the members in the BU, the members of BTS, and ARMY themselves. This interrelatedness comes from a complex simultaneous recognition of marketing impulses and genuine fellow feeling, a longing for something better than the hollowness of capital accumulation and the human destruction it leaves in its wake. Through the affectionate viewer, that destruction can be recognized, mitigated, or even undone—by another rewatch, through consumption of new content, and in myriad fan-generated reconfigurations. In restoring order to the BU's fragments, ARMY form the organizing principle and the center of the BU: the one space and time in which all seven members survive and come back together again. ARMY's collective longing animates the transmedia event that is BTS.[20] In sum, ARMY's heart is where BTS lives on forever.

Notes

1   *Doolset Lyrics* translates this line as "Please reach your hand to save me, save me," lending support for an in-universe request for help from the members in character to ARMY themselves. RM's later line "Thank you ' 우리'가 돼 줘서" (Thank you for becoming "us") can then be read not only as gratitude to the listener for joining ARMY but also as a hint at ARMY's constitutive role in the BU. (In the 2021 NPR Tiny Desk performance of "Save ME," there is a deliberate pause after this line, as several members repeat "Thank you," further cementing both line and song as clear addresses to ARMY.)

2   The BU uses the members' given names for the characters they play in the BU. Thus, the names in parentheses are the members' stage names as listed under "Cast" in the "Euphoria" music video. Divergences from the members' stage names in this paper refer to their BU characters; any changes in given name spelling reflect character name romanization in

花樣年華 *The Most Beautiful Moment in Life: The Notes 1*, English version, and are noted as such.

3   *The Notes* is a series of BU-related Twitter posts and printed notes included in the physical album releases of the *LOVE YOURSELF* and *MAP OF THE SOUL* series and compiled as two printed books in 2019, published by Big Hit Entertainment in four versions: English, Korean, Japanese, and Spanish. This chapter references the English version of these printed books. See BTS Wiki, s.v. "The Most Beautiful Moment in Life: The Notes," and "花樣年華 THE NOTES 1," at Fandom.com, last modified, respectively, August 30, 2022, 13:34, and June 21, 2021, 14:08, https://bts.fandom.com /wiki/The_Most_Beautiful_Moment_in_Life:_The_Notes and https://bts .fandom.com/wiki/The_Most_Beautiful_Moment_in_Life:_The_Notes_1.

4   花樣年華 *The Most Beautiful Moment in Life: The Notes* 1 and 2 form a two-book narrative of the BU published by Big Hit. Presented as a series of confessional journal entries written by the characters, *The Notes'* elliptical narrative fragments must be made coherent by their readers, a process that recalls the filling of plot-based lacunae required by the music videos and the stitching together of these narratives with the rest of the BU.

5   Jenkins, *Convergence Culture*, 97–98.

6   Lee, BTS, *Art Revolution*, 111.

7   See Vernallis, *Experiencing Music Video*, for more.

8   McCain, "Today Your Barista Is."

9   Moran's gesture prompted backlash against both RPF writers and Moran herself, for using fan work without permission for shock value. For context, see Bethan Jones's article, "The Ethical Hearse: Privacy, Identity, and Fandom Online."

10   Busse, "I'm Jealous"; Thomas, "Fans Behaving Badly?"; and Piper, "Real Body, Fake Person" all argue for analyzing RPF as a complex, well-informed fannish activity, acting at the level of canonical celebrity text manipulations such as biographical films.

11   While the convention of the group or member "concept," or trope-reliant, media-friendly public persona, is a widespread tactic of East Asian idol industries, its extension into complex virtual settings was less common at the time of HYYH's initial propagation. Alongside earlier virtual idol avatars (such as the vocaloid Hatsune Miku) and later phenomena like aespa's virtual avatars and the SM Culture Universe, this transmedia propagation method has since become an increasingly common way to gain and hold fan attention.

12   This happy ending's inaccessibility seems to hold true in *The Notes*, although the ending for the *Save ME* webtoon, another iteration of the HYYH timelines, is slightly more open.

13   RUN's opening scene holds filmic affinities with Dogme 95 techniques, and with Michelangelo Antonioni's 1964 film *Red Desert* (*Il deserto rosso*) and Jia Zhangke's 2006 film *Still Life* (三峽好人), specifically in a shared reflection of social disintegration through landscapes and miniatures of industrial detritus.

14   See Berlant's *Cruel Optimism* for more on this topic, including an expansion of physically marked "slow death," to index the impersonal social structures responsible for mundane experiences of oppression and the emotional weight of that mundanity as an accelerant of physical deterioration.

15   Big Hit Entertainment, 花樣年華 *The Most Beautiful Moment in Life: The Notes 1*, 144. *The Notes* romanizes Jin's character's name as *SeokJin*, with capital J.

16   The music video's full name is "Euphoria: Theme of Love Yourself 起 Wonder." Alongside the "Prologue," it is arguably a short film set to music, rather than a showcase for the song.

17   The "Prologue" short film also uses the same recording of "Clair de Lune" as a backdrop to V's slow, traumatized handwashing, but does not deploy the song as a definitive structuring device.

18   Big Hit Entertainment, 花樣年華 *The Most Beautiful Moment in Life: The Notes 1*, 144.

19   Roberta Pearson's early dichotomization of online fan behaviors into historical (data collecting) and mythological (narratively focused) forms of fandom collapses in this analysis of ARMY's role in the BU.

20   With thanks to Michelle Cho for this definition.

Works Cited

Berlant, Lauren. *Cruel Optimism*. Durham, NC: Duke University Press, 2011.

Bernstein, Robin. *Racial Innocence: Performing American Childhood from Slavery to Civil Rights*. New York: New York University Press, 2011.

Big Hit Entertainment. 花樣年華 *The Most Beautiful Moment in Life: The Notes 1*. Seoul: beORIGIN, 2019.

BTS [방탄소년단]. "Euphoria: Theme of Love Yourself 起 Wonder." Directed by Choi Yongseok (Lumpens) and Lee Wonju (Lumpens). HYBE / Big Hit Entertainment, April 5, 2018. YouTube video, 8:52. https://youtu.be/kXovO4vlJuU.

BTS [방탄소년단]. "I NEED U OFFICIAL MV (Original ver.)" Directed by Choi Yongseok (Lumpens). HYBE / Big Hit Entertainment, May 10, 2015. YouTube video, 5:33. https://youtu.be/jjskoRh8GTE.

BTS [방탄소년단]. "RUN Official MV." Directed by Choi Yongseok (Lumpens). HYBE / Big Hit Entertainment, November 29, 2015. YouTube video, 7:30. https:// youtu.be/wKysONrSmew.

BTS [방탄소년단]. "Save ME." Translated by *Doolset Lyrics*, June 25, 2018. https:// doolsetbangtan.wordpress.com/2018/06/25/save-me/.

Busse, Kristina. "'I'm Jealous of the Fake Me': Postmodern Subjectivity and Identity Construction in Boy Band Fan Fiction." In *Framing Celebrity: New Directions in Celebrity Culture*, edited by Su Holmes and Sean Redmond, 253–67. London: Routledge, 2006.

Jenkins, Henry. *Convergence Culture: Where Old and New Media Collide*. New York: New York University Press, 2006.

Jones, Bethan. "The Ethical Hearse: Privacy, Identity, and Fandom Online." *Learned Fangirl*, March 25, 2016. http://thelearnedfangirl.com/the-ethical-hearse -privacy-identity-and-fandom-online.

Lee, Jiyoung. BTS, *Art Revolution*. Translated by Stella Kim, Myungji Chae, Jiye Won, and Shinwoo Lee. Seoul: Parrhesia, 2018. English translation published in 2019.

McCain, Katharine Elizabeth. "Today Your Barista Is: Genre Characteristics in the Coffee Shop Alternate Universe." PhD diss., Ohio State University, 2020.

Pearson, Roberta. "It's Always 1895: Sherlock Holmes in Cyberspace." In *The Fan Fiction Studies Reader*, edited by Karen Hellekson and Kristina Busse, 44–60. Iowa City: University of Iowa Press, 2014.

Piper, Melanie. "Real Body, Fake Person: Recontextualizing Celebrity Bodies in Fandom and Film." *Transformative Works and Cultures*, no. 20 (2015). https://doi.org/10.3983/twc.2015.0664.

Thomas, Bronwen. "Fans Behaving Badly? Real Person Fic and the Blurring of the Boundaries between the Public and the Private." In *Real Lives, Celebrity Stories: Narratives of Ordinary and Extraordinary People across Media*, edited by Julia Round and Bronwen Thomas, 171–85. New York: Bloomsbury, 2014.

Vernallis, Carol. *Experiencing Music Video: Aesthetic and Cultural Context*. New York: Columbia University Press, 2004.

11 · "Black Guy Reacts to BTS for the First Time": Provocations from a Black ARMY — Jheanelle Brown

To be a Black ARMY is to contend with the specter of Blackness in BTS's music. In K-Pop, challenges, tensions, and contradictions arise regarding issues of race, representation, and power. K-Pop is deeply indebted to Black American (henceforth referred to simply as "Black") music, especially hip hop. This debt is a shadow present in much of Korean pop music, by idols and non-idols alike.[1] As a Black person, I am sensitive to the ways in which Blackness and Black music is performed and often appropriated by non-Black people. There are countless examples of K-Pop idols reducing Blackness to dreadlocks, corn-rows, box braids, or the superficial use of materialistic or violent lyrics, as if Blackness is merely an aesthetic.

I have unresolved feelings about being protective of Black music *and* being a K-Pop fan (most significantly of BTS). I constantly question if I am partici-pating in the erasure of Black people in Black music as an ardent fan of BTS, other K-Pop acts, and non-Black folks performing Black music in general. Am I losing sight of that politically important protectionism by praising BTS Rap Line's technical and lyrical prowess, the Vocal Line's R&B-inflected turns, or the dynamism in their soul and hip-hop-oriented choreography? Am I betray-ing other Black artists and the history of Black music by citing my love for BTS? How do I honor Blackness in Black music performed by non-Black people?

My protectiveness of BTS exists alongside my protectiveness of Blackness. I became ARMY in April 2018, right before the *LOVE YOURSELF* 轉 *'TEAR'* album comeback. As is common in ARMY narratives, I found BTS when I needed them most. I was sad during that time, and some of the first BTS songs I encountered

("Save ME," "Stigma," "Euphoria," and "Singularity") helped me face the melancholy that had consumed me. Their music allowed me to honor my feelings. Lyrics such as "The phantom pain that tortures me remains still," from "Singularity," embodied my heartbreak. Writing this chapter in 2022, in the aftermath of heartbreak and the pandemic, I know that the last four and a half years of my life have been enriched by the wonder of BTS's musical artistry—their poetic lyricism, the melancholic sonic character of many of their songs—their singular world-building, and the joyous nonmusical content in their variety shows and livestreams. I love when the Rap Line lets loose. I love the fact that BTS have recorded covers and interpolations of Young B and DJ Webstar's "Chicken Noodle Soup" and Puff Daddy, Faith Evans, and 112's "I'll Be Missing You." I recognize that by and large after their debut-era concept, BTS doesn't lean on attempts to perform Blackness through gesture, AAVE (African American Vernacular English), or dress.[2] Thus, I'm deeply protective of them. This protectiveness manifests by making sure folks know that the members are musical artists, with depth and a wide creative spectrum, and that their relationship to Black music isn't appropriative. But the specter of racism as non-Black artists using Black music remains.

As a Black ARMY, how do I navigate this tension between love and critique? How do I square the deep cognitive dissonance I feel at K-Pop concerts with the lingering mistrust between Black and Korean communities in the US, or the manifest anti-Blackness in the Korean community (especially where I live, which bears the scars of the 1992 Los Angeles uprisings)? How do I balance my anxiety about people interpreting my BTS fandom as a Korean fetish—being a Koreaboo—with the deep resentment I feel toward my friends who judge my love for BTS? I believe that most people (in the West, as well as most Black people) perceive K-Pop to only be appropriation of Black music and nothing more, so there is a racial critique, one of perceived self-hatred—sometimes implied, sometimes explicit—about my love for them. Additionally, I am in my thirties and teenagers are assumed to be the primary demographic for boy bands. Lastly, there is the perception that K-Pop isn't good music. But it is the assumption of self-hatred that affects me the most. I often censor myself because most of my friends seem uninterested in or hostile to my engagement with K-Pop, which has been a space for me to think through the complexities of creative lineages, cultural appropriation, and identity.

The difficulty of reconciling the tensions I feel slightly abate when I engage and think through Black fan texts about BTS. One of the sites that allows me to explore these internal conflicts—the tension between love and critique—are BTS reaction videos, particularly those created by cisgender/

heterosexual Black men. Sometimes I watch them as a fan, sometimes as a critic, often as both. In reaction videos, people record themselves watching and reacting to audiovisual media content, sometimes for the first time. Generally, the content plays simultaneously within the same frame in a separate picture-in-window that is generally positioned at the bottom or top of the frame. The reactor is either minimized in the foreground or maximized in the background so that the audience can watch the original media and the live reaction at the same time.

Numerous YouTube channels are dedicated to reactions to BTS content. Due to BTS's massive online global fan base, many YouTubers experience an increase in traffic (views, comments, subscribers, likes) after posting BTS reaction videos and subsequently post more BTS reaction videos. Most of the videos show a spectrum of opinions and emotions that are ostensibly unfiltered, though sometimes edited. But reactions are also just that—reactions, rather than theses or resolutions or answers. Because of this sense of immediacy, there is a blurriness that mirrors my own relationship to BTS and K-Pop as a whole. Through these videos, I watch as people work through intellectual and emotional responses to music videos and other video content released by BTS that have been meaningful to me. I feel less helpless contending with questions around race, performance, and power as a BTS fan because I witness others grapple with the same issues, while still arriving at an appreciation of BTS or even becoming a part of the fandom. Because non-Black fans are not burdened with questions and conflicted emotions around BTS's relationship to Blackness and Black music in the way that I am, seeing myself reflected in these videos is validating. I feel the burden I carry as a Black fan being shared with other Black ARMY as I watch reaction videos made by Black reactors.

I started watching BTS reaction videos a few months before the pandemic shutdown but began to view them in earnest in April 2020, when YouTube became my best friend during the isolation of the pandemic. It was exciting to see other Black folks publicly enjoying BTS's music. I was drawn to YouTube reactors who think of themselves as active participants in Black culture: who use Black slang (especially the n-word), make reference to Black pop culture jokes, perform versions of normative masculinity, and are naturally funny. Most of my friends weren't interested in engaging with BTS, so reaction videos filled that void and created a larger community outside of my fandom friend group. Black reactors sat with racialized tension while also finding value and joy in BTS's music and performance. I felt a deep satisfaction watching them be doubtful at first but ending up cosigning and enjoying BTS's music.[3]

Aside from not feeling alone, I gravitated to these videos because of the sense of community activated by the discussions they inspired. As I watched and read comments on the videos, I found myself asking new questions: What are the expectations that non-Black fans have of Black reactors when reacting to music that is indebted to Black musical traditions? How do fans respond to Black male reactors' negative reactions or complicated readings of BTS music and performance? How and why does watching Black male reactors give me a sense of relief?

"I'm Pretty Sure This Is Going to Be Gas, but If It's Not, I'm Not Going to Lie"

"What should I title this? Black Man Experiences K-Pop for the First Time?" You-Tuber Sebastine jokingly asks in his reaction video posted on January 6, 2021. His opening question plays on a common trope found in YouTube reaction video titles, where reactors juxtapose a part of their identity with the subject of the content they are reacting to. Titles like "Black Guy Reacts to K-Pop for the First Time," or "Ex-Ballet Dancer Reacts to BTS—Black Swan," advertise the unique perspective or expertise the reactor will offer. It is a common clickbait strategy to direct traffic to a video.

Sebastine is one reactor that I find particularly compelling. I found his videos in April 2021. I had already been watching lots of reaction videos, but I found Sebastine funny and refreshing—crude and subtle in equal measure, with a very strong DMV (DC/Maryland/Virginia) accent that made me nostalgic for my eight years living in Washington, DC. The first video I watched on Sebastine's YouTube channel, "This is the Most Beautiful Moment in My Life . . . Part 2 (Album Review)" (uploaded in April 2021, three months after he began reacting to BTS music videos and songs), featured him clipping a lavalier mic to his beard, finding pants to put on just so he could get up and dance on camera, because the song "RUN" has what he describes as "bounce in this b*tch."[4] It was exciting to see a young Black man experience joy in unexpected things. As it was my first time watching any of his videos, I was interested in what or who brought him to BTS, what other artists or genres he listens to, and how that would color his analysis of BTS. It was gratifying to hear him talk about the craft of album sequencing and offer a critical analysis of the album as a discrete object deserving of engagement. Sebastine compared the album sequencing and the overall emotional landscape of *The most beautiful moment in life pt.2* to how he felt the first time he listened to Kanye West's *My Beautiful Dark Twisted Fantasy* (widely considered West's best album).

In the comments section of his videos, his identity as a Black man and his reference to Black music provoked a set of assumptions about who the fans of BTS are, which often excludes straight, cisgender Black men. Boy band fans are largely assumed to be teenage girls and young women.[5] Black fans of all genders are often left out of representations of ARMY (or hide their fannishness).[6] Sebastine initially played on his Black (male) identity to attract his viewers. Even I assume that he has a certain authority regarding hip hop *because* he is a Black man. But Sebastine also confirms his own reciprocal assumptions about whom he believes to be a typical K-Pop fan when he states:

I am so confused as to why K-Pop is so f*****g popular. Why do y'all n****s love that shit so much? . . . But at the same time, I ain't no b*tch. I'm always open to listening to new music, but if it's ass, and I think it's ass n***a I'm not afraid to say that. . . . Let's piss off some fans today. I don't care about no g*ddamn fans, I'm a grown ass man![7]

Sebastine differentiates himself ("grown ass man") from the young women and girls who are assumed to be ARMY. In these assumptions lies a tension: As a Black ARMY who is femme, I am caught between wanting to challenge and interrogate the expectations I imagine being placed on Black male reactors and the pride I feel when I see a Black man recognize that BTS makes music heavily indebted to Black cultural production in a respectful way.

K-Pop scholar Crystal S. Anderson claims that global, non-Korean fans function as an unofficial music press that legitimizes K-Pop in relation to Black musical influences.[8] Fans place more weight on the content that Black male reactors produce—because they are Black, American, and men. Black men are viewed as racially "authentic" and credible sources of Black culture. This credibility bolsters BTS's legitimacy, especially when they rap or sing R&B or soul-centric songs. As a result, there are a host of expectations that fans project onto Black male YouTube reactors. But what happens when some of these reactors do not unquestioningly praise BTS?

Like any YouTuber wanting to increase his viewership, Sebastine acknowledges he titled his reaction video "Is BTS Overrated?" as clickbait, but in that admission, he makes himself appear honest and therefore a reliable narrator. Thus, we believe his positive and negative reactions: they aren't just a performance. After reacting positively to "Dynamite," and somewhat positively to "DNA," Sebastine reacts negatively to the rap verses in "Boy with Luv":

Can y'all please not ruin this song for me? I was liking the song . . . but then the n***a [SUGA] started rapping. . . . These vocals are crazy. I'm not gon' hold you, I'm not f***ing with the rapping, but I'm f***ing with the vocals in the back, the vocals in the back be saving these songs. . . . What the f*** did I just see? I mean I'm glad it's not all seven of them just rapping.[9]

When I looked at the comments in response, I saw that many people assumed that the Black men would gravitate toward the group's hip-hop-centric songs or the rap verses in general. User "Jimin's exposed shoulder" observes, "This is the first time I have ever watched someone dislike bts' [Rap Line]," with user "Euphoricblackcats" adding, "its [embarrassing] right!" User "Pan" says, "I was so excited for Yoongi's part, i thought you would like it, but when you said he ruined the song, i literally left." When Black male reactors start posting reaction videos to BTS songs, enthusiastic ARMY (who I assume to be mostly non-Black) are quick to recommend Rap Line songs. In these recommendations, Black men are positioned as gatekeepers of hip hop, but if they don't immediately applaud or acknowledge the rappers' skills, commenters question their hip-hop bona fides. User "disgusTAEd" comments, "i mean, opinions are okay but do you know that bts's rapline is THE BEST [RAP LINE] IN THE ENTIRE KPOP?? well, you should know then." This is particularly interesting because Sebastine's overall opinion is that "bts is gas! I f***s with you n*****. I understand why y'all love this sh*t so much!"[10]

In his next video, "I'm ARMY Now . . . Listening to BTS for the First Time Again!," Sebastine responds to the pushback, stating, "When I listen to pop songs, and a rap verse just comes out of nowhere, it kind of throws me off. . . . I'm giving it another try. I'm pretty sure this is going to be gas, but if it's not, I'm not going to lie. This time I'll actually listen to the raps. And I'm not gonna be close-minded."[11] Sebastine reacts positively to "Fake Love," "Not Today," and "Mic Drop (Steve Aoki Remix)" (see figure 11.1). After the first few seconds of j-hope's opening verse in "Mic Drop (Steve Aoki Remix)," he pauses, saying, "Without rap, you wouldn't get none of this sh*t. Without the influence, you wouldn't get none of this sh*t. I'm not saying this to disrespect, but without Black culture, you wouldn't get none of this moe!"[12] Sebastine acknowledges the foundational Black music genealogy that undergirds much of BTS's music (and K-Pop in general). Like Sebastine, I never lose sight of the fact that BTS wouldn't be the group they are without the influence of Black music. But for some new ARMY, this may not be something they recognize.

As Sebastine continues to watch the "Mic Drop" video, he ends up loving it: "Talk ya muthaf****n shit man! I'm not downplaying none of they shit! Them

Don't need to see you anymore. This is the last farewell

11.1 · Sebastine reacts to BTS's "Mic Drop." Screenshot from "I'm ARMY Now ... Listening to BTS for the First Time Again!"

n****s work hard and they get they sh*t. F**k the haters. I'm not one of them!"[13] As a Black male reactor he is expected to perform a function: to legitimize BTS, specifically Rap Line, as credible and talented rappers. He doesn't do that initially, upsetting the expectations of ARMY. On the one hand, the racialized projections of Black men as gatekeepers of hip hop place Sebastine in a position of power to grant authenticity to BTS rap verses. On the other hand, his perceived authority is undermined when it doesn't live up to the audiences' expectations. But as Black ARMY, I appreciate the space he provides to consider what the rap verses are actually adding to the songs. I am also disappointed that most of the comments shut down any productive conversation around how to examine and interrogate rap performance, especially by non-Black people. Black reactors are thus a space for me to feel validation but also a space to examine the specter of Blackness when it comes to K-Pop.

There are instances of reactors explicitly questioning perceived instances of cultural appropriation. Reaction videos are a forum in which genuine feelings about cultural appropriation are expressed—which is one of the reasons I turn to them. Unfortunately, due to the limitations of social media interactions, potentially fruitful discussion is sometimes shut down. During reaction channel Losers Clubs first BTS reaction, two of the four regular members, Cody and Terrell (both Black men), react favorably to the "ON" official music video. The majority of comments were positive—they commented on how funny

Cody and Terrell are, suggesting other videos for them to react to.[14] In their second BTS reaction video, this time to j-hope's "Chicken Noodle Soup" (featuring Becky G) music video, Cody and Terrell are joined by Cody's brother. Expressing skepticism from the start, Cody's brother calls out j-hope's hairstyle as appropriative, which (I agree) mimics dreadlocks, saying, "Let's get this off the screen! Does he have dreadlocks? Stop playing with me, man, everybody wanna be black."[15] Cody's brother's honest and heartfelt critique, however, did not resonate with many of Losers Club's viewers. User "Army Purple bts" comments: "We understand a good criticism, so don't just say I don't like them without giving any reason . . . some of us are mature enough to handle it . . ." (see figure 11.2).

This moment captures a key racial tension around cultural appropriation and power that was dismissed by casting it as ignorance and hate. I believe there should be room for exploring and questioning the history of appropriation and where BTS lands in that story—the ways it fails or succeeds. For instance, there were also commenters who identify as Black and do not find j-hope's hairstyle appropriative, stressing that they are gel twists and not actual faux dreadlocks. They pointed out that DJ Webstar and Young B (the producer and rapper of the original song) were paid well for the sample clearance, j-hope made sure to shout them out during the song's promotion, and more generally that j-hope and BTS consistently reference their Black musical influences. These are all true, important, and necessary actions for non-Black artists who perform Black music. But at the same time, they do not negate instances of racial and cultural markers that are appropriative.

I do think that j-hope's hairstyle is appropriative and was disappointed in him and the larger HYBE/BIGHIT staff for their choices. I never watch the "Chicken Noodle Soup" video past the point where it features j-hope's hair styled in faux dreadlocks. Sometimes I'm also embarrassed that I even watch the video at all or love the members despite their appropriative mistakes. Am I betraying Black music by loving BTS when they participate in the history of appropriating Blackness? The instances in which Black male reactors push back on the Rap Line's skills, or something they interpret as appropriative, point to unresolved interracial tensions. Of course, these unresolved tensions are much bigger than BTS reaction videos or the presence of Black music in K-Pop, but unpacking the tensions through reactions to BTS can be constructive.

Sitting with the racial tensions that BTS reaction videos bring up, I often feel like I'm meeting a point of stasis as I contend with the sometimes prob-

11.2 · Losers Club reacts to BTS's "UGH!" Screenshot from "BTS—UGH! | REACTION."

lematic nature of their performances. Sometimes, I have to step away from my computer. In these moments my love for BTS meets my critical awareness of the history of the appropriation of Black music. I must compartmentalize my emotions because I do not have easy answers or solutions. I am learning to embrace the conflict within me.

Neither Sebastine nor Losers Club have easy answers either. Sebastine is now ARMY (and a fan of multiple K-Pop groups). The members of Losers Club are also ARMY. I sense a similar tension, especially in Sebastine's videos, between love and critique. The strain is reassuring—there are fellow Black ARMY critically engaging BTS while publicly loving them. I can look inward and hold my personhood, which is deeply entangled with my Blackness, with grace and complexity.

A Postscript

I completed the first draft of this chapter directly after leaving j-hope's Lollapalooza (a.k.a. "Hobipalooza") headlining performance on Sunday, July 31, 2022, in Chicago. During his performance of "Chicken Noodle Soup," I was anxious that he might repeat the hairstyle from the music video. Thankfully, he did not. j-hope's performance did not disappoint. It stood in sharp contrast to the Kid LAROI's (a white Australian rapper who performed before him) in that he didn't prop up his set by performing Blackness. The Kid LAROI tried to sound Black by using African American Vernacular English in his lyrics and onstage banter. Not only was this absent from j-hope's set, but his influences were stated, both visually and verbally (with a flickering image of Ol' Dirty Bastard's face as a transition into his "Shimmy Shimmy Ya"–sampled song "What If . . ." and shouting out DJ Webstar and Young B, the original artists behind "Chicken Noodle Soup"). I don't want to overly praise musical artists for citing their Black musical references, but it is important, it matters, and it is not always done. BTS has always been consistent about this throughout their career.

It took me weeks to process the performance. j-hope was phenomenal, assured, nimble, and mesmerizing, and I am not alone in this assessment. In their reaction to j-hope's performance of "Daydream" at Lollapalooza, Losers Club continue their inside jokes of being related to BTS members; "I was there, I can give you a recap," Devin jokes.[16] Sebastine reacted to the full performance: "Are you serious, bruh? Are you serious? Are you serious? . . . j-hope is *him* I don't give a f*ck what nobody says! He really shut that [thing] down. What else needs to be said?"[17] I found an immense joy in sharing these feelings with Black reactors as a community of Black critical thinkers and fans of BTS.

After "Hobipalooza," I unlocked a deeper level of awe in what BTS continually brings me. Being Black and loving BTS has allowed me to think about the contours of Black music—how it travels globally and how other Black people interpret the ways it travels. Watching Black men's BTS reaction videos has given me space to examine my own projections, assumptions about straight Black masculinity, and the complexity of my own emotional investment in BTS. More broadly, the tensions Black male reactors grapple with around race, gender, and music have forced me to embrace a level of complexity that has challenged who I am as a thinker and consumer. On an emotional level, their recognition of the humanistic and poetic qualities of BTS's music and the care they imbue into their craft have solidified my attachment to the members. With the joy I feel for BTS comes more tension, and now I know that the line between love and critique is a productive space to live in.

Notes

1. See Anderson, *Soul in Seoul*, for scholarship on K-Pop citational practices regarding Black American music.

2   O'Reggio, in "The Dark and Wild Past of BTS," provides a close reading of BTS's debut-era Mnet reality show *American Hustle Life*, as well as a discussion of racialized and gendered stereotypes that structure the show.

3   See Chatman, "I Know That Song!," for several case studies on Black fans reactivating a connection to the Black musical tradition through K-Pop music and music videos.

4   Sebastine, "This Is the Most Beautiful Moment in My Life . . . Part 2 (Album Review)," April 17, 2021, YouTube video, 10:42, https://www .youtube.com/watch?v=MLLRwB6YzzA.

5   Sterling Wong, "Black K-Pop Fans Come Out of the Closet," *Daily Beast*, April 14, 2017, https://www.thedailybeast.com/black-k-pop-fans-come -out-of-the-closet; K-Ci Williams, "(Fan)boy with Luv: BTS Have Male Fans Too," *Medium*, July 1, 2020, archived July 26, 2020, at Archive.org, https://web.archive.org/web/20200726232713/https://medium.com /@kci_w/fan-boy-with-luv-bts-have-male-fans-too-ba91832859ed.

6   Yoon, "These Portraits Show That the BTS ARMY Is Not a Monolith."

7   Sebastine, "Is BTS Overrated?," January 6, 2021, YouTube video, 10:30, https://www.youtube.com/watch?v=SnUlO21rvMQ&t=459s.

8   Anderson, *Soul in Seoul*, 26.

9   Sebastine, "Is BTS Overrated?"

10   Sebastine, "I'm ARMY Now . . . Listening to BTS for the First Time Again!," January 7, 2021, YouTube video, 10:42, https://www.youtube.com/watch ?v=DRWIKGoE3sw&t=33s.

11   In this context, *gas* means "good a** s**t."

12   Sebastine, "I'm ARMY Now."

13   Sebastine, "I'm ARMY Now."

14   Losers Club, "BTS ON OFFICIAL MV | REACTION," March 7, 2020, YouTube video, 9:32, https://www.youtube.com/watch?v=G1VMsTwdqCQ.

15   Losers Club, "J-Hope Chicken Noodle Soup (feat. Becky G) MV REACTION," March 12, 2020, YouTube video, 6:15, https://www.youtube.com/watch?v =8ISZhm4NTB4.

16   Losers Club, "j-hope Daydream @ Lollapalooza 2022 | REACTION," August 14, 2022, YouTube video, 7:47, https://www.youtube.com/watch?v =dTFaGCypvpc.

17   DMV slang that refers to a person. Sebastine, "Never Let J-Hope at Lollapalooza AGAIN! (Full Performance Reaction)," August 2, 2022, YouTube video, 1:16:46, https://www.youtube.com/watch?v=uRNToyGA8hc&t=2836s.

Works Cited

Anderson, Crystal S. *Soul in Seoul: African American Popular Music and K-Pop*. Jackson: University Press of Mississippi, 2020.

Chatman, Dayna. "I Know That Song! Black Fans and the Familiarity of K-Pop." *Flow*, May 2, 2021. https://www.flowjournal.org/2021/05/iknowthatsong/.

O'Reggio, Ciarra. "The Dark and Wild Past of BTS: Identity Building through Binary Formations in *American Hustle Life*." *Crossings* 5 (2021): 103–30.

Yoon, Hannah. "These Portraits Show That the BTS ARMY Is Not a Monolith." *Time*, February 7, 2022. https://time.com/6122609/bts-army-photos/.

12 · "Your Story Becomes Our Universe": Fan Edits, Shitposts, and the BTS Database — Jaclyn Zhou

In April 2022, Twitter user @jkssope tweeted, "there's specific monumental events in army twt that you just had to be there for," prompting thousands to reply with cherished ARMY Twitter moments—almost as many, it seems, as there are ARMY. One such moment raised by a number of fans was "when the BU game was released, they should've known we'd never take that shit seriously" (Twitter user @_kookism_).

"The BU game" refers to BTS *Universe Story*, a visual novel released in late 2020 by HYBE and Netmarble, South Korea's largest mobile game developer. Visual novels are a genre of illustrated interactive fiction whose gameplay is generally limited to allowing players to click to progress through a scene, and occasionally giving players choices for how the story should continue. Users play a storyline within the titular "BTS Universe" or "Bangtan Universe," a HYBE-sanctioned transmedia narrative featuring alternate versions of the BTS members that have been pieced together over a number of music videos, short films, and more. However, BTS *Universe Story* is also a sandbox game—a game that provides an open-ended environment for design and interaction. A set of sophisticated editing tools enables players to create and share their own visual novels about BTS as detectives, vampires, high school students, and so on. Producing a story in BTS *Universe Story* is a labor- and time-intensive process of selecting from a range of backdrops; dressing and arranging 3D animated characters; adding gestures, motions, and facial expressions; writing dialogue and narration; and choreographing shots, camera angles, and transitions. Other users can spend tickets, a kind of in-game currency that can be purchased with real money or accumulated through play, to access these stories, some of which were written by creators recruited in advance of the game's release.

How, then, did ARMY neglect to "take that shit seriously"? They employed this unprecedented set of tools to create fan edits, often using popular memes originating outside the fandom, and shared them online. A fan edit is a type of video created by selecting images and clips of a fannish object, editing them together, and setting them to audio of one's choice. Fan edits can take many different forms—from anime music videos (AMVs) to fully reedited versions of feature films. While AMVs and other long-standing forms of fan edit are still flourishing, a specific type of fan edit has gained a kind of supremacy, particularly in English-speaking K-Pop, anime, and video game fandoms. These edits are shorter, often mere seconds long, and adapted to mobile production and consumption—they are created on smartphone editing apps rather than, or in addition to, computer editing software, circulate on primarily mobile platforms like TikTok and Twitter, and as such have aesthetically adapted to these formats, such as using aspect ratios that work better in portrait mode for smartphone viewing. They often make use of memes, popular audio clips, and social media trends. They are generally focused on snippets of individual characters and relationships, and they only rarely address overarching plot structures or themes.

The edits made with BTS *Universe Story* are largely of this kind. Fans produced these edits by first building the scenes frame by frame in the app, recording the screen as they clicked through each frame, then using editing tools outside of the app to layer audio onto the screen recording. Within days of the game's release, these videos, many of which appeal to a style of nonsensical online humor that can only be described as "shitposting," flooded English-speaking ARMY Twitter, TikTok, and YouTube.[1] In one eleven-second edit, Jimin dances in a burning subway car and asks the viewer, "Is he bothering you, queen?" This edit is based on a meme in which the line is superimposed over an image of a random face or a clip of someone breakdancing. In another, this one using a popular TikTok audio, SUGA berates a generic man for being born in the 2000s ("two thousand and—"), incredulously responding, "And? There's more? You got a compound sentence for an age, my dude."[2]

On the one hand, BTS *Universe Story* is a literal example of what Azuma Hiroki famously referred to as "database" consumption, a seminal theory of *otaku*, or anime and manga fans, that has been crucial to later understandings of Japanese and Asian media fandoms. What is being sold to *otaku*, Azuma argues, is not a discrete media text, or even a set of related media texts (à la transmedia) but a database: "an aggregate of information without a narrative, into which all viewers could empathize of their own accord and each could read up convenient narratives."[3] While BTS *Universe Story* cannot literally provide an aggregate of all information pertaining to BTS, the product is functionally a set of digital files (image files, audio files, and so on) that can be rearranged to "produce" an infinite number of perfectly legible versions of BTS. And once a BTS text has been made, the app provides a platform for its reentry into the database to become part of the app's (and subsequently HYBE's) "official" offerings. This is the promise behind the app's slogan: "Your story becomes our universe."

On the other hand, while fans did in fact take BTS *Universe Story* and produce new texts with it, many of those texts were deemed (in a celebratory or at least fond tone) to be "not taking that shit seriously." If an edit of Jimin dancing in a burning train is not "serious," what is it? Much of the literature on fandom's creative practices, while always acknowledging what is playful, humorous, or ironic about fandom, has focused productively on what is "serious" about fan work. For example, Francesca Coppa discusses how vidders have disidentified with sexist objectification and violence in mainstream media.[4] She argues that "a vidder can tailor-make her media to be as she likes it, and can convey her preferred reading of a text by showing us exactly what and how she sees. . . . This customization of the visual text is particularly important for women and people of color, who often find their desires marginalized. In vidding, their priorities are central."[5]

However, I argue that there is a rapidly expanding body of fan works, such as memes and GIF sets, that convey little of the maker or her priorities and are often intentionally nonsensical—not at all "serious." When consumed in quantity, they give fans a sense of having penetrated the abundance of material surrounding the source text without necessarily imparting onto fans any particular information about, or interpretation of, that text. Invoking Azuma's theorization of database consumption and James Hodge's "vernacular genres," a proliferation of new, networked image genres responding to the felt ubiquity of computing in twenty-first-century life, I am tentatively calling these fan works "database genres." But they could just as easily be called, and have been called, shitposts. Shitposts are intended to be humorous and eye-catching, but are purposely not incisive. They are social—meant to be seen and circulated as the basis of many online communities—but are by definition meaningless. Shitposts convey nothing in particular but, through an affective register of bewildered amusement, enroll viewers into a kind of public culture.

In this chapter, I discuss the ways in which BTS *Universe Story* shitposts and other fan works operate as database genres to negotiate the rapidly expanding and increasingly unwieldy BTS database for fans old and new.

The Idol Database

Azuma argues that, rather than a "grand narrative" that connects all the texts and objects in any given franchise, the database is a "grand nonnarrative"—it exists behind and enables all works within it, but, as it does not have a driving story, allows for a theoretically infinite amount of narrative divergence. In fact, there is often little connection or even outright conflict between various texts within the franchise, but this is not necessarily experienced by fans as a betrayal of expectations or a rupture of a coherent whole, given that there was no such whole to begin with. *Otaku*, then, are less interested in the "entire world" of the fannish object than they are in "settings and character designs as objects for excessive interpretation or 'reading up' (exemplified in derivative works), and for *chara-moe*."[6] "Read-up" here means something like "read into." As for *chara-moe*, it refers to a powerful affective attachment to a character, or an aspect of a character (such as, for example, clumsiness or cat ears).[7] Given the lack of emphasis placed on a unified canon, the source text is viewed "not as a privileged original but as a simulacrum at the same level as derivative works."[8] That is to say, since any text is "judged not by its distance from an original but by its distance from the database," derivative works may appear as equally legitimate as the ostensible source text.[9] As such, the database is constantly changing—not a fixed canon, but a loose collection of information from which data is pulled out and "read-up," derivative work is made, and new data reinserted.[10]

Indeed, the ability to produce derivative work that is indistinguishable from the "original" is precisely what BTS *Universe Story* sells. Recall that it is, first, a visual novel, and, second, a sandbox for producing visual novels. Visual novels comprise a constrained set of backgrounds, character images, outfits, and limited animation effects. These elements are shuffled and reused (this reuse becomes very obvious after only a few scenes) to produce the multitude of "shots" in a visual novel. If this sounds familiar, it is because it is the exact process by which users produce stories in the BTS *Universe Story* sandbox, simply on the other side of the increasingly fuzzy producer-consumer divide. In fact, as Azuma notes, visual novel fans have often generated software to pull out the "raw material" of the game, organize them into actual databases, and allow others to rearrange them into new scenes: fan-made sandboxes. BTS *Universe Story* allows fans to produce works that have a shared materiality (the same "raw material") in a shared technical apparatus (the app) as the "original," via the exact same process through which all visual novels are made, which then reside on an officially sanctioned platform.

Azuma's theories can be usefully applied to celebrity fandom insofar as celebrities are themselves less individuals than they are aggregates (of their professional work, public statements, press, rumors, and so forth). Contemporary celebrity is what Anthony Elliott and Ross Boyd call "fame emptied of content."[11] That is, a gap exists between a celebrity's fame and what she is famous for—if she is famous for any specific thing at all. Indeed, fame that holds specific content at arm's length is crucial for what Suk-Young Kim has termed the "kaleidoscopic" nature of K-Pop: how K-Pop depends on multimedia performance and on the versatility of its performers as not just singers, rappers, and dancers, but also actors, fashion icons, and television and Internet personalities to reach global audiences.[12] As Patrick Galbraith notes about J-Pop, which has both heavily influenced and been heavily influenced by K-Pop, "Although they sing, dance, act and model, an idol's talent lies not in singing, dancing, acting or modeling per se, but rather in 'idoling,' or being an idol for fans."[13] As such, just about anything done in the course of "idoling" could, and does, serve as an entry point into idol fandom—variety show appearances, social media presence, fan work, and other extra-musical content often bring new fans into the fold. New fans will find some object to "read-up," affectively attach to, and use as a foothold from which to expand their knowledge of the database. As for existing fans, given that *chara-moe* has arguably been the basis of celebrity fandom long before it could be said to be the basis of anime fandom, they will be interested in anything related to the stars they like, whether or not there is any relation to the rest of the "world" of the star.

Database Genres

As online fan spaces have increased and the technological capability of fans to produce new forms of fan work has improved, any given large fandom has now accumulated a database that is far too expansive to ever be fully consumed by individual fans, and many new fans find it difficult to even begin to engage. BTS is no exception—or rather, BTS is the rule. Even officially produced content has exceeded easy consumption, let alone fan-produced content (there are, as of November 2023, approximately 196,000 BTS stories on the popular fan-fiction site Archive of Our Own). What is a fan to do?

I'd like to suggest that this abundance is negotiated by a category of fan works that might well be described as "database genres." In addition to fan edits (itself a broad category that encompasses a diverse set of texts), fandom Tumblr formats like text message and fake quotes blogs, GIF sets, and image macro memes might at times be included in this category.[14] I take inspiration here from Hodge's theorization of "vernacular genres," a set of relatively new image forms that have arisen online in response to the anxieties of "always-on computing," the ambient "too-muchness" of always being plugged into a network whose speed and scale far outstrips human perception.[15] Selfies, GIFs, supercuts, and other "practices of mindlessness" help manage these anxieties by establishing a relation between self and network that is simultaneously social and impersonal, not per se about individual self-expression, and not per se about connections to specific people, but rather about a sense of connection in general that is largely devoid of substantive content. For Hodge, these images constitute a "genre" based not necessarily on shared formal traits, but on shared modes of reception and the social context of their proliferation: "[B]y calling the text a generic instance, we reach an agreement, tacit or explicit, about the sorts of feelings, actions, meanings, and effects that this instance may solicit (or not)."[16]

The anxieties of networked life in general are beyond the scope of this chapter, but we might narrow Hodge's useful concept to think about modes of fannish media that hinge less on the idea of the "transformative" experience, as it has been celebrated in fandom and fan studies, than on public yet impersonal performances of connection to a database. To return to the Twitter thread with which the chapter opens, we can call the thread itself a database fan work whose primary purpose was to assemble a collection of events—with the goal of quantity, not consensus or explanation—and to enable public performances or private feelings of "I was here." Or, to step further back, "these things happened." There is something phatic, then, about these fan works: that is, emphasizing the sheer act of communication itself rather than any communicated content. The phatic call of vernacular genres, Hodge says, "[sustains] a powerfully persistent—if simultaneously ambient and soft—libidinal promise of connection."[17] Database genres form an affective channel—if "ambient and soft"—between a fan and a database, representing and radically compressing the abundance of the database, and asserting the possibility of intimacy with it despite the fact that the kind of knowledge that fans desire is no longer possible.

At first glance, it may seem odd to classify a crowdsourcing Twitter thread together with labor-intensive fan edits, but fan edits are more often than not collections of clips of an idol set to music and effects based on *chara-moe*. Indeed, the most popular platforms for online dissemination, such as TikTok, Twitter, and Tumblr, reward such edits, which are often short and meant to be consumed in quantity (as with potato chips, you can't have just one). Edits such as a BTS *Universe Story* video of Jung Kook striking a pose and, in close-up, asking the viewer "Are you lost, baby gorilla?" circulate widely among ARMY, are watched, rewatched, compiled, shared and loved, but provide no particular elaborations on, and lead to no particular reinterpretations of, Jung Kook's character. But in its capacity as a shitpost, the work is attractive precisely for that reason. It is perhaps no coincidence that a majority of online shitpost meme groups are connected to specific fandoms or media texts. These groups inundate fans with communications that appeal precisely because they are both about the fannish object and about nothing.

Database genres are neither transformative nor affirmational—not in the way we normally mean, anyway. They affirm neither the legitimacy of original authorship nor the inviolability of the source material, but instead assert the sheer possibility of a relationship with the database. They transform the database via recombination—adding new material and permutations of the same material; popularizing new memes, audios, trends and challenges; introducing crossover fandoms—but cannot always be said to offer any personal reinterpretations. "Impersonal" does not mean that fans, their attachments, and their desires are somehow absent from fan work, just that the work in question is not always about performing subjectivity: this is me; this is a peek into my reading of the text. It is not, to return to Coppa, about "the representation of the woman who looks [that is, the vidder]."[18] Nor is it precisely about "what and how she sees." It is simply that we are all seeing, and that there is so, so much to see.

Conclusion

Understanding these fan works as conceptually distinct from more frequently studied works like fan fiction helps us consider fandom's varying affective registers and the different forms of the social that result. Anna Wilson has argued that "fan fiction cultivates intimacy between readers and the original source text or canon through a focus on affect."[19] This is certainly true of database genres. What is different is that for Wilson, fan fiction's ability to cultivate that intimacy depends not only on affective reception but ultimately on emotionally charged content: "Affective hermeneutics direct focus toward moments of high emotion in a text that stimulate equally strong feelings in the reader; these heighten a sense of empathy, connection, or intimacy between the reader and the characters in the text." While fandom is most often associated with hot feelings—love, devotion, but also hatred—database genres do not particularly appeal to moments of high emotion. In other words, database genres do not speak to "the feels": ardent emotions of all flavors that, while sometimes difficult to label precisely, are said to form the foundation of fannish engagement. In addition to feels, then, the phatic address of database genres is also one type of affective glue that produces fan collectivities.

Fandom's most celebrated aspect, by both scholars and fans, is that it is social and that its sociality is based on shared fannish feeling. The version of sociality that is most often focused on in fan studies, in reaction to the much-derided loner stereotype of the media fan, focuses on fan community-building: the connections made with other fans via fan clubs, conventions, and social media, fandom's gift economy, mobilization toward activism, and so forth. However, this focus on fan community often has the effect of individualizing fans: this form of the social relies on the existence of a subject who performs their identity as a fan via their online and offline activity. This fan then communicates with and feels proximity to other individuals. The object of devotion, then, is understood in the end as a medium through which interpersonal connections are made. But a large part of the experience of being a fan, I believe, lies in the nonindividual—or what Hodge calls the "impersonal," or what Félix Guattari has called the "pre-personal" nature of affect—social.[20] This sociality is not about the concrete and specific interpersonal connections fans might make with each other, nor is it about the individual relationship one might have with a text. Instead, it is formed through the communication between fans and the fannish database.

The work of database genres lies in the dredging up, "reading-up," recombination, recontextualization, and wide dissemination of database elements, and the reshaping of the fannish database. Here we arrive at a contradiction. Database genres are primarily about addressing the "too-muchness" of fandom: they bring fans closer to the database in a reduced form. However, they also exacerbate the too-muchness of fandom by literally contributing new objects to the database. Subsequently, we arrive at objects such as YouTube compilations of BTS *Universe Story* shitposts or Twitter accounts dedicated entirely to reposting *chara-moe* edits of various idols—the database genre's database genres. As databases expand, so do the fan works that attempt to mediate them, helping fans old and new maintain an always tenuous grasp on the fannish abundance. This chapter offers the term and concept of database genres as one possible name for that effort at mediation.

Notes

1   The purest definition of *shitposting*, a term that arose in the 2000s on sites like 4chan, is the act of posting irrelevant, pointless, nonsensical, or otherwise annoying content in an online conversation (for example, on a forum) in order to derail and hijack that conversation. In the lead-up to and aftermath of Donald Trump's election in 2016, this form of shitposting, as practiced by an increasingly vocal and hostile right wing, has received a great deal of attention. However, *shitpost* has also come to refer more generally to online content that is humorous precisely because it is absurd, random, and not properly joke-like in any discernible sense.

2   For those wishing to see more, or to relive the early days of the game's release, examples of BTS *Universe* edits have been efficiently gathered and can be watched via Twitter threads and YouTube compilations. See, for example, two compilations by YouTube user YouKnowBTS? that were posted within a week of the game's release. "Armys going crazy with BTS Universe game—a compilation (help me breath 😂 😂)," YouTube video, 12:45, September 24, 2020, https://www.youtube.com/watch?v=mECJB1tXjtU; "Armys going MORE cRAzY with BTS Univers game and it's LEgiT memes this time (help me breath pt.2 😂)," YouTube video, 7:59, September 28, 2020, https://www.youtube.com/watch?v=STSmYDq6vRs.

3   Azuma, *Otaku*, 38.

4   "Vidding" is the widespread fan practice of editing together video clips from one or more sources, such as TV shows or films, and setting the clips to music. The resultant video is called a "vid," and those who make vids are called "vidders."

5   Coppa, "An Editing Room," 124.

6   Azuma, *Otaku*, 37.

7   The term *moe* arises from and most famously describes the relationship between male fans and cute, often young, female characters, though it is used more broadly among female fans of Boy's Love manga. In theory, contrary to its usage in English-speaking fandom, *moe* is not a trait proper to the character, it is a feeling held by the fan. As such, *moe* can be

felt toward anybody whether or not they are a stereotypical "*moe* character" or, more derogatorily, "*moe* blob." Azuma is even more interested in how *moe* is felt not toward characters per se, but character elements that can be detached and recombined, such as the aforementioned cat ears, or glasses, or other paraphernalia.

8 Azuma, *Otaku*, 38.

9 Azuma, *Otaku*, 61.

10 In fandom, "canon" refers to the source text(s) and the officially sanctioned content contained within. To quote Fanlore, a wiki maintained by the Organization for Transformative Works, "canon is what fans agree 'actually' happened in a film, television show, novel, comic book, or concert tour."

11 Elliott and Boyd, "Celebrity and Contemporary Culture," 4.

12 Kim, "What Is K-Pop?"

13 Galbraith, "'Idols' in Japan, Asia and the World," 202.

14 Tumblr has given rise to, or at least been the major home of, a number of distinctive fannish formats. Some blogs, for example, use the visual mode of text message screenshots to present imagined interactions between characters. These text messages might be wholly original to the poster, reenact memes or scenes from other media, or pull content from sources such as *Texts From Last Night* (a blog launched in 2009 that collects, for the most part, texts from the wee hours of the morning that should probably not have been sent). A GIF set is a curated selection of GIFs that are somehow related, for example, focusing on the same character's notable moments throughout a series, or recapping a specific scene. Many of these formats and their role in various fandoms have been explored elsewhere, so they are largely outside the scope of this chapter.

15 Hodge, "Vernaculars," 221.

16 Hodge, "Vernaculars," 224.

17 Hodge, "Sociable Media."

18 Coppa, "An Editing Room," 128.

19 Wilson, "The Role of Affect in Fan Fiction."

20 Guattari, *The Guattari Reader*, 158.

Works Cited

Azuma, Hiroki. *Otaku: Japan's Database Animals*. Minneapolis: University of Minnesota Press, 2009.

Coppa, Francesca. "An Editing Room of One's Own: Vidding as Women's Work." *Camera Obscura: Feminism, Culture, and Media Studies* 26, no. 2 (2011): 123–30.

Elliott, Anthony, and Ross Boyd. "Celebrity and Contemporary Culture: A Critical Analysis of Some Theoretical Accounts." In *Routledge Handbook of Celebrity Studies*, edited by Anthony Elliott and Ross Boyd, 3–25. Oxfordshire, UK: Routledge, 2018.

Galbraith, Patrick W. "'Idols' in Japan, Asia and the World." In *Routledge Handbook of Celebrity Studies*, edited by Anthony Elliott and Ross Boyd, 202–14. Oxfordshire, UK: Routledge, 2018.

Guattari, Félix. *The Guattari Reader*. Edited by Gary Genosko. Oxford: Wiley-Blackwell, 1996.

Hodge, James J. "Sociable Media: Phatic Connection in Digital Art." *Postmodern Culture* 26, no. 1 (2015). https://doi.org/10.1353/pmc.2015.0021.

Hodge, James J. "Vernaculars." In *A Concise Companion to Visual Culture*, edited by A. Joan Saab, Aubrey Anable, and Catherine Zuromskis, 221–37. Hoboken, NJ: Wiley, 2020.

Kim, Suk-Young. "What Is K-Pop?" Lecture presented at University of Southern California Korean Studies Institute, Los Angeles. May 7, 2016. YouTube video, 43:26. https://www.youtube.com/watch?v=bA5rG7l1ang&ab_channel=USCKSI.

Wilson, Anna. "The Role of Affect in Fan Fiction." *Transformative Works and Cultures* 21 (2016). https://doi.org/10.3983/twc.2016.0684.

13 · Jung Kook's Button, or the GIF That Keeps on Giving — Mimi Thi Nguyen

In March 2022, on the third and final night of BTS's *PERMISSION TO DANCE ON STAGE* tour in Seoul—their first live concert performances in Korea since the COVID-19 pandemic began—Jung Kook's cropped black tuxedo jacket captured the attention of fans all around the world. During their high-octane performance of "Fake Love," the jacket (worn over a body chain and nothing else) was held together by a single, heroic button, the others having come undone, unintentionally. Video of the performance was immediately clipped and endlessly reproduced across social media as animated GIFs or seconds-long captures shared on mobile electronic devices, through apps such as Instagram, Twitter, and TikTok, with an asynchronous audience of dispersed spectators. ARMY (BTS's fandom) could watch again and again as the garment gaped with every movement, revealing glimpses of Jung Kook's leanly muscled chest, a nipple, or a near-armpit.[1]

Watching the GIFs and videos proliferating across my social media accounts, I was reminded of film scholar Linda Williams's study of pornography. Describing the invention of cinema, the particular pleasure she calls "the frenzy of the visible" follows from the desire to see and know more of the human body.[2] *Frenzy* does indeed describe the tempo of these near-immediate responses from ARMY to any media from or about BTS, but just as germane is the more deliberate drumbeat of temptation metering this media itself. Here I mean not the pace of release (BTS is almost guaranteed to release something every few days, whether an MV, a trailer, an interview, a VLIVE stream, behind-the-scenes footage, a dance rehearsal, and so forth), but the teasing disclosure. In *The Pleasure of the Text*, French critic Roland Barthes queries:

Is not the most erotic portion of a body where the garment gapes? In perversion (which is the realm of textual pleasure) there are no "erogenous zones" (a foolish expression, besides); it is intermittence, as psychoanalysis has so rightly stated, which is erotic: the intermittence of skin flashing between two articles of clothing (trousers and sweater), between two edges (the open-necked shirt, the glove and the sleeve); it is this flash itself which seduces, or rather: the staging of an appearance-as-disappearance.[3]

This "flash itself which seduces" is part of BTS's repertoire, of course.[4] From the teaser and the ensuing tension to the anticipation of release, the choreography of idol presence is built into the K-Pop industry (tightly managed debuts and launches), into the PR machine (comeback trailers after just months between albums), and into the performances themselves. Or, as one report from the Seoul concerts puts it, "The members wore a wide variety of clothes that had the ARMY at the edge of their seats, including a lot of mesh."[5] A bared shoulder here, a comely clavicle there—ARMY reliably preserves these flashes in looping images, separated from the original performance and circulated, downloaded, reframed, and reincarnated, as each hypnotic performance becomes an interminable striptease.

In *A Lover's Discourse*, Barthes argues that a beloved body (knowingly, sometimes) entices another—in this case, Jung Kook's body, beloved by ARMY—in ecstatic fragments: "What fascinates, what ravishes me is the image of a body in situation. What excites me is an outline in action, which pays no attention to me."[6] It is this, *the outline in action, which pays no attention to me*, that names Jung Kook's button as a relay between the idol and his GIF.

Tease

If, as filmmaker and theorist Mila Zuo writes, "Stardom, [as] an amplification of the actor as mythic and exceptional, engages the eye through an incitement to stare and an intensification of the gaze," it should be no surprise that the visual is key to the K-Pop idol.[7] Indeed, the *visual* is an industry term naming those idols who are tasked to bear the burden of that gaze because of their ostensibly exceptional beauty. BTS's visuals (here, more broadly construed) are intensely managed and manufactured, as with other industrial stars from other corners of the world. Cultural geographer Youjeong Oh observes, "Given the image-based idol production system, potential K-Pop idols are basically blessed with extraordinary good looks. Such natural beauty, however, is a mere resource to be processed further. The *gihoeksa* [management company] makes use of various production skills to develop the appearance of each idol through fashion, hairstyle, makeup, and accessories under the umbrella of a group concept."[8] As such, particularly "visual" idols might take center in the dance formations or concept photo shoots. Famously first recruited for his lovely face, BTS's Jin often mockingly introduces himself as "Worldwide Handsome." It is a bold, joking declaration, often accompanied with a laugh, a wink, or a flying kiss to the spectator who might be ARMY, or ARMY to come.

The PERMISSION TO DANCE ON STAGE tour was much anticipated after a planned, and then canceled, world tour in 2020—the year the pandemic became a global catastrophe, and some of us were in various degrees of quarantine (depending on our employment status, and our states' readiness to mitigate contagion). Inaugurated in Los Angeles, polished in Seoul, and completed in Las Vegas, these stadium performances featured (as is common for most shows of this scale) colossal video screens and meticulously planned camerawork that allow concertgoers to catch movements and details that they otherwise would not see at all. Otherwise dwarfed by the scale of these venues, these screens amplify facial expressions and gestures in their individual corporeal dimensions to yield a just-barely mediated intimacy (the members are *right there*). Even if one's seat is at a distance (as even most of the "good ones" are), we are able to admire a curled lip, an unscripted encounter (Jimin and V's laughter, and Jung Kook's giggling chagrin, when he fails to complete a move on behalf of an injured Jin during the stage choreography for "Butter"), or an accidental wardrobe mishap, each central to the ephemeral and fleeting nature of the "live" moment.[9]

Of course, seemingly spontaneous situations for *the flash which seduces* are central to the idol apparatus and its bids for love and attention from an observer.[10] Earlier in their career, BTS often deployed ballet-trained member Jimin as a b-boy with bared abs in MVs for "No More Dream" or "We Are Bulletproof, Part 2," in which the members in their now-familiar V-formation join Jimin in jerking their oversized T-shirts and sports jerseys up and down in unison. And in livestream footage of the members, Jung Kook is teased for his liberal use of body oil for the PTD stage performance of "Fake Love." (When SUGA reveals this new information during a livestream to much laughter, Jung Kook replies, wide-eyed, "I always put it on," and RM responds, "Are you grilling steak?")[11] And following its announcement during FESTA 2022, chapter 2 in BTS's career has included many more casual glimpses of flesh—for instance, V's full-length mirror selfie in pajama bottoms and Jin's sun-kissed back, baring his new "7" tattoo on his left rib cage, on their respective Insta-gram accounts; Jimin's bared chest in the "Set Me Free" MV from his solo debut EP; and, of course, Jung Kook's sculpted abs, only loosely clad in denim, for his Calvin Klein campaign.[12]

And yet BTS is more modest than some of the other masculine idol groups, in comparison. Other idols (sometimes called "beast idols") might perform or pose shirtless, such as Wonho, formerly of MONSTA X, whose social media is absolutely littered with photographs of his hard, muscular body. Jackson Wang, formerly of Got7, stages his solo performances in what I can only com-pare to a *Magic Mike* revue. In contrast, it is an event worth remarking upon (and swooning for) if j-hope wears mesh, Jung Kook loses a button, Jimin bares a shoulder, or RM is caught on someone's phone pulling off his jacket as he jogs backstage after a particularly vigorous choreography, flashing his sweat-gleaming biceps.[13] Theirs is a carefully crafted dance of deliberate dis-closure in which the presence of clothes (and other obstructions) implies at times their absence. The classic striptease of a burlesque dancer, revealing glimpses of her nude body beneath the diaphanous covering of swirling os-trich feathers or giant fans held by other dancers or herself, might be a pre-cursor to frequently repeated images of BTS members, languid and longing behind sheer fabrics or screens. A catalog of such visuals is nigh impossible (there are a lot), but there is V in the "Singularity" MV, V again in the "Blood Sweat & Tears" MV, and one of the concept photo shoots for the *Proof* anthol-ogy album, to name just a few.

The French have much to say about desire and its solicitations, from Barthes to Jean Baudrillard, who proposed, "Seduction does not consist of a simple appearance, nor a pure absence, but the eclipse of a presence," and that "absence here seduces presence." Seduction, he suggests, is the play of appearances and signs, an "aesthetics of disappearance" rather than the rev-elation of truth or reality.[14] This drama of seduction might be not just in the content, but also the medium. In searching for his mother, Barthes confessed that, when he looks at a photograph, he sees "only the referent, the desired object, the beloved body."[15] Through this medium, he suggested that love, "extreme love," enabled him to "erase the weight of the image," to see not the photograph but the object of his desire.[16] At the same time, Barthes could not dismiss the actual *thing* before him: "I am delighted (or depressed) to know that the thing of the past, by its immediate radiations (its luminances), has really touched the surface, which in its turn my gaze will touch."[17] Decades later, film theorist Laura Marks observes of video's sensorium in relation to its low resolution and manipulability: "Part of the eroticism of this medium is its incompleteness, the inability to ever see it all, because it's so grainy, its chiaroscuro so harsh, its figures mere suggestion. . . . But haptic images have a particular erotic quality, one involving giving up visual control. The viewer is called on to fill in the gaps in the image, engage with traces the image leaves."[18] The animated GIF that loops the moment a garment gapes is one such sensory solicitation.

In writing about cinema, French philosopher Gilles Deleuze revels in the antihistorical bent of the close-up, which can also be said about the GIF that tears "the image away from spatio-temporal coordinates in order to call forth the pure affect as the expressed."[19] As an immaterial transfer of data and affect, the GIF might capture a referent and also distressingly lose it (there is no there there). Because of its looped nature, there are necessarily gaps in the animated image—whatever comes before or after the moment captured in the GIF is not pictured, though it could be guessed at, or pieced together from other footage (including other GIFs). This cyclical staging of an appearance-as-disappearance facilitates what Roger Hallas (in his essay on AIDS and gay cinephilia) calls "a fetishistic preoccupation with the moment, the detail, the fragment."[20] And in this case, the GIF is an instrument for the striptease that is never ending.

Loop

What are the erotics of this closed circuit of looped time? Focusing on Jung Kook's button, GIFs allow for prolonged contemplation of a singular and spontaneous moment of intermittence, in which *the garment gapes* but never quite comes entirely undone. One GIF might focus on the moment at which Jung Kook realizes his jacket has come nearly undone, and smiles; another, the moment he lifts the jacket in the choreography to flash his abdominals but, of course, they are already bare. This, from a thousand angles, stopped or slowed at a particular nanosecond, blurred in resolution or movement (one GIF might be the zoom motion pushing closer to Jung Kook's bared chest from a still image), or captioned with commentary ("This day will never be forgotten," or "That button is my enemy").

The aesthetic possibilities of the looped image of the flash of skin once the button gives way belong to an uncanny, libidinal economy operating within both a choreography of movements and their technologically mediated reprise. Even we—the audience, ARMY—are a part of this industrial machine. Like other K-Pop entertainment corporations and music labels, Big Hit Entertainment generates a *lot* of BTS content, from music videos (MVs), reality series (the multiseason game show *Run BTS!*, the travel show BON VOYAGE, the quarantine show IN THE SOOP), livestreams, performances, digital games, photocards and deco kits, commercials for other corporate collaborations, and on and on, which ARMY adopts and sometimes alters into other forms. (Unsurprisingly, there is a flourishing subculture—and trade—of fanart and fiction.) Youjeong Oh observes that this circular mutuality is built into the forms of mediated intimacy the idol industry solicits from fans: "This collaborative and discursive consumption process produces secondary content such as captured images, short movies, GIF images, and SWF images that are then further distributed on various media, particularly online social media due to their virality and spreadability."[21]

In particular, fan cam GIFs of live concerts highlight a passage across multiple thresholds or barriers—the separate spaces of the operator (who films), the spectator (who is the operator but also all those who can be anticipated as audience), and the "world" of the performer, who is on a stage but also projected on thirty-foot screens in a stadium—to forge an impossible relationality with and through the monumental form of j-hope's smolder, or V's cheeky wink. Immediately after any concert (sometimes during, depending on network connectivity), audience members upload myriad fan videos, even though professional DSLR or video cameras are prohibited. Because of the scale of these venues (stadiums seating in the tens of thousands), many GIFs are made from video of the colossal screens and use close-up effects, either at the time of filming or afterward, during editing. These initial screens inflate and mythologize their seemingly otherworldly beauty, while the secondary screen—my phone, your phone—shrinks that beauty into plentiful details we can hold in our hands. High cheekbones, dewy porcelain skin, big luminous eyes, and glimpses of tattoo ink are captured in miniature, small enough to pocket, while also rendered more durable (we can revisit this moment again and again).[22] In both instances, as film scholar Mary Ann Doane observes in her study of the close-up, *Bigger Than Life*, the shamelessly disruptive scalar qualities of these techniques add further dimensions to this mediated intimacy: "Unlike the tracking shot, which because it is the result of an actual camera movement appears to transport the spectator along with the camera through a physical space with depth and varying perspectives, the zoom, as a mechanical movement changing the focal length of the lens, flattens and abstracts space. It is not a *real* movement."[23] Here, there is a double movement that is not a real movement, though it is real enough to produce a desirable encounter with *the outline in action, which pays no attention to me*. We stare, because they will never catch us looking, and we keep staring, long after the enrapturing moment.

Such encounters are looped into GIFs, self-enclosed images set apart from a narrative structure, that solicit and *sustain* particular sensations. In "The Affect of Animated GIFs," Sally McKay writes, "The cyclical repetition and the viewer's hypnotic engagement is reinforced as the animation repeats again and again and again, creating an immersive effect. It is entirely up to the viewer to determine how much time to spend with the GIF, and it is the value of the affective experience alone that makes up the criteria for lingering or leaving."[24] In other words, the GIF that keeps on giving will do so for as long as a viewer might wish to stay in that specific moment—Jung Kook's fateful performance in "Fake Love," for instance. McKay cites art historian Mieke Bal, who describes animated GIFs like cinematic close-ups, as "abstractions isolating the object from the time-space coordinates in which we were moving as if 'naturally.' A close-up immediately cancels out the whole that precedes it, leaving us alone, thrown out of linear time, alone with a relationship to the image that is pure affect."[25]

Both machines for the suspension of time, the close-up and the loop create a tight circuit of intimacy and enclosure. But even while GIFs may induce a kind of cloistered trance in between the face and the screen (my own 3 a.m. scrolling through BTS-centric Instagram tells me that this is a real possibility), they also address us as ARMY, as "adorable representatives" engaged in practices that make up a multitude, a collectivity.

ARMY

In his 2002 experimental short film *K.I.P.*, Nguyen Tan Hoang videotapes a television screen as an attached VCR plays a rental porn video featuring '70s gay porn star Kip Noll. Where previous renters have rewound "the good parts" (presumably scenes of orgasmic pleasure, but perhaps not), he films himself watching these same moments in the glare of the television screen, a ghostly presence transposed over the bared flesh of the performers and the glitches, drop-outs, and poor resolution that is the consequence of the material decay of the magnetic reel. *K.I.P.* is about the shared experience of watching over and over again "the good parts" with an unknown number of others, a collectivity in absentia.

Without temporal sequence or complete disclosure, these GIFs specialize in selective movements that give life to desire through the anticipation of what is already to come *again*. That such desire is also communal, while asynchronous, is all the more striking. GIFs, of course, exist as immaterial (to us) data, but we can observe this collectivity of audience in the numbers—the views, the hearts, the comments, the reposts. An ARMY who cares enough might clip and reedit moments from live performances, reality shows, livestreams, or behind-the-scenes shooting sketches, adding subtitles and soundtracks before uploading it to a platform to share with others. *A GIF is never a GIF for one, but a GIF for many*. As sharing GIFs or videos is inherent to their full affective resonance (whether one desires to be *with* BTS, or *like* BTS, or something in between), our phones each connect us to a commons, a free, indeterminate space without property or enclosure.[26] Or, as Asian German video artist Hito Steyerl writes about the "poor image," the image that is "compressed, reproduced, ripped, remixed, as well as copied and pasted," "Its optical connections—collective editing, file sharing, or grassroots distribution circuits—reveal erratic and coincidental links between producers everywhere, which simultaneously constitute dispersed audiences."[27] These GIFs and clips build alliances as they move, soliciting translation or commentary, creating publics or disputes. We are bonded as ARMY, or as ARMY with particular affinities (often aesthetic, sometimes erotic, occasionally political), through the circulation of these visual images across global networks, a shared history of encounter with our idols.

At the PTD concerts in Las Vegas a month later, Jung Kook's stage costume for the "Fake Love" and "Black Swan" performances was swapped for a sturdier garment. Worn over thin, silver body chains encircling his waist, the cropped jacket featured a stiff, corset-like bodice and curved bow's hem (with boning and busk fasteners) that, with arms down at his side, covered his navel, but with arms raised, bared it. This costume change resulted in fewer fortuitous accidents, though just as many GIFs and images were produced of his obliques, and lower back (the intermittence between the bottom of his jacket and the top of his pants).

BTS both produces and solicits expressive forms that each promise an account of a historical situation and the world; consider the lyrics of "Spring Day" (a memorial to the *Sewol* ferry disaster and, implicitly, a critique of governmental and corporate neglect), or "Life Goes On" (a melancholic ballad about quarantine, isolation, and time out of joint), or the copious commentaries about *what BTS means*. That is to say, BTS is so often the occasion or event for questions about singularity, exemplarity, contextualization, and expertise. The idol group is remarkable in itself as a richly intertextual phenomenon, but BTS is also oft-cited as a signal illustration, explanation, problem, or claim about X for our consideration. It is as such that these GIFs, these fan-generated temporal loops, also express something significant about the forms of singularity found in the moment, the detail, the fragment—at which BTS excels in generating, endlessly—that demand the constancy of our attention.

Notes

1   Many thanks to my coeditors who supplied the adjectives and superlatives for this chapter. Because GIFs are low resolution, I did not try to capture stills from one for this chapter. However, there are plenty of fan cams on YouTube featuring this particular moment, such as this one posted by I DARE U JK, though attribution is vague: https://www.youtube.com/watch?v=8h5_5dPCu4E.

2   Williams, *Hardcore*, 36.

3   Barthes, *The Pleasure of the Text*, 9.

4   Not just BTS's repertoire, specifically, but that of both K-Pop idols and other pop stars, generally.

5   Bishnoi, "BTS' Jungkook Sends ARMY in a Tizzy."

6   Barthes, *A Lover's Discourse*, 193.

7   Zuo, *Vulgar Beauty*, 8.

8   "As *gihoek* means planning or designing, the *gihoeksa* creates performers from scratch through its 'in-house' production system. In addition, the *gihoeksa* controls every aspect of the idols' public image and career, including the coordination of artistic and media content, macro- and microscheduling (i.e., deciding when to release a new album, stream a concert, or announce a television show lineup), and long-term market planning." Oh, *Pop City*, 112.

9   For more on liveness, see Kim, *K-Pop Live*.

10   It is beyond the scope of this chapter, but these bids for love and attention are not simply about a desire to be *with* an idol, it is just as likely a desire to be *like* one. To be as beautiful, as luminous, to be a beloved body too—BTS also inspires gender envy, especially among queer and trans ARMY.

11   McDonald, "BTS Cracked Up at Jungkook's Secret to Making His Abs Stand Out on Stage."

12   At FESTA 2022, the annual celebration of their debut, BTS announced a temporary hiatus of most group activities as the members stagger their mandatory military enrollment. Dubbed "chapter 2" in their story, this "hiatus" has resulted in a deluge of solo activities, from singles, albums, MVs, sponsorships, fashion editorials, and more.

13   Pham, "These BTS Wardrobe Malfunctions Prove That the Boys Are Professionals Through and Through."

14   Baudrillard, *Seduction*, 34.

15   Barthes, *Camera Lucida*, 7.

16   Barthes, *Camera Lucida*, 12.

17   Barthes, *Camera Lucida*, 81.

18   Marks, *Touch*, 11, 13.

19   Deleuze, *Cinema 1*, 96.

20   Hallas, "AIDS and Gay Cinephilia," 93.

21   Oh, *Pop City*, 115–16.

22   ARMY often express the desire to put a member (or two) in their pockets, which suggests the aesthetic of cuteness is just as key as the striptease to their appeal. For more on cuteness as an aesthetic category, see Ngai, *Our Aesthetic Categories*.

23   Doane, *Bigger Than Life*, 4.

24   McKay, "The Affect of Animated GIFs."

25   Bal, "Exhibition as Film," 81.

26   Here I am drawing on Lauren Berlant's concept of the commons. Berlant, *On the Inconvenience of Other People*.

27   Steyerl, "In Defense of the Poor Image."

Works Cited

Bal, Mieke. "Exhibition as Film." In *Exhibition Experiments*, edited by Sharon Macdonald and Paul Basu, 71–93. Oxford: Wiley-Blackwell, 2007.

Barthes, Roland. *Camera Lucida: Reflections on Photography*. Translated by Richard Howard. New York: Hill and Wang, 1982.

Barthes, Roland. *A Lover's Discourse: Fragments*. Translated by Richard Howard. New York: Hill and Wang, 1978.

Barthes, Roland. *The Pleasure of the Text*. Translated by Richard Miller. New York: Hill and Wang, 1975.

Baudrillard, Jean. *Seduction*. Translated by Brian Singer. Montreal: CTheory, 1990.

Berlant, Lauren. *On the Inconvenience of Other People*. Durham, NC: Duke University Press, 2022.

Bishnoi, Priyadarshni. "BTS' Jungkook Sends ARMY in a Tizzy as a Sudden Wardrobe Malfunction Exposes More Than He Signed Up for during PTD Day 3." *Zoom*, March 13, 2022. https://www.zoomtventertainment.com/korean/korean-entertainment-kpop-news-bts-jungkook-sends-army-in-a-tizzy-as-a-sudden-wardrobe-malfunction-exposes-more-than-he-signed-up-for-during-ptd-day-3-article-90185807.

Deleuze, Gilles. *Cinema 1: The Movement-Image*. Translated by Hugh Tomlinson and Barbara Habberjam. Minneapolis: University of Minnesota Press, 1986.

Doane, Mary Ann. *Bigger Than Life: The Close-Up and Scale in the Cinema*. Durham, NC: Duke University Press, 2022.

Hallas, Roger. "AIDS and Gay Cinephilia." *Camera Obscura* 18, no. 1 (2003): 85–127.

Kim, Suk-Young. *K-Pop Live: Fans, Idols, and Multimedia Performance*. Stanford, CA: Stanford University Press, 2018.

Marks, Laura U. *Touch: Sensuous Theory and Multisensory Media*. Minneapolis: University of Minnesota Press, 2002.

McDonald, Amy. "BTS Cracked Up at Jungkook's Secret to Making His Abs Stand Out on Stage." *Korea Boo*, March 19, 2022. https://www.koreaboo.com/news/bts-jungkook-abs-fake-love-stage/.

McKay, Sally. "The Affect of Animated GIFs (Tom Moody, Petra Cortright, Lorna Mills)." *Art F City*, July 16, 2018. http://artfcity.com/2018/07/16/the-affect-of-animated-gifs-tom-moody-petra-cortright-lorna-mills/.

Ngai, Sianne. *Our Aesthetic Categories: Zany, Cute, Interesting*. Cambridge, MA: Harvard University Press, 2012.

Oh, Youjeong. *Pop City: Korean Popular Culture and the Selling of Place*. Ithaca, NY: Cornell University Press, 2021.

Pham, Jason. "These BTS Wardrobe Malfunctions Prove That the Boys Are Professionals Through and Through." *Stylecaster*, August 14, 2020. https://stylecaster.com/bts-wardrobe-malfunctions/.

Steyerl, Hito. "In Defense of the Poor Image." *E-flux* 10 (November 2009). https://www.e-flux.com/journal/10/61362/in-defense-of-the-poor-image/.

Williams, Linda. *Hardcore: Power, Pleasure, and the "Frenzy of the Visible."* Berkeley: University of California Press, 1999. First published 1989.

Zuo, Mila. *Vulgar Beauty: Acting Chinese in the Global Sensorium*. Durham, NC: Duke University Press, 2022.

III "Not Today"

GEOPOLITICS AND ACTIVISM

It is something of a truism to tie the emergence of *Hallyu* and consequently BTS's ascension with the rise of Korean "soft power," the name given to the social and cultural influence of persuasion, as opposed to "hard" military force or political coercion. Yet, BTS's emergence is more complex and contradictory than the South Korean government's cultural-political strategy can capture, exceeding the sheer weight of the band's contributions to national GDP or the K-Pop industry's power to commodify youthful rebellion.

The chapters in this section illuminate how BTS emerges from and engages with the geopolitical dimensions of the world around us, as well as how people around the world utilize BTS to grapple with their specific conditions. The group's messages lend themselves to thinking about and acting upon injustice both in and outside of South Korea. This may feel contradictory, given BTS's present position at the apex of a culture industry designed to squeeze profit from its workers' blood, sweat, and tears. But perhaps it is precisely because the band members themselves are caught in, and continue to rage against, this structure, that their evolving struggles resonate all the more with the lives of their vastly diverse fans. BTS have long incorporated their poignant underdog story into their body of work, inspiring not only confidence and love of self, but conviction in the struggle, whatever the struggle might be. As the lyrics of "Not Today" insist, "Yeah we are extra / But still part of this world," mapping their tribulations to South Korea's social inequities, while also connecting their fight to their fans' battles. BTS's anthems of rebellion—challenging the audience to fly, run, walk, or crawl, and "gear up" toward "a new world," or refusing to "endure it a little more"—have been translated to concerns and campaigns seemingly distant from the South Korean contexts that first inspired the members. While they might be constrained in terms of what they can explicitly critique in South Korea (the high-pressure educational system and rigid class hierarchies; less so mandatory military conscription or anti-LGBTQ violence, though they have not ignored these either), BTS has found opportunities to lend their celebrity to support other causes. Their efforts land in uneven ways, and oftentimes, it is ARMY who take up where BTS must leave off.

The first two chapters in this section situate BTS within South Korea–US relations that have been defined by Cold War conflict, military occupation, Asian labor migration, and the legacies of this continuing alliance. In "Empire Goes On: Transpacific Circuits of Care Work," Vernadette Vicuña Gonzalez links the gendered labor of entertainment and hospitality to post–Cold War tourism economies in Asia and the Pacific, locating BTS within this geography. Reading the band's consumption of a hula dance performance on holiday in Hawai'i for the travel show BON VOYAGE, alongside the killings of Asian masseuses in Atlanta during the pandemic and their own roles as ambassadors of Korean culture and tourism, Gonzalez foregrounds a circuit of racialized care work to contextualize BTS's travels. In "Like a Criminal Undercover: Love, Hate, and the Performance of Inclusion," Rachel Kuo follows the coverage of BTS's 2022 visit to the White House to shed their starlight on rising anti-Asian violence. Kuo examines the limitations of BTS's positioning against Asian hate in the United States within the context of broader US imperial ambitions in Asia, cautioning us to consider the state's love of BTS against its ongoing support of other forms of racial violence.

The BTS fandom often take the band's messages and make them their own. Many of these deployments take place online, where ARMY create local and translocal communities *and* evade surveillance, practices that were intensified during the COVID-19 pandemic. Andrea L. Acosta's contribution, "Recoding the Bot: ARMY and Digital Transgression," reflects on the equivalencies that are often made between the online "bot" and ARMY, usually to discredit BTS's popularity as the result of mechanistic, horde behavior. Parsing the deeply racialized figure of the "bot" illuminates the very human investments behind digital strategies of resistance and antisurveillance that have sparked solidarities with Black Lives Matter and antifascist movements. In "Break the Structure: BTS ARMY Digital Activism and State Surveillance in Indonesia's Omnibus Law Protest," Karlina Octaviany grapples with how Indonesian ARMY's social media practices created a space to protest a controversial Omnibus Law in 2020 that proposed the removal of labor protections and rights. Despite state policing and harassment, Indonesian feminists consolidated support for protesters arrested by the police, shedding light on the relationship between K-Pop and activism outside South Korea. "From Purple to Pink: The Filipino ARMY for Leni and the Fight for Good Governance" describes a similar set of tactics used by Philippine ARMY to counter misinformation during the 2022 national elections. From political messaging through BTS memes to fundraising with BTS-themed campaign "merch," Allison Anne Gray Atis, Noel Sajid I. Murad, and Hannah Ruth L. Sison recount their involvement as ARMY during Leni Robredo's campaign challenging the autocratic Rodrigo Duterte administration and his anointed successor and how they used the seeds of hope and humor to sustain youth participation during the election season.

The harsh realities of social inequality, capitalist exploitation, and political repression tragically produce all too many incidents of rage and grief, which ARMY refract through BTS. Alptekin Keskin and Mutlu Binark's chapter, "'Yoongi, Can You Hear Me?': Demanding Justice for #Melisa and ARMY Activism in Turkey," delves into how Turkish media attempted to deflect critiques of intimate violence by laying blame on the corrupting influence of K-Pop for the suicide of a young BTS fan. They examine how Turkish ARMY navigated the shoals of social media to seek justice for her death. The section ends with Michelle Cho's "'Spring Day': Nostalgia, Pop Mediation, and Public Mourning," an analysis of the group's 2016 single and music video "Spring Day" and fan-produced videos about the music video as an allegory for the 2014 *Sewol* ferry tragedy, in which a South Korean ferry capsized, killing more than 300 passengers, 250 of whom were high school sophomores on a field trip. Cho details how Korean and international fans engage in a form of networked-yet-informal social justice work by contextualizing the local South Korean and global-systemic, geopolitical conditions that caused the disaster, demonstrating the song's ability to enable collective grief and public mourning across a translocal fandom.

14 · Empire Goes On: Transpacific Circuits of Care Work — Vernadette Vicuña Gonzalez

... lessons of hula hands in the "dream place"

An interlude in BON VOYAGE, BTS's 2016–19 reality travel series that follows the seven members as they vacation around the world, captures the linked gendered and racial desires that entertainers in Asia and the Pacific navigate. The moment is tucked into the seventh episode of season two, which takes place in Hawai'i. "Enjoy a hula dance" features the members attending dinner and a stage show after a day packed with tourist activities. In the episode, there is a sustained focus on a female hula dancer and BTS's admiration of her performance. The juxtaposition of BTS as Korean entertainers with the dancing bodies of Hawaiian women illuminates the indispensability of gendered care work in smoothing out post–Cold War interstate relations and narratives of partnership and peace between the United States and its allies in Asia and the Pacific. The provision of hospitality, pleasure, diversion, and healing through care work was a crucial part of the machinery of imperial occupation in the region. It continues through to the present and was undertaken mostly by Indigenous and Asian women. BTS's work as entertainers is also woven into this story. Their encounters with these other forms of care work provide an entry point for understanding how histories of empire and militarism continue to shape the experiences of many Asian care workers moving through the world today.

Near the end of their trip to the islands, the band members visit the Polynesian Cultural Center, a forty-two-acre cultural theme park on O'ahu that houses seven Pacific "island cultures." Dressed in bright aloha shirts,

BTS members sit down for a lūʻau followed by a stage performance of song and dance from "Polynesia." Adorned in feathered headdresses, six women perform a Tahitian dance. Their rapid-fire sensual hip movements are accentuated by low-slung decorative belts. A hula kahiko (a traditional hula) follows, performed by male dancers to a percussive chant. Their rhythmic stomps, chest slaps, and sharp gestures emphasize their oiled musculature. Impressed, BTS members comment on the performance using touchpoints familiar to K-Pop: the fitness of the dancers' bodies, the synchronization of their steps, and the charisma of the dancer who is the "center."

Smiling in anticipation, V announces, "This is the one, this is it," calling his bandmates' attention to the line of women who glide onstage to a wistful song, accompanied by an ʻukulele. The dancers are dressed in purple bandeaus and floor-length skirts, and their hair, accessorized with white orchids, is pulled back tightly from their faces. The BTS members imitate the characteristic undulating arms and "hula hands" of the dancers. Jimin points out the attractiveness of one particular dancer's eyes as the camera cuts to a three-quarter framing of her body. The dancer gracefully reaches her arms outward in invitation as she sways to the music. As typical of the hula ʻauana style, a modern version that gained traction in the twentieth century with the expansion of tourism in the islands, the dancer's movements are sinuous, evoking romance and femininity. Her captivating smile is direct, and her welcoming gaze complements the mood. BON VOYAGE editors insert a caption describing her "honey dripping eyes," a Korean expression for eyes that are full of love and affection.[1] The members exclaim in admiration, with SUGA appreciatively adding, "She should have debuted as an idol group member." They tease V—offscreen, it seems one of the dancers winks or waves to him—and the editorial caption cheekily comments that "it feels like winning the lottery." At the end of the day, the members reflect on the performances, again commenting on the female hula dancers' skill and charisma, and conclude they had witnessed "idol members in Hawaiʻi."

That BON VOYAGE Hawaiʻi and BTS cannot help but linger on the hula dancer's "honey-dripping eyes" illustrates the success of her performance. V's anticipation of the attractions of the hula—This is the one, this is it—demonstrates the effective translation of hula into a register of tourism and how central its eroticized invitation is to the fantasy that tourism sells. BTS's time in Hawaiʻi reflects just how potent the idea of Hawaiʻi-as-paradise remains despite the deep social inequalities, environmental devastation, and military occupation that shape life in the islands. Earlier in the "hula" episode, RM looks out on the blue expanse of ocean from a sandy beach and observes, "Isn't Hawaiʻi anyone's dream place?" This dream place for tourists, however, is the result of the overthrow of the Kingdom of Hawai'i in 1893 by a foreign sugar plantation oligarchy in collusion with the US military. Haunani-Kay Trask, a critic of Hawai'i's dependence on tourism, argues that "lovely hula hands" prostitute Native Hawaiian culture for the pleasure of tourists, masking the pain of Hawai'i's occupation with entertainment that implies invitation, welcome, and, thus, consent.[2]

Hawai'i was the destination most wished for by the band members in interviews that preceded *BON VOYAGE*'s first season.[3] Indeed, V and j-hope returned for vacations after the 2021 *PERMISSION TO DANCE ON STAGE* Los Angeles concerts. Tourism's reinterpretation of aloha (the greeting, the sentiment of love, the "honey-dripping eyes") as consent is instrumental to the erasure of this historical and ongoing dispossession of Native Hawaiians. Today, Hawai'i's economy is deeply dependent on tourism, despite the fact that its profits flow to nonlocal corporations, while squeezing the value out of Indigenous and Asian settler labor and cultures.[4] Ideas of the "dream place" elide how the islands serve as headquarters for the US Indo-Pacific Command, which oversees over half of the world's surface and population in the geostrategic "Asia-Pacific" region and holds military exercises for the United States' hemispheric allies every two years in the waters off Honolulu. On O'ahu, nearly one quarter of the island's land mass is under US military occupation.

In the face of this reality, the idea of Hawai'i as a "dream place" is held together by evidence of happy natives through displays such as hula. In these performances, Asian, Pacific Islander, and Native Hawaiian women—interchangeable in an economy that traffics in multiculturalism to erase Indigenous dispossession—are especially positioned as natural hosts. Their presence in hula and in other feminized service occupations is visible as entertainment but erased as labor, belying years of training. The hula dancer's equation with hospitality resonates with BTS and other tourists, because it underscores commonly held beliefs about who does this kind of work and why certain women are best suited for it. An observation that BTS members repeat throughout the second season is their impression of how "relaxed" and "peaceful" everyone seems to be in Hawai'i. While this might be a commentary on the contrast with their high-octane life as K-Pop idols, it obscures the work it takes to create the fantasy of peace and relaxation in occupied, militarized territory, and why that work is essential to the status quo.

This kind of labor is something BTS is intimately familiar with. Toward the end of the performance at the lū'au, three of the members (V, Jimin, and j-hope) are called to the stage to dance a hula led by a group of children, while

RM, SUGA, Jin, and Jung Kook look on and tease their bandmates for awkwardly dancing out of sync. Their comical attempts at hula inadvertently reveal how much work goes into the stage work of fantasy. BON VOYAGE's main conceit of capturing the spontaneous unscripted charm of the band works in much the same way, deflecting our gaze from the never-ending labor of BTS crafting their relatable and fun-loving image, while simultaneously boosting Hawaiian tourism. The staged spectacle that BTS takes part in occludes an itinerary dictated by sponsorships from Hawaiian Airlines and Blue Hawaii helicopter tours and the band's obligation in turn to promote local tourism.

BTS's exploits in BON VOYAGE further endeared the band to their growing international fandom and also augmented their official role as Seoul Tourism ambassadors, a role which overlapped with the show's airtime. As avatars of Korean allure, BTS has come to play a similar role to Hawai'i's iconic hula girl for South Korea's growing international tourism market.[5] The Korean state recruits the world's most recognizable K-Pop idols into the work of welcome and hospitality that helps stabilize the region's interstate relations, while concealing the realities of a militarized Korean peninsula (even as they ultimately have to serve mandatory military service in very visible ways). In the hula episode, BTS's recognition of their fellow entertainers, and their brief appearance on the hula stage, points to their common roots and overlapping routes in the post–Cold War landscape of Asia and the Pacific.

. . . lessons of healing hands in a nightmare place

BON VOYAGE, with its documentation of some of the band's intercultural encounters outside of Asia, lent credence to what BTS later had to say about anti-Asian violence. The band explicitly weighed in on what it means to be Asian in the world as the global-historical event of the COVID-19 pandemic manifested in intensified animus and desire around Asian bodies. In the most shared tweet of 2021, the band released a statement following the fatal March shootings of eight people in Atlanta massage parlors, six of whom were Asian women (and four of whom were Korean). The group denounced the hatred and violence stoked by pandemic race mongering and shared their own pain of being targeted by anti-Asian discrimination during their travels. Their addition to the #StopAsianHate campaign detailed how the members "endured expletives" and were "mocked for the way [they] look." They testified that they, too, had been subject to the pain and indignity of prejudice. Coming from young, highly successful cosmopolitans, the statement was a sobering reminder of the persistence and reach of anti-Asian racism, as much as it was a gesture of solidarity: "What is happening right now cannot be dissociated from our identity as Asians."[6]

BTS leveraged their visibility to augment the stories behind the alarming rise of anti-Asian violence. The way they framed Asianness as *the* explanation for the tragedy in Atlanta, however, limited the potential and scope of their critique. The rise of anti-Asian violence manifested in distinctly gendered ways: Asian women are by far the primary targets of this violence. The gendered occupation of those who were killed is just as instrumental as Asianness in understanding the workings of this violence; all six Asian women worked at the two massage parlors targeted by the shooter. These factors are interconnected. In some ways, BTS's stratospheric success made other commonalities that they had with the women who were killed less evident: their labor and circulation in the world as entertainers and their feminization due to this labor and their Asianness. Yet BTS—at the apex of global popular entertainment—and near-anonymous Korean massage workers share overlapping, if deeply asymmetrical, circuits of labor mobility that are generated by US-Korea post–Cold War relations.[7]

Unlike the moment in *BON VOYAGE* where V calls attention to the invitation of the hula dancers' hands and eyes, BTS's statement does not remark on or identify with the hands providing relief and pleasure in massage parlors in the deep US South. This kind of intimate care work is perhaps too shamefully yoked with prostitution—a perverse kind of hospitality that is the constant and regulated companion to US militarization in Asia and the Pacific, including US bases in South Korea. Linking the Atlanta massage workers to the hula dancers of *BON VOYAGE* and BTS as entertainers makes visible the complicated relations that the gamut of care work sustains in the region.

The Atlanta killer's perception of Asian women as objects of sexual temptation has roots in the US Asian exclusion laws of the late 1800s, which framed Chinese women as prostitutes to prevent them from immigrating for "immoral purposes"—logics akin to Calvinist missionaries' views of Hawaiian women dancing hula. These ideas were recycled during twentieth-century US wars in Asia, which translated racialized fantasies into service, entertainment, and care work occupations for women in Asia and the Pacific, as well as Asian migrants to the United States. The presence of Korean women in massage parlors in Atlanta is a direct outcome of these histories.

The relocation of the Korean military camptown sex industry within US borders was precipitated by transpacific movements of labor and the racial-sexual fantasies that traveled with them. Historian Yuri Doolan notes the surprising and little-known fact that 90 percent of the "massage parlors, saunas and health spas operating as fronts for the illegal sex trade" adjacent to US military bases in the South were staffed by a Korean workforce that was made up of GI brides.[8] Since the end of World War II, but especially in the 1970s and 1980s, the immigration of GI brides reproduced the camptown economy on US soil. Korean club owners, seeking to move their businesses stateside with the waning US military presence in South Korea, brokered marriages between South Korean women and American soldiers. They brought over women who were forced by poverty and exploitative conditions in South Korean camptowns to seek a better life elsewhere, only to fall into further debt bondage in the United States. The illegal sex trade capitalized on even legitimate marriages: 80 percent of GI marriages ended in divorce, creating a pool of vulnerable women with no financial safety net. Massage parlor work—even with, and perhaps because of, its dubious connotations—was the most available opportunity for them to gain a financial foothold.

Although women make up a large number of Korean migrant workers to the United States, their labor as entertainers is of a vastly different order than that of BTS and the hula dancers at the Polynesian Cultural Center. While BTS might enjoy touring or documenting travel-as-work as a large part of how they connect to their global fandom, other workers in the broad category of entertainment—such as the Korean women in Atlanta and women who continue to work in the camptowns in South Korea—have devastatingly distinct experiences of care work and mobility. In the United States, Asian massage workers are not just targets for deranged shooters but also for misplaced anti-trafficking ordinances. The persistent structural links that tie Asian women in the United States to militarized sexualized labor at US bases around the world have resulted in their criminalization, policing, and deportation, rather than in measures that might alleviate the conditions of poverty and vulnerability that drive them to exploitative kinds of work.[9]

Shoring up the interstate collaborations that ensure the circulation of different kinds of care work and its necessity for the continued militarization of Asia, the South Korean government created the E-6 visa specifically to allow businesses "catering to US troops to import migrant 'entertainers' under the guise of tourism law."[10] In South Korea's camptowns, Filipino, Russian, Uzbek, and Kazakh women have taken the place of South Korean women in nightclubs and massage parlors.[11] In comparison to the hula girl dancing, or even BTS's work attracting tourists to South Korea, the position of women "entertainers" in the US South and South Korea, while legitimated by visas, is profoundly vulnerable and exploitative, a secret these states would rather keep under wraps.

A little over a year after the Atlanta shootings and their original #StopAsianHate statement, BTS was invited to the White House to meet with President Biden, in order to help raise awareness about anti-Asian hate as part of Asian American, Native Hawaiian, and Pacific Islander Heritage Month. Traveling to the United States, using their own passports and funds and not as official representatives of the South Korean government, the trip further bolstered BTS's status as global K-Pop ambassadors for diversity and inclusion. Yet, they remained proxies for the South Korean state. Their presence in the White House demonstrates the ways in which a militarized "entertainment-diplomatic complex" has always operated in support of the state, from providing entertainment for troops during wartime to generating goodwill for interstate alliances during times of peace.[12] In a BANGTANTV episode later released about their White House visit, we see the members get camera-ready, rehearse their lines, and discuss their order and positioning for the press conference, highlighting the shared showmanship of politics and entertainment.[13] Lining up in their tailored black suits in front of the White House press corps, and then meeting with the president to bring attention to US hate crime legislation, the band members embodied the fantasy of Korean soft power.

The structural conditions underpinning the Atlanta killings are, of course, impossible to address in a tweet or a brief publicity-laden White House visit, or to amend by calling on the "right to be respected." Their resolution calls for more than educational exposure to different cultures, because these conditions sustain the very dynamic of US-Asia relations. At the same time, BTS's statement about their own experience of anti-Asian hate is an occasion to think about the incongruity of this moment: a male K-Pop group speaking up to decry racial violence in a country that is not theirs. Some critics were quick to point out that it was not their place—a different version of *go back to where you came from*. And yet, perhaps, there is no more apt place for the Asian entertainer to go than back to the heart of empire.

... lessons of finger hearts in korean places

BTS's popularity (and that of *Hallyu* more broadly) is only the most recent instance of how Asians have long provided entertainment and comfort for life under capitalism, especially during times of increased precarity and pain.

During the pandemic, their growing fandom turned to BTS for assurance that "life goes on." After the disappointing cancellation of their widely anticipated *MAP OF THE SOUL* world tour, BTS recorded their album *BE*, which was presented as a panacea for the trauma and isolation of the pandemic. *BE* became a source of emotional care that many of their fans turned to in the face of systemic governmental neglect and incompetence.

BTS's body of work during the pandemic represents another kind of gendered Asian care work that sustains people even as it remains entangled in empire. The band members provided comfort to their fans as beautiful men singing words of solace. They extended scenes of normalcy and home through their pandemic version of a travel series, *IN THE SOOP*, which showcased them eating and cooking together in the bucolic South Korean countryside, offering content that lifted the spirits of old and new fans alike. BTS members tapped into a different but related kind of care work that they themselves had consumed, through their enjoyment of hula, or that they had empathized with, however imperfectly, in their advocacy of Asian massage workers.

As travel restrictions began to loosen in 2021–22, BTS further solidified their image as cultural ambassadors for South Korea, broadening their uplifting message in service of their nation. Pandemic-era BTS members traveled with the imprimatur of honorary ambassadors, as spokespeople for youth and mental health at the United Nations. Each member was presented with diplomatic passports and appointed by President Moon Jae-In as a "special presidential envoy for future generations and culture," based on their collective success in delivering "messages of comfort and hope to the entire world."[14] This particular moment demonstrated the state's recognition of the finger heart—the shorthand of K-Pop's cultivation of love and care for its fans—as a diplomatic strategy in support of liberal values on the global stage. Here we see BTS translating the labor they do as entertainers into roles as honorary delegates, following a tradition of cultural ambassadorship laid out by other state-artist collaborations during and after the Cold War.

BTS's steadying presence and hopeful message were swiftly translated to a wish for a "return to normal" by the pandemic-ravaged South Korean economy. In 2021, just as the pandemic began to ebb, the City of Seoul and the Seoul Tourism Organization unveiled a promotional campaign, "Your Seoul Goes On," a hopeful play on *BE*'s lead-off single, "Life Goes On." Incorporating the phrase *Eo-gi-yeong-cha*, a Korean onomatopoeia reminiscent of traditional work songs, the campaign drew on the idea of pushing forward together despite obstacles, a sentiment frequently expressed by BTS members during their reflections at the end of each BON VOYAGE season. The video produced for the campaign intersperses close-ups of BTS members, styled in a mix of modern and traditional Korean clothing with footage of different districts of Seoul. A rousing score accompanies cuts of Koreans in action in different trades and occupations, many having to do with the arts and service industries that cater to tourists. It ends with the BTS members lined up, gazing at the camera, extending an invitation to visit. South Korean marketing leaned into the band's image—and their "honey-dripping eyes," and the power of the finger heart—to build anticipation and desire for postpandemic travel. At the two in-person concerts that BTS held in Los Angeles and Las Vegas (in 2021 and 2022 at the first signs of the pandemic's retreat), the Korea Tourism Organization hosted promotion booths. A repeating spot, advertising "The Rhythm of Korea," played alongside a selection of BTS's music videos in the stadium before each concert, further linking BTS to the idea of tourism to Korea.

In late 2022, even as debates continued over the possibility of military exemptions for BTS, the band was deployed as the official public relations ambassador (and a central attraction) for the city of Busan's bid to host the 2030 World Expo. As the band members took the stage in Busan in October 2022, their allure as symbols of care, pleasure, and healing was tightly woven to the city's extension of hospitality to the tens of thousands of fans who flocked to Busan from all over the world, and the tens of millions who watched the concert online or followed social media accounts of fellow fans about their experiences. As the seven most visible hosts to the visiting national and global community, BTS members helped craft an invitation to the city through their ability to connect, welcome, assure, and enthrall, linking their work of entertainment and their brand of care work to the larger state project of the world exposition. The Busan concert captured BTS at the height of their fame and popularity, singing, rapping, and hip-thrusting for the delight of their fans *and* in the service of the city and nation's prosperity.

The sheer scale of the Busan concert's impact—the numbers of Korean and international fans it attracted, the transformation of an entire city in the image of BTS, the breakdown of HYBE's livestreaming infrastructure due to an unprecedented fifty-million-strong global audience—points to BTS's stratospheric popularity and how the band's message of care genuinely resonates with the fans. In the span of two hours, BTS brought together a global audience not only to derive enjoyment from their performance but also to imagine and rehearse the future exposition. However, the concert also illuminated the unsettling power of entertainers as providers of care, healing, and release for a mostly female fandom, a demographic that unsurprisingly overlaps with the global care work population. With the stage and political spotlight on their love and attentiveness to their fans, seven young Asian men made clear the indispensability of Asian care work to regional, state, and inter-state relations and economies. Often discounted as mere entertainment or illicit acts taking place in the shadows of massage parlors or nightclubs, here in its most visible form of the most famous performers in the world, the foun-dational work and potential reach of the labor of care work writ large is clear. We see how it operates as a sustaining force for imperial and extractive systems that simultaneously use, denigrate, and abandon the people assigned to this kind of labor. In understanding its value, power, and scale, we may also find a way to move forward as we craft new models of solidarity and labor justice across Asia and the Pacific that can encompass and cherish our differences.

Notes

1   Thanks to Michelle Cho for her translation of this phrase.
2   Trask, "'Lovely Hula Hands.'"
3   BTS: BON VOYAGE, season 1, episode 0. The episode was released on June 22, 2016, as a teaser for the first season and was available on VLIVE.
4   Aikau and Gonzalez, introduction to Detours, 1–3.
5   Oh, Pop City, 2–13.
6   @BTS_twt, "#StopAsianHate #StopAAPIHate. We send our deepest con-dolences to those who have lost their loved ones . . . ," March 29, 2021, 9:48 p.m. https://twitter.com/BTS_twt/status/1376712834269159425.
7   Two of the women were of Chinese descent, which gestures to different, if overlapping, geopolitical structures at play.
8   Doolan, "Transpacific Camptowns," 33–34.
9   Shih, "The Trafficking Deportation Pipeline," 57–61.
10   Doolan, "Transpacific Camptowns," 48.
11   Lee, Service Economies, 130.
12   Choi and Maliangkay, "Introduction: Why Fandom Matters to the Inter-national Rise of K-Pop," 6.
13   BANGTANTV, "[EPISODE] BTS (방탄소년단) Visited the White House to Discuss Anti-Asian Hate Crimes," October 5, 2022, YouTube video, 15:22, https://www.youtube.com/watch?v=xjfw_fNRfds.
14   "President Taps BTS as Special Envoy ahead of UN Session Next Week," Korea Times, September 14, 2021, https://www.koreatimes.co.kr/www /nation/2021/09/113_315530.html.

Works Cited

Aikau, Hōkūlani K., and Vernadette Vicuña Gonzalez. Introduction to *Detours: A Decolonial Guide to Hawai'i*, edited by Hōkūlani K. Aikau and Vernadette Vicuña Gonzalez, 1–13. Durham, NC: Duke University Press, 2019.

Choi JungBong, and Roald Maliangkay. "Introduction: Why Fandom Matters to the International Rise of K-Pop." In *K-Pop: The International Rise of the Korean Music Industry*, edited by JungBong Choi and Roald Maliangkay, 1–18. Abingdon, UK: Routledge, 2015.

Doolan, Yuri W. "Transpacific Camptowns: Korean Women, US Army Bases, and Military Prostitution in America." *Journal of American Ethnic History* 38, no. 4 (2019): 33–54.

Lee, Jin-kyung. *Service Economies: Militarism, Sex Work, and Migrant Labor in South Korea*. Minneapolis: University of Minnesota Press, 2010.

Oh, Youjeong. *Pop City: Korean Popular Culture and the Selling of Place*. Ithaca, NY: Cornell University Press, 2018.

Shih, Elena. "The Trafficking Deportation Pipeline: Asian Body Work and the Auxiliary Policing of Racialized Poverty." *Feminist Formations* 33, no. 1 (2021): 56–73.

Trask, Haunani-Kay. "'Lovely Hula Hands': Corporate Tourism and the Prostitution of Hawaiian Culture." In *From a Native Daughter: Colonialism and Sovereignty in Hawai'i*, rev. ed., 136–47. Honolulu: University of Hawai'i Press, 1999. First published 1991.

15 · Like a Criminal Undercover: Love, Hate, and the Performance of Inclusion __ Rachel Kuo

On May 31, 2022, the last day of what is formally called Asian American, Native Hawaiian, and Pacific Islander Heritage Month in the United States, BTS visited the White House to discuss the issue of "anti-Asian hate crimes, Asian inclusion, and diversity" with President Joe Biden.[1] Biden's invitation came amid broad calls to #StopAsianHate following highly visible incidents of anti-Asian violence throughout the COVID-19 pandemic. These acts of violence included physical violence against the elderly and the March 2021 mass shooting in Atlanta that targeted Asian-owned spas and massage parlors.[2] Mass media coverage, social media posts, and data collection and reporting projects (with Stop AAPI Hate being the most well known) have narrativized both the spectacle and scale of anti-Asian violence through highlighting individual incidents and attacks. At the same time, such narratives and projects also reproduce the notion that anti-Asian violence continues to remain invisible (and underreported) to a broader public eye. To this end, the White House's invitation to BTS was embraced and celebrated in media coverage and by their fan base as delivering a powerful message against racism on a global scale. And yet, their visit to the White House and its surrounding publicity obscure the ways in which racial violence against Asians is constituted and sustained through longer histories and contemporary forms of US empire, including ongoing US military occupation in Korea.

The aftermath of the Atlanta spa shootings seemingly sparked swift performances of "taking seriously" anti-Asian violence through national statements of solidarity and local law enforcement responses, such as the deployment of special units and creation of task forces.[3] In a speech in the days following the murders, Biden said, "Hate and violence often hide in plain sight. . . . Our silence is complicity. . . . We have to speak out."[4] Using a similar frame, BTS members released a #StopAsianHate statement, written in both Korean and English about their own painful experiences with discrimination as Asians, in one of the most widely circulated posts on Twitter that year. In the statement, BTS observes, "We have endured expletives without reason and were mocked for the way we look. But these experiences were enough to make us feel powerless and chip away our self-esteem. . . . What our voice must convey is clear. We stand against racial discrimination. We condemn violence."[5] Months later, Biden signed the COVID-19 Hate Crimes Act in May 2021 to address and respond to anti-Asian violence and racism.[6] The act sought to affirm the federal government's intolerance of hate through the expansion of crime data reporting initiatives and provision of diversity training to law enforcement to better recognize hate crimes.[7] A year later, during BTS's visit, Biden further emphasized the importance of "speaking out" against the lurking danger of hate in the US. He said to the members, "Talking about eliminating hate is important. . . . This is an important month here in America. A lot of our Asian American friends have been subject to *real* discrimination."[8]

Yet, what is "real" discrimination and what are its forms that demand attention and intervention? What does it mean to refer to hate as the primary frame for understanding racial violence? As journalist Seth Berkman observed, the same day that BTS visited the White House, home care workers in New York City, many of whom are Asian migrant women, came together to protest exploitative conditions including twenty-four-hour work days and unpaid back wages.[9] This protest garnered little attention in a media landscape hypervigilant to anti-Asian violence, especially in comparison to the high-profile coverage of BTS at the White House.[10] Such slow forms of economic violence and precarity that affect many Asian migrants are often rendered invisible and unaddressed through the spectacle of anti-Asian hate.[11]

BTS's visit to the White House offers an example of the discourse of inclusion and performativity of "stopping hate" politics that have come to dominate mainstream Asian American and antiracist political discourse in the US in the past several decades. Anti-hate discourse moralizes and reduces racism to interpersonal violence resolved through individual recognition and punishment. "Stopping hate" and institutional diversity and inclusion measures that legitimize state intervention are demonstrated through the juxtaposition of two official videos documenting BTS's visit: one produced by the US White House and the other by HYBE Corporation. Bringing intertextual readings of these videos with related media showcases the interconnectedness of anti-Asian hate in the US and US imperial exploits in Asia.[12] In other words, what is often imagined and depicted as problems of individualized racial hatred against Asians and Asian Americans depends upon the reproduction of such hatred through carceral and geopolitical state violences. The staged encounter between the White House and BTS offers an entry point for observing how the US domestic criminalization of hate is a carceral measure that represents and performs "good" antiracist politics. Taken together, these examples also illuminate contradictions and tensions within Asian American politics, which are often obscured by the mainstreaming of #StopAsianHate as the primary form for recognizing Asian American injury and redress.

Performing the Contradictions of Inclusion

Composed of a press briefing and conversation with Biden and Vice President Kamala Harris, BTS's visit was memorialized through an official White House release of a poppy, trailer-style video overlaid with snippets from their discography and key interview excerpts and quotes.[13] Several months later, in early October 2022, the band's official YouTube channel released footage of the visit, tracing the band's travels from Incheon Airport in Seoul to Washington, DC.[14] Much of the content in the behind-the-scenes *Bangtan Bomb* episodes edited and produced by HYBE highlights the band's preparation for music videos, live performances, and concerts. In this way, the original White House's video is analogous to an official music video release, highlighting the visit as a staged performance with the White House playing the role of the welcoming, inclusive nation-state and BTS standing in as representative of a racially marked population vulnerable to racist violence. The behind-the-scenes video functions as a means for HYBE (representing both state and corporate interests) to showcase BTS members as grateful and dutiful participants in a performance of obligation to the US as the generous host, even as BTS members demonstrate the theatricality of their role.

The beginning of the White House video immediately highlights the artificiality of the encounter as Biden welcomes the members gathered around a couch in the Oval Office. "I figured I'd make you feel at home," he says, before turning to a tablet on the side table to play a music video. The pop beats of their second English-language single "Butter" come on—*I got that superstar glow so, oooh.* The video cuts to footage of all the members walking in slow-motion across red carpets and marble floors and posing in front of columns and portraits at the White House, showcasing the stateliness and significance of the visit and location.

The stylized nature of the entire visit, documented through the highly edited video, demonstrates the politics of appearance behind "stopping anti-Asian hate." During their conversation in the Oval Office, Biden and Harris emphasize the language of hate in describing the toll of racism on individuals. For example, Harris says, "Hate and prejudice are meant to make people afraid and for people to feel alone without power." Biden adds to this by telling the members of BTS, "Hate only hides. When good people talk about it and say how bad it is . . . it goes down. It's not just your great talent, it's the message you're communicating." Here, Biden again highlights the necessity of "speaking out" against hate. On behalf of the members, RM replies, "Thank you sincerely for your decision, such as signing the COVID-19 Hate Crimes Act into law." This particular exchange legitimizes the act as the solution to anti-Asian violence, as well as demonstrates indebtedness to a benevolent state.[15]

The documentation of anti-Asian racism through the pandemic has included differing forms and degrees, from verbal harassment to physical attacks and confrontations. Public attention and discussion of anti-Asian racism has sparked important conversations about its day-to-day tolls and material impacts. My argument does not dismiss the very real feelings of grief, fear, and anger that people are experiencing. However, the public condemnation of particular manifestations of racism has promoted solutions where "respect" and "anti-hate" politics are enforced via carceral systems of policing, prosecution, and punishment.[16] In signing the COVID-19 Hate Crimes Act, Biden describes anti-Asian hate as a "critical problem of hate crimes being underreported." He frames this problem as a consequence of both a lack of resources and training for law enforcement in accurately identifying crimes to the FBI, and cultural and language barriers between police and communities for crime reporting.[17] The idea that hate is "hiding"—that there are undercover racist criminals waiting to be caught and that we can fix racism by making racist incidents more visible—is the undergirding logic of the act, which can only be "solved" by strengthening law enforcement mechanisms.

BTS's White House visit functions as an allegory for the state performance of antiracism and its false promise of diversity and inclusion.[18] HYBE's behind-the-scenes segment featuring the press briefing offers a further example of this. Every aspect of the briefing is highly choreographed, including their rotational order of speaking. In the video, the members express collective nervousness and rehearse the performance of their speech, such as how they will walk in and stage themselves around the position of the microphone. Jin is tasked with delivering the line, "Today is the last day of the AANHPI Heritage Month. We join the White House to stand with the AANHPI community and celebrate." Neither "AANHPI" nor "heritage month" have a direct translation in Korean, so his line is a hybrid of English and Korean. In the video, there are several shots of him practicing the line over and over again, and he asks RM for help with pronunciations. Throughout his rehearsal, the other members tease him by shouting out random combinations of letters, such as "ANHHH" or "AANHNH."

Jin's struggles with the acronym inadvertently demonstrate a tension between saying something correctly versus something making sense. In this case, the representative inclusion of Asian American, Native Hawaiian, and Pacific Islander categories is a contradictory one; the subsumption of Native Hawaiian and Pacific Islander through the AANHPI categorical acronym constitutes exclusion via mechanisms of inclusion.[19] This shorthand to celebrate cultural heritage erases historical and contemporary forms of violence that come with "including" Hawai'i and different Pacific Islands into US statehood and territories, including seizures of land and displacement, military occupation, and nuclear testing. Further, the "power of diversity" functions as US propaganda to legitimate the annexation of Hawai'i as a state through the frame of multiculturalism to counter characterizations of the United States as a racist empire.[20]

The official White House and HYBE videos are mutually performative constructions, in which the former seeks to promote a vision of global interdependence and the latter reveals state machinations and orchestrations in the deployment of culture as a tool of political ideology. Historically, US leveraging and abstraction of political organizing and agitation for Black and Third World liberation during the Civil Rights and Cold War era established a metanarrative of the US as an antiracist savior, upholding ideals of democracy and freedom in order to stabilize global political and economic power in the fight against communism.[21] At the same time, this self-image masks historical US expansion into Asia through military intervention and economic agreements. The combined circumstances of BTS's visit, with their cultural prominence as global pop stars bringing heightened attention to anti-Asian violence in the US, symbolically uses them as representatives to address state management of racism while occluding state violence in both domestic and international arenas.

The message of inclusion that BTS offers during the visit then is delivered not just through their speeches and lyrics, but also through the presence of their bodies in the White House. Not only do they serve as transnational subjects representing US and Korean allied relations, but their attendance also functions as a generic stand-in for a racialized Asian otherness. This racialization is always in relation with the state's shifting constructions of allies and enemies; the current US "friendship" with South Korea comes hand in hand with the normalization of military "protection," as well as economic sanctions and restrictions against the threat of North Korea in an unending war.[22] The White House video symbolizes this "friendship," while the HYBE video focuses on their preparation for the visit to draw attention to the work and their labor as they navigate these racialized positions. BTS's representative inclusion and recognition within US popular culture and national politics demonstrate a mutual dialectic between their social significance, due to the cultural and economic value of their "talent" and "success," and the continued staging of their foreignness through their role as cultural ambassadors.

Reflections on Inheritances of Anti-Asian Hate

"Stopping hate" at home disavows historical and ongoing US war and intervention in Asia.[23] In other words, the existence of violent exclusions elsewhere is masked by the "promise of inclusion" that sustains an idealized liberal image of US culture as welcoming of difference.[24] And yet US state violence overseas has long marked Asians as "objects of racial hatred" in order to sustain carceral regimes of war and occupation, deportation and detention, that manage and criminalize Asian and Asian diasporic populations in relation to the US nation-state.[25] Policies and public sentiments figuring Asian peoples as friend *or* foe buttress one another. For example, after their defeat in World War II, Japan transformed from a wartime enemy into an ally in the fight against communist China, including hosting US military bases that later supported military expansion into Korea and Vietnam.

In the 1980s, anti-Asian violence spiked when Japan's rapid economic growth was seen as a threat to US economic power and the reason for its economic recession.[26] This violence included the murder of Chinese American Vincent Chin by two white Detroit autoworkers, who had been laid off and blamed their unemployment on the rapidly expanding Japanese auto industry. In 1988, President Ronald Reagan responded to Chin's murder

prior to signing the tenth Asian / Pacific American Heritage Week proclamation. In his remarks, he reiterated the model minority myth, extolling
the value of Asian work ethic and talent for US nation-building, while highlighting racial hostilities exacerbated by geopolitical conflicts through US
trade policies.

> Any practice of racial discrimination against any individual violates the
> law, is morally wrong and will not be tolerated. . . . A few years ago, in
> Detroit, Vincent Chin, a citizen of Chinese-American heritage, was beaten
> to death by two men enraged over car imports from Japan. Political dif-
> ferences over trade policy are one thing, and we can debate them, but
> racially-tainted appeals cross a very dangerous line. They're an affront to
> this country, and they threaten the tranquility and safety of all of us here
> at home.[27]

I bring up the history of Chin's killing by two white men because it is simultaneously perceived as a lesser-known story by those outside of Asian
American political formations, while also serving as an often retold and hy-
pervisible (and perhaps canonical) case of anti-Asian violence, typifying the
racialization of Asian foreignness in a period of heightened xenophobia. Further, Chin's killers were sentenced to just probation and a $3,000 fine, causing
an uproar. Rather than questioning the legitimacy of state systems of justice,
much of the public outrage, including in some Asian American organizing
spaces, was in response to the lack of severity in sentencing. The emphasis on adequate punishment continues to shape some advocacy and policy
approaches to violence in the present. Throughout 2020 and 2021, as more
visible incidents of anti-Asian violence made headlines, a doubling down on
hate crimes legislation and law enforcement responses swiftly emerged as
public sentiments materialized into state actions. Calls to "stop Asian hate" revealed a desire for visibility and recognition through increased data collection
and prosecution that harkened back to the sentiment of unresolved justice for
Vincent Chin.[28]

Anti-Asian racism cannot be disentangled from US state projects of war-
making and economic competition. The murder of Vincent Chin in the 1980s
occurred amid racial anxieties and resentment over technological development and accelerated economic growth in East Asia, including Japanese
technology industries and rising economies in Hong Kong, Singapore, South
Korea, and Taiwan (then dubbed "Asian Tiger economies"). During this time,

the Reagan administration also began a racially charged "chip war" with Japan over control of the semiconductor industry.[29] This landscape fomented anti-Asian sentiment with corresponding physical violence and attacks. Decades later, in 2020, in addition to incendiary commentary racializing the COVID-19 virus as an Asian disease, the Trump administration was also embroiled in conflicts with China's multinational technology corporation Huawei over the semiconductor trade. Such industry conflicts also carried over to the Biden administration, leading to new policies to "counter China," including a block on exports of semiconductors and chip-making equipment. The ban has also been described as a national security measure to hinder Chinese military weapons and technology development. Such economic sanctions are part of an arsenal of war and empire, and while they target industries, they have a human cost. Both "trade wars" and military build-up in Asia are tied to US imperialism, but this connection is elided in the popular framing of racism as a domestic problem of individual malice.[30] Looking back to Reagan's statement, that "racially tainted appeals cross a very dangerous line" and are an "affront" and "threat" to domestic safety, pushes us to reconsider the criminalization of racist expressions and actions as a state response to anti-Asian racism. Different modalities of US geopolitical conflicts in Asia contribute to racial tensions domestically, yet these violences are disavowed in declarations that hate has "no place in America."[31]

Speaking Out on Love and Hate

Throughout the White House visit, BTS members appear hyperaware of their role as performers, carefully playing their roles as spokespeople without actually saying anything too politically substantive. The HYBE video includes footage of the members hanging out together in their pajamas, prior to their visit, to discuss how they will approach the press briefing. "Whatever the question, we just give that answer in English," Jung Kook jokes, adding that he'll reply to every question with the answer, "Music is always . . ." as all the members laugh at his antics. The line also inspires a reflexive hilarity at the promise of music as a neutral communicative and affective medium that can solve any problem.[32] So while BTS's lyrical messages can provide entry points in which fans participate and mobilize politically, their overall messages are fluid and ambiguous.[33] The visit to the White House is not the first time BTS members have served as youth representatives for South Korea or as envoys of a global politics, including performances at the United Nations to spread generically malleable messages of "love" and "unity." International leveraging of BTS's fame to promote the vague rhetoric of empowerment and belonging, or to "raise awareness" about mental health and kindness, fails to take responsibility for multiple crises and state-facilitated actions (and inaction) that compound racialized precarity.

BTS's global LOVE MYSELF campaign and multiyear partnership with UNICEF to #EndViolence function as the other side to their role as messengers "speaking out" against hate. The 2019 "BTS LOVE MYSELF" music video depicts youth of different racial and ethnic backgrounds being bullied by their peers, but moved by BTS's music and message as a "force for good," they are able to overcome these challenges by choosing to love themselves. In this joint campaign, global problems of violence become reduced to the problem of one's eroding self-esteem. Solutions focus on neoliberal measures of individual choice: to "choose respect, choose support, choose kindness."[34] The individual focus on choice, in which oppression is linked to poor self-esteem, and the solution is self-empowerment, simultaneously absolves states of social responsibility while also positioning states to govern and enforce those choices through a "regime of morality."[35] The governance of moral feelings such as love, respect, and hate also obfuscates the ways in which state regimes of global peacekeeping depend upon the mutual entanglement of humanitarian aid, militarism, and colonial control.[36]

The desire for individual recognition and belonging through mainstream media and politics, found in concerns with Asian visibility in Hollywood and identity-based electoral representation, has constrained political imaginations around narrow bids for state and institutional incorporation. The empty, feel-good promises of securing diversity and inclusion through raising "awareness" and ending racism by stopping hate both *deracialize* and *depoliticize* structural violence. Further, the overemphasis on individual prejudice and bias as the driving forces of racism occludes how sanctioned diversity and domestic civil liberties rely on state apparatuses of racial violence, including law enforcement and the criminal court system.[37] The mainstreaming of "stop Asian hate" as the means to channel so-called solidarities with Asian American communities thus obscures other political possibilities.

Reading BTS's visit to the White House as a performance of statecraft offers us one site in which to interrogate both the limitations and dangers of "stopping hate" discourses, underwritten by carceral regimes. We all desire worlds in which we can be safe and well, but this world cannot be secured by the violent apparatuses of police or military. In response to the image of Biden posing with BTS, while holding up finger hearts as a show of solidarity against anti-Asian violence, Notdutdol, an organizing collective against US imperialism and for Korean reunification, tweeted, "Cute pic! Can you send Biden a message for us? Get US troops out of our homeland!"[38] The cheekiness of the post strategically draws attention to ongoing US military occupation as a predominant modality in which anti-Asian violence takes place.

In December 2022, HYBE announced that BTS's oldest member Jin would comply with the law and enlist in the South Korean military to perform his mandatory service, with the rest of the members to follow. Earlier that year, I remember talking to different friends in Asian American political organizing spaces, who were also part of ARMY, on building up more anti-imperial and antimilitaristic campaigns across BTS fandom. Yet, I do wonder, what politics might be possible across a disparate and dispersed community held together by a collective commitment and love for an idol? BTS's compulsory service has already sparked some online discourses about ongoing US military involvement and occupation in Korea that undergirds mandatory conscription.[39] Perhaps "raising awareness" and "speaking out" in this case may draw further attention to the violences of US empire that have remained largely invisible, and push toward political imaginations beyond carceral solutions. Such political futures are possible and "yet to come."

Notes

1   Press briefing by Press Secretary Karine Jean-Pierre, members of BTS, and National Economic Council director Brian Deese, May 31, 2022, Washington, DC, https://www.whitehouse.gov/briefing-room/press -briefings/2022/05/31/press-briefing-by-press-secretary-karine-jean -pierre-members-of-bts-and-national-economic-council-director -brian-deese-may-31–2022/.

2   As widely reported by mainstream media outlets, the spas were targeted for posing a "sexual temptation." Reporting also emphasized the Atlanta Police Department's failure to understand the shootings as racially motivated, which focused attention onto police competency in understanding hate crimes. The overemphasis on police response also elided other analytical frameworks by Asian American feminist organizers, including the intertwining of US military occupation in Asia, creation of local sex industries, and racialized sexualization of Asian women; historical and contemporaneous forms of criminalizing Asian

women's sexuality through legislation such as the Page Act of 1875; and police raids of massage parlors and spas.

3   For criticisms of police responses in the aftermath of the Atlanta shootings, including the deployment of local law enforcement as undercover plain clothes units to Asian neighborhoods, see Hamid and Kuo, "Towards Collective Safety."

4   Joe Biden, "Remarks by President Biden at Emory University," March 19, 2021, Atlanta, Georgia, https://www.whitehouse.gov/briefing-room /speeches-remarks/2021/03/19/remarks-by-president-biden-at-emory -university/.

5   @BTS_twt, "#StopAsianHate #StopAAPIHate," Twitter, March 29, 2021, 9:48 p.m., https://twitter.com/bts_twt/status/1376712834269159425?lang=en.

6   The act builds on existing state mechanisms of protection through hate crimes legislation. This includes the Matthew Shepard and James Byrd Jr. Hate Crimes Act in 2009. Passed under the National Defense Authorization Act, this act links the expanded enforcement of "tolerance" and "equality" to categories of gender, sexuality, and disability alongside military expenditure. See Reddy, *Freedom with Violence*.

7   For in-depth discussion of data collection and crime reporting in relation to anti-Asian violences, see Kuo and Bui, "Against Carceral Data Collection in Response to Anti-Asian Violences."

8   Soo Youn, "Inside BTS's Landmark White House Visit to Denounce Anti-Asian Hate." Italics added.

9   The campaign against the twenty-four-hour work day in New York State includes significant testimony by Chinese migrant workers on grievances against the Chinese-American Planning Council (CPC), an outwardly progressive nonprofit, for violation of bargaining agreements. Notably, CPC's advocacy under #StopAsianHate has included participation in the NYC Commission for Human Rights' Day of Visibility to engage community members on how to report hate crimes. On the home care attendants' grievances, see discussion of Chan et al. v. Chinese American Planning Council Home Attendant Program, Inc., and Chu et al. v. Chinese-American Planning Council Home Attendant Program, Inc., in "The Nonprofit War on Workers, Part I. Weapons of Labor Violence: An Analysis of the Chinese-American Planning Council's Legal Tactics to Exploit Workers," by Ron T. Kim, State Assembly of New York, January 4, 2022.

10   Berkman, "We Were Supposed to Help Asian Migrant Women—Instead We Got Police."

11   Kuo and Bhaman, "Attacks on Asian Women Are Fueled by Criminalization, War and Economic Injustice."

12   This chapter primarily focuses on East Asia. Much can also be said about US wars and interventions in Southeast Asia as well as War on Terror

regimes, including the coupling of anti-hate measures and antiterrorism measures that build on post-9/11 national security infrastructures that have targeted and policed Muslim, Arab, and South Asian communities in the United States.

13   The White House (@WhiteHouse), "President Biden and Vice President Harris Welcome BTS to the White House," June 4, 2022, YouTube video, 4:50, https://www.youtube.com/watch?v=fHFgJux7MzM.

14   BANGTANTV, "[EPISODE] BTS (방탄소년단) Visited the White House to Discuss Anti-Asian Hate Crimes," October 5, 2022, YouTube video, 15:22, https://www.youtube.com/watch?v=xjfw_fNRfds.

15   See Baik, "Unfaithful Returns."

16   See Rodríguez, "The Asian Exception and the Scramble for Legibility."

17   Joe Biden, "Remarks by President Biden at Signing of the COVID-19 Hate Crimes Act," May 20, 2021, https://www.whitehouse.gov/briefing-room /speeches-remarks/2021/05/20/remarks-by-president-biden-at-signing -of-the-covid-19-hate-crimes-act/.

18   See also Melamed, *Represent and Destroy*; Lowe, *Immigrant Acts*; Ahmed, *On Being Included*; Duggan, *Twilight of Equality?*

19   Hall, "Which of These Things Is Not Like the Other."

20   Saranillio, *Unsustainable Empire*.

21   Dudziak, *Cold War Civil Rights*.

22   On the cost of sanctions, see Nodutdol's 2020 zine "Sanctions of Empire," https://nodutdol.org/sanctions-of-empire/. Additionally, in 1988, Ronald Reagan had also designated the DPRK (North Korea) as a state sponsor of terrorism.

23   See Baik, "Unfaithful Returns"; Kim, *The Interrogation Rooms of the Korean War*.

24   Lowe, *Immigrant Acts*.

25   Hamid and Kuo, "Towards Collective Safety."

26   Anti-Asian violence during this time is also tied to the aftermath of the US war in Vietnam.

27   Ronald Reagan, "Remarks on Signing the Asian / Pacific American Heritage Week Proclamation," May 3, 1988, Public Papers of the President: Ronald Reagan, 1981–1989, Ronald Reagan Presidential Library, https://www.reaganlibrary.gov/speeches.

28   See also Tseng-Putterman, "On Vincent Chin and the Kind of Men You Send to Jail."

29   In 1987, Reagan raised tariffs on Japanese exports to $300 million, ratio-nalizing the economic sanctions due to Japan's "third-country dumping" and lack of US access to the Japanese market. The "chip war" itself was an assertion of US empire and exceptionalism disguised as aspirations for economic globalization. See Ronald Reagan, "Statement on the Japan–United States Semiconductor Trade Agreement," March 27, 1987, Public

Papers of the President: Ronald Reagan, 1981–1989, Ronald Reagan Presidential Library, https://www.reaganlibrary.gov/speeches.

30   Tseng-Putterman, "Policing the Borders of Anti-Asian Violence."

31   For examples of this discourse, see "Remarks by President Biden at the United We Stand Summit," September 15, 2022, White House, Washington, DC., https://www.whitehouse.gov/briefing-room/speeches-remarks /2022/09/15/remarks-by-president-biden-at-the-united-we-stand -summit/.

32   On music as a cultural apparatus that translates ideologies into "easily absorbed emotions," see Klein, *Cold War Orientalism*, 93.

33   Cho, "BTS for BLM."

34   HYBE LABELS, "BTS (방탄소년단) LOVE MYSELF Global Campaign Video," July 29, 2019, YouTube video, 2:29, https://www.youtube.com/watch?v =Eo_mo5vA7tw.

35   See Baik and Kaisen, introduction to "Korea and Militarized Peace," on the discursive echoes of South Korean president Moon Jae-In's national security adviser stating that North Korea should "make the right choice" toward peace by accepting US military presence in ending war in 2018. See also Lee, "Beauty between Empires."

36   Nguyen, "The Biopower of Beauty."

37   On racial liberalism, the legitimization of state violence, and critiques of domestic hate politics from internationalist frameworks, see Tseng-Putterman, "Policing the Borders of Anti-Asian Violence." See also Whitlock and Bronski, *Considering Hate*.

38   @Notdutdol, "@bts_bighit Cute pic! Can you send Biden a message for us? Get US troops out of our homeland!," Twitter, June 1, 2022, 2:07 p.m., https://twitter.com/nodutdol/status/1532061408611168257.

39   통일까지 투쟁 (@hermit_hwarang), "BTS wouldn't have to do compulsory military service if it weren't for the US," Twitter, October 17, 2022, 1:37 p.m., https://twitter.com/hermit_hwarang/status/1582063148533657601; @PinayYonsei, "The US empire maintains anti-communist foreign policies of encirclement," Twitter, October 17, 2022, 11:30 a.m., https://twitter .com/PinayYonsei/status/1582031388190347264.

Works Cited

Ahmed, Sara. *On Being Included: Racism and Diversity in Institutional Life*. Durham, NC: Duke University Press, 2012.

Baik, Crystal Mun-hye. "Unfaithful Returns: Reiterations of Dissent, U.S.–Korean Militarized Debt, and the Architecture of Violent Freedom." *Journal of Asian American Studies* 18, no. 1 (2015): 41–72.

Baik, Crystal Mun-Hye, and Jane Jin Kaisen. Introduction to "Korea and Militarized Peace." *Social Text*, December 21, 2018. https://socialtextjournal.org /periscope_article/11908-2/.

Berkman, Seth. "We Were Supposed to Help Asian Migrant Women—Instead We Got Police." *Nation*, September 8, 2022. https://www.thenation.com /article/activism/aesthetic-asian-activism-police/.

Cho, Michelle. "BTS for BLM: K-pop, Race, and Transcultural Fandom." *Celebrity Studies* 13, no. 2 (2022). https://doi.org/10.1080/19392397.2022.2063974.

Dudziak, Mary L. *Cold War Civil Rights: Race and the Image of American Democracy*. Princeton, NJ: Princeton University Press, 2011.

Duggan, Lisa. *The Twilight of Equality? Neoliberalism, Cultural Politics, and the Attack on Democracy*. New York: Beacon, 2004.

Hall, Lisa Kahaleole. "Which of These Things Is Not Like the Other: Hawaiians and Other Pacific Islanders Are Not Asian Americans, and All Pacific Islanders Are Not Hawaiian." *American Quarterly* 67, no. 3 (2015): 727–47.

Hamid, Sarah T., and Rachel Kuo. "Towards Collective Safety: Transformative Methodologies." SSRN. *First Monday: Special Issue on Online Harm and Abuse*, September 7, 2022. https://papers.ssrn.com/sol3/papers.cfm ?abstract_id=4212651.

Kim, Monica. *The Interrogation Rooms of the Korean War: The Untold History*. Princeton, NJ: Princeton University Press, 2019.

Klein, Christina. *Cold War Orientalism: Asia in the Middlebrow Imagination, 1945–1961*. Berkeley: University of California Press, 2003.

Kuo, Rachel, and Salonee Bhaman. "Attacks on Asian Women Are Fueled by Criminalization, War and Economic Injustice." *Truthout*, March 23, 2021. https://truthout.org/articles/attacks-on-asian-women-are-fueled-by -criminalization-war-and-economic-injustice/.

Kuo, Rachel, and Matthew Bui. "Against Carceral Data Collection in Response to Anti-Asian Violences." *Big Data and Society* 8, no. 1 (January–June 2021). https://doi.org/10.1177/20539517211028252.

Lee, Sharon Heijin. "Beauty between Empires: Global Feminism, Plastic Surgery, and the Trouble with Self-Esteem." *Frontiers: A Journal of Women Studies* 37, no. 1 (2016): 1–31.

Lowe, Lisa. *Immigrant Acts: On Asian American Cultural Politics*. Durham, NC: Duke University Press, 1996.

Melamed, Jodi. *Represent and Destroy: Rationalizing Violence in the New Racial Capitalism*. Minneapolis: University of Minnesota Press, 2011.

Nguyen, Mimi Thi. "The Biopower of Beauty: Humanitarian Imperialisms and Global Feminisms in an Age of Terror." *Signs* 36, no. 2 (Winter 2011): 359–84.

Reddy, Chandan. *Freedom with Violence: Race, Sexuality, and the US State*. Durham, NC: Duke University Press, 2011.

Rodríguez, Dylan. "The Asian Exception and the Scramble for Legibility." *Society and Space*, April 8, 2021. https://www.societyandspace.org/articles/the-asian-exception-and-the-scramble-for-legibility-toward-an-abolitionist-approach-to-anti-asian-violence.

Saranillio, Dean Itsuji. *Unsustainable Empire: Alternative Histories of Hawai'i Statehood*. Durham, NC: Duke University Press, 2018.

Tseng-Putterman, Mark. "On Vincent Chin and the Kind of Men You Send to Jail." Asian American Writers' Workshop, *Margins*, June 23, 2017. https://aaww.org/vincent-chin-the-kind-of-men/.

Tseng-Putterman, Mark. "Policing the Borders of Anti-Asian Violence." ROAR *Magazine*, April 29, 2021. https://roarmag.org/essays/anti-asian-racism-american-imperialism/.

Whitlock, Kay, and Michael Bronski. *Considering Hate: Violence, Goodness, and Justice in American Culture and Politics*. New York: Beacon, 2016.

Youn, Soo. "Inside BTS's Landmark White House Visit to Denounce Anti-Asian Hate." *Teen Vogue*, June 1, 2022. https://www.teenvogue.com/story/bts-white-house-visit-2022.

16 · Recoding the Bot: ARMY and Digital Transgression

— Andrea L. Acosta

On Sunday night, April 3, 2022, CBS aired the annual Grammy Awards to a reported audience of just under 9.6 million total viewers.[1] Nielsen, the company that measures audience data for much of the US music industry and its associated media, included in this count both those who watched the broadcast directly on CBS and those who livestreamed the show via Paramount+ and other platforms. Nielsen did not include, however, the uncountable thousands of viewers watching the Grammy Awards through illegal and pirated livestreams online. While nearly every major award show and sports game sees unsanctioned streams crop up on the internet, the 2022 Grammy Awards experienced particularly high numbers of unofficial viewers on account of BTS. The group's nomination and performance at that year's ceremony prompted the spread of several unauthorized links to the show across social media, allowing fans who otherwise lacked access to the official broadcast, both in the US and abroad, to view the ceremony live.

A predictable game of cat and mouse between fan streamers and copyright enforcers ensued: the former uploading pirated streams across different platforms, the latter racing to report and remove them for violation of copyright and platform terms of service. But while copyright enforcers worked quickly (one of the fandom's most well-known anonymous streamers had a live feed taken down within the first five minutes of the show), fans worked faster, setting up two (or more) new streams for every single link taken down. For every platform that responded quickly to copyright claims, another existed that would take more time to do so. For every fan account reported, a second backup account existed—and if the backup account failed, dozens more fans were willing to step in.

I take this flexibility and platform-savvy intelligence as representative of ARMY's collective digital power—a power manifested throughout the fandom's history as it supported the rise of BTS in the US and other Western music industries. ARMY moves so proficiently online, in fact, that outside observers and algorithms alike have understood fans to be more "bot" than human. The *bot*, a general term for digital automated agents, refers on a technical level to a program that performs artificial labor online with varying capacities for "adaptability," "reasoning," and "autonomy."[2] In a more figurative sense, however, the bot signals the undesired and undesirable presence of the nonhuman in digital space: the security threat of phishing email, the intrusive text of online advertisement, the unsettling sense that a fellow user might not be as human as they seem. These derogatory associations merge with the bot's technical reputation for proficient labor and efficiency to create a figure that exists on the fringe of digital citizenship.

Correspondingly, the routine association of ARMY with bots has often worked to the disadvantage of both the fan community and BTS members themselves. Take, for instance, the February 2020 incident when YouTube discarded nearly 40 million views from a newly released BTS video as part of "standard precautions taken against bots"—a move that, at the time, directly affected a fan-organized effort to set a new music video debut record and lowered BTS's official streaming count overall.[3] Fans looping the video too many times, or otherwise viewing it *too* repetitively, triggered the (mis)reading of fan activity as bot activity by the algorithm designed to filter such views out. In this and several similar incidents across Spotify, Apple Music, and other streaming platforms, fans' systematic, proficient, or purposeful engagement with BTS's music is relentlessly coded as artificial, either as the automated work of bots or as an excessively "bot-like" bid to achieve certain chart results at the expense of so-called organic music consumption.

As BTS fans moved to forge a legitimate space for Korean artists in Western music markets, the association of BTS's fandom with bots or bot-like tactics largely functioned as a rhetoric of industry exclusion. A comment by one *Billboard* staff writer in a published 2021 roundtable on the US Billboard Hot 100 Chart illustrates this framing particularly well: "As long as BTS is going to sell as many copies as they need to stay on top each week," they remark, "No. 2 debuts are basically the new No. 1 debuts."[4] The comment renders BTS's achievement of staying at the number one position for multiple weeks inorganic—a result of chart manipulation and overzealous purchasing by fans—in comparison to the implicitly passive, and thus more organic or genuine, achievement of other artists on the chart. Tellingly, the roundtable puts forward no equivalent suspicion of US recording companies and their own gamified methods of promotion, advertising, and purchasing strategies for placing artists on the Billboard Charts. Media narratives such as these—with their ambiguous suggestions of illegitimacy or artificiality, their saying-without-saying that BTS does not organically or naturally belong—have been a staple of BTS's Western industry success since the band's US breakthrough in 2017.

That a discourse of artificiality and bot metaphors emerged around an Asian act breaking through into a US arena of cultural power is no coincidence. The figure of the bot (and its predecessor, the robot) has historically underwritten techno-orientalist imaginings of Asian identity and continues to do so in ways both obvious and subtle. By "techno-orientalist," I mean the association of futurity and technology with Asian bodies in a way that, while it might seem progressive, nonetheless reproduces a "representational containment" of Asian identity.[5] Far from a flattering comparison, it works to render Asians "predictable" and "reified as Oriental" through the terms of the robotic: strange in its alterity and, ultimately, unincorporated into, or undesired by, Western ideas of normative belonging.[6] The conflation of the bot with K-Pop and K-Pop's associated fandoms is simply the most recent iteration of a historically racialized trope, updated for the digital era.

Understanding this to be the case, I am interested not only in the way the bot functions in a techno-orientalist vein but also in how BTS fans work to reclaim and redeploy the techno-orientalist figure of the bot toward their own ends. The relentless flexibility and platform-savvy intelligence of ARMY online frequently underwrites the strength of their digital power. I maintain, in fact, that the dismissive remarks of Western commentators respond to the profound cultural impact BTS fans have achieved through precisely these bot-like methods. In this sense, while I acknowledge BTS fans have expended significant time and energy on rejecting the label of the bot—arguing for their own humanity in the face of an industry that routinely denies it—I ask instead what the bot can offer. Rather than rejecting the label of the bot as a derogatory one, what power do fans uncover by its embrace?

Namely, if the bot is a figure leveraged for racist and techno-orientalist exclusion, we might reimagine it as open to reclamation by the minoritarian communities targeted by such exclusions. José Esteban Muñoz's "minoritarian"—a broad term that refers to subjects who exist at a remove from normative power or social belonging—responds well to the way online K-Pop fan demographics are often complicated and multifaceted, yet largely self-identify as a majority nonwhite, femme, and queer community.[7] This is not to say that BTS fans do not include majoritarian subjects as well but rather that the large-scale issues facing the fandom, and its conflation with Asian culture by outside observers, routinely place the fandom at odds with Western systems of power and belonging. In this context, fans' deliberate and voluntary bot-like behavior functions as a useful praxis of moving within and against the systems they choose to influence. Of these systems, the US music industry represents the most common object of critique but, as was made evident during the Black Lives Matter protests of 2020, the same techniques can and have been deployed by BTS fans in contexts of broader political movements.

With this history in mind, performances of "botness" online might work not just in a conservative and capitalist vein—that is, as a strategy for consuming commercial music more effectively—but also as a fundamentally minoritarian and distinctly digital mode of engagement with the political.[8] Understanding the bot as a venue for minoritarian strategy or protest opens it to the possibility of reclamation from techno-orientalist work and, critically, (re)frames it as an available method for subversive movement and creative escape, particularly for people of color online. Attending to the ways BTS fans perform botness uncovers, too, the way such performances might deconstruct the boundary between human and bot that polices who may be considered human—and who is otherwise delegitimized or excluded.

Spam and/as Protest

In the years since BTS's 2013 debut, ARMY has leveraged strategies of anonymity, spam, and obfuscation, as well as their savvy understanding of platforms and algorithms, to achieve their goals. Spam in particular has emerged as a shared aesthetic form, community in-language, and style of humor for the fandom. Its ubiquitous aesthetic (keyboard smashes, repetitive posting, a hyperbolic, almost advertisement-esque affect) across ARMY's digital spaces positioned spam as an early and intuitive tool for fandom protest and political organizing. Accordingly, in the immediate aftermath of the police murder of George Floyd in May 2020, fan-authored spam emerged as a primary tactic by which ARMY voiced support for the Black Lives Matter cause. Fans on Twitter (a platform known within the ARMY community for having an organized group of fans that perform significant promotional work and discourse management around BTS-related media) responded to the growing political movement with a coordinated spam-like campaign targeting Twitter's Worldwide Trend list.

For context, ARMY was by this point well versed in leveraging Twitter's Worldwide Trends list toward goals such as promoting new music releases, celebrating award show wins, or revising mainstream media narratives about BTS. In each case, fans communicated an agreed-upon message or hashtag en masse through the global fanbase network across Twitter. For this political effort, then, they needed only to deploy an existing network to hijack white-supremacist-trending topics toward their own ends. The strategy relied on sheer numbers and repetitive persistence to overwhelm hashtags like #WhiteLivesMatter, #BlueLivesMatter, and #AllLivesMatter with falsely tagged K-Pop videos and photos, to the point where the Twitter algorithm began to categorize hashtags like #WhiteLivesMatter under the "K-Pop" category of Trending Topics.[9] While the strategy proved controversial—some fans, including several Black fans, made the point that flooding the tag with K-Pop content effectively boosted the hashtag and prolonged the trend life of a distressing phrase—the collective effort did functionally drown out the misinformation, racist conversation, and right-wing organizing under these hashtags. Fans pushed the same technique across other platforms and communities, as users on Instagram and TikTok used the strategy to perform similar work. On May 30, 2020, for instance, K-Pop fans and TikTok users teamed up to spam the Dallas, Texas, police department's local surveillance app, iWatchDallas, with videos of K-Pop idols to protect protesters who would otherwise be exposed to arrest.[10] The spam initiative in this case worked in concrete and direct ways, as the app crashed within a day and forced the Dallas Police Department to find alternate routes of protest surveillance.

The value of this type of spam-oriented, bot-like protest is perhaps most evident in the right-wing response to (and visible confusion over) K-Pop fans' political activity online. One Twitter user posted in June 2020, "SPAM & CHINA INFILTRATION ALERT!: WHEN U SEE ANY kpop HASHTAG/TREND DOWNGRADING OUR PRESIDENT, ITS [sic] REALLY FAKE BOTS FROM CHINA TRYNIG [sic] INTO OUR PAGES. . . . WHEN U SEE "KPOP" BULLSHIT, REPORT IT 4 ABUSE OR SPAM."[11] The racist slippage between Korean and Chinese nationalities—and the accusation that media from the former operates as a front for the cyberwarfare of the latter—represented a common line of argument from right-wing users in response to K-Pop fans' viral protest activity. A different tweet posted two days later asked, "What are all these 'anime' 'kpop' Chinese bots popping up all over twitter against Trump? A few months back you never saw this."[12] The messy conflation of K-Pop fans with "SPAM," "CHINA," "FAKE BOTS," and Japanese "anime" captures the coordinates of racist imaginings around Asian presence in US cyberspace. Yet, this orientalist conflation offers, perversely,

an opportunity for obfuscated movement. When other users and outside observers cannot immediately parse the origin of digital activity—whether it is
done by bots or humans, Korean nationals or Black American K-Pop fans—it
becomes difficult to interrupt or track down the individuals involved and even
more difficult to strategize against them. Indeed, despite spamming the surveillance app in Dallas and mobilizing against other surveillance initiatives,
there has been to date no known retaliation against, or direct punishments
for, fans' various spam attacks—likely due to the legal and logistical difficul-
ties of tracking down the participants in an anonymized global digital campaign. In this way, the techno-orientalist conflation of humans with bots, and
the confusion it generates around user identity, worked as an asset to digital
protest.

Moving in the Gaps

BTS fans therefore take up not only spam's ability for practical and concrete
disruption but also its refusal to be pinned down. As Finn Brunton reminds us,
the filters designed to identify and prevent spam are relentlessly imperfect
and in perpetual need of development. They depend on constant feedback
to achieve a certain threshold of success due, in fact, to the very *impossibility*
of a reliable set of criteria to distinguish bots from humans.[13] Bot behavior,
after all, is not static. It evolves alongside, and in response to, the programs
designed to filter it out. In the resulting feedback loop, spambots find increasingly sophisticated ways of bypassing spam filters, while filter programs develop increasingly nuanced criteria for parsing bot from human. The resulting
gap between the movements of bots online and their identification by filter
programs creates something beyond just the conservative idea of a security
weakness in the system. It also generates a productive opacity and refusal of
legibility. A user might deliberately pass as bot instead of human—or develop
a program that seems human when it is not. The opaque movement these
misreadings make possible, and the digital subterfuge they enable, opens
distinct avenues of protest and influence online. Even acknowledging the
vulnerability of such avenues to bad-faith actors and conservative interests,
it is worth underscoring their equal possibilities for minoritarian grassroots
organizing online.

ARMY realizes such possibilities acutely. They conduct acts of protest in
precisely this space between movement and identification online, playing
with the bot's categorical confusion between artificial and human to gener-

ate a profound opportunity for disguise. In doing so, fans take up not only the digital savvy of the bot but its evasion of fixed identity, its investment in evolving ahead of, or deftly slipping past, the official systems that seek to manage it. BTS fans' performance of botness in such moments imbues spam, and the figure of the bot, with political and minoritarian force. In the process, fans implicitly collapse the binary that traditionally holds bot and human apart to expose instead a newly intermediate figure, that of the human-*as*-bot. Ultimately, the human-as-bot offers a model of digital subjecthood whose in-between identity prompts a rethinking of the raced, gendered, and techno-orientalist boundaries of the "human" that have informed digital subjecthood from the start. To break these boundaries is to make room for stranger and more liminal possibilities of what it means to define the human in digital space.

Notes

1   David Bauder, "Grammys Barely Move the Needle in Television Ratings," Associated Press, April 5, 2022, https://apnews.com/article/grammy -awards-duke-blue-devils-mens-basketball-entertainment-sports -business-4bbb1ba9c9e2f2a23c2385de3f6ca34e.

2   LeBeuf, Storey, and Zagalsky, "Software Bots."

3   Brendan Wetmore, "YouTube Responds to BTS Video View Concerns," *Paper*, February 28, 2020, https://www.papermag.com/bts-on-views -youtube-delete.

4   Billboard Staff, "Five Burning Questions: Lil Nas X and Jack Harlow's 'Industry Baby' Debuts at No. 2 on the Billboard Hot 100," *Billboard*, August 3, 2021, https://www.billboard.com/pro/lil-nas-x-industry-baby -five-burning-questions/.

5   Roh, Huang, and Niu, *Techno-Orientalism*, 3.

6   Roh, Huang, and Niu expand on techno-orientalism's relationship to the originary concept of Edward Said's "orientalism" with the following: "Whereas [Said's] imagined 'Orient' frames the present through the past by detaining the East in a timeless limbo of stagnation in service to the West's desire for self-identification, techno-Orientalism sheds light on technology as the operational mechanism of Orientalism" (*Techno-Orientalism*, 3). See also Nakamura, *Cybertypes*, 63–64.

7   Muñoz, "Introduction: Performing Disidentifications," 1–8.

8   Taina Bucher uses the term *botness* to refer to a mode of behavior or style of speech associated with algorithms and automated technology. Bucher, "About a Bot: Hoax, Fake, Performance Art," *Media/Culture Journal*

17, no. 3 (2014), https://www.journal.media-culture.org.au/index.php
/mcjournal/article/view/814.

9   @My_Meatloaf, "gotta love the kpop stans for taking over," Twitter,
June 3, 2020, 12:38 p.m., https://twitter.com/My_Meatloaf/status
/1268218060701347843.

10   Zoë Haylock, "K-Pop Stans Spammed the Dallas Police Department's
App with Fan Cams," *Vulture*, June 1, 2020, https://www.vulture.com
/2020/06/k-pop-stans-crashed-dallas-police-app-with-fan-cams.html.

11   @CBRLTWPMluvsMCS, "SPAM & CHINA INFILTRATION ALERT," Twitter,
June 14, 2020, 7:24 p.m., https://twitter.com/CBRLTWPMluvsMCS/status
/1272308956963061760.

12   @killiansdad66, "What are all these 'anime' 'kpop' Chinese bots popping
up all over twitter against Trump? A few months back you never saw
this," Twitter, June 16, 2020, 7:24 p.m., https://twitter.com/killiansdad66
/status/1273079041721950208 (account has since been suspended).

13   Brunton, *Spam*, 126.

Works Cited

Brunton, Finn. *Spam: A Shadow History of the Internet*. Cambridge, MA: MIT Press,
2013.

LeBeuf, Carlene, Margaret-Anne Storey, and Alexey Zagalsky. "Software Bots."
Software Technology 35, no. 1 (January/February 2018): 18–23. http://chisel
.cs.uvic.ca/pubs/lebeuf-IEEESoftware2018.pdf.

Muñoz, José Esteban. "Introduction: Performing Disidentifications." *Disidentifications: Queers of Color and the Performance of Politics*, 1–8. Minneapolis:
University of Minnesota Press, 1999.

Nakamura, Lisa. *Cybertypes: Race, Ethnicity, and Identity on the Internet*. New York:
Routledge, 2002.

Roh, David S., Betsy Huang, and Greta A. Niu, eds. *Techno-Orientalism: Imagining
Asia in Speculative Fiction, History, and Media*. New Brunswick, NJ: Rutgers
University Press, 2015.

17 · Break the Structure: BTS ARMY Digital Activism and State Surveillance in Indonesia's Omnibus Law Protest _ Karlina Octaviany

On October 5, 2020, Indonesian BTS ARMY protested the Omnibus Law, a controversial bill ostensibly about job creation, passed by the House of Representatives (Dewan Perwakilan Rakyat, or DPR). The 1,000-page bill proposed the amendment of 79 existing laws and 1,200 clauses, simplifying bureaucracy for foreign investors at the expense of environmental and labor protections.[1] Promoted as a bill encouraging job creation, the controversial law cut minimum wages and removed sick leave provisions, severance pay, and job security amid the COVID-19 pandemic and subsequent massive layoffs. Met with protests and acts of civil disobedience even as the bill was being drafted in January 2020, the Omnibus Law was abruptly passed three days before schedule and before a final copy was available to citizens for public consultation and transparency.

On October 6, the police announced that 5,198 people had been detained in protests around the country. Two days later, October 8, 15,000 more demonstrators took to the streets in over forty cities, resulting in clashes with the police. The protests led to uprisings in Jakarta and other cities and, without any proof, students were blamed for acts such as setting fire to public facilities. The protesters comprised a coalition of fifteen activist groups and trade unions, and included ARMY and other K-Pop fans, especially ARMY university students. The online student movement against Indonesia's House of Representatives and the government began, over social media in 2019, with the hashtag #ReformasiDikorupsi (#ReformCorrupted). Reformasi Dikorupsi was a movement protesting the revision of the Criminal Code or RKUHP in the Indonesian Legal System and the revision of the KPK (Corruption Eradication Commission) Law by the House of Representatives that would weaken the nation's anti-corruption agency. The revisions included articles that would characterize online protest as a crime of undermining the government and creating public unrest. Criticism of the government could be reframed as causing civil disorder, and protesters could face up to four years of jail time. And yet the student movement continued to protest the Omnibus Law.

Online, BTS ARMY was at the vanguard of K-Pop fans who opposed the Omnibus Law and deployed trending hashtags #MosiTidakPercaya (vote of no confidence), #DPRRIKhianatiRakyat (House of Representatives betrays the people), and #TolakOmnibusLaw (reject Omnibus Law). ARMY circulated pictures of student protests with signage declaring their ARMY affiliation, such as "I'm ARMY of BTS, but today I'm ARMY of Indonesian people" or flashing their ARMY Bomb light sticks at demonstrations (see figure 17.1).[2] Anonymous ARMY also released a social media statement against the Omnibus Law, appropriating BTS's positive message to encourage others to act on social issues of inequality. Due to social distancing measures during the COVID-19 pandemic, many ARMY activists posted photos from the 2019 RKUHP protest captioned with #TolakOmnibusLaw. In an interview with one of the anonymous ARMY activists about their post, they joked about not seeing a "meatball seller" in front of the house.[3] During Soeharto's dictatorship (1968–98), students who participated in political movements were surveilled by government intel disguised as street hawkers. Activists often joke about fried rice or bakso/meatball sellers in front of one's house as code for government surveillance.

In response to the Omnibus Law protests online, Indonesia's National Police Chief issued an order to ban political rallies from October 6 to October 8, citing the pandemic, and released instructions for "cyber patrols" to monitor protest planning, "clear hoaxes" related to Omnibus Law counternarratives, and framing protesters as antigovernment agitators and rioters. This chapter examines ARMY activists' social media practices during the Indonesia Omnibus Law protests to consider how ARMY digital activism maps the potential of contemporary collective action and, correspondingly, how it illustrates the power of state surveillance against fandom and other social movements.

ARMY's digital activism against the Omnibus Law was challenged by state-sanctioned social media restrictions. National police gathered intelligence to detect popular opposition to the law, which led to surveillance and cyber patrolling. Following the massive protest on October 8, cyber police used the

#HIDUPMAHASISWA

AKU ARMY NYA BTS ♥
TAPI HARI INI
AKU JADI ARMY NYA
RAKYAT INDONESIA

#HIDUPMAHASISWA

17.1 · BTS ARMY protest sign stating, "I'm ARMY of BTS, but today I'm ARMY of Indonesian people," with hashtag #HidupMahasiswa. Photograph courtesy of Luciana, 2019.

2008 Electronic Information and Transaction (ITE) Law to arrest leaders of a new group of Islamic and national activists called the Save Indonesia Coalition, and seven administrators of a WhatsApp group, an Instagram account, and a Facebook page. All were accused of using social media to incite protests that were framed as riots by the Indonesian government.

The government's response to the protests was reminiscent of the horrors of President Soeharto's dictatorship.[4] Soeharto's repressive regime silenced protesters by using propaganda to cast protesters as rioters and anarchists. To suppress the student movement, the regime threatened students with university suspension, kidnapping, and random shooting by the Indonesian Army. Perpetrators of these crimes still have not faced trial. The current government is using similar approaches in the digital sphere, framing protesters as antigovernment and using "cyber patrol" to hunt for protesters.

Cyber patrolling makes use of the 2008 ITE Law, and in particular the defamation articles that allow the government to restrict information and criminalize freedom of expression. According to a position paper written by a coalition of civil society organizations working with the Institute of Criminal Justice Reform, between 2016 and 2020, 96.8 percent of cases, or 744 people, were convicted under articles 27, 28, and 29 of the ITE Law, while 88 percent of cases resulted in imprisonment.[5]

The Southeast Asia Freedom of Expression Network (SAFEnet) has found that public officials are the primary group using the problematic defamation articles to limit information exchanges by shutting down internet access, hacking, and cyberattacks. Using both the Indonesian National Cyber and Encryption Agency and the cybercrime agency within the National Police, the Indonesian government has targeted political protesters by labeling political dissent as a "hoax."[6] The Omnibus Law protests led to an increase in digital attacks on activists, labor unions, and students, presumably by the state. These attacks included the hijacking of WhatsApp numbers and Twitter accounts, as well as doxing and threats made to individuals on WhatsApp and Instagram accounts. Due to state surveillance in Indonesia, the research for this chapter was conducted with safety protocols in place to maintain the anonymity of the activist movement in Indonesia.

Since 2019, before the start of the COVID-19 pandemic, BTS ARMY in Indonesia had already begun showing their growing influence in demonstrations. ARMY were part of the massive street demonstrations that took place in front of the DPR. ARMY protesters uploaded pictures and videos with BTS-related posters quoting RM's UN speech and flashed their ARMY light sticks. Protesters were able to pressure the DPR to halt efforts to revise the RKUHP in 2019, but the DPR revived it in 2022. The Indonesian ARMY were able to further influence the conversation on social media, becoming key opinion leaders and reaching high engagement rates. With only 133 followers, an Indonesia ARMY account, @BEAUTIFULYOONGO, became a top influencer with 11,491 engagements for the 2019 Reformasi Dikorupsi (Reform Corrupted) movement.

Following the fandom's familiar digital strategies for boosting and trending BTS, Indonesian ARMY, also called "Indomy," posted comments with the hashtags on hit tweets, created fan-edits of video demonstrations with BTS songs like "Baepsae" (Silver Spoon) and "Not Today," and built Twitter threads to raise awareness and educate followers and fans alike.

A fan-edited video of "Baepsae" using images of the labor movement gained more than 4,000 views and another using images of the 2019 student protests went viral with more than 35,000 views.[7] The lyrics from "Baepsae" discuss class conflict, oppression in the education system, labor exploitation, and an unjust social order. "Baepsae" refers to a Korean proverb: "If a *baepsae* (a small Korean bird with short legs) tries to walk like a *hwangsae* (a stork), it will break its legs." To translate this into a social allegory, the "baepsae" is a disadvantaged person of low status, and the stork is an elite. The fan-made video gave Indonesian translations of the lyrics, emphasizing the context of "baepsae" as "rakyat jelata" or "proletarian" students, "gold spoon" as "teachers receiving bribes" who forbid students from protesting, and "stork" as the "corrupted high-level government officials and legislative members." Citing the lyrics "the regulation must be changed" in the face of the current regime, the video also shared news articles that described police brutality against student protesters and a university chancellor's threats of sanctions against the students.

Online protests also reused edited video of "Not Today" from the 2019 Reformasi Dikorupsi protests, using the lyrics "Today we fight!" The video included news coverage framing the student movement as "riots," while also providing advice from student movement leaders for avoiding riot allegations and reminders of the importance of democracy for practicing responsive and participatory policymaking. A report titled *Social Network Analytics of Omnibus Law*, published by Drone Emprit, found that academics, NGOs, student organizations, activists, and K-Pop fans made up a large part of the protesters.[8] Researchers found that K-Pop fans who used K-Pop avatars, especially BTS members, as their profile pictures on Twitter, became the top influencers who dominated the conversation against the Omnibus Law. Researchers described a process through which K-Pop fans, who might not have understood the Omnibus Law, learned about the bill through social media and then mobilized their power in numbers to raise the protest hashtags as "Worldwide Trending Topics" on Twitter.[9]

Indonesian ARMY are well aware of the pitfalls of invoking BTS in their political activism. Cast as "crazy," just a bunch of "teenagers" or "stupid girls" involved in fan wars, ARMY activists are often undermined by traditional media, government officials, and netizens. Some ARMY considered the danger of associating BTS with local political movements, fearing backlash to the artists and fandom. Yet using ARMY fandom identity for a collective movement builds strong bonds among individual members. Trust built from daily intimacy through online interaction can create community with potential to affect other arenas of social life. Arts researchers Chang Woongjo and Park Shin-Eui found that the use of social media has intensified fandom, describing BTS ARMY as a "digital tribe."[10] The "ava K-Pop," or online personas of fandom accounts, consist of diverse people from students protesting on the street to feminist and youth activists doing advocacy work. Behind the online movement, many ARMY participants are also activists on the ground, working on diverse concerns linked to BTS, such as youth oppression, restrictive gender norms, and mental health wellness.

When the hashtags for #TolakOmnibusLaw began trending on social media, activists moved through encrypted channels to coordinate BTS ARMY for street mobilization. However, ARMY works like a "rhizome," a decentralized and leaderless community, which made it hard to coordinate and mobilize offline.[11] Learning from previous digital communications demonstrations such as Reformasi Dikorupsi in 2019, activists were aware of "cyber patrols" even while the pandemic made it harder to coordinate offline. In 2019, the Indonesian government suspended all data packages to access social media in the country due to massive demonstrations online and in the street, during which approximately 1,365 student activists were arrested.[12] As a consequence, the student movement learned to use VPNs to avoid government blocking, manipulating the location of the protesters from IP addresses outside Indonesia. The VPN hacks circulated through social media posts by key influencers so the public could continue to monitor the movement through social media.

Later, during the 2020 protest, ARMY activists circulated guidelines on digital safety for protesters on social media. Instructions on how to avoid online surveillance, use VPNs, and access legal aid were provided along with other safety protocols for online and offline demonstrations. On ARMY Day in 2021, Indonesian ARMY held workshops sharing their expertise on personal data protection and cyberattack prevention. In the background, ARMY who also work as activists organized meetings, provided emergency response to chaotic conditions, advocated for arrested protesters, and supported protesters experiencing trauma after state violence.

Fandom Knowledge Transfer for Digital Activism

ARMY activism enabled Indonesian youth to gain knowledge about politics and engage in political protest through digital "connective action."[13] This "new political generation" learns about critical issues by mixing digital media, pop culture, and online youth identity in fandom discussions. After online protests began trending posts on Twitter, the media picked up the posts and circulated news about the involvement by K-Pop fandom. This created a backlash against K-Pop fans. Supporters of the Omnibus Law claimed that ARMY did not understand the bill and only protested because protest was a popular trend on social media. In response, K-Pop fans and youth activists organized Zoom webinars to discuss the Omnibus Law and strategize their digital activism. The promotion of the webinar was spread through closed K-Pop chat groups and networks to circumvent state surveillance.

During the webinar, members of the K-Pop fandom participating in digital activism realized that the trending hashtags lacked context, and agreed to insert their own opinion when posting trending hashtags. ARMY shared their perspectives on the Omnibus Law by presenting on controversial chapters in the bill, ranging from wage theft to gender injustice. Other participants in the webinar shared digital strategies to create a schedule for posting tweets to maximize effectiveness.

While non-ARMY activists questioned the authenticity of ARMY's involvement in the Omnibus Law protests as well as their understanding of complex issues, ARMY responded with criticism of NGOs and activists who used jargon such as "destroying hegemony." ARMY activists use a term called "baby language" as a strategy for explaining complex issues in easy-to-digest metaphors or social media threads. To do so, ARMY activists turn BTS lyrics and memes into protest signs. For example, people made signs with the lyrics "Win No Matter What" from "ON," and the slogan "Ava Korea also students, Indonesia Number One, *Oppa* Number Two,"[14] with funny photos of RM (a.k.a. Kim Namjoon), BTS's leader and spokesperson.[15] People also used quotes from BTS's 2018 UN speech, such as one sign that read, "No matter who you are, where you from, your skin color, your gender identity, SPEAK YOURSELF!— KIM NAMJOON period!!"[16]

The use of humor within the context of fandom jokes and wordplay speaks to the grassroots efforts to build solidarity among youth who identify as ARMY. The anonymity provided by ARMY affiliation creates an inclusive space for online expression. This allows civilians to voice their concerns in an otherwise risky political environment that is unsafe. ARMY affiliation made it possible for people from diverse backgrounds to participate in the protests, without the need for individuals to join political protest groups or legally formalize as civil society organizations. The informality of ARMY activism is preferable to traditional forms of organizing, with an "informal network of social actors" in scattered and loose linkages between anonymous individuals, influencers on social media, fan accounts, and a fan base.[17] This informal co-alition makes it difficult for the government to shut down all protest activities because new groups and accounts can form and grow. The network allows for the circulation of essential resources, safety information, and professional expertise to support protests as a form of solidarity for a common goal. This form of organizing is an alternative to traditional models of structured mobilization. While the Indonesian government can blacklist NGOs for criticizing government policies, the government cannot control ARMY activists in the same way because ARMY is not a singular entity.

Digital Activism vs. State Surveillance

ARMY is a female-dominated fandom and being a part of it comes with the risk of being subjected to patriarchal views of women's activism. AwasKBGO, an online platform initiative focused on preventing online gender-based violence (OGBV), found that female human rights activists were subjected to OGBV, such as hate comments attacking gender identity, trolling, condescending comments, and hate speech.[18]

ARMY activists were treated in a quite similar fashion across political allegiances. Viral trolling by ARMY activists made non-ARMY activists question the motives and credibility of ARMY activists in condescending comments. ARMY was criticized for using BTS songs in discussions about Indonesia's future and were told that ARMY should use Indonesian or patriotic songs. Supporters of the Omnibus Law characterized ARMY as unpatriotic Indonesians obsessed with South Korean musicians. Media and netizens often label ARMY as "militant" in their protection of BTS in fan wars. ARMY activists were accused of using protests against the Omnibus Law as an excuse to promote BTS songs instead of an opportunity to discuss real issues.

At the same time, ARMY activism was so effective that new ava K-Pop accounts sprung up to spread propaganda supporting the Omnibus Law, accounts which were later detected as fake ava K-Pop accounts. An ARMY activist observed in an interview:

Perhaps there is a potential risk with intruders, fake ava K-Pop accounts. But we can detect if the accounts' content is not reflecting K-Pop fandom. Ava K-Pop accounts have no tendency of hardline politics attitudes for Omnibus Law. If they are infiltrated by mimicking ava K-Pop, it will be easier to detect. Because they will only post based on what they need the narrative to be. Fandoms have genuine need to share their feeling. Accounts without cute BTS contents, K-Pop accounts who focus only on politics, it's impossible.[19]

Notably, donation and charity campaigns have become a regular feature of the fandom to support diverse causes, though these online campaigns are again not without risks. ARMY's #MatchAMillion donation for the Black Lives Matter movement in the United States gained global attention after raising USD$1 million in twenty-four hours. In Thailand, ARMY raised 173,744 baht to support the pro-democracy protest.[20] Due to the safety situation in Indonesia, ARMY activists protesting the Omnibus Law were more cautious after the singer and activist Ananda Badudu was arrested for fundraising in support of the 2019 Reformasi Dikorupsi protest.[21] Through discussion on social media posts, Indonesian ARMY came to a consensus and decided not to open public fundraising efforts under the name of ARMY as a fanbase, but ARMY could give donations through personal channels as individuals.

ARMY activism was a way for youths to participate in a political discussion from which they were otherwise excluded, even though the Omnibus Law would have a direct impact on their lives. Lobbying against the Omnibus Law to the House of Representatives is done behind closed doors, and only senior activists and international NGOs have access. As affected stakeholders, youth were overlooked and not invited to the discussion—so they used their skills to create their own spaces to be heard. The Omnibus Law protest showed a different perspective on ARMY's supposed "militancy" as part of a larger social movement.

Media highlighted ARMY's role in leading the protest movement to take action to raise awareness. Non-K-Pop activists reached out to ARMY to join forces to mobilize. Civil society organizations against the Omnibus Law involved ARMY when giving statements for press releases. The media also covered the importance of ARMY fandom in implementing digital activism against the Omnibus Law. The joint forces of ARMY and other K-Pop fandoms forced the media and other activists to realize the potential of ARMY as a new civil society power outside of NGO and activist affiliations.

Conclusion

Amid a global pandemic, Indonesian ARMY's activism had a major impact in accelerating awareness of the Omnibus Law and consolidating social opposition. Indonesian ARMY used translated and altered BTS lyrics to apply their critiques to local contexts and deployed sophisticated knowledge of social media algorithms and their manipulation. ARMY also pooled their collective expertise to create safe spaces for connecting and learning with inclusive language and easy-to-digest anecdotes to discuss concerns about the law.

Fandoms therefore can use their knowledge of social media platforms for digital activism and mobilizing public pressure for policy change. Though protests failed to cancel the Omnibus Law, ARMY involvement in Omnibus Law digital activism shows the promising future of using K-Pop fandoms to mobilize grassroots power and expose the threat of digital state surveillance. To this end, agents of civil society must learn from ARMY and develop meaningful participation through inclusive language and knowledge sharing, while also fighting the stigma that weakens the potential for ARMY fandom to become involved in movements. Furthermore, more powerful agencies such as NGOs also need to provide risk mitigation against online gender-based violence and legal rights assistance to ensure the safety of participating youth.

With rising political tensions and future presidential elections, ARMY digital activism has the potential to become a new force in the social movement ecosystem in Indonesia. In doing so, Indonesian ARMY activists insist that ARMY put humanity in the forefront of their movement: "ARMY is a home and family. When we know another ARMY experiences life-threatening conditions, we see the matter as cross-border, no longer nation, but as a human. We can see basic human instinct when we see others in danger and our willingness to help."[22]

Notes

1   CNN Indonesia, "Imbas Demo Omnibus Law, Ditangkap Polisi hingga Orang Hilang."

2   Paramitha and Firmansyah, "Ngakak!"

3   Anonymous ARMY activist, Instagram direct message to the author, May 30, 2017.

4   Hamid and Hermawan, "Indonesia's Shrinking Civic Space for Protests and Digital Activism."

5	Institute for Criminal Justice Reform et al., *Kertas Kebijakan*.
6	Hamid and Hermawan, "Indonesia's Shrinking Civic Space for Protests and Digital Activism."
7	Multifandom Ketcjeh, "BTS—Baepsae (Silver Spoon) Lirik Video Tolak UU Omnibus Law"; Ethereal Flower, "Dewan Penghianat Rakyat."
8	Rahman, "Ruu Omnibus Law Disahkan, K-Popers Strike Back."
9	Rahman, "Ruu Omnibus Law Disahkan, K-Popers Strike Back."
10	Chang and Park, "The Fandom of *Hallyu*, a Tribe in the Digital Network Era."
11	Lee, BTS, *Art Revolution*.
12	BBC News Indonesia, "Demo Mahasiswa."
13	Sastramidjaja, "Indonesia."
14	*Oppa* is Korean for *older brother*.
15	Paramitha and Firmansyah, "Ngakak!"
16	Translation by the author.
17	Grant, "Informal Social Movements," 252–53.
18	Awas KBGO is an online platform initiative from SAFEnet focusing on consultation and support for privacy and digital security to prevent OGBV (abbreviated KBGO in Indonesian). See "Services," Awas KBGO (website), accessed February 7, 2024, https://awaskbgo.id/layanan; SAFEnet, *Kami Jadi Target*.
19	Interview with ARMY activist in Indonesia by the author, April 8, 2021.
20	Khaosod English, "K-Pop Fans Raise Millions for Pro-Democracy Protest."
21	Nugraha and Afifa, "Police Arrest Ananda Badudu in Ties to Students Protest's Funding."
22	Interview with ARMY activist in Indonesia by the author, April 8, 2021.

Works Cited

BBC News Indonesia. "Demo Mahasiswa: Sebagian Pedemo Sudah Dilepaskan, Banyak Yang Masih Ditahan." October 15, 2019. https://www.bbc.com/indonesia/indonesia-50039337.

Chang, Woongjo, and Shin-Eui Park. "The Fandom of *Hallyu*, a Tribe in the Digital Network Era: The Case of ARMY of BTS." *Kritika Kultura* 32 (2019): 260–87. https://doi.org/10.13185/kk2019.03213.

CNN Indonesia. "Imbas Demo Omnibus Law, Ditangkap Polisi hingga Orang Hilang." October 13, 2020. https://www.cnnindonesia.com/nasional/20201013082314-12-557691/imbas-demo-omnibus-law-ditangkap-polisi-hingga-orang-hilang.

Ethereal Flower. "Dewan Penghianat Rakyat, DPR Penghianat Indonesia || BTS—'Baepsae' 뱁새 (Silver Spoon) [SUB INDO]." October 6, 2020, YouTube video, 3:53. https://www.youtube.com/watch?v=Dve9Uv_VUR4.

Grant, Robert. "Informal Social Movements." In *Conventions, Treaties and Other Responses to Global Issues*, edited by Tom Cioppa, 249–63. Vol. 2 of *Encyclopedia of Life Support Systems*. Oxford: EOLSS/UNESCO, 2009. Available at https://www.eolss.net/sample-chapters/c14/E1-44-03-08.pdf.

Hamid, Usman, and Ary Hermawan. "Indonesia's Shrinking Civic Space for Protests and Digital Activism." Carnegie Endowment for International Peace, November 17, 2020. https://carnegieendowment.org/2020/11/17/indonesia-s -shrinking-civic-space-for-protests-and-digital-activism-pub-83250.

Institute for Criminal Justice Reform et al. *Kertas Kebijakan: Catatan Dan Desakan Masyarakat Sipil atas Revisi UU ITE*. April 15, 2021. https://icjr.or.id/wp -content/uploads/2021/04/kertas_posisi_revisi_UU_ITE.pdf.

Khaosod English. "K-Pop Fans Raise Millions for Pro-Democracy Protest." October 19, 2020. https://www.khaosodenglish.com/net/2020/10/19/k-pop -fans-raise-millions-for-pro-democracy-protest/.

Lee, Jiyoung. BTS, *Art Revolution*. Translated by Stella Kim, Myungji Chae, Jiye Won, and Shinwoo Lee. Seoul: Parrhesia, 2019.

Multifandom Ketcjeh. "BTS—Baepsae (Silver Spoon) Lirik Video Tolak UU Omnibus Law." October 6, 2020. YouTube video, 4:09. https://www.youtube.com /watch?v=gMdOclVRnt4.

Nugraha, Ricky Mohammad, and Laila Afifa. "Police Arrest Ananda Badudu in Ties to Students Protest's Funding." Tempo.co English, September 27, 2019. https://en.tempo.co/read/1252937/police-arrest-ananda-badudu-in-ties -to-students-protests-funding.

Paramitha, Tasya, and Wahyu Firmansyah. "Ngakak! Deretan Poster Kocak K-Popers Ikut Demo Tolak Omnibus Law." Viva.co.id, October 9, 2020. https://www.viva.co.id/showbiz/gosip/1310379-ngakak-deretan-poster -kocak-k-popers-ikut-demo-tolak-omnibus-law.

Rahman, Andi. "Ruu Omnibus Law Disahkan, K-Popers Strike Back." *Drone Emprit Publications*, October 6, 2020. https://pers.droneemprit.id/ruu-omnibus -law-disahkan-k-popers-strike-back/.

SAFEnet. *Kami Jadi Target: Pengalaman Perempuan Pembela HAM Menghadapi Kekerasan Berbasis Gender Online (KBGO)*. Jakarta: Awas KBGO, 2022. https://awaskbgo .id/ppham/.

Sastramidjaja, Yatun. "Indonesia: Digital Communications Energising New Political Generation's Campaign for Democracy." *ISEAS Perspective*, no. 16 (March 2020): 2–6. https://www.iseas.edu.sg/wp-content/uploads/2015 /11/ISEAS_Perspective_2020_16.pdf.

18 · From Purple to Pink: The Filipino ARMY for Leni and the Fight for Good Governance — Allison Anne Gray Atis, Noel Sajid I. Murad, and Hannah Ruth L. Sison

Picture this. A sea of pink made up of a hundred thousand Filipinos marching in the streets, chanting the name "Leni! Leni! Leni!" Brimming with bright hope for the future, this might be the most passionate the crowd has ever been in their lives. Waving banners representing different social groups, from the professional to the absurd, they proudly proclaim themselves to be "Doctors for Leni!," "Artists for Leni!," or "Those with Allergic Rhinitis for Leni!" As part of the Pink Movement in the Philippines during the 2022 national election campaign season, BTS fans formed an important part of Philippine history—a revolution that unified millions of Filipinos in fighting for their political and social dreams. With their light sticks held high, shouting at the top of their lungs, BTS fans in the Philippines showed up as "ARMY for Leni." Embodying the opening lyrics of BTS's single "Not Today," in which RM growls, "All the underdogs in the world / A day may come when we lose / But it is not today / Today we fight!" Filipino ARMY were fighting for a better future for the Philippines by trying to prevent the son of a former dictator from being seated in the highest position of government. ARMY for Leni's hopes were pinned on Maria Leonor "Leni" Robredo, the sitting vice president during the 2022 national election and the lone female candidate for president. Leni Robredo's "Pink Movement" was inspired by the color pink's many meanings, which was translated into one of her main slogans, "*Kulay Rosas Ang Bukas*" (Our tomorrow is pink), symbolizing the yearning for a rosier future. Not long after the campaign announcements, supporters referred to themselves as *Kakampink*, a mash-up of the Tagalog word *kakampi*, roughly translated in English as "ally or teammate," and the word *pink*. The creativity expressed through this portmanteau was rapidly translated into different platforms, forms, outlets, and styles to express support for Robredo.

As vice president under her political opponent Rodrigo Duterte, Robredo was given a small budget. Budget proposals made by the Office of the Vice President were cut by the Department of Budget and Management. Lawmakers made calls to have her budget increased but to no avail. Robredo stated that her office would do their best with whatever budget was given to them.[2] In the aftermath of typhoons that caused massive destruction and major internal displacements, and the rising number of deaths under the COVID-19 pandemic that led to the weakening of the country's healthcare system, Robredo successfully initiated programs for housing and resettlement, poverty reduction, relief operations, and medical frontliner assistance. She took swift and strategic actions to address the needs of those most affected in spite of her limited budget. Leni's brand of leadership—being a leader of the people, for the people—was translated into her campaign and her platforms through slogans summarizing these commitments to truth telling and radical love: "*Sa Gobyernong Tapat, Angat Buhay Lahat*" (With an honest government, all lives are uplifted) and "*Mas Radikal ang Magmahal*" (It is more radical to love).

The 2022 Philippine national election campaign season ran from February 8, 2022, until election day on May 9, 2022, and it was a culturally and historically defining moment for the country. In addition to rallies and events in support of the presidential candidates, the election featured an online battle of misinformation and disinformation regarding the political candidates and their respective platforms. Many different groups, such as KPOP Stans 4 Leni, LGBTQIA+ for Leni, and Creatives for Leni, actively supported Robredo's presidential campaign by participating in creative actions and initiatives in online and offline spaces. Filipino ARMY worked alongside these groups to campaign for good governance, accountability, and transparency.

The Philippines has been the subject of many studies on the spread of misinformation and disinformation, and the 2022 campaign was no exception. The authors of this chapter, as well as being ARMY and Kakampinks, are media and communication scholars, teachers, and practitioners—active witnesses for years to the jarring realities of misleading media campaigns. The Pink Movement thus sought to support a leader who would actively confront aggressive disinformation tactics and the oppressive policies of the Duterte administration. Leni Robredo was viewed to be that leader, as suggested by the moniker the "People's Campaign," which is how news outlets referred to the movement and to which Robredo's camp aspired.[3] From simple gestures of placing pink decorative stars and posters on houses to changing profile photos on Facebook to pink and proactively engaging with people to discuss what was fact and what was not (regardless of the dangers that came with doing so), people were committed to expressing their support. One simple act led to a collectively greater one—being part of online social groups, volunteering, being part of various offline initiatives. Having seen Robredo's record as a beleaguered vice president, "Let Leni Lead!" became a call to action that many Kakampinks, including ARMY, held on to for hope, inspiration, and real unity.

Since 2016, the Philippines has gone through immense changes under the government of Rodrigo Duterte, driven by his vitriol and brazen bravado. His so-called iron fist led to the launch of the infamous "war on drugs" that claimed the lives of thousands. Ironically, some of these unfortunate victims were known to be his staunch supporters. In addition, he silenced multiple media companies that resisted his tyrannical form of government and opposed his removal of due process. He routinely jailed his critics and even publicly insulted world leaders. His administration created a massive troll farm designed to spread hate and misinformation online in order to create division among citizens. The misinformation was effective, causing Filipinos to question reality, truth, and history. In the election for a new leader, Robredo was viewed as the candidate who was clearly opposed to Duterte's legacy and his political (and literal) heirs.[4] As Robredo's campaign gained increasing traction, so did the online attacks attempting to discredit her work, such as claims that typhoon relief goods were of subpar quality, that her projects favored only the elite, and that her positions on sociopolitical issues were weak. The aggressive tactics of Duterte's camp, prevalent since the 2016 election campaigns, unsurprisingly built on the misogyny of his presidency and "often targeted high-profile women, such as current Vice-President and 2022 presidential candidate Leni Robredo."[5]

For the Kakampinks, the 2022 Philippine national election campaign was not only a battle to replace Duterte's iron fist with Robredo's radical love; it was a battle over truth and history. Robredo's strongest opponent for the presidency, Ferdinand Marcos Jr. (also known as Bongbong Marcos, or BBM), is the son of the late dictator Ferdinand Marcos Sr. and his wife, Imelda Marcos. Marcos Jr. was invested in historical revisionism and rewriting the legacy of his parents and their infamous conjugal dictatorship, known as the Marcos martial law era. In an attempt to erase the murky past of the Marcos family, Marcos Jr. used the infrastructure and practices established by Duterte to run a relentless propaganda campaign against Robredo.

So Can We Get a Little Bit of Hope? The ARMY for Leni

Soon after Robredo filed for her candidacy in October 2021, many of her supporters formed groups identified with her campaign. ARMY for Leni was a subgroup of the Kakampinks that organized through their mutual love of Robredo and BTS. Like the rest of the Kakampinks, they were dedicated to countering the Marcos camp's disinformation campaign but also participated in large-scale campaign activities in support of Robredo. With over 90,000 members, ARMY for Leni volunteered in various missions, donated funds and relief goods, attended rallies, and spread support for Robredo through each of their own networks. Members of ARMY for Leni connected with each other and the campaign not only through in-person events but also through social media.

ARMY for Leni (which changed to ARMY for Leni and Kiko during the height of the campaign season to include her running mate) started a Facebook page that brought together thousands of Filipino ARMY. By connecting BTS fans who were active supporters of Robredo, the Facebook page became an information hub for Robredo's campaign materials and served as a community of practice—a group of people with a collective identity who come together for a social purpose. Not only did the group function as the main source of knowledge and information about Leni's political platform, it was also a site where people could exchange thoughts ranging from Leni's actual campaign to their mutual love for BTS.

The group's Facebook posts called for volunteers to help with both the online and offline activities for the campaign (see figure 18.1). The design of the page reflects the visual and practical merging of Kakampink values of radical love and ARMY *borahae* (a neologism meaning "I purple you," coined by BTS's V as an expression of love). The dominant purple of BTS and ARMY bleeds seamlessly into the pink of Kakampinks to signify the blending of these communities and their values. The page's message exemplifies ARMY and Kakampink's use of social media campaigns in the effort to drive real, on the ground, movement. In some ways, ARMY for Leni can be likened to recent international, organized fandom efforts, most of which were either spearheaded or supported by ARMY, such as the #MatchAMillion for Black Lives Matter, the sinking of the Trump rally in Tulsa, Oklahoma, crashing the Dallas Police Department app, and the sabotaging of racist Twitter hashtags at the height of the Black Lives Matter movement.[6] These online sociopolitical mobilizations, often carried out through social media platforms, grew exponentially due to constraints caused by the COVID-19 pandemic.

ARMY for Leni and Kiko
5 Nov 2021 · ⚙

Change starts within us, with our votes.

Help us achieve a better Philippines. Join us at AFL:
https://t.co/9qZyZDKyzo 💜🎀

#ARMYforLeni #ARMYforPH #LetLeniLead2022

ARMY for Leni
is looking for volunteers!

I believe that real change
lies in the mirror

Change, RM & Wale

How to be a Kakampink ARMY? 🔍

Sign up here
tinyurl.com/AFLVolunteers

👍❤ 30   3 shares

18.1 · ARMY for Leni and Kiko Facebook page call for volunteers. Screenshot from Facebook.

While social media mobilizations did not originate with Kakampinks or ARMY for Leni, ARMY practices had established the effectiveness and impact of such tactics—from fundraising for a local cause to responding to natural disasters. With this experience, ARMY for Leni were able to organize volunteer-driven initiatives such as fundraising activities for underprivileged communities, house-to-house campaigning, mural paintings, and the creation and sale of BTS-inspired merchandise to support Robredo. For ARMY for Leni, the pandemic conditions in the Philippines, and the lack of government-organized relief efforts during the course of the political election season, led to the emergence of mutual aid and volunteer efforts that tied Robredo's message of radical love to material action. Volunteers went out of their homes during the pandemic to provide aid to the less fortunate and survivors of natural calamities, and to advocate for Robredo. The need to provide immediate aid offered an opportunity for a grassroots approach to improving quality of life and was associated with Robredo-led programs and projects.

ARMY for Leni's online battles were just as important as its offline efforts. One goal of Filipino ARMY was to battle the disinformation campaigns of the opposition's trolls through fact-checking over social media. The Marcos camp employed internet trolls and disseminated fake news to assassinate Robredo's character. For instance, BTS was used by the opposition to push the Marcos agenda. From blatantly manipulated photos on Facebook posts claiming BTS members like Jimin supported Marcos Jr. to posts comparing RM's leadership style to Marcos Jr.'s and satirical posts claiming that Jung Kook was the twin of Marcos Jr.'s eldest son, there was a surfeit of absurd fake news that leveraged BTS's popularity. The ARMY for Leni group made sure that these were called out as fake and did their part in sharing and disseminating what was real and factual. A specific online campaign created by another group, KPop Stans 4 Leni, was shared by ARMY for Leni for its clever message design in dealing with online trolls and disinformation. Using songs and messaging from BTS, they asked if fake news made people feel "UGH" and the need to clean up the digital "Mikrokosmos" by telling trolls "Not Today." The post also provided ways to identify a troll's "DNA," suggested how to "Make It Right," and reminded everyone to *LOVE YOURSELF.*[7]

ARMY for Leni leveraged a multitude of intertextual content and pop culture references in posts and comments to help Robredo's political message go viral. Its Facebook page members used memes that were easily identifiable to ARMY and also the general Filipino audience. One such "memeified" moment was a video edit of excerpts of Robredo's speech during a presidential debate superimposed over instrumental BTS music. In the short video, Robredo seemingly raps her vice-presidential achievements during the pandemic in the rapid-fire style of Agust D (the solo alter ego of BTS's SUGA), backed by the driving baseline of his single "대취타 (Daechwita)." The fact that this song describes the toppling of a tyrant resonates with this political moment. The caption on the post also connects "LENI SUNBAENIM" with "Agust D" using an X, which gestures to the artistic and political collaboration implied in the "music video."

ARMY for Leni used humor as an effective political tool on social media. Another meme repurposed a popular 2022 Grammy Awards moment that went viral among ARMY—when V whispered to Filipino American pop star Olivia Rodrigo during the prologue to their "Butter" performance (see figure 18.2). ARMY fans all over the world wondered what V whispered in her ear. In a still image of the flirtatious exchange, set in a hot pink background, that question is answered by V's injunction to "LET LENI LEAD," one of Robredo's slogans.

18.2 · A recontextualized meme of the still shot from the famous 2022 Grammy Awards segment featuring BTS's V and Olivia Rodrigo. Screenshot from Facebook.

This moment demonstrates how Robredo volunteers campaigned on the ground—instead of using aggressive and hard-sell tactics, they approached people with love, kindness, and humor, the soul of Robredo's campaign message. The meme was particularly effective given Filipinos' identification of Olivia Rodrigo as one of our own, especially among Gen Z Filipinos. According to the *Philippine Star*, a national newspaper, she is the "Rodrigo we're all proud of."[8]

As fans enmeshed in Korean pop culture, ARMY for Leni harnessed their strengths as fans in producing merchandise, organizing events, and streaming music, merging their fandom savvy with their political message. The group created "merch" using designs created by ARMY for Leni members to raise money for the Leni-Kiko campaign (see figure 18.3). The designs incorporated references to BTS, such as the whale and line drawings reminiscent of the *LOVE YOURSELF* trilogy album cover art. Other items for sale included posters, masks, pins, baller bands, and sticker sets.

ARMY for Leni also turned to their streaming prowess as BTS fans to support their political "idol." Tactics often denigrated by music critics and fans of other musical performers as chart manipulation included mobilization through streaming parties. ARMY for Leni boosted campaign songs composed

18.3 · Popular campaign merchandise—the Leni-Kiko ARMY Kit. Screenshot from Facebook.

ARMY for Leni and Kiko
18 Feb · ⚙

🎤HAPPY HOBI DAY🎤

WTS LFB PH

🎤LENI KIKO ARMY KIT🎤
PHP 550
ETA: MAR 12
MOP: GCash
MOD: SDD or Courier
🔗tinyurl.com/AFLKits

Get your own kit now and complete your #hopefit 😊

#ARMYforLeni #LeniKikoArmyKit
#RosasAngKulayNgBukas #LeniAngatSaLahat
#10LeniRobredo #7KikoPangilinan #LeniKiko2022

Product Details

LENI – KIKO ARMY KIT

LENI-KIKO ARMY KIT
FULL SHOT

1 TARP

LENI – KIKO ARMY KIT
DETAILS

1 TARP

🎤ONLY 🎤EXCLUSIVE
LENI – KIKO ARMY KIT
PHP 550

Purchase Notice

2. PINS
+5

Add to Cart

203

6 comments · 28 shares

by Kakampink volunteers to the top spots on music-streaming platforms. The songs "Kay Leni Tayo" ("Let's go for Leni") and "Rosas" ("Rose" or "Pink") both snagged top spots in the Philippine charts on music-streaming platforms Spotify and iTunes, proving the power of politicized Filipino fandoms but also drawing from specific ARMY streaming tactics to boost BTS. That Robredo is herself a BTS fan is notable, and her message of love, healing, growth, and hope converged with those associated with BTS. As the end of the campaign approached, and the intensity of the political stakes were highlighted, it almost seemed as if the K-Pop idol and the political "idol" became one through the support and streaming of ARMY for Leni. "Kay Leni Tayo" even surpassed Jung Kook's single "Stay Alive," which was released around the same time on iTunes Philippines, perhaps due to the urgency of ensuring that Robredo received the *daesang* (top award) of the presidency on election day.

As a community of thousands, the ARMY for Leni collectively participated in rallies and campaign events in specific locales around the archipelago. At multiple rallies across the country, each host city held the "Olympinks," a healthy competition showing which city had the highest number of Kakampinks attending. The final campaign in Makati boasted almost a million Kakampinks in attendance. From wide fields in the provinces to the city streets of metro Manila, Kakampinks showed up for their candidate.

ARMY for Leni was a significant player among a larger landscape of groups supporting Leni organized through K-Pop fandoms. Many socially conscious initiatives of the ARMY for Leni group entailed partnerships with other groups organized around K-Pop fandoms, such as Blinks for Leni, CARATS for Leni, ONCE for Leni, NCTzens for Leni, and Reveluvs for Leni. ARMY for Leni joined a K-Pop event for Leni in Manila called the KFiesta, which engaged different K-Pop fandoms and individuals with the shared vision and interest for good governance.[9] Bringing ARMY Bombs and their ARMY for Leni banners, Filipino ARMY were present in all of these rallies, side by side with fans holding different light sticks and wearing merch representing other K-Pop groups. These fandoms—which are usually in competition with each other over their beloved group's chart position, media exposure, popularity polls, or awards on a regular day—found a way to set aside their differences and unite for an important cause. These fandom partnerships reflected what BTS had succinctly described during their 2021 United Nations speech as the "Welcome Generation," the generation who "instead of fearing change . . . says 'welcome' and keeps pushing ahead." In campaign rallies leading to election day, ARMY for Leni, like other Kakampink groups around K-Pop fandoms, shared COVID-19 masks, secured booths to sell their merch and meet with fellow ARMY, and played their group's songs to uplift the mood and prepare us for our battle for good governance.

ARMY for Leni was predominantly made up of young people new to the political scene (see figure 18.4). The playful intertextual language of Generation Z was prevalent in the social media posts of the ARMY for Leni group. Terms like *kween* and *boss*, as well as Korean words like *seonbaenim* (a term

18.4 · "Put Your Light [sticks] Up!": Allison Anne Gray Atis (*left*) and her sister Arradine (*right*), holding an ARMY Bomb, during the Pink Rally in Pasig City, Philippines. Photograph by Allison Anne Gray Atis.

describing someone more senior and experienced in a group) to refer to Robredo and Pangilinan, were popularized by K-Pop and demonstrate ARMY for Leni members' playfulness in the expression of both their collective partisan political identity and their K-Pop fan identity. K-Pop affiliation proved to be an effective way to engage more youth in the political dialogue, and also sparked the curiosity of Filipinos belonging to older generations. Parents became more involved in the political discussions their children—who were often first-time voters—were having with them. At rallies we attended, a common sight was young ARMY for Leni members accompanied by their parents. They shared stories about how their parents were pleasantly surprised that the music of BTS and K-Pop in general were the vehicles through which their children were discovering the political sphere. These political expressions became the parents' introduction to BTS. Suddenly (though not unexpectedly), listening to and appreciating BTS, especially their message of love, healing, growth, and hope, became a family affair distinct from the Marcos tradition.

Until the Spring Day Comes Again

Despite the massive concerted efforts of the Pink Movement, Marcos Jr. won the election. Even though a number of political analysts predicted that his camp would win, the results still came as a shock, especially to Kakampinks. For those eager to experience a different form of leadership built on compassion and transparency, the first week after the election was dark and depressing as the shift from being hopeful to hopeless was terrifying.

Many ARMY for Leni had surprisingly left their comfort zones to actively campaign for Leni. Thousands of Filipinos and Kakampinks had not been this active during past electoral campaigns. Their involvement was driven by a desire to resist oppression, and Robredo had become a remarkable symbol of that fight. Robredo lost not because she was not the best fit for the position, nor because Kakampinks failed her as part of the voting population. She lost in an election backed by millions of pesos' worth of aggressive disinformation tactics.

Life does go on, as the BTS song of the same title notes. Despite the heartbreaking results, Leni Robredo continued to share her message of positivity and inspiration. At a thanksgiving rally held after the election, she called on all the Kakampinks to continue fighting, not for her, but for good governance. On top of this, their camp also introduced the formation of the "*Angat Buhay*" program, which literally translates as "Lift Lives." This program aimed to uplift the lives of many Filipinos and build on the momentum of incredible volunteerism and selflessness spurred by the movement. Most groups supporting Robredo were rejuvenated by this call and changed their names from "for Leni" to "for good governance."

As BTS raps in "Not Today," "A day may come when we lose." Drawing on these lyrics, the ARMY for Leni and Kakampinks may have lost, but they fought hard. Until then, guided by the message of BTS, these people will continue to fight the good fight for a better future for all. *Their moment is yet to come.*

Notes

1   BTS, "Not Today," *You Never Walk Alone*, lyrics transcript, Big Hit, 2017.
2   Mercado, "'Smallest Budget in Bureaucracy.'"
3   Aytona, "Centering the Marginalized"; Cepeda, "Robredo-Pangilinan Want a 'People's Campaign'"; Subingsubing and Ramos, "Robredo."
4   Robredo was elected vice president during Duterte's term as the president. In the Philippines, the president and vice president are elected separately and can come from different political parties.

5   Grounds and Koff, "Disinformation, Disruption, and the Shifting Media Ecosystem in the 2022 Philippines Election."

6   Bruner, "How K-Pop Fans Actually Work as a Force for Political Activism in 2020"; Frenkel, "TikTok Teens and K-Pop Stans Say They Sank Trump Rally"; Park et al., "Armed in ARMY"; Sinha, "K-Pop Stans Successfully Sabotaged Trump's Tulsa Rally."

7   The words with emphasis are titles of BTS tracks.

8   Philstar.com, "The Rodrigo that we're all proud of! 👋 Filipino-American singer Olivia Rodrigo's hit single 'Drivers License' became the first song to surpass 1 billion streams in 2021," Facebook, April 2, 2021, https://www.facebook.com/philstarnews/posts/the-rodrigo-that-were-all-proud-of-filipino-american-singer-olivia-rodrigos-hit-/10165779727190713/.

9   POP!, "A K-Pop Event Like No Other."

Works Cited

Aytona, Pheelyp. "Centering the Marginalized: A People's Campaign." *Rappler*, April 17, 2022. https://www.rappler.com/voices/imho/opinion-centering-marginalized-people-campaign/.

Bruner, Raisa. "How K-Pop Fans Actually Work as a Force for Political Activism in 2020." *Time*, July 25, 2020. https://time.com/5866955/k-pop-political/.

Cepeda, Mara. "Robredo-Pangilinan Want a 'People's Campaign' in 2022." *Rappler*, October 11, 2021. https://www.rappler.com/nation/elections/robredo-pangilinan-want-people-campaign-2022-polls/.

Frenkel, Sheera. "TikTok Teens and K-Pop Stans Say They Sank Trump Rally." *New York Times*, June 21, 2020. https://www.nytimes.com/2020/06/21/style/tiktok-trump-rally-tulsa.html.

Grounds, Kelly, and Madelyn Koff. "Disinformation, Disruption, and the Shifting Media Ecosystem in the 2022 Philippines Election." Asia Pacific Foundation of Canada, May 5, 2022. https://www.asiapacific.ca/publication/election-watch-philippines-dispatch-4-social-media-use.

Mercado, Neil Arwin. "'Smallest Budget in Bureaucracy': Solons Push for Higher OVP Budget." *Philippine Daily Inquirer*, September 14, 2020. https://newsinfo.inquirer.net/1335074/smallest-budget-in-bureaucracy-solons-push-for-higher-ovp-budget.

Park, So Yeon, Nicole Santero, Blair Kaneshiro, and Jin Ha Lee. "Armed in ARMY: A Case Study of How BTS Fans Successfully Collaborated to #MatchAMillion for Black Lives Matter." *Proceedings of the 2021 CHI Conference on Human Factors in Computing Systems* (May 2021): 1–14. https://dl.acm.org/doi/10.1145/3411764.3445353.

POP! "A K-Pop Event Like No Other: KFiesta Brings Fans Together as a Force for Political Activism." POP!, April 29, 2022. https://pop.inquirer.net/327553/a

-k-pop-event-like-no-other-kfiesta-brings-fans-together-as-a-force-for
-political-activism.

Sinha, Charu. "K-Pop Stans Successfully Sabotaged Trump's Tulsa Rally." *Vulture*, June 21, 2020. https://www.vulture.com/2020/06/k-pop-stans
-successfully-sabotaged-trumps-tulsa-rally.html.

Subingsubing, Krixia, and Marlon Ramos. "Robredo: Rare Force and Flair of 'a
People's Campaign.'" *Philippine Daily Inquirer*, May 7, 2022. https://
newsinfo.inquirer.net/1593333/robredo-rareforce-and-flair-of-a-peoples
-campaign.

19 · "Yoongi, Can You Hear Me?": Demanding Justice for #Melisa and ARMY Activism in Turkey — Alptekin Keskin and Mutlu Binark

On September 5, 2020, a fifteen-year-old Turkish girl named Buse Melisa Kılıç committed suicide in response to her father's psychological abuse. In the aftermath, it came to light that Melisa, a high school student and a fan of BTS, had posted messages on her Twitter account addressed to SUGA (a.k.a. Yoongi). Turkish media subsequently ran a headline asking who was responsible for Melisa's death—"the father or Yoongi." The tenor of such media coverage deflected attention away from the father's responsibility in his daughter's death and shifted the blame onto K-Pop and its fandom. Such a framework dramatized the tragedy in such a way that dampened public debate and shielded perpetrators of domestic violence, which is widespread in Turkey. In this case, however, K-Pop fans quickly launched a Change .org campaign calling for the father's punishment. By refusing the distraction caused by the media's fabricated controversy, Turkish BTS fans (or T-ARMY) raised the public's interest in seeing the father brought to trial. Referred to by the hashtag #Melisa, this online campaign differed from the fundraising campaigns that are normally organized by T-ARMY. The #Melisa campaign politicized the so-called private sphere in the first highly visible campaign about domestic violence within Turkey. This is significant due to the erosion of women's rights under an increasingly authoritarian regime. For supporters of the Change.org campaign, the abuse within the family reflected the indifference of the state. In the face of this terrible event, T-ARMY raised their collective voice to exhort the public to fight for women's rights and create public pressure on the Turkish government to act against domestic violence and violence against women.

Turkish BTS fans are well-organized on social media and in the real world. T-ARMY's digital activity is generally hosted on Twitter, with hashtag campaigns celebrating the birthdays of BTS members and comeback activities of BTS. Among Twitter communities, the BANGTAN TURKEY account has 185,000 followers, while the BTS ARMY TURKEY account has 125,000 followers and the BTS Galaxy Turkey account has 76,000 followers. Many individual ARMY accounts share their affective connections to BTS on Twitter and Instagram and follow BTS-related topics day by day and hour by hour on social media flows, with ARMY being the most active of the K-Pop fan groups in Turkey. But T-ARMY also use social media for digital activism to address social issues, organizing fundraisers in support of foundations that work for disability rights, contributing to cancer treatments, and raising awareness of environmental issues such as forest fires. Besides making donations, T-ARMY members contributed to campaigns calling for the support of the firefighting efforts through such hashtags as #helpturkey, #globalcall, and #havadanmüdahaleis (#todistinguishfireswithairsupport), during the devastating wildfires that ravaged Turkey's Aegean and Mediterranean regions in August 2021.

Most members of T-ARMY are women between fourteen and twenty-five years old who live primarily in metropolitan cities, but T-ARMY is not a homogeneous group, and members hold different political views and religious beliefs.[1] Ethnographic and microscale studies have focused on the popular cultural consumption practices of female members of T-ARMY who attend religious high schools, but it cannot be said that all members are conservative and hold strong Islamic beliefs. T-ARMY has a broad membership base that also includes mothers in their forties and fifties and academics who hold secularist beliefs. For this reason, T-ARMY's campaigns refrain from referring to the political polarization of Turkish politics. For the most part, T-ARMY as a whole does not claim support in their digital campaign materials for either the ruling Justice and Development Party (JDP), led by President Recep Tayyip Erdoğan, or any opposition parties. Campaigns with political bents usually address problems outside of Turkey in order to ensure group harmony among T-ARMY.

Through donation campaigns and through targeted political critique of issues outside Turkey, T-ARMY members seek to legitimize the consumption of a "foreign" popular culture in the eyes of the Turkish public. They organize hashtag campaigns against the oppressive practices of the Chinese government against the Uyghur ethnic population in the Xinjiang Autonomous Region, and the Israeli government's repression of Palestinians in Gaza. BANGTAN TURKEY raised concerns over the acts of violence in East Jerusalem directed against the Palestinians with such hashtags as #PalestiniansLivesMatter, #FreePalestine, #SavePalestine, #AlAqsaUnderAttack and #GazaUnderAttack.[2] These campaigns, which support Muslim communities in other locales, do not include criticism of the Turkish government and are not viewed as being directly related to domestic politics. This kind of activism contributes to a positive public image of T-ARMY.

The #Melisa campaign was the first event organized by T-ARMY to protest domestic violence, demonstrating to the Turkish public that the K-Pop community could raise its voice and take a political stand on local issues. The campaign also served to unite K-Pop fans in Turkey. Similarly, the increase in domestic violence against women in Turkey attracted the attention of defenders of women's rights and nongovernmental organizations supporting gender equality, which brought more support to the petition.

It should be noted that these activist campaigns are not carried over to the streets. The limitation of social movements and demonstrations to online spaces in Turkey is not only true for T-ARMY but for all social and political movements under the increasing authoritarianism of the JDP and Erdoğan's regime. Under his regime, public gatherings in which opposing views are espoused are banned, often through intervention by police force. Since 2018, the JDP—a conservative Islamist party—has intensified its cultural and political policies in support of institutions and practices that support the Islamic religion.[3] These practices and policies include opening Hagia Sophia as a mosque, expanding the number of religious high schools, and increasing the budget of the Presidency of Religious Affairs much higher than that of the Ministries of Interior and Foreign Affairs. Furthermore, the JDP has emphasized the role of women in the family as good mothers and wives in its policies since coming to power. In March 2021, President Erdoğan announced the exit of Turkey from the Istanbul Convention, an agreement aimed at preventing and combatting violence against women, to which Turkey was once a leading signatory. He claimed that the principles of the Istanbul Convention were detrimental to family values. The #Melisa campaign was nourished by this social conjuncture of concern over the growing Islamization of the public sphere and unabated violence against women. T-ARMY's Change.org and hashtag campaigns reflected the social mood.

Melisa's Conversation with SUGA and the Media Coverage of Her Death

For an ARMY member, BTS's Twitter account @BTS_twt has three functions: it allows fans to follow the group members and their activities; it facilitates communication with the group members; and it generates communication and social interaction among the fans themselves. For Melisa, the BTS Twitter account functioned as a place to chat with SUGA, albeit in a one-sided way, since BTS members rarely respond to specific fans. Since 2019, Melisa had mentioned BTS's Twitter account on her own account (@onabunagecityok). She used her tweets to SUGA—whom she called Yoongi, his actual name—like a personal diary, highlighting the abuse she had been enduring for one and a half years. Written in Turkish, her tweets described the seriousness of the psychological problems she had developed as a result of domestic violence. She explained that her father considered her love of K-Pop to be an addiction. Her account tracks the ways in which she identified Yoongi as a source of psychological support, as someone she could confide in about the violence she was subjected to, the damage to her self-confidence, and her fear of her father. With no access to social support for the psychological violence she experienced at home, she turned to a public figure and a public forum. In one tweet, Melisa expressed that she endures more pain every day because she lacked the courage to kill herself. In her tweets to SUGA, she often said that she was more afraid of her father than dying. On the day of her death, she announced on her Twitter account that she intended to take her own life. Melisa's tweets were read by some ARMY members who responded by saying that life was precious and that they understood her suffering. But these posts were not enough for Melisa to overcome her sense of loss.

Her tragic death attracted the attention of the media because she had posted about her intentions to kill herself on her Twitter account. The fact that Melisa was a member of T-ARMY and a fan of SUGA allowed the media to connect the event to negative qualities often associated with K-Pop. SUGA's own self-disclosed suicide attempt in the past was used by the media to frame Melisa's death as proof that the tragedy was caused by the negative influence of K-Pop on impressionable youth.

On September 6, 2020, the daily newspaper *Akşam*—a mouthpiece of the JDP administration—ran the headline "Melisa killed herself . . . Who is responsible? The father or Yoongi?" The story emphasized that SUGA, from whom Melisa had sought help on social media, had also attempted suicide at the age of fifteen and mentioned several other K-Pop stars who had died by suicide in recent years.[4] In the same newspaper, two days later, journalist Mustafa Kartoğlu penned an article titled "Has Yoongi heard, and will he be sad? I don't think so. . . ."[5] Writing about Melisa's suicide, he implied that Yoongi's posts may have led Melisa to take her own life and blamed Yoongi for producing lyrics that promote death by suicide and depression among the younger generations. "In other words," he said, "Melisa chose a singer whom she admired with whom to share her painful experience. The innocence of her communication is obvious, but the musician cannot be said to be similarly innocent."[6] The journalist's report completely disregarded the psychological violence that Melisa suffered at home.

Rather than identifying the larger problem of domestic violence, the journalist shifted focus to an easy scapegoat: the consumption of foreign cultural products as a result of cultural imperialism. Kartoğlu's article stigmatized K-Pop and accused K-Pop idols of inciting misbehavior in young people and causing a decline in social morality, with androgynous outfits and sexy performances on stage. He claimed that young Turkish people who listen to K-Pop are moving away from national values and religion (Islam) and are abandoning heteronormative gender values. The journalist's point of view is based on a belief in a hypodermic needle model of mass media usage, in which the consumption of popular cultural products has a direct and immediate effect on the individual.[7] This model of cultural influence induces moral panic about the social impact of foreign cultures. In this respect, Kartoğlu's point of view reflects the mainstream media representations of K-Pop fandom in Turkey.

There is a growing anti-K-Pop discourse in Turkish mainstream media, fueled by fears of nonnormative gender representation and moral panics about LGBT+ identities. Several conservative and Islamist media portals in Turkey use homophobic and transphobic hate speech when referring to K-Pop idols, stigmatizing the intense interest in the Korean language and Korean cultural centers as a "Korean Epidemic." Korean cultural content, considered far removed from the dominant cultural norms in Turkey, is framed as cultural corruption and a threat to Turkish Islamic nationalism, as promoted under the rule of the Justice and Development Party.[8] As a result of this excessive condemnation of K-Pop, there is continuing public pressure to cancel performances by K-Pop cover groups, as well as concerts by K-Pop groups in Turkey. For instance, the concert by the K-Pop boys group Mirae, organized jointly by the Ministry of Culture and Tourism and the Korean Cultural Center in Ankara in May 2022, was targeted by a pro-government journalist who launched a Twitter campaign against the concert, suggesting K-Pop promoted homosexuality. Without providing any explanation, the ministry withdrew its support for the event. Concerts of local artists who make K-Pop-style music are accused of perversion and their performances have also been canceled. For example, Pinkeu Hilal (one of two Turkish singers working in the K-Pop industry) was scheduled to perform in Kayseri on July 30, 2022, but the concert was called off.[9]

"RIP Melisa from ARMY. We Purple You!" and the Digital Activism for Melisa

After Melisa's death, K-Pop fans launched a Twitter campaign using the hashtags #Melisa, #notsuicideitismurder (#intihardeğilcinayet), and #justiceformelisa (#melisaiçinadalet). Generating more than ten thousand tweets, fans politicized the private sphere through digital activism. T-ARMY members specifically blamed Melisa's death on her father and demanded his arrest and prosecution for domestic violence. A T-ARMY member launched a Change.org campaign titled "Hand in Hand for Melisa," which was signed by 91,868 people.[10] The campaign called for an investigation of Melisa's tweets and the prosecution of her father under Article 84 of the Turkish Penal Code, which states that any person who publicly encourages others to die by suicide is to be punished with three to eight years imprisonment. In other words, it is a crime to encourage a depressed person to believe that their life is worthless and to end it. According to the Turkish Penal Code, since the crime of suicide is not among those subject to complaint, it is directly investigated by the prosecutor's office, and there is no time limit for complaint regarding these crimes. As a result of the Melisa campaign and the media coverage it attracted, the local prosecutor filed a civil lawsuit and the father was taken into custody and briefly detained, but he was subsequently released due to a lack of evidence.

The comments on the Change.org campaign came from ARMY all over the world, with almost fifteen hundred comments written in multiple languages, including English and Spanish, expressing feelings of sorrow, grief, and support: "This is totally unbelievable because her father blamed her just because she listened to K-Pop. . . . And the Turkish peoples are blaming BTS SUGA for it Who doesn't even know. We want justice for Melisa"; "I'm signing because i want justice for Melisa her father gave her a gun to kill herself it's truly wrong, that's nothing wrong to like a K-Pop, her father mentally abused her. . . . #Justiceformelisa"; and "I'm signing because I'm also a BTS fan and this action is not right, BTS has saved many lives like hers through their music which spreads the message of loving your true selves, may she Rest In Peace. We

Purple you girl." A common theme running throughout the comments was the shared sentiment that listening to BTS does not encourage suicide; rather, BTS's music is a source of mental and emotional support. Several comments stated that parents who violate the rights of their children should receive the necessary punishments, while others emphasized that adolescents should be free to follow their tastes and desires.

For the first time T-ARMY members, commenting in Turkish, voiced their anger at the state and judicial bodies for their lack of response to acts of violence against women. The need to support digital activism and create public pressure to ensure justice in Turkey was also seen in the comments. Other members mention that some young people are prevented by their families from listening to K-Pop. One T-ARMY member made the following comment when signing the petition:

> I'm signing because my heart is on fire. I can't tell if it's real or a nightmare. Talking to the sky when she goes out and smokes on the balcony every night really bothers me. The tragic death of Melissa has been bothering me for 3 weeks and the state does nothing about it. Maybe she was the future of the country, maybe she would be a very good mother. . . . Melisa pulled the trigger, smoked her cigarette for the last time, listened to her music for the last time, and cried inside her world for the last time. . . . I'm begging you, don't let this go. . . . I'm so sorry for God's sake.

The outrage and sadness online were loud and clear. To even further assess how T-ARMY responded to Melisa's abuse and subsequent death, we interviewed four T-ARMY members who signed the petition. One stated:

> When I heard about the Melisa incident, I was up all night. Every tweet Melisa posted before she died appeared on my home page. Mine was one of the tweets giving Melisa the biggest support. . . . The fans living in the same neighborhood as Melisa were sought, and they were asked to inform the police. There was a stigma related to K-Pop in Turkey. But her one-way discussions with Yoongi revealed that she was a victim of domestic violence. It had nothing to do with K-Pop.

Another participant voiced her approval of Melisa's strong emotional attachment to SUGA:

Melisa's death was really sad. We really mourned for days, but it had nothing to do with BTS or any of their members, or anyone else. That girl chose the path of suicide because she had family problems. All she wanted was to send a cry for help on social media. At that time, she wanted to open up herself to them because she felt close to BTS. No one was aware of her pain until she died by suicide.

All four T-ARMY members mentioned BTS's own agenda of self-love and mental health wellness. Accordingly, Melisa's choice to seek help from SUGA can be considered a reflection of her sense of being part of something that contributed to both her desire for self-acceptance and self-confidence. T-ARMY interviewees observed that the Change.org campaign highlighted a social problem, but instead of discussing the reason for the campaign, Turkish media took the event out of context and used it as an opportunity to pathologize and misrepresent the K-Pop fandom. For T-ARMY, those larger forces responsible for Melisa's suicide were the education system and the social environment, both of which failed to help Melisa address the psychological pressure she faced. The Turkish media, on the other hand, turned a blind eye to the social problems and used K-Pop fandom as a scapegoat.

T-ARMY's Change.org campaign demonstrates how K-Pop fans in Turkey are not cultural dopes who mindlessly consume foreign lifestyles as framed by Turkish media. Instead, T-ARMY are active citizens who are aware of their political, social, cultural, and civil rights. The Melisa campaign stressed the desire among T-ARMY members for individual freedom within the family and for the legal punishment of acts of violence against women. Due to the increasingly authoritarian governance in Turkey, the state has become the main actor violating both private and public rights. The democratization and application of the rule of law by the state are necessary changes if young people are to breathe free in this country.

In 2021, one year after Melisa's suicide, her name was taken up by defenders of women's rights in their social media celebrations to mark International Working Women's Day, with references also to T-ARMY's campaign. According to the 2017–20 Violence against Women and Gender Equality report, around 120,000 women were victims of violence in 2020, while the Ministry of Internal Affairs put the number of women who lost their lives to violent acts at 234.[11] Hashtags memorializing the names of murdered women, including #pinargultekin, #eminebulut, #sulecet and #CerenÖzdemir, were used alongside the #Melisa hashtag in International Women's Day celebrations. The silence of the state and the ruling party in the face of domestic violence has come under criticism from opposition parties and NGOs supporting gender equality. Found in the comments supporting the Change.org campaign were statements that the ruling party condones the murders of women and sees no place for women in social life.

T-ARMY has not forgotten Melisa and continues to demand justice for her with the #whereisjusticeformelisa (#Melisanınadaletinerede) hashtag in the Twittersphere. In a society in which child abuse and domestic violence tend to remain hidden, T-ARMY's Melisa campaign served to bring social "private" issues into the public sphere through popular culture. It is apparent that the social and political power of K-Pop fans is important in highlighting the problems in society and in creating public pressure for their resolution. Despite the gradual decline in democracy, constraining the ability to organize and hindering the organization of anti-government campaigns, T-ARMY took a distinctly political stance in Turkey by launching the #Melisa campaign. This campaign served to demonstrate the possibility of uniting people with different political views and beliefs around an issue related to the rights of children and women. In this regard, T-ARMY's digital activism gives us hope for the advocacy of democratic rights in the Turkish public sphere.

Notes

1   Keskin, "Güney Kore K-Pop Popüler Kültürü ve Türkiye'deki Yansımaları," 133.

2   BANGTAN TURKEY (@BTSTurkey), "Medyanın konuşmadığı, herkesin sustuğu bu katliamlara lütfen biz susmayalım," Twitter, May 11, 2021, 7:08 a.m., https://twitter.com/BTSTurkey/status/1392074234340552707.

3   With the constitutional amendment in 2018, the parliamentary system in Turkey has been transformed into a new administrative structure in the form of the leadership of the president, who has organic ties to his political party and the parliament, functioning as an advisory board. In practice, the president is the head of the executive board. Since 1923, when the Republic of Turkey was founded, to 2018, the presidency was legally neutral. But with this transition President Erdoğan became Turkey's most powerful leader. For a detailed discussion of Turkey's political regime, see Esen, "Competitive Authoritarianism in Turkey under the AKP Rule."

4   Ertan Altan, "Melisa canına kıydı . . . Sorumlu baba mı Yoongi mi?," *Akşam*, September 6, 2020, https://www.aksam.com.tr/guncel/melisa -canina-kiydi-sorumlu-baba-mi-yoongi-mi/haber-1107385.

5   Mustafa Kartoğlu, "Yoongi duyar da üzülür mü? Sanmıyorum . . . ,"
         Akşam, September 8, 2020, https://www.aksam.com.tr/yazarlar/mustafa
         -kartoglu/yoongi-duyar-da-uzulur-mu-sanmiyorum/haber-1107933.
6   Kartoğlu, "Yoongi duyar da üzülür mü? Sanmıyorum."
7   Berger, Essentials of Mass Communication Theory.
8   Yavuz and Öztürk, "Turkish Secularism and Islam under the Reign of
         Erdoğan."
9   Arzu Geybullayeva, "Concerts Are Becoming a Political Battleground in
         Turkey," Global Voices, May 31, 2022, https://globalvoices.org/2022/05/31
         /concerts-are-becoming-a-political-battleground-in-turkey/.
10   Change.org, "Melisa için el ele," September 5, 2020, https://www.change
         .org/p/melisa-için-el-ele-melisa-nın-tweetlerinin-incelenmesini-ve
         -babasının-türk-ceza-kanunu-madde-84-uyarınca-cezalandırılmasını
         -istiyoruz-intihardeğilcinayet.
11   Yüksel-Kaptanoğlu, Violence against Women and Gender Equality 2017–
         2020, 28–31.

Works Cited

Berger, Arthur Asa. Essentials of Mass Communication Theory. Thousand Oaks, CA:
        SAGE, 1995.
Esen, Berk. "Competitive Authoritarianism in Turkey under the AKP Rule." In The
        Routledge Handbook on Contemporary Turkey, edited by Joost Jongerden,
        153–67. London: Routledge, 2021.
Kartoglu, Mustafa. "Yoongi duyar da üzülür mü? Sanmıyorum . . ." [In Turkish.]
        Akşam, September 8, 2020. https://www.aksam.com.tr/yazarlar
        /mustafa-kartoglu/yoongi-duyar-da-uzulur-mu-sanmiyorum
        /haber-1107933.
Keskin, Alptekin. "Güney Kore K-Pop Popüler Kültürü ve Türkiye'deki Yansımaları:
        Sosyolojik Bir İnceleme." PhD diss., Istanbul S. Zaim University, 2022.
Yavuz, M. Hakan, and Ahmet Erdi Öztürk. "Turkish Secularism and Islam under
        the Reign of Erdoğan." Southeast European and Black Sea Studies 19, no. 1
        (2019): 1–9.
Yüksel-Kaptanoğlu, İlker. Violence against Women and Gender Equality 2017–2020.
        Ankara: CEID, 2018.

20 · "Spring Day": Nostalgia, Pop Mediation, and Public Mourning

— Michelle Cho

"Spring Day," BTS's much-loved 2016 single and music video, has been widely acknowledged as an audiovisual tribute to the victims of the sinking of the marine vessel *Sewol* (*Seweolho*) on April 16, 2014, on a routine journey from the port of Incheon to Jeju Island in South Korea. Three hundred and four of the ship's four hundred and seventy-six passengers perished. Two hundred and fifty of the victims were sophomores at Danwon High School in Ansan, Gyeonggi province, a satellite city southwest of Seoul, who were on what should have been a celebratory class trip. These hundreds of lives lost, aboard an overloaded ferry that capsized twenty kilometers from shore, ignited a firestorm of public grief, anger, and recrimination in South Korea. The accident took place in calm waters, and initial news reports of the incident claimed that all passengers had survived in a straightforward rescue operation. In reality, the vessel lacked safety protocols, and individuals and institutions at every level, from the ship's crew to the dispatchers, coast guard, police, broadcasters, military, and political leaders, failed to act, in a staggering display of incompetence, negligence, and greed.[1]

The disaster revealed the pervasive corruption that had led to deregulation and unenforced safety measures, as well as the ineptitude of military and civil agencies that hesitated to mount a rescue mission under an unclear chain of command.[2] Government agencies persistently deflected responsibility for the failed rescue and blamed the news media and the precariously employed ferry captain and crew for the public outcry following the accident. Politicians and bureaucrats also tried to intimidate the government's critics into silence, especially the bereaved parents of the teenaged disaster victims. Despite calls to salvage the ship to investigate the accident and search for missing victims' remains, the *Sewol* remained submerged until March 23, 2017, just days after the high court upheld the impeachment of then president Park Geun-hye. Park's many failures of leadership include an unexplained absence from national command on the day of the incident, which contributed to a populist, direct-action protest campaign of historic proportions—the Candlelight Protests of 2016–17 (촛불 집회)—to impeach and remove her from office. A month before the *Sewol* was finally reclaimed, BTS released the track and music video "Spring Day," their most successful ballad to date, and South Korea's most perennially popular hit single of the last decade.[3]

This chapter investigates "Spring Day's" intertexts, references, images, and lyrics, as well as the uptake of "Spring Day" as a *Sewol* allegory by Korean and international fans alike. "Spring Day" facilitates collective grief and public mourning through its multilayered vision of lost time, which routes the longing for restitution through its assemblage of media references that center nostalgia's utopian dimension and the latter's centrality to memorialization projects. I contend that this strategy is a hallmark of BTS's oeuvre, which highlights the concept, embodiment, sentiments, and semiotics of youth—arguably the nostalgic object par excellence.[4] "Spring Day" also evinces a characteristic mode of Korean popular media's use of intertextuality to activate communal affect—the co-feeling or shared sentiment for which popular culture provides a common form.[5] The emphasis on shared affect as a means of consciousness-raising is demonstrated by the uptake of the allegorical interpretation of "Spring Day" in fan-produced videos. "What you STILL DON'T KNOW about BTS SPRING DAY MV," authored by "Italian ARMY" and posted on April 30, 2017, demonstrates how fans relate to the group's content in a transitive mode that underscores contemporary global media's emphasis on vicarious experience.[6] The video essay explicates the *Sewol* allegory by illustrating fan theories and commentary with clips from the music video. "What you STILL DON'T KNOW" also splices together Korean television news footage and international K-Pop news coverage to teach non-Korean fans about the *Sewol* tragedy and to facilitate mourning of the victims through the remixing of archival and popular media content. Reading BTS's music video alongside fan-produced media expands the allegorical parameters of "Spring Day" and reveals its potential to catalyze a translocal politics of fandom that centers shared affect, emotion, and experience.

Pop Memorialization

The twentieth century's wars and their overwhelming scale of human loss have resulted in the ubiquity of memorials in modern life.[7] What is at stake, though, in public mourning? How and for whom is a memorial successful, as a sufficient and necessary response to collective tragedy? In South Korea, controversies over public memory work concern both domestic events, such as mass casualties resulting from war, political persecution, or failed infrastructure, and international conflicts concerning postcolonial redress, including the commemoration of so-called Comfort Women—young women and girls who were forced into sexual slavery by the Japanese imperial army when Korea was a Japanese colony.[8] Often, memorials raise debates over historical revisionism, that is, whose version of history becomes legitimized by public recounting. In cases of what anthropologist Lisa Yoneyama terms "transborder redress culture," disputes tend to arise at the level of interstate trade and diplomatic relations.[9] Yet, the state does not always speak for the interests of victims, which leads to conflicts between governments and civil society, nation-states and their citizens.

This is the case in attempts to redress the *Sewol* tragedy. In the months after the incident, *Sewol* activists became embroiled in the already polarized climate of South Korean party politics, as the public also began to tire of news coverage that exploited footage of the passengers' pleading calls for help to their parents and panicked farewells as the waters began to rise in their cabins—media footage that was often retraumatizing. In the face of the government's refusal to investigate higher-level collusion, the families' demands for proper response met institutional stonewalling, leading to interminable mourning, or the circulation of rage and indignation that has no end and no possible release.[10] Debates about the *Sewol* victims' proper memorialization have continued to pit individuals against the state, which summarily removed a memorial site in 2022 that was built by *Sewol* families in the public plaza near Seoul City Hall.[11] The rationale given for removing parents, supporters, and protesters from sites of remembrance in the capital city that had operated for years is that a government-funded memorial is being built in Ansan, even though objections by residents and *Sewol* families remain unaddressed.[12]

In the absence of an agreed-upon and effective public forum to grieve the victims of *Sewol*, "Spring Day" offers one possible site—an iterative and sensory popular memorial, supercharged by the "stickiness" of fan affect, that unites its audiences in solidarity and shared remembrance.[13] In the process, "Spring Day" expands the act of mourning by processing it through the

aesthetics of nostalgia. While this gesture broadens the memorial's referent, the pop culture assemblage of "Spring Day" enfolds a larger community
into the shared act of remembrance. "Spring Day" was not the only product
of the South Korean commercial culture industries to memorialize the *Sewol*
victims. Other idol pop groups like Red Velvet, f(x), and the Ark also released
singles whose lyrics and/or music videos referenced the South Korean public's
harrowing condition of suspended grief. However, what is unique about BTS's
"Spring Day" is the way in which the music video's interwoven references expand the processing of grief beyond the *Sewol* families, while at the same time
highlighting *Sewol* as the song's primary referent. In the video's multilayered
citations, along with its widespread global reception, we can see the ways in
which "Spring Day" innovates on the role of public culture to memorialize collective loss, while creating new, transitive modes of shared experience.

Pop Mediation: *Sewol* Youth, Nostalgia, and Utopian Critique

The "Spring Day" music video begins with BTS member V standing on a train
platform and then stepping onto the snowy train tracks that symbolize time's
linear progression, drawing the group members away from the past and in-
exorably forward toward an adult future. As V leans down to rest his ear on
the tracks, the camera zooms into a close-up of his pensive face, and the faint
sounds of a train fade into the song's opening bars. This opening sets the video's retrospective and nostalgic mood. The scenes that follow briefly flash
back to playful adolescent bonding, followed by more contemplative images
to signify the shift to adulthood, as the video places each of the members in
multiple sites of remembrance. The video's primary settings are the Hotel
Omelas, a laundromat, a large mountain of clothes, a train car, a stairwell, the
outdoor settings of snowy train tracks, a deserted beach, an empty lot with
a rusty carousel painted with the words "You Never Walk Alone," and, at the
video's climax, a wintery field at dusk with a lone, leafless tree.

The major literary reference in "Spring Day" is American science fiction
writer Ursula K. Le Guin's short story "The Ones That Walk Away from Omelas" (1973), which conjures a classless, utopian society, full of joy, beauty, and
virtue, in which a lone child suffers in neglect and squalor. As they come of
age, each of Omelas's citizens not only learn of the child's miserable existence
but also that it is the necessary condition of their own happiness. The child,
in all its pathos, is the ritual sacrifice that enables the good life shared by the

rest of the society's inhabitants.[14] While most come to accept the dictum that the child's suffering is a necessary evil, some citizens choose to leave, forgoing the benefits of their complicity. Le Guin's evocative text has been frequently read, anthologized, and taught since its publication. However, its enigmatic approach to utopia and morality, as well as its rhetorical strategies to implicate the reader in cocreating both Omelas's wonders and the afflictions of its suffering child, has rarely received sustained exploration as in BTS's "Spring Day."

The full title of Le Guin's story is "The Ones Who Walk Away from Omelas (Variations on a Theme by William James)," and she has credited American psychologist William James's critique of utilitarianism with inspiring her (anti-)utopian tale.[15] In his essay "The Moral Philosopher and the Moral Life" from 1891, James proposes the following scenario:

> If the hypothesis were offered us of a world in which . . . millions [were] kept permanently happy on the one simple condition of a life of lonely torture, what except a specifically and independent sort of *emotion* can it be which would make us immediately *feel*, even though an impulse arose within us to clutch at the happiness so offered, how *hideous a thing would be its enjoyment* when deliberately accepted as the fruit of such a bargain?[16]

Here, James writes against a prescriptive and categorical moral philosophy based on utilitarian principles, to instead privilege affect as a guide to moral action. This prompt led Le Guin to write "Omelas" as an attempt to illustrate James's proposition using the full capacities of narrative prose to evoke emotion and sensory experience. Written in 1973 as Americans bore witness to the devastating impacts of the Vietnam War (shortly following on Hiroshima and the Korean War), "Omelas" is at once a fable and a political statement, criticizing the United States' self-deluded myths of moral rectitude that rationalized the nation's prosperity as a global good.[17] Going beyond the generic reading of the story that lionizes the ones who leave as taking an individualized stand against an unjust society, the insistence on transindividual experience in "Spring Day" makes mourning the vulnerable and powerless an inevitable, shared responsibility, no matter the personal relationship one might have to the event.[18]

Alongside Le Guin's parable, cinematic reference points lend aesthetic and ideological significance to the music video (MV), especially through the leitmotif of train tracks, from Lee Chang-dong's 1999 film, *Peppermint Candy*, to the dystopian action film *Snowpiercer* (2013) by Bong Joon-ho. Lee's film, which similarly begins and ends with the sights and sounds of a train, thematizes youth destroyed by national tragedy by tracking the life of a young conscript who loses his innocence in the violent events of the Gwangju Uprising in 1980, and continues down an overdetermined path toward suicide in the film's present. *Snowpiercer*, which "Spring Day" cites both lyrically and visually, sets its science fictional dystopia on a train containing the last survivors of a calamitous, engineered ice age—humanity's last-ditch attempt to reverse global warming. *Snowpiercer*'s train, a symbol of the industrial age that initiated the era of human-caused climate change, circumnavigates the globe in perpetual motion. The train is revealed to be maintained by a dispossessed Black child from its expendable laboring class, young and thus small enough to maneuver within the confines of its dangerous engine. Thus, "Spring Day" anchors Le Guin's "psychomyth" to the racialized child laborer in *Snowpiercer* and *Peppermint Candy*'s traumatized youth of South Korea's dictatorship era—both those murdered by the state and those conscripted to inflict this murderous violence—who were sacrificed to the nation's economic-developmentalist mandates. The video weaves a citational tapestry that centers the vulnerable, exploited child as the victim of capitalist predation on a global scale. These intertextual references echo Le Guin's and James's emphasis on felt suffering, against the calculating, instrumental logic of utilitarianism that sacrificed the *Sewol* victims to the market tyranny that has driven South Korea's postwar economic miracle.

The quick cutting and alternating scenes in "Spring Day" are matched to the members' verse lines in the song, creating a shift in perspective that destabilizes conventional narrative expectations—the point is not to designate fixed character roles to the BTS members; instead, they alternate as the song's speaker. The direct address to the listener/viewer in "Spring Day" begins with "I miss you / 보고싶다," as RM delivers the line while facing the camera and breaking the cinematic fourth wall. The variability of the speaker and addressee continues in the lines that follow in the first verse as well as in the chorus. The lyrics are sung either by individual members or pairs, as the camera follows each member as they move through the MV's varied settings. In this way, "Spring Day" distributes the "I" position across all the group members to depict a structure of shared experience that nevertheless captures interiority and individualized regret and loss, as conveyed in the lyrics. An important formal quality of the lyrics and vocal arrangement consists of the shifting vocal delivery of the first- and second-person mode of address, even in the most dialogic section of the song, where SUGA and Jimin duet in verse four:

s: Is it you who changed?

ɟ: Is it you who changed?

s: Or is it me who changed?

ɟ: Or is it me who changed?

s: I hate this moment, this time flowing by. We are changed, you know?
Just like everyone, you know?

ɟ: *in harmony*. Just like everyone, you know?

Although SUGA and Jimin engage in call-and-response as a sonic pair, Jimin echoes SUGA's words, rather than answering his queries, and then his voice joins SUGA in the line "Just like everyone, you know?" Grammatically, the lyrics blend SUGA and Jimin into a single semantic subject, but the song's delivery makes their intersubjectivity perceivable, creating a holding space for both members to be addressing each other and the audience at the same time. The speaker/addressee positions remain mobile, with the floating "I" activated by multiple subjects/group members, in turn. This contrasts with the song's collective ending, where the members' voices join in unison on the "wo-o-oh, wo-o-oh, wo-o-o-o-oh" refrain that concludes the song on a hopeful and triumphant note.

The song builds on the romantic trope of lost innocence to emphasize the transindividual over the personal impacts entailed by coming of age, namely, the shifting terrain of peer relations in the transition from youth to adulthood. The poignant tribute to friendship in "Spring Day" preserves the intensity of grief that issues from even this most ordinary loss, opening this act of memorialization to all, yet grounding it in the specific sociohistorical context of *Sewol* youth, whose lives were the casualties of unevenly distributed risk in neoliberal South Korea.[19] Bridging the monumental and the quotidian—the *Sewol* and the losses of friendship entailed by growing up—diminishes neither; instead the gesture extends the gravity of the *Sewol* to a large, international public, refuting the South Korean government's framing of the tragedy as affecting only the victims' immediate families, who were, at the time of the music video's release, facing conspiracy-laden accusations of holding the nation hostage to unreasonable demands for restitution and framed as enemies of the public good. "Spring Day" functions as a popular memorial that liberates the fixed rhetorical positions otherwise found in memorial sites that place victims on one side and survivors on the other, or install the state as addressee to the national public. Instead, the transindividual aesthetic structure, both lyrically and visually, in "Spring Day," not only expands the mourning collective, but unsettles the victim-witness relation.

The continuous movement in "Spring Day"—registered aurally by the intermittent rumblings of the train—resolves in stillness in two tableaus that signal the utopian desire for the members' reunion, where they can pause their relentless forward motion, hurtling toward adulthood in progressive, capitalist time. The first tableau unites the group on the mountain of clothes, now turned into a landscape feature of a beautiful and seemingly mythical setting that is nonetheless tinged with absence, as represented by the discarded garments. The second utopian space is the MV's ending memorial site—the train's final destination. Here the utopian form is that of nostalgic remembrance: facing the future with a collective commitment to honoring the past.

Transcultural Public Mourning

"What you STILL DON'T KNOW," first posted in 2017 and updated in 2021, carefully assembles visual and thematic resonances between media accounts of the *Sewol* disaster and an exegesis of the "Spring Day" music video's narrative and images, with the aim of urging other BTS fans to learn about the incident, the catastrophic failed rescue, and the ensuing activism to hold the government to account. YouTube user Italian ARMY takes pains to persuade viewers of their video essay to *feel* the injustice of the situation, especially by including media clips of family members pleading with authorities in the immediate aftermath of the ship's capsizing to rescue their drowning children, only to be met with indifference.[20] The clips openly display government actors' active obstruction of efforts by fishermen and the ROK Navy to rescue passengers, in favor of the ill-equipped salvage company that was officially designated as the contracted entity to conduct the response—a result of the state's outsourcing of passenger safety to private enterprise. In so doing, the video materializes the suffering and helplessness of the *Sewol* victims, emphatically centering the tribute to *Sewol* in "Spring Day."

"What you STILL DON'T KNOW" reconstructs an explanatory narrative of the event, while also organizing its account of the *Sewol* tragedy through its decryption of the music video's multiple thematic references and material symbols of the incident. To take one example, the video edits a sequence of match cuts that juxtaposes a newspaper photograph taken through one of *Sewol*'s portholes of a diver entering the doomed ship with the music video image of BTS member Jin filmed from inside the washer in the laundromat setting (see figures 20.1 and 20.2). Italian ARMY's video deploys this method of matching the mise-en-scène to *Sewol* media coverage in explanations of

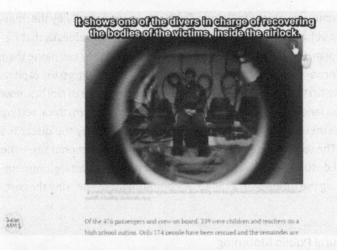

It shows one of the divers in charge of recovering the bodies of the victims, inside the airlock.

Of the 476 passengers and crew on board, 339 were children and teachers on a high school outline. Only 174 people have been rescued and the remainder are

The porthole does not remind you of something?

20.1 & 20.2 · Screenshots from Italian ARMY's "Spring Day" video essay "What you STILL DON'T KNOW about BTS SPRING DAY MV."

other "Spring Day" elements, such as the yellow ribbons tied to the carousel in front of which BTS member Jung Kook stands suspended in time, with sped-up footage of other BTS members circling around and behind him. "What you STILL DON'T KNOW" links the music video's set design to photographs of *Sewol* mourners tying lengths of yellow ribbon onto impromptu memorial sites in the weeks following the tragedy.

In another example, "What you STILL DON'T KNOW" inserts photographs of French artist Christian Boltanski's 2010 art installation *Personnes*, the inspiration for another set piece in the "Spring Day" music video—a mountain of used clothing that many have interpreted as commemorating *Sewol* victims.

Personnes evokes the haunting scenes of genocide, as noted in the *Guardian*'s review of the installation: "Boltanski has always been maker of monuments and memorials. His medium is the human trace and the memento mori."[21] The reference to *Personnes* in "Spring Day" most firmly anchors the music video to the tradition of socially critical, public art that seeks to intervene in the cultural field of collective memory work and memorialization.[22] These elements of the fan video testify to its author's keen attention to formal details in their research of *Sewol* coverage, fan discussion of the music video's intertexts, and their viewing of "Spring Day." By bringing these moments into contact with the domestic media reportage of *Sewol*, "What you STILL DON'T KNOW" reiterates the sticky images and sounds in "Spring Day" as an affective memorial to the *Sewol* tragedy, reading both image composition and thematic content as evidence of the music video's allegorical impulse. Ultimately, "What you STILL DON'T KNOW" recodes fan activity—analyzing BTS content—as the work of collective memory, enlisting scores of witnesses of *Sewol*'s affective intensities to the ethical act of remembrance prompted in turn by Le Guin's, Lee's, Boltanski's, and Bong's visions of refusal and revolutionary change.

Myriad filmed reactions to "What you STILL DON'T KNOW" can be found on the video-sharing platform YouTube; viewers who learn of the *Sewol* for the first time express tremendous sympathy, shock, and indignation. Fan responses knit the *Sewol* tragedy into the sphere of contemporary youth movements, connecting South Korea's *Sewol* generation with Americans traumatized by the unceasing violence of school shootings, Thai and Burmese democracy activists, ARMY for Leni, Indonesia's anti-corruption protesters, and others whose positions are not merely analogous but are intimately bound by the network of forces that have yielded the global scope of antidemocratic governance, austerity, and heightened physical and economic risk in everyday life.[23]

While it is not necessary that all MV viewers learn about *Sewol*, "Spring Day" and its fan-made paratexts create sites of consciousness-raising through shared sentiment. The music video's visible reception through explainer videos like "What you STILL DON'T KNOW" extends the process of memorialization in ways that continue calls for accountability, focusing attention on the structural conditions and social malaise that led to the *Sewol* disaster. Focusing on affect wrests us away from instrumental and transactional logics of valuing human life, instead highlighting the transitive mode of feeling that characterizes fandom as a ground for ethical engagement and political action. Although fan affectivity has been denigrated as irrational and antimodern, especially when it is understood as a form of populist derangement,

"Spring Day" and its reception offers an unprecedented example of the ways in which pop consumption and collective memorialization can converge. The acts of co-feeling evoked by "Spring Day" allow us to consider how popular culture facilitates and shapes our understanding of the worlds we inhabit, and our shared responsibilities to remember and advocate for the most vulnerable among us.

Notes

1   Jae Jung Suh's essay "The Failure of the South Korean National Security State" catalogs the infuriating details of the botched response and the collusion between regulators and the shipping industry that led to the *Sewol*'s dangerously overloaded state, bearing twice the maximum officially permitted cargo and manned by an untrained captain and crew that abandoned ship after instructing passengers to "stay still" in their cabins as the ship sank.

2   See sociologist Yoonkyung Lee's "The Sewol Disaster" and anthropologist Hyeon Jung Lee's "From Passive Citizens to Resistant Subjects." Both scholars' analyses of the causes of and responses to the *Sewol* disaster support cultural critic Eric Cazdyn's assessment of what he calls the "post-post-Cold War moment," which operates according to "the unapologetic logic of the capitalist market, which is not at liberty to suspend the rule of profit and expansion under any circumstance." Cazdyn, "Anti-anti," 336.

3   "Spring Day" collected the Song of the Year Award at the 2017 Melon Music Awards (Melon is one of the country's main music streaming platforms and music charts) and topped all of the major music charts in South Korea during the week of its release. As of February 2022, the song had accomplished the unprecedented feat of appearing on the weekly Melon Top 100 singles chart every week since its release, for 260 consecutive weeks.

4   BTS's breakthrough success on the Korean pop charts dates to the group's embrace of a nostalgic concept of youth in the *The most beautiful moment in life / Hwayangyeonhwa* album series, during 2015–16. They continued to center their coming-of-age concept on their follow-up full-length album, *WINGS*, and the special repackage of *WINGS—YOU NEVER WALK ALONE*, which capped the *WINGS* era with "Spring Day" in 2017.

5   For the South Korean culture industries at large, this transnational commercial strategy also serves as a vision of cultural exchange across media markets. See Choi and Raley's discussion of the "cham" effect in their essay "K-Streams."

6   "BTS Spring Day MV EXPLAINED | Sewol Ferry, Snowpiercer & Survivors," February 21, 2017, YouTube video, 8:55, https://www.youtube.com/watch?v=Tye1ONFeKis; Italian ARMY, "[2021] What you STILL DON'T KNOW about BTS SPRING DAY MV," April 30, 2017, YouTube video, 17:04, https://www.youtube.com/watch?v=FrT4a_Fw6pE.

7   Writing in 1995, German art historian Andreas Huyssen states that in the last years of the twentieth century, he was "struck by the surprising popularity of the museum and the resurgence of the monument and the memorial as major modes of aesthetic, historical, and spatial expression" (3), as part of a veritable "memory boom of unprecedented proportions" (5). Huyssen, *Twilight Memories*, 3, 5.

8   Other debates focus on cultural memory of the Gwangju Uprising, the Jeju Massacre, and the Korean War. On memorializing Gwangju, see Shin, *The Cultural Politics of Urban Development in South Korea*. On the Jeju Massacre, see Hun Joon Kim, *The Massacres at Mt. Halla*.

9   Yoneyama, *Cold War Ruins*, 12. For discussions of the current dilemmas of transborder redress culture vis-à-vis historical revisionist tendencies in post-1990s Japan, see *Cold War Ruins*, 111–46.

10   Jinah Kim calls the *Sewol* survivors' ceaseless grief "insurgent melancholia," affirming "the power of the parents' mourning and the way they demanded accountability from the state" as "particularly important given the orientalist attitudes in the initial global media coverage and political analysis of the event, which blamed the victims and their adherence to the Confucian value in listening to authority, translated as the inability of Korean youth to think for themselves." Kim, "The Insurgency of Mourning," 85.

11   As of the ninth anniversary of the tragedy in April 2023, disputes between *Sewol* activists and Seoul city were ongoing, with families of the victims of the October 2022 crowd crush tragedy in Itaewon joining with *Sewol* families against city officials' removal of their memorial sites and altars. The Seoul city government is now charging *Sewol* families for the rent and maintenance of a temporary memorial site in front of the Seoul Metropolitan Council. See Yu Gyeong-seon, "Are Memories and a Memorial Something Illegal That Must Be Removed?," *Kyunghyang Shinmun*, April 17, 2023, https://english.khan.co.kr/khan_art_view.html?artid=202304171456247.

12   See Jin Chang-Il and Lim Jeongwon, "Sewol Memorial Unfinished Due to Disputes and Resistance," *Korea JoongAng Daily*, April 17, 2022, https://koreajoongangdaily.joins.com/2022/04/17/national/socialAffairs/Sewol-Sewol-ferry-disaster-Sewol-anniversary/20220417152539331.html.

13   In *The Cultural Politics of Emotion*, feminist critic Sara Ahmed uses the metaphor of "stickiness" to describe the quality of signs and concepts that accrue significance via affective transference in public discourse.

Ahmed defines stickiness as a characteristic of objects and signs that are "saturated with affect, as sites of personal and social tension" (20). Further, she writes, "signs become sticky through repetition" (91). My thoughts on "stickiness" in relation to "Spring Day" and its shared reception are spurred by Jinsook Kim's reference to Ahmed's "stickiness" to synthesize the material and metaphorical import of spontaneous, sticky-note memorials. These participatory memorials have become part of a repertoire of public speech and commemoration in South Korea, after tragedies such as the Gangnam Station murder in 2016. See Jinsook Kim, "Sticky Activism."

14   Sarah Wyman points to Le Guin's reference to the "scapegoat trope as a 'psychomyth,' ushering in the notion of communally held descriptors and moral directives" in Le Guin's text "Myth and Archetype in Science Fiction." Wyman, "Reading through Fictions," 231n7.

15   Amelia Z. Greene explains that Le Guin "mirrors the scenario that James originally posits in 'The Moral Philosopher and the Moral Life' in order to test the reader's tolerance for the utilitarian position that the suffering of a few individuals is acceptable if it ensures the happiness of many." Green, "Variations on a Theme by William James," 219.

16   James, "The Moral Philosopher and the Moral Life," 333, emphasis added. In her introduction to "The Ones Who Walk Away from Omelas," in *The Wind's Twelve Quarters*, Le Guin writes that in James's scenario "the dilemma of the American conscience can hardly be better stated" (277).

17   This was an especially repugnant fiction in the wake of America's "hot" war in Vietnam, Laos, and Cambodia, which followed upon the bipolar world system's violent inception in the Korean War. See anthropologist Heonik Kwon's important reframing of Cold War historiography that refutes the characterization of the period as an era of fragile peace through brinksmanship in a binary world system. By centering the so-called peripheries of the decolonizing world in *The Other Cold War*, Kwon concludes that the Cold War was decidedly "hot" beyond North America and Europe, that is to say, across most of the globe.

18   Against the reading of "Omelas" that "Le Guin supports the noncompliance of the ones who *walk away*," Wyman asserts that Le Guin would "likely place emphasis on the incarcerated *lost soul*," rather than "offering a utilitarian excuse." Wyman, "Reading through Fictions," 228.

19   The study of risk in modern, industrialized societies is an influential area of research with particular relevance for analyzing globalization's impacts on people and their environments. German sociologist Ulrich Beck initiated the discourse with his 1992 book *Risk Society: Towards a New Modernity*.

20   Italian ARMY, like many fan-creators, puts little identifying information on the "About" page of their YouTube channel, but the video narration is

in Italian, which suggests that Italian ARMY is part of BTS's multilingual, global fandom. In the "What you STILL DON'T KNOW" video description, Italian ARMY credits several other fan Twitter accounts for providing subtitles in Spanish, French, Korean, and Russian.

21 Laura Cumming, "Christian Boltanski: Personnes," *Guardian*, January 16, 2010, https://www.theguardian.com/artanddesign/2010/jan/17/christian -boltanski-personnnes-paris-review.

22 Huyssen includes the work of Christian Boltanski in his catalog of contemporary artists who "return to history, the new confrontation of history and fiction, history and representation, history and myth that distinguishes contemporary aesthetic productions from most of the trends that made up the post-1945 neo-avantgardes" (*Twilight Memories*, 88). Suk-Young Kim reads the reference to Boltanski in "Spring Day" in part as a call to end exploitative, fast-fashion practices that so clearly demonstrate the environmental and human costs of economic global-ization. See Kim, "Beauty and the Waste."

23 Heartbreaking comparisons can be made between the *Sewol* trag-edy and the school shooting in Uvalde, Texas, in 2022. In both cases, officers and rescue agencies delayed action, in a spectacular display of institutional and moral failure. See Emma Tucker, "Police Failed to Act Quickly in Uvalde. Experts Say Their Inaction Allowed for the Massacre to Continue and Led to Catastrophic Consequences," CNN, May 29, 2022, https://edition.cnn.com/2022/05/28/us/failure-by-uvalde-police-to-act -quickly-led-to-catastrophic-consequences/index.html.

Works Cited

Ahmed, Sara. *The Cultural Politics of Emotion*. 2nd ed. Edinburgh: Edinburgh Univer-sity Press, 2014.

Beck, Ulrich. *Risk Society: Towards a New Modernity*. Translated by Mark Ritter. Thou-sand Oaks, CA: SAGE, 1992.

Cazdyn, Eric. "Anti-anti: Utopia, Globalization, Jameson." *Modern Language Quarterly* 68, no. 2 (2007): 331–43.

Choi, Eunjin, and Rita Raley. "K-Streams: Global Korea and the OTT Era." In "The Hallyu Project," edited by Yin Yuan. Cluster, *Post45: Contemporaries*, February 23, 2023. https://post45.org/2023/02/k-streams-global-korea -and-the-ott-era/.

Greene, Amelia Z. "'Variations on a Theme by William James': Varieties of Religious Experience in the Writing of Ursula K. Le Guin." *William James Studies* 13, no. 2 (2017): 217–39.

Huyssen, Andreas. *Twilight Memories: Marking Time in a Culture of Amnesia*. New York: Routledge, 1995.

James, William. "The Moral Philosopher and the Moral Life." *International Journal of Ethics* 1, no. 3 (1891): 330–54.

Kim, Hun Joon. *The Massacres at Mt. Halla: Sixty Years of Truth Seeking in South Korea.* Ithaca, NY: Cornell University Press, 2014.

Kim, Jinah. "The Insurgency of Mourning: *Sewol* across the Transpacific." *Amerasia Journal* 46, no. 1 (2020): 84–100.

Kim, Jinsook. "Sticky Activism: The Gangnam Station Murder Case and New Feminist Practices against Misogyny and Femicide." JCMS: *Journal of Cinema and Media Studies* 60, no. 4 (2021): 37–60.

Kim, Suk-Young. "Beauty and the Waste: Fashioning Idols and the Ethics of Recycling in Korean Pop Music Videos." *Fashion Theory* 25, no. 1 (2021): 53–73.

Kwon, Heonik. *The Other Cold War.* New York: Columbia University Press, 2010.

Le Guin, Ursula K. "The Ones Who Walk Away from Omelas." In *The Wind's Twelve Quarters*, 277–86. New York: Harper and Row, 1975.

Lee, Hyeon Jung. "From Passive Citizens to Resistant Subjects: The Sewol Families Stand Up to the State." In *Challenges of Modernization and Governance in South Korea: The Sinking of the Sewol and Its Causes*, edited by Jae-Jung Suh and Mikyoung Kim, 187–207. Singapore: Palgrave Macmillan, 2017.

Lee, Yoonkyung. "The Sewol Disaster: Predictable Consequences of Neoliberal Deregulation." In *Challenges of Modernization and Governance in South Korea: The Sinking of the Sewol and Its Causes*, edited by Jae-Jung Suh and Mikyung Kim, 33–48. Singapore: Palgrave Macmillan, 2017.

Shin, HaeRan. *The Cultural Politics of Urban Development in South Korea: Art, Memory and Urban Boosterism in Gwangju.* New York: Routledge, 2020.

Suh, Jae Jung. "The Failure of the South Korean National Security State: The Sewol Tragedy in the Age of Neoliberalism." *Asia-Pacific Journal: Japan Focus* 12, no. 40 (2014). http://apjjf.org/2014/12/40/Jae-Jung-Suh/4195.html.

Workman, Travis. "Mediating Neo-Feudalism." *Postmodern Culture* 31, no. 3 (2021). https://doi.org/10.1353/PMC.2021.0003.

Wyman, Sarah. "Reading through Fictions in Ursula Le Guin's 'The Ones Who Walk Away from Omelas.'" ANQ: *A Quarterly Journal of Short Articles, Notes and Reviews* 25, no. 4 (2012): 228–32. www.doi.org/10.1080/0895769X.2012.720854.

Yoneyama, Lisa. *Cold War Ruins: Transpacific Critique of American Justice and Japanese War Crimes.* Durham, NC: Duke University Press, 2016.

INTERLUDE · "Magic Shop": So Show Me, I'll Show You (My Fanart)

Fan-produced artwork stands out as one of the most generative and generous forms of public engagement with popular culture. Fans use a variety of forms, including video and audio edits, storytelling, performance art, song and covers, illustrations in various mediums, poetry, and even pastry, to express the gratitude, love, desire, and connection they feel for certain artists or texts, as well as for other fans who might share their affinities.[1] The world of K-Pop is no exception. K-Pop is a vast intertextual universe by design, providing fertile ground for an array of invited, as well as unexpected, responses and readings. As many of the contributions in this volume observe, BTS inspires a truly monumental level of devotion from their fans, and fan-produced artwork exists in deep symbiosis with the members. The lyrics to their 2018 single "Magic Shop"—"You gave me the best of me / So you'll give you the best of you"—illustrate the dynamic parasocial relationship that BTS cultivates with ARMY. Just as BTS members offer inspiration for fan creativity, so, too, do fans move BTS's artistry; V revealed in 2022 that Jimin's tattoo of the phases of the moon was inspired by a fan's portrait imagining such ink inscribed down his spine.

While just a minuscule sample of the transmedia archive that ARMY has produced since 2013, the art curated here demonstrates how BTS fans create and circulate their art and labor as a means of appreciating beauty, forging community, expressing generosity, and speaking from the margins of official cultures. Art often demonstrates how, as Mimi Thi Nguyen writes, "Consumption and interpretation are . . . highly constrained but nonetheless enabling sites of subject and discourse formation."[2] Fanart necessarily emerges from social histories that can at times illustrate the conditions and circumstances for an idol's publicity; for an idol themself as part of a cultural inheritance or a culture industry; and for the fan to reflect upon their own relationship to that inheritance or industry that constitutes an idol's popularity.

Fans work from scripts not of their own making—photo shoots, performances, animations, interviews, fashion editorials, tabloids, fansites, hours and hours of video or streaming content, and so much more—but also stretch their imaginative powers to transform these original materials through their labors. Rosanna Hall's digital painting *My Universe* (plate 1) is emblematic of fanart that lovingly details the physical beauty (or "visuals," in the industry parlance) of idols. Against a backdrop of intergalactic cloud formations, portraits of BTS members make up the "stars" in a heavenly constellation, referencing themes about celestial bodies and the meaning of existence found in much of BTS's oeuvre. Carolina Alves's digital illustration *Crimson Blooming* (plate 2) draws inspiration from an individual photo shoot in the 2021 *Vogue Korea* special issue on BTS, featuring a scarlet-clad Jimin posed against a pale pink backdrop. Typical of her figurative art, her portrait removes facial details, yet Jimin is easily recognizable because of fans' deep familiarity with each of the members. Replacing the pink backdrop with a creamy peach, she arranges blooming crimson flowers and ripe pomegranates around Jimin, the centerpiece in an abundant bouquet of beauty. For <*Archive for Bangtan Universe—YET TO COME*> (plate 3), JIN Youngsun combines fresco and frescography technique with the form of a folding screen to create an archive of BTS's musical journey. The work references the narratives, symbols, and images of their discography from their early SKOOL LUV AFFAIR album to their more recent "Yet To Come" single. When folded, the images are hidden from view, and when fully spread out, it opens up to a panorama inspired by BTS's body of work. The 2017 full-length album YOU NEVER WALK ALONE (a repackage of BTS's second studio album, WINGS) inspired Yuni Kartika's "*Spring Day*" (plate 4), named after the melancholy lead track. In a loving homage to "Spring Day" and its contemplative nature, Kartika's thread painting of the iconic oceanside bus stop photograph was created using a hand embroidery technique using strands of embroidery floss (traditionally cotton or silk thread) to blend together colors for a painterly effect.

Other fans also bring a wealth of other knowledge to reflect on how we might otherwise "see" our idols or to deepen our reception of their body of work. Maria Mison's *Diary of Youth: "Justice"* (plate 5) is a featured card from a BTS tarot project that reinterprets imagery from the band's music videos and performances into the classic Rider-Waite-Smith Tarot. A tarot reader themself, Mison designed the cards with their project partner, Mara Andres, to be used for the intuitive and self-contemplative practices via story-laden images that undergird tarot. The layers of BTS lore in each design add to and complement the traditional meanings of a usual tarot deck. Kaina "Kai" Bernal's digital print *Cultural Rebellion Pt. 1* (plate 6) captures the creative energy of BTS's massive Latinx fandom. Bernal turns to nostalgic images of candy from her Mexican American childhood to imagine, through food (so often the "prize" in any given *Run BTS!* episode), a bridge to another culture whose language she does not understand. In doing so, she illustrates a hybrid and uniquely Latinx presence and visual vocabulary within K-Pop fandom.

Fanart often centers the individual fan's love of BTS, while not eliding the contradictory aspects of their consumption of a commodity-image of an idol. Johnny Huy Nguyễn's *Minority without a Model* (plate 7), a full-length dance theater work, is an autobiographical exploration of gender, race, and desire through the performer's lived experiences as a cisgender, heterosexual Southeast Asian man in the context of anti-Asian exclusion and violence in the United States. The moment captured in the photograph of this performance features a dance cover of BTS's "DNA," where Nguyễn meditates on the tensions between BTS's representation of Asian idol masculine beauty, the absurdity of trying to emulate their desirable "look," and the underlying feelings of invisibility that underpin such an undertaking. Other fan labors use the resources made available to them through K-Pop and BTS to generate utopian fantasies and counter social erasure. The selected panel from Havannah Tran's twenty-page digital zine, *BTS Stands for Bisexuals, Trans Folks, & Sapphics* (plate 8), riffs on a long-practiced queer tradition—stanning—to grapple with questions of expression and visibility in a society that would rather not see, let alone honor, queerness. Both an homage to BTS, and the members' concept photos prompting gender envy and style inspo (slang for inspiration), as well as a love letter to her queer friends, many of whom became ARMY during the pandemic, the digital zine is at once an opportunity for joy and community, but also a meditation on love and queer possibility. Drawing on her background in graphic design and illustration, Ameena Fareeda's *Namjooning* (plate 9) is part of a series of posters created for each individual member of BTS. Envisioning them as pages in a scrapbook, Fareeda tailors each poster to reflect some part of each member's persona; in *Namjooning*, she illustrates a term coined by RM to describe activities he enjoys in his leisure time. The term embodies the sentiment that walks in nature, reading, and going to art museums are activities that ARMY can enjoy "with" him.

In a digital economy, memes are now ubiquitous communicative devices, condensing a wide array of complex emotions, ideas, or information for viral circulation. Among fans, memes are often palimpsestic messages that mine and modify familiar materials for new interpretations or affects. Ever since Marcel Duchamp drew a mustache and goatee on a postcard image of Leonardo da Vinci's *Mona Lisa* (c. 1503–6) and renamed the work *L.H.O.O.Q.* or *La Jaconde* (1919), artists have been remixing well-known artworks, and the meme is a perfect format for that labor. In *Namjoon and the Sirens* (plate 10), Amanda Lovely inserts an image of RM (Namjoon) into a digital reproduction of Herbert James Draper's *Ulysses and the Sirens* (1909). The humorous connection between RM's attempt to escape the seductive sounds of the Sirens from Homer's *The Odyssey* both resonates with BTS's sly song "Pied Piper" ("I'm here to save you / I'm here to ruin you"),[3] "Home," and sits alongside BTS's own references to Greek antiquity in "Dionysus" and Draper's *The Lament of Icarus* (1898), which also appears in the music video of "Blood Sweat & Tears." In their *Being cute / Pays mah bills* (plate 11) meme (featuring a press photograph of SUGA), Prerna Subramanian comments on "cuteness" as a commodity aesthetic in which BTS often partakes—and lampoons—as K-Pop idols but inquires further about the racial and gendered dimensions of such performances. "How can cuteness be reparative, and not be a regurgitation of devaluing femininity while embracing it only when it softens the edges of a masculine presenting person?" Her work as the Instagram meme account @btsabolitionmemes is not about being a "killjoy," but instead invoking what adrienne maree brown calls pleasure activism or joyful militancy.[4] Gracelynne West's *Learning Radical Love through* BTS (plate 12) observes that while K-Pop is deeply entrenched in capitalism, a number of the members—SUGA, RM, V, and Jin, in particular—have challenged prevailing structures of extraction and self-commodification in their songs and in their words. In posting these valentines to her Instagram account @joonsmelanindrop, she sought to highlight those sentiments and allow ARMY who "feel seen" through these memes to redefine radical love.

Fans also draw from the well of BTS inspiration to create art that comments on the reciprocal relationship between BTS and ARMY and between ARMY among themselves, and sometimes actively generates aid for causes that fans hold dear. Sophia Cai's crocheted and knitted plushies, BFFs *(Butter Friends Forever)* (plate 13), are inspired by the *BANGTAN BOMB* video where the seven members of BTS each decorate their own copy of the album.[5] Cai made these hand-holding pair of albums (the two colors in which one might purchase them) in the spirit of solidarity and shared joy during a period of isolation and uncertainty. Cai's albums were auctioned in 2021, with part of the proceeds going to PS Mutual Aid, an Australian organization that supports low- and no-income households without access to government support during the COVID-19 health crisis. Similarly, Inez Amihan Anderson and Mimi Thi Nguyen's ink-and-digital drawing, *Light It Up Like Dynamite* (plate 14), references the murder of George Floyd and the protests against anti-Black police violence that broke out in its aftermath, in the same summer of BTS's first English-language single. Anderson and Nguyen's art mashes up the bright, saturated colors and nostalgic Americana of BTS's "Dynamite" music video with an illustration of a burning police car, "borrowed" from a T-shirt used to raise funds for those arrested in the 1979 White Night Riots (another anti-police uprising), to conjure abolitionist dreaming.

Finally, this interlude ends with Yutian Wong's photograph, called *Gifts* (plate 15), of some of the "freebies"—stickers, photocards, candies, bookmarks, magnets, doodles, hand-beaded bracelets customized with members' names, and even a crocheted tangerine—received from ARMY at BTS concerts or film screenings. These souvenirs enact a utopian aesthetics of being in a world together with others, taking shape in the encounter with a smiling stranger, holding out their hand.

Notes

1   Other forms of emotional attachment—including disgust, scorn, and sometimes outright hatred—do appear in fanart in general, of course.
2   Nguyen, "Bruce Lee I Love You," 276.
3   Lyrics for "Pied Piper," translated by Genius English Translations, September 18, 2017, https://genius.com/Genius-english-translations-bts -pied-piper-english-translation-lyrics.
4   brown, *Pleasure Activism*.
5   BANGTANTV, "[BANGTAN BOMB] 'Butter' Album Unboxing—BTS (방탄소년단)," July 11, 2021, YouTube video, 23:06, https://www.youtube.com/watch?v =s3cJxUop66E.

Works Cited

brown, adrienne maree. *Pleasure Activism: The Politics of Feeling Good*. Chico, CA: AK, 2019.

Nguyen, Mimi Thi. "Bruce Lee I Love You: Discourses of Race and Masculinity in the Queer Superstardom of JJ Chinois." In *Alien Encounters: Popular Culture in Asian America*, edited by Thuy Linh Nguyen Tu and Mimi Thi Nguyen, 271–304. Durham, NC: Duke University Press, 2007.

Plate 1 · Rosanna Hall, *My Universe*, 2021.
Digital painting with Procreate.

Plate 2 · Carolina Alves, *Crimson Blooming*, 2022. Digital illustration with Procreate.

Plate 3 · JIN Youngsun, *Archive for Bangtan Universe—<YET TO COME>*, 2022. Fresco and frescography, aluminum honeycomb panel installed in folding screen, 180 × 160 cm.

Plate 4 · (*above*) Yuni Kartika, "*Spring Day*," 2022. Cotton floss, cotton calico, beechwood, and acrylic.

Plate 5 · (*opposite*) Maria Mison, *Diary of Youth: "Justice,"* 2022. Mixed media, 2.75 × 4.75 in., 1 of 79 cards.

Plate 6 · Kaina "Kai" Bernal, *Cultural Rebellion Pt. 1*, 2020.
Digital print, 18 × 26 in.

Plate 7 · Johnny Huy Nguyễn, *Minority without a Model*, 2021.
Dance theater still.

Plate 8 · Havannah Tran, *BTS Stands for Bisexuals, Trans Folks, & Sapphics*, 2020. Panel from digital zine, created in Clip Studio Paint and Adobe InDesign.

STYLE
MY HAIR,

AND DO MY MAKE-UP.

SO WHEN I SCREAM OVER CONCEPT PHOTOS
AND AIRPORT FITS, WHAT I'M SAYING IS THIS IS WHAT I
ASPIRE TO BE, AS A CURRENTLY POORLY DRESSED FUTCH.

Plate 9 · Ameena Fareeda, *Namjooning*, 2021.
Digital art/illustration, 8 × 10 in.

Plate 10 · Amanda Lovely, *Namjoon and the Sirens*,
2022. Instagram post, created in Photoshop.

Being cute

Pays mah bills

Kstyle

Representation in yt supremacist institutions doesn't mean meaningful change besties, wanna join us in sharing mutual aid, instead?

@joonsmelanindrop

Plate 11 · (*opposite*) Prerna Subramanian, *Being cute / Pays mah bills*, 2023. Instagram post, created in Canva.

Plate 12 · (*above*) Gracelynne West, *Learning Radical Love through BTS*, 2023. Instagram post, created in Canva.

Plate 13 · Sophia Cai, *BFFs (Butter Friends Forever)*, 2021. Cotton yarn, plastic eyes, cardboard, polyfill, approximately 16 × 15 × 4.5 cm (each).

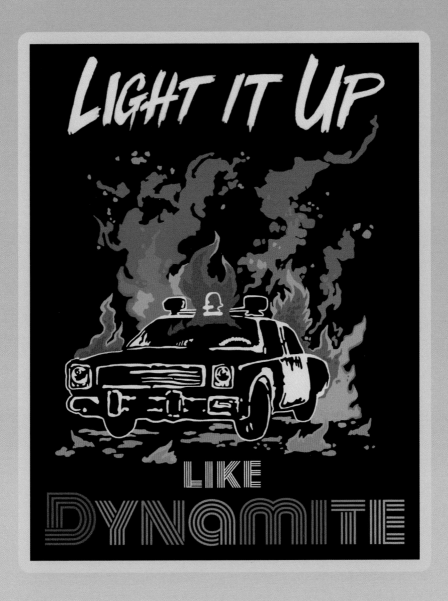

Plate 14 · Inez Amihan Anderson and Mimi Thi Nguyen, *Light It Up Like Dynamite*, 2020. Ink drawing, digital coloring.

Plate 15 · Yutian Wong, *Gifts*, 2023. Digital photograph.

IV "You Never Walk Alone"

FANDOM AND COMMUNITY

After the agony and angst found on their second studio album, WINGS, BTS described their 2017 release of YOU NEVER WALK ALONE as "a message of warm consolation and hope for the suffering youth of this generation." Such messages of camaraderie and care, whether mining feelings of anger in "No More Dream" or offering solace in "Life Goes On," have long been a part of the power of BTS.[1] During a 2016 fan meeting, member V (known among the members and the fans for sometimes speaking in "TaeTae," a fantastical dialect of his own invention) coined "*borahae*," or "I purple you." The phrase combines two Korean words—*bora* (violet) and *saranghae* (I love you)—to mean, "I'll love you till the end of days," because as V explained, purple (violet) is the last color of the rainbow. His explanation signaled the importance of ARMY as a band of confidantes so strong in their affections that they deserve a new logic and language of love. This is just one example of how BTS together and individually address, with precise attention to detail, our affective attachments to each other.

It is impossible to write about BTS without addressing how their existence as idols is saturated with love and desire. Whether it be how the members express their feelings—about their haters, their struggles and sacrifices as idols, and their relationships with each other and ARMY—or how the fans understand such feelings and their own fierce attachments, love and desire define BTS's every chord and movement. From hard stans (those who view BTS in a sexual way), fan-fiction fantasies (ranging from fluffy to explicitly sexual), "shipping/anti-shipping" wars, to art, faith, pedagogy, and political action, BTS is often a catalyst for voicing and even transfiguring erotics, meanings, and values. The chapters in this section illuminate how attachments to BTS facilitate acts of love, fantasy, friendship, safety, collaboration, lust, art, and hope. In doing so, their authors give voice to the promise found in "you never walk alone," demonstrating the dynamism of BTS as a phantasmatic force.

Focused on how ARMY engage their star texts, idol performances, elaborate story worlds, and thematic arcs across BTS's body of work, a number of the chapters address desire in its multiple dimensions and forms. Sara Murphy's "The Skinship Diaries" ponders the allure of physical and emotional intimacy as a woman whose autoimmune disease prevents her from a life of touch. Narrating the complex nexus of loss and pleasure she feels when watching the members of BTS engage in moments of affection, Murphy observes how, through skinship, BTS illustrates a tactile life not limited to traditional notions of sex and sexuality. In "'Gender DOES NOT Exist Outside of Patriarchy': Flower Boys, Gender Envy, and the Radical Possibilities of JIMIN GENDER," S. Heijin Lee examines the intersection between South Korean and North American constructions of masculinity and how North American fans perceive BTS member Jimin as a gender category unto himself. Rani Neutill interviews Gen X women in "Permission to Desire" to consider an encounter with oneself through new objects that rewrite the story of one's libidinal, unconscious, and symbolic life. She describes a collective reckoning among Gen X women with how the media of their youth produced often-demeaning images of East Asian men and how BTS has subsequently reshaped their desires. In "Fifty Shades of Butter: Consensual Nonconsent in BTS Fan Fiction," Raymond San Diego examines a subgenre of self-insert fan fiction featuring BTS. Closely reading the nuanced address of consent in these stories, San Diego details the ways in which these fan fictions move away from often-reductive conceptions of consent, enabling a demystification of sexual desire altogether.

Profuse in their encouragement to each other and their fans, BTS also inspires among ARMY a commitment to care and communion (despite how conflict also exists within the fandom and between fandoms). Bangtan Scholars cofounder Courtney Lazore's "Bangtan Scholars and the Ethics of Care" examines the principles that guide the creation and activity of many ARMY-initiated groups and, in particular, Bangtan Scholars, a collective dedicated to connecting and supporting the wide range of ARMY researchers. Sophia Cai brings together BTS and ARMY as a case study for applying fandom as an expanded curatorial methodology. Focusing on two recent curatorial projects, "*Sincerely Yours, ARMY*: Exploring Fandom as Curatorial Methodology" suggests that fandom and fan culture might offer a novel lens through which to rethink intersections of art and identity outside of traditional exhibition formats, art institutions, and circuits. And, as Muslims in various parts of the world continue to face discrimination and violence, Mariam Elba argues that BTS fandom can serve as a safe haven in the midst of Islamophobic policies and worldviews. Her chapter, "The Digital ARMY-*Ummah*: Faith and Community among Muslim BTS Fans," shows how a common interest in BTS drove the formation of an online Muslim ARMY community that provided support for each other while dismantling stereotypes about Muslims.

Finally, UyenThi Tran Myhre draws fierce hope from BTS and their embrace of both destruction and creation, a duality also found at the heart of abolitionist movement building. By following the threads of her own origin stories as a Minneapolis-based abolitionist, a daughter of Vietnamese refugees, and as ARMY, "'Let Us Light Up the Night': BTS and Abolitionist Possibilities at the End of the World" explores how encounters with BTS and their work can illuminate and inform abolitionist principles and practices for a "moment yet to come."

Note

1   "No More Dream" was the lead single from BTS's debut album, *2 COOL 4 SKOOL* (2014). The lyrics criticize the dead-end "dream" of steady but unfulfilling employment imposed by societal norms.

21 · The Skinship Diaries

_ Sara Murphy

January 4, 2020, is the first day of the thirty-fourth annual Golden Disc Awards (GDAs), a two-day ceremony in Seoul that honors achievements in the South Korean music industry. BTS will go on to win the top awards: Album of the Year for *MAP OF THE SOUL: PERSONA* and Song of the Year for "Boy with Luv (작은 것들을 위한 시) feat. Halsey." As the members—lusciously decked out in Givenchy—watch the proceedings from their seats on the side of the stage, Jung Kook taps V, who sits hunched over in front of him, on the side. V turns, and Jung Kook catches his eye. They share a glance. Without speaking, V slowly leans back, relaxing against Jung Kook's chest. Jung Kook encircles V with his right arm and, after a beat or two, tightens his grip and rests his chin on V's head. They stay like that for a while, V tapping out a rhythm on his thigh as he stretches out his legs and sinks deeper into Jung Kook's body.

Three months later, I sit in my bed, replaying this moment over and over again on YouTube.[1] I notice the little things: How Jung Kook moves to make room for V after they lock eyes. How Jung Kook follows it with a tiny nod of invitation, permission. How V melts into Jung Kook, sliding down his body as if slouching in a seat. How Jung Kook doesn't break the embrace even though he has to crane his neck over V's head to see the stage. It's seamless, this silent conversation, and it fills my chest with warmth. V and Jung Kook look beautiful, as do their gestures: movements as smooth as a choreographed dance. I smile.

Watching them is alluring, but my joy and enchantment is tempered by a sense of emptiness and isolation. Air brushes coldly against my exposed arms, and the headboard of my bed is stiff behind my back. I try to remember the last time someone held me like that, moving their bodily instinctually to touch mine. It takes a while, but finally the memory comes. Freshman year at college. Sitting on the coarse, cheap, brown carpet in my dorm room, I stared at the TV as my friend Tom cradled me. Silently, we watched the bird's-eye footage of high schoolers running out of their school with their hands behind their heads, arms pointed out like angle brackets. April 20, 1999. The school shooting at Columbine, Colorado. Comfort in crisis.

V and Jung Kook do not need the excuse of a watershed event in American gun violence to give and receive comfort through touch. In K-Pop, that familiarity and ease with physical contact is called skinship. Originally coined in Japan to refer to tactile intimacy between a mother and child, in South Korea the concept of skinship has expanded to encompass any skin-on-skin contact that demonstrates affection or closeness.[2] In K-Pop, skinship between (same-sex) group members through holding hands, hugging—and, yes, leaning into each other—is a vital part of fan service.[3] I get the appeal. When I see Jung Kook embrace V at the GDAs, or RM put his arm around Jin, or j-hope wake up Jimin by climbing into bed and spooning him, I feel the same vicarious joy that comes from watching the protagonists in a romantic comedy finally smooch. As ARMY, I'm invested in V's and Jung Kook's happiness, and it comforts me to see them comfort each other. But that joy is lined with a jealous sorrow, because watching them reminds me how absent touch is in my own life, and of the blend of chance and choice that has denied me such pleasure.

When my town of Asheville, North Carolina, shuts down due to the COVID-19 pandemic on March 17, 2020, I am two months shy of my fortieth birthday. Perennially single, my last and longest relationship ended in the autumn of 2004 after eight months. I live with my mother and stepfather, an arrangement that isn't strange to us given my mother's Iranian roots; extended families frequently share households in our culture. I prefer my parents to roommates; in this costly region, their spacious house in the mountains is nicer than anything I could rent. Prior to the pandemic, to give us all some room to breathe, I spent what otherwise would have been rent money on a couple months of international travel each year. Solo, of course. Though I sometimes found it lonely, as an only child I have long been used to entertaining myself. I planned my trips around brief visits to friends in cities like Shanghai and Vienna and then struck out on my own. It's because of one of these trips—two months in Asia that included two weeks in South Korea—that I am a fan of BTS. When I returned to the United States in June 2019, I missed the bustle and historical sites of Seoul, the temples and spas in Busan. In lieu of booking a return trip, I decided to delve into one of the prized exports from South Korea—*Hallyu*, or the Korean wave. Never much of a film watcher, I chose K-Pop instead, and discovered the video for "Boy With Luv (작은 것들을 위한 시) feat. Halsey."

I have never looked back. Though the music hooked me, I quickly noticed how tactile the members are with each other. Dressed in shiny pink silks, they joyfully drape their arms around each other as they shout to the camera at the end of the video. In "피 땀 눈물 (Blood Sweat & Tears)," SUGA grabs Jimin's hand and pulls him like a child dragging his friend along as they run out of the art gallery. This physical intimacy is so different from the aloofness of the bands I used to obsess over, those of the '60s British Invasion in my adolescence and Radiohead and Blur in my twenties.

By the time the pandemic arrives in the US, I desperately need not just BTS's music but also shows like BTS BON VOYAGE and Run BTS!, where their skinship—cuddling in bed, holding hands, or giving and getting piggyback rides when walking—is on full display. I spend hours watching, knowing it will be a long time before I touch anyone outside my household. I have lived with ulcerative colitis, an autoimmune inflammatory bowel disease, since the age of ten. For two decades, I have taken immune-suppressing medication. Twice in my life, I spent a week in the hospital after catching a garden-variety virus my body could not shake. In February 2020, I suffered a three-week-long bout with the flu. No hospital, thankfully, but I barely left my bed. When I took my first walk in three weeks, I managed only twenty minutes instead of my usual hour a day. As the transmissibility of COVID-19 and its deadly consequences become clearer, I know that this virus could kill me. The rhythm of my life disappears, as time blurs into one long, suspended day with no change of scenery. Instead of helping my elderly parents with errands, they shop for me. Each time they return, the air feels rife with potential contagion. I wipe down packages of salad mix with Lysol. I agonize over whether I should urge them to change their clothes, as a friend in Italy—where the virus had already left a devastating trail of death—does every time she enters her home. BTS's joyful embrace of each other's bodies provides a welcome contrast to the protective bubble I am forced to erect around myself.

Though I half fear I will go mad, I remember: *I have done this before.* In high school, I was so acutely ill that leaving the safety zone of my bedroom and bathroom created a constant hum of anxiety. I developed a series of mental and physical rituals to distract me from the cramps in my gut and the feeling that I was about to soil myself; most often, I crossed the fingers of my left hand and dug my thumbnail into my index finger, using self-inflicted pain to forget the pain I could not control. My senior year, I would drive the five minutes home (we were allowed to go off-campus for lunch) to sip chicken broth with a couple of carrots. I sometimes fell asleep at the kitchen table, and once on the toilet. Even though I only ate at dinnertime, I still had bloody diarrhea as much as ten times a day.

Back then, the Beatles kept me company. They had a song for every one of my shifting moods: "Strawberry Fields Forever" when I was low, "She Said She Said" for my sneeringly angry moments, and "Something" and "Here, There, and Everywhere" when I felt sappy and romantic. A moody and bookish teen, I fed my adoration of them through not just sonic but scholarly immersion. As I played *Rubber Soul*, *Revolver*, *Abbey Road*, and the *1967–1970* compilation affectionately known as "the Blue Album" on my boom box, I paged through pictures of John, Paul, George, and Ringo in the various biographies, illustrated discographies, and other books that made up my small but carefully curated collection. Cocooned by these sights and sounds, I disassociated from my uncontrollable, pain-wracked body. I would stare at pictures of Paul (my favorite) with his orange-haired girlfriend, Jane Asher, and fantasize it was my hand he was holding. At that age, my only experience of romantic touch was an awkward first kiss my sophomore year. I had crushed on Will (a pseudonym) for months and felt like the luckiest girl in the world when I realized that my attraction was reciprocated for the first time in my life. But when he leaned in to make out with me on our first date, every alarm bell in my brain blared GET AWAY. Instead of sweet and soft, his tongue was thick and slimy, a snake-like muscle that clogged my mouth. I ghosted him without explanation for the (mercifully short) rest of the school year, hiding behind friends until he got the hint. To deal with that disappointment, I played "For No One" on repeat, mouthing along as Paul sang, deadpan, "She says that long ago she knew someone / But now he's gone, she doesn't need him."

Now, in the naive first spring of the pandemic, it is BTS rather than the Beatles who keep me company. There's a lovely symmetry in that, since BTS channeled the Fab Four's iconic 1964 appearance on *The Ed Sullivan Show* for their May 2019 performance on *The Late Show with Stephen Colbert*, complete with Beatles-esque suits and a black-and-white filter.[4] Similarly, BTS has undergone an evolution in their music over the years. MAP OF THE SOUL: 7 shows a growth in the maturity and complexity of songwriting that echoes the Beatles' progression from bubblegum love songs to genre-breaking concept albums like *Sgt. Pepper's Lonely Hearts Club Band*. There are also crucial differences. BTS members confidently wear makeup and perform intensely choreographed dances, aware of but unfazed by Anglo-American culture, which sees such behavior as effeminate and weak. On red carpets in Los Angeles, they unapologetically place their arms around each other. In interviews, they rest their hands on each other's thighs or shoulders. John and Paul never did that in public.

I, too, have changed since my Beatles days. My colitis has been in remission for fifteen years, my last relapse in 2005. I meditate daily, eat lots of plants, and take exercise seriously, all habits that make my body the healthiest it has ever been. Except for my heart, which aches with loneliness, and my skin, which is starved for touch. It has been eighteen years since my one and only real romantic relationship, four years since I last experienced the touch of mutual desire, which lasted only ten days. I have failed myself, too afraid and ashamed of my body's inadequacies to find a romantic partner. The result has been a life deprived of touch. Not just sexual or romantic touch—as I age, the opportunities for platonic touch with male and female friends beyond hugs of greeting and farewell have dried up. So, when I see Jung Kook hold V at the Golden Disc Awards, it's like spotting an oasis after days of dehydration in the desert. Never mind that I can only experience that touch vicariously. A mirage of an oasis creates happiness and hope, too.

* * *

When I think back to January to August 2004—the brief span of my first love and only relationship—one memory sticks out. Nighttime in his bed, my arm slung over his waist, my nose buried in his white T-shirt, my knees tucked into his as we spooned on his rarely washed sheets. I floated on happiness, confident I knew what shooting heroin felt like. I told myself to drink the feeling in, stave off my sleep to cherish it. Greg (a pseudonym) was leaving in August to pursue his PhD in another country. Who knew, after he was gone, when I would next feel this way again?

I felt that ecstasy even though our sex life was, in many ways, a disaster. Vaginal sex felt like my muscles were being ripped apart like fabric seams. Ashamed of this physiological failure, I didn't tell Greg until weeks after we had started dating. Concerned, he insisted we slow down until it felt good. He put extra lube on his condom each time. It got to be bearable but never pleasurable. I got used to faking it.

Then, one day, he gingerly informed me that, compared to his other partners, it was clear that my pleasure wasn't actually orgasmic. He bought me a vibrator in the hope that it might help; I only let him try it once. I couldn't bear any reminder of the fact that, yet again, my reactions and experiences of sexual touch were abnormal. Deficient. Wrong. My colitis was in remission, and even the acne that had once prompted a man to announce to a full train car that he could "fix" my face had calmed. Yet there was never going to be a time when my body wasn't fucking up somehow.

The urinary tract infections didn't help. One led to a full-blown kidney infection, complete with a night in the hospital, where I was told I had a heart murmur. I discovered I was allergic to codeine when I threw up the Tylenol-3 they prescribed me after discharge. My immunosuppressants were making me far too vulnerable to every infection, and the clock was counting down to Greg's departure date. Even though those drugs kept the worst of my symptoms at bay, I stopped them. I put myself and my health behind my desire to keep him and his love.

In the end, I lost both. He left, as he said he would. And two years later, I relapsed and went back on the immunosuppressants.

My first and only love taught me two indelible lessons about my body. Greg's adoring, lustful touch made me believe that my body was touchable, lovable, capable of giving (if not receiving) pleasure. But not lovable enough: he had left me. I never managed to trust anyone else not to do the same, feeling a perverse gratitude when anyone wanted to bother with my body. Their interest never lasted long, especially once they noticed that I couldn't come on command and felt how inexpertly my hands fumbled against their own skin. The second lesson I learned after all those infections was that romantic love and touch were a hazard to my health. I could let someone permeate the boundaries of my body and suffer consequences I couldn't anticipate: yet another manifestation of my sexual dysfunction, perhaps, or an STD. Or, I could go back to my usual position of solitude and protect that delicate equilibrium of remission. A skin starved of touch was a loss I knew, one I could bear however painful. The longer I stayed single, the taller the obstacles to learning how to have healthy, nourishing romantic intimacy became. A man who would be patient enough with my intimacy hang-ups and a compatible partner seems like a unicorn. I don't even want my body, so why would someone else? And, if they did, what would that say about their judgment?

* * *

When I first start obsessively watching BTS skinship videos, I can only see them through the lens of my own bittersweet and nostalgic memories of romantic touch. My favorite BTS skinship videos are the ones made by ARMY seeking to prove that a particular ship is "real"—in other words, that they are a romantic couple. (The implication is that anything less than romantic partnership is somehow *not* real.) That Golden Disc Awards moment I watch so much comes from a sixteen-minute "analysis" of V and Jung Kook's interactions at the ceremony, complete with slow-motion and still photos and interpretative commentary. I find myself nodding in agreement when I read comments under the video like, "Anyone who says their relationship isn't real is blind. The love and adoration in their eyes is so obvious."[5] I want their relationship to be "real," because the most intoxicating touch I've ever felt was with a romantic, sexual partner. Because I love BTS, I want the members to experience that joy, too. It's the most I can hope for, since I have already given up on that possibility for myself.

The more I watch, however, the more I read the comments from ARMY. Many of them resist the romantic readings of various shippers, arguing that skinship is not perceived in Korea as essentially romantic. Some openly express their desire that men in their cultures could perform skinship among friends without shame and hesitation. "I wish healthy examples of male affection and connection like this were more prevalent," one writes, decrying "the harsh 'gotta be tough to be a man / can't show weakness or be in touch with my emotions' persona."[6] At first, I nod along. But I soon realize that the "healthy . . . affection and connection" that I and other ARMY see in skinship is something I want not just for the members but for *me*. BTS's skinship has shown me an alternative world of touch I've never known: one that enjoys physical intimacy without the pressure of sexual expectation.

I tried to create that experience twice in my life. Once in both high school and college, I tried to link arms with girlfriends as we walked together. Both times, we barely made it twenty feet before I felt their arms go tense and rigid under my own, their discomfort making my skin buzz.

Those fleeting, failed attempts are such a contrast to the casual confidence with which BTS reach out and grab each other, as if they have no boundaries of consent to navigate. The way RM slings his arm around Jin's shoulder as they walk back to their seats after picking up an award at the Mnet Asian Music Awards 2019. How Jung Kook rubs V's thigh as they sit next to each other in early *MAP OF THE SOUL: 7* interviews. How Jimin and j-hope joyfully spoon Jung Kook when he collapses on one of the futons in Jeonju Cultural Village where they film their 2019 Summer Package. There's no question in their minds that their members won't welcome the touch. Even SUGA (incidentally, my bias), who more often than not makes faces and squirms when hugged, indulges V like a permissive parent and consents to be carried, piggyback, on stage at the 2019 Golden Disc Awards. A moment between SUGA and V ("Taegi," as fans of the pair's interactions call them, a portmanteau of their birth names Taehyung and Yoongi) that I find particularly poignant takes place in 2017, during the second season of the travel show *BTS BON VOYAGE*. At the end of the fifth episode, the members are tasked with pairing up for what the staff calls a "friendship tour" around Hawai'i.[7] The staff suggest making it more interesting for ARMY by creating pairs usually not seen together. So, rather than pairing V with Jung Kook or Jimin, the members suggest that he spends the day with SUGA. "We usually have different opinions," SUGA acknowledges. He therefore declares that whenever they disagree, they will solve it by "holding hands." He demonstrates, clasping V's hand as V hangs his head in embarrassed laughter. I love this moment because SUGA isn't just putting up with V's penchant for skinship. As a *hyeong*, or elder, he knows that the power balance between him and V makes his statements about how often they disagree not just embarrassing but potentially hurtful. So, even though SUGA has his own hesitations around touch, he uses it to soften his words because he knows it will comfort V. When SUGA holds V's hand, I see a touch that I long to experience myself. Uncomplicated, supportive, organic touch that doesn't harm. Touch that doesn't make me feel broken and defective, abnormal and lacking. Touch that's playful, and low stakes, and not bound up with fears of infection and rejection. Touch that holds and heals, comforts and calms. In short, skinship. It's bittersweet to watch, simultaneously heartwarming and heartbreaking.

Because even if I could gather with my friends tomorrow and confidently ask for and receive the back hugs, hand-holding, and spooning I long for, I wouldn't. Despite what Psy claims in the SUGA-produced 2022 hit "That That (prod. & feat. SUGA of BTS)," the pandemic is not over as I write these words in the autumn of 2022. The American disability activists I follow on Twitter express their anguish at getting left behind as life in the United States broadly returns to prepandemic masklessness. The risk of long COVID feels too great to socialize beyond Zoom or occasional outdoor walks with friends willing to make the drive up the mountain road to my home.

In the children's story *The Velveteen Rabbit*, it's the loving touch of a child for their favorite toy that transforms the frayed stuffed bunny into a real rabbit. We're supposed to feel joy when the toy transforms into a living creature, but I never lost a sense of sadness that he would no longer have the constant, adoring touch of the boy who loved him. In the book's final illustration, the living bunny leaps for joy, but the other rabbits watch from afar, uncertain of this new addition to their woods.[8] As a child, I slept for years with piles of stuffed animals, cloaking me in a sense of community and closeness I didn't have at school. Years later, when I was in the hospital for a week during my sophomore year of college, the resident advisor for my dorm floor brought me the softest stuffed elephant I'd ever felt. Alone in my room after visiting hours ended, I'd curl around it and pull it to my stomach, the plush soothing against my skin as my insides twisted painfully. That elephant is long gone, its fur having hardened with age. But, thanks to BTS, I have a surrogate to spoon in the absence of a beloved, breathing body. Every night, I clutch my own stuffed bunny: the pink rabbit Jung Kook designed for LINE FRIENDS called Kooky. Soft and giving against my skin, it reminds me that, imperfect as my body may be, I am real.

Notes

1   AnalisandoTaeKook, "GDA 2020 Taekook analysis [vkook]," February 8,
        2020, YouTube video, 16:15, https://youtu.be/IcQrydm13kc.
2   Gregory, "Skinship." According to *Word Spy*—the source for Gregory's
        working definition—the word first appears in the *Nihon Kokugo Daijiten*,
        the Japanese equivalent of the *Oxford English Dictionary*, in 1971. *Word
        Spy*, s.v. "skinship," February 3, 2003, https://wordspy.com/index.php
        ?word=skinship.
3   Choi, "Gender, Labor, and the Commodification of Intimacy in K-Pop."
        Choi presents skinship as part of a larger marketing strategy appealing
        to desires that Korean female K-Pop fans express in venues like slash
        or same-sex fan fiction. However, her work, while valuable, focuses on
        Korean K-Pop fans, and this chapter examines skinship from a North
        American perspective.
4   Gemmill, "BTS Re-created a Legendary Beatles' Performance."
5   Comment by Maria in AnalisandoTaeKook, "GDA 2020 Taekook analy-
        sis [vkook]," February 8, 2020, YouTube video, 16:15, https://youtu.be
        /IcQrydm13kc.
6   Comment by LietSayri in Pinkkoyaa Films, "BTS Being Cuddly," Decem-
        ber 27, 2021, YouTube video, 10:49, https://youtu.be/WNsdzOWtDAo.
7   "BTS Bon Voyage Season 2 Episode 05," September 4, 2022, BiliBili video,
        51:44, https://www.bilibili.tv/en/video/2044531042.
8   Nicholson, "At Last! At Last!"

Works Cited

Choi, Stephanie. "Gender, Labor, and the Commodification of Intimacy in K-Pop." PhD diss., University of California, Santa Barbara, 2020. https://escholarship.org/uc/item/5xj1r230.

Gemmill, Allie. "BTS Re-created a Legendary Beatles' Performance When Playing 'Boy with Luv' on *The Late Show with Stephen Colbert*." *Teen Vogue*, May 16, 2019. https://www.teenvogue.com/story/bts-beatles-boy-with-luv-late-show-stephen-colbert.

Gregory, Chris. "Skinship: Touchability as a Virtue in East-Central India." HAU: *Journal of Ethnographic Theory* 1, no. 1 (2011): 179–209. doi.org/10.14318/hau1.1.007.

Nicholson, William. "At Last! At Last!" In *The Velveteen Rabbit, or How Toys Become Real*, by Margery Williams. Garden City, NY: Doubleday, 1922. https://digital.library.upenn.edu/women/williams/rabbit/rabbit.html.

22 · "Gender DOES NOT Exist Outside of Patriarchy": Flower Boys, Gender Envy, and the Radical Possibilities of JIMIN GENDER — S. Heijin Lee

On October 10, 2020, during the first (of two) *MAP OF THE SOUL ON:E* pay-per-view streaming concerts, Park Jimin performed his solo track "Filter." The performance and subsequent concert photos revealed that Jimin had written the word *Illecebra* on his right hand and *Arcanus* on his left. Social media platforms were abuzz with ARMY deciphering that the former is a feminine noun meaning "enticement" while the latter is a masculine one that means "keeper of secrets." That Jimin had chosen both types of gendered nouns to adorn his hands was deeply meaningful to ARMY, as illustrated by Twitter user @gajaaegiyagaja's tweet: "The fact that illecebra is a feminine term and arcanus is a masculine term blows my mind. JIMIN REALLY SAID JIMIN GENDER."[1] (See figure 22.1.) The tweet exemplifies North American ARMY's fascination with Jimin as an arbiter of a new gender formation. Accordingly, this chapter seeks to understand the regional specificities of how JIMIN GENDER is conceptualized among fans through an analysis of contemporary North American fan discourse on Twitter. What is JIMIN GENDER and why is it so meaningful to North American ARMY? After locating JIMIN GENDER within the genealogy of Korea's "flower boy" aesthetic, I argue that JIMIN GENDER offers North American ARMY a visual language for reimagining new ways of performing gender and, as such, signifies the radical possibilities of a genderqueer world.

Since the late 1990s, *Hallyu*'s (the Korean Wave) "soft masculinity" has been heralded as one of the defining features that has made it so popular

🥴🪓 shira (rest)
@gajaaegiyagaja   ...

The fact that illecebra is a feminine term and arcanus is a masculine term blows my mind. JIMIN REALLY SAID JIMIN GENDER

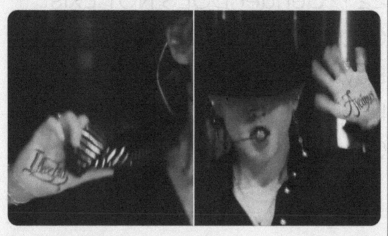

12:59 AM · Oct 11, 2020

22.1 · @gajaaegiyagaja's tweet exemplifies North American ARMY's fascination with Jimin as an arbiter of a new gender formation.

in different parts of the world. The emergence of gentle, well-coiffed, wholesome, and good-hearted leading men—characterized as the Korean "metrosexual"—gave rise to the *kkonminam* or "flower boy," an alternative to the excessively heteropatriarchal men who had until then dominated Korean cultural productions.[2] According to Sun Jung, several sociohistoric factors coincided to create the *kkonminam* aesthetic. First, the 1997 IMF crisis, and the unemployment it engendered, caused a crisis over traditional gender roles, thus forcing open spaces for new ways for Korean men to "do" gender.[3] Around the same time, the South Korean government loosened decades-long restrictions on Japanese cultural imports that stemmed from continued animosity due to Japan's colonization of Korea from 1910 to 1945. These cultural imports included *shōjo manga* that featured androgynous *bishōnen* (Japanese for beautiful boys).[4] Because of Japan's pop cultural dominance at the time, *shōjo manga* was wildly popular with young girls in many Asian countries and, eventually, this aesthetic was popularized in K-dramas and then taken up by K-Pop to create a pan–East Asian soft masculinity.[5] In the early 2000s, the *kkonminam* was exemplified by idol groups like TVXQ!, SHINee, and Super Junior. By the end of the 2010s and with the emergence of *Hallyu* 2.0, a new more aggressively masculine aesthetic termed *jimseungdol* or "beast idol," exemplified by 2PM's muscular physiques and acrobatic b-boy dance performances, emerged as a way of standing out against an oversaturated market of flower boys.[6] *Kkonminam* had by then, however, left its mark in creating a standard for Korean men as gentle, beautified, and perfectly styled, especially in comparison to typical American male celebrities. Today, the *kkonminam* is no longer seen as pan–East Asian as it once was but, rather, as a hallmark of K-Pop particularly among fans outside of Asia.

As *Hallyu* scholars have pointed out, K-Pop's versatile masculinities are about more than just aesthetics. In some parts of Asia, they have come to represent a racialization of race, class, and geopolitics. Sun Jung's 2005 interviews with the Japanese housewife fans of Bae Yong Joon of *Winter Sonata* fame, arguably the first super army of *Hallyu* fans, illuminate how—because Japan once colonized Korea—their fandom is mediated through a postcolonial gaze that sees Bae's masculinity as "nostalgic," "retrospective," and thus, a "simulacrum of Japan's past."[7] Yet, according to Dredge Byung'chu Kang, in Thailand, Thai gay men have not only emulated the *kkonminam* aesthetic due to *Hallyu*'s dominance there, but have sought romantic partnerships with "white Asians" like Koreans whose "whiteness" signifies advanced economic development and urban cosmopolitanism.[8] For lesbians in Thailand, "the practice of 'soft' masculinity facilitates new queer gender and sexual possibilities," including new couplings between *tom* (akin to butch lesbian) and *tom* that were previously unimaginable.[9] While sexuality and desire intersect with soft masculinity unevenly and in different ways in different parts of Asia, as these examples illustrate, *Hallyu*'s soft masculinity has engendered new ways of being and longing that are shaped by larger colonial histories and geopolitical relationships between Korea and Asia at large.

Outside of the contexts of Asia, *Hallyu*'s soft masculinity is filtered through a different set of racialized and gendered meanings. In the west, K-Pop joins exceedingly commonplace popular representations like the literary trilogy *Crazy Rich Asians* and its filmic adaptation that features "a global, mobile Asian capitalist class," or what Grace Hong calls "a particularly twenty-first-century incarnation of Model Minority discourse" that associates Asian diasporic populations with Asian capital and affluence.[10] While the domestically demarcated and historical version of the model minority reduces Asian American humanity to their hard work and obedience, global model minority discourse indexes a neoliberal shift in which transnational Asians have come to signify mobility through tropes that are predicated on the excessive consumption afforded by speculative capital.[11] It is within this milieu that K-Pop has become so intimately associated with high fashion, an association that began in 2009 when Louis Vuitton signed on as the clothing sponsor for G-Dragon's debut album.[12] The partnership between Louis Vuitton and YG Entertainment (G-Dragon's management company) intensified when the world's largest luxury brand invested $80 million in YG in 2014.[13] While the deal soured with the 2019 Burning Sun Scandal involving several YG celebrities, it is within this larger context between K-Pop and luxury branding that BTS first collaborated with Louis Vuitton in 2019 and became their brand ambassadors in 2021.[14] More recently in 2023, Jimin became the ambassador for both Dior and Tiffany & Co.[15]

As @gajaaegiyagaja's tweet, with which I began this chapter, illustrates, North American ARMY sees JIMIN GENDER as fluid, one that can contain both the masculine (*arcanus*) and the feminine (*illecebra*). A slew of tweets asserting variations of "Jimin is my gender" illustrate that K-Pop's long-standing link to luxury commodities and Jimin's own association with Tiffany & Co. and Dior make it difficult to separate that fluidity from high-end fashion. In a February 2023 tweet, Twitter user @mygfluffs writes "JIMIN IS MY FAVORITE GENDER" and posts a picture of Jimin from *Esquire*'s photo shoot, dressed in pastels sitting atop a mattress surrounded by flowers.[16] Another tweet by @jhihro just a few months later proclaims that "my favourite gender is jimin" while a *Vogue Korea* black-and-white short video loops close-ups of Jimin's face as well as the Tiffany & Co. jewelry adorning his fingers, neck, and wrists.[17] While K-Pop idols do not symbolize either postcolonial nostalgia or economic developmentalism as they do in Asia, they are associated with luxury in North America, which becomes intimately tied to both Jimin's presentation of gender fluidity and fans' desiring of it. In other words, in such tweets fans express a desire not only for Jimin's gender (to which we will return) but also for the affluence that undergirds it.

Fans desire Jimin's gender, however, because they see it as an alternative to hegemonic masculinity and femininity. With the exception of a few pop icons such as Prince and David Bowie whose "prettiness" and gender fluidity did little to change mainstream gender norms, music industries outside of East Asia have historically privileged aggressive displays of masculinity that mirror the hegemonic gender norms of the culture. North American ARMY are often attracted to BTS precisely because they see the idols as alternatives to hegemonic gender ideals (which have historically excluded Asian masculinity) offering instead something new to the Western pop cultural landscape. As Crystal Anderson has shown, the binary opposition between *kkonminam* and *jimseungdol* masculinities within K-Pop idol groups has been overstated. Anderson contends that idol groups like TVXQ! display overlapping rather than exclusionary masculinities that are hybrid and transnational.[18] It is precisely these overlapping masculinities embodied by Jimin that North American ARMY determine as "new." For instance, Twitter user @sleepingkook tweets: "I used to think I only liked masculine men until I saw park jimin and realized femininity in men can be so gorgeous and now I am extremely attracted to it. Anddddd he has that duality in which he can hold the utmost masculinity as well, it's sooo hot."[19] Significantly, @sleepingkook points out overlapping masculinities in JIMIN GENDER by using the word *duality* to describe "femininity in men"—something that is typically outside of the realm of "masculine men." Other ARMY, however, do not emphasize a duality within JIMIN GENDER but rather, simply posit Jimin *as* masculinity. In a June 5, 2022, tweet, for example, Twitter user @yexelyn2573 tweets a picture of Jimin wearing a white sleeveless sweater, his muscular arm exposed to the viewer, contrasting with the soft gaze with which his eyes look sideways into the camera, peeking from beneath his slightly tousled, highlighted hair.[20] The words THE MASCULINE MAN . . . accompany the photo. While Jimin falls outside of traditionally Western notions of hegemonic masculinity, @yexelyn2573 asserts Jimin as *the* face (and body) of masculinity. These sentiments are echoed by other Twitter users such as @SincerelySugaa, who says, "This [Jimin] is no longer big dick energy it's on its own plane of fucking existence."[21] First introduced to the American lexicon to describe Anthony Bourdain after his passing in 2018, "big dick energy" is a colloquialism that refers to masculine energy that is confident in a respectful rather than toxic way.[22] While still patriarchal in how it attributes confidence to male genitalia, the tweet suggests that Jimin surpasses and even transforms the spectrum of masculinity into something perhaps more respectful and more flexible. In these ways, BTS—and Jimin especially—affirm North American ARMY's desire for gender fluidity during a historical moment when the concept is being normalized among the millennials and Gen Z who make up the majority of BTS's fanbase.

This queering of Jimin relies, however, on Western assumptions about Asian masculinity. Jimin's gender performance is decontextualized in the West, and fans often read male idols as nonbinary or make assumptions about their sexuality because of their softer aesthetics when, in fact, there is no association between gender presentation and sexuality in Korea. As previously mentioned, pan–East Asian soft masculinity can be traced back to the 1990s, and within the Asian context, both *bishōnen* and *kkonminam* are seen as firmly masculine and heterosexual though soft. In the West, however, Jimin's masculinity is filtered through a racialized lens that always already sees Asian male bodies as feminized in relation to white and black men and certainly, the *kkonminam* aesthetic reinforces existing stereotypes about feminized Asian masculinity.[23] Yet, BIGHIT (and later the umbrella entertainment corporation HYBE) strategically capitalizes on North American fans' racialized and gendered expectations.[24] Since the onset of *Hallyu* 3.0 in 2020, when the target audience for South Korean media shifted to the West, BTS's image has softened—a transition that is encapsulated in their metamorphosis from "Boy *in* Luv," a single from their 2014 *SKOOL LUV AFFAIR* EP, to "Boy *with* Luv," their 2021 hit collaboration with Halsey.[25] "Boy in Luv" begins with Jung Kook chanting "I want to be your oppa," while "Boy with Luv" begins with Jimin singing "I'm curious about everything, how's your day?"[26] The latter centers that object of the boys' affection rather than the boys themselves, a shift that is also reflected in the aesthetic image of the members, changing from a more hip-hop-influenced hard masculinity to a softer feminized one. Fanart by @lin.csa documents this transformation by showing "Old Jimin" wearing a backward cap, a black sleeveless jersey, and jeans with boots, shaking hands with a blond "New Jimin" wearing a long-sleeved white blouse with ruffled sleeves, black slacks, and loafers.[27] New Jimin's lips are prominently pink, pouting, and slightly smiling. Notably, New Jimin greets Old Jimin with his hand in his pocket, looking relaxed and assured. The fluidity and ease in @lin.csa's art from old to new can be read as a queering gesture that signals transformation as growth.

This queering gesture, one that narrates Jimin's transformation from hegemonic to soft masculinity as positive change, undergirds BTS's allure for many North American fans, many of whom are queer youth of color themselves.[28] In other words, despite long-standing ideas that boy bands are simply stand-ins for female adolescent desire, North American ARMY tweets illustrate that fans do not so much want to be *with* Jimin as they want to *be* Jimin, which is a stark departure in how we imagine the role of boy bands. Gooyong Kim asserts that in proffering a non-threatening "fantastical masculinity," BTS—like other boy bands before them—play on "female desires for intimacy" and, as such, BTS members' alternative masculinities do "not challenge fundamentally unequal relationships between men and women" nor do they "contribute to the formation of a more gender equal society."[29] When we do not assume that ARMY are necessarily female *and* widen our view of North American ARMY's investments in Jimin from simply "female desires for intimacy," we see that ARMY's desires exceed what can be overly simplified as romantic love or intimacy. Reading fan tweets through the lens of "gender envy" illuminates how Jimin opens up a world of gendered possibilities for North American ARMY. ARMY's "gender envy" tweets join a recent phenomenon across social media through which people who identify as nonbinary and trans share expressions and performances of gender they would like to emulate. The "gender envy" tag on TikTok, for example, has accumulated more than 236.8 million views and yields TikToks of a range of images including flowers, inanimate objects, androgynous icons, as well as K-Pop idols from Stray Kids, Seventeen, BTS, and more.[30] As @gajaaegi-yagaja's tweet shows us, ARMY desire a new gender formation that does not alienate the feminine from the masculine but instead contains both as JIMIN GENDER. As such, North American ARMY tweets often emphasize that ARMY want, not to possess Jimin romantically, but rather, to possess his gender. A May 2021 tweet by @promiserendpty includes a short video of Jimin posing playfully at a photo shoot and reads: "this jimin gives me so much gender envy!!!!!!! why can't I be him???????"[31] @itboypop's February 2023 tweet states plainly their desire not for Jimin but his gender as well: "no cause the gender envy I get cause jimin is actually crazy sometimes I just wanna roll on the floor because I can't have his gender."[32] Twitter user @HopeBriMino213's May 2023 tweet attributes their envy to his fluidity: "Gender envy is so real. The way Jimin is thee [sic] gender envy for everyone regardless of their gender! I LOVE how he embodies femininity, masculinity and gender fluidity so well."[33] A May 2021 @princessa_jota tweet shows how, like the Thai *toms* of which Kang writes, Jimin is reshaping and expanding lesbian gender performance: "I don't often experience gender envy but every time I look at Jimin something in my little lesbian heart goes bonk."[34] A March 2023 tweet by @enbyoonji (see figure 22.2) illuminates how Jimin provides trans people a template for gender outside of the binary. Posting a picture of Jimin posing in a white tank top, @enbyoonji writes: "jimin has one job and that's to feed trans ppl gender envy."[35] Thus, while Jimin may not change the structures of gender inequality, his gender performances provide a visual language from which ARMY reshapes and reimagines theirs.

Like boy band members before him, Jimin is ultimately an object of desire upon which ARMY can project their fantasies. Unlike the fans of most other boy bands, however, the ARMY fandom includes those who proj-

mez 🏳️‍⚧️ FESTA 🖤 LOCKDO... · 3/23/23 · · ·

jimin has one job and that's to feed trans ppl **gender envy**

♡ 1   ↻ 1   ♡ 18   ↓|| 475   ↑

22.2 · Jimin's gender performances provide a visual language from which ARMY reshape and reimagine theirs.

ect their fantasies about Jimin's radical feminist politics. An August 2019 @lovelybangta tweet includes a scene from *Run BTS!*, BTS's reality show, in which the members take a selfie together. The tweet includes the following translation:

JM [JIMIN]: let me check how it came out

JK [JUNG KOOK]: Men shouldn't check selfies

JM: What's the point in that?

TH [TAEHYUNG]: Men take selfies but shouldn't check them

JH [J-HOPE]: men don't do that

JM: There u go again . . . what the heck is "men"?

To which @lovelybangta concludes, "Jimin really said fuck gender stereotypes."[36] My own translation of the dialogue within the scene differs from the one included in @lovelybangta's post, which transcribes Jimin's final words as "what the heck is 'men'?"[37] While he is emphatic, I translate him as saying "what is 'men'?" or "what is a man?" Though this difference may be ever so slight, my version conveys a less definitive urgency to his query. As such, and perhaps because of the translation, @lovelybangta projects onto Jimin a radically political interpretation of his words in which Jimin adamantly eschews gender stereotypes altogether. Certainly, such interpretations are aided by some of Jimin's fashion and adornment choices. In a 2020 photo shoot, Jimin was photographed with tattoos he drew on himself, including the bigender symbol. Around the same time, he was also photographed wearing a sweater that says both "Radical Feminist" and "Gender Equality." In the context of an idol system wherein idols are not outrightly political (at least not domestically), especially when it comes to gay rights since Korea is still by and large homophobic, Jimin never explains these choices. Yet, ARMY use these fashion and adornment choices to validate their fandoms. @taegiberry95's tweet includes a picture of Jimin in the sweater and with the bigender symbol and concludes that these acts evidence that "yes we stan the right man!!"[38] In other words, in the eyes of North American ARMY, radical feminist politics makes their idol the "right man," deserving of their affection and devotion.

As I hope to have shown, JIMIN GENDER is more than a set of versatile marketed masculinities. It is an intense interplay between Jimin and North American ARMY in which ARMY queer his gendered performances and make meanings accordingly. As such, while JIMIN GENDER does not necessarily transform the structures that maintain gendered power, it catalyzes the imagining of a world in which there are new possibilities, forms, and expressions of gender that young people today are concurrently inventing and, in some cases, fighting for their lives to live. Such possibilities are encapsulated by fan fic on a tumblr in which misa-ndry imagines a one-on-one interview with Jimin. In response to asking him why he chose the bigender symbol as a tattoo, imaginary Jimin responds: "Gender does not exist outside of patriarchy."[39] Imaginary Jimin thus articulates the politics and promises that JIMIN GENDER embodies. In this way, BTS allows us to imagine that our idols are not merely our fantasy love interests but, rather, the harbingers of radical revolutions to come.

Notes

1   ☺ 🦐 shira (rest) (@gajaaegiyagaja), Twitter, October 11, 2020, 6:59 a.m., https://twitter.com/gajaaegiyagaja/status/1315245717192142848.
2   Lim, "The Trend of Creating Atypical Male Images in Heterosexist Korean Society."

3   Jung, *Korean Masculinities and Transcultural Consumption*, 29.

4   Jung, *Korean Masculinities and Transcultural Consumption*, 30.

5   Sun Jung argues that the pan–East Asian soft masculinity is a result of a "paradigm of Japanisation." In other words, Japan's past colonial dominance and cultural dominance in the late 1990s and early 2000s created a pan–East Asian soft masculinity that became hegemonic at the time. Jung, "The Shared Imagination of Bishōnen, Pan–East Asian Soft Masculinity."

6   Asian media outlets first coined the term *Hallyu* 2.0 in August 2010 to describe the "second invasion of Hallyu," which since then has been the domain of teens and twentysomethings and uses social media sites such as YouTube, Facebook, and Twitter as its backdrop. Jin, "New Perspectives on the Creative Industries in the Hallyu 2.0 Era." See also Yi, "How K-Pop Empowered Men Everywhere to Embrace Make-Up."

7   Jung, *Korean Masculinities and Transcultural Consumption*, 30.

8   Kang-Nguyễn, "Eastern Orientations."

9   Kang-Nguyễn, "The Softening of Butches."

10   Hong, "Speculative Surplus," 108.

11   While K-Pop is a lucrative export industry, there is perhaps nothing more speculative than "idol speculation," or the high risk / high rewards investments based on the speculation of fan preferences. *Financial Times*, "K-Pop: Idol Speculation."

12   "Korean Media Cites G-DRAGON as the Reason Why High-Profile Luxury Brands Enlist Korean Idols," allkpop.com, May 4, 2021, https://www .allkpop.com/article/2021/05/korean-media-cites-g-dragon-as-the -reason-why-high-profile-luxury-brands-enlist-korean-idols.

13   Stutz, "Louis Vuitton to Invest $80 Million in K-Pop Culture Factory YG Entertainment."

14   Duc Tran, "BTS: The Phenomenon of Luxury Brand Collaborations— Essential Homme," March 27, 2023, https://essentialhomme.net/bts-the -phenomenon-luxury-brand-collaborations/.

15   BLACKPINK has continued YG's partnerships with high-end retailers with Jennie representing Chanel and Rosé representing YSL Saint Laurent, to name just a few. Duc Tran, "BTS: The Phenomenon of Luxury Brand Collaborations—Essential Homme.

16   lee♡⁷ FESTA ⫽ (@mygfluffs), Twitter, February 7, 2023, 6:55 a.m., https://twitter.com/mygfluffs/status/1622927059466223616.

17   晶 (@jhihiro), Twitter, March 14, 2023, 11:19 p.m., https://twitter.com /jhihiro/status/1635480829886631938.

18   Anderson, "That's My Man!," 118.

19   cy⁷ YOONGI IN 9 DAYS (@sleepingkook), Twitter, December 6, 2021, 9:40 p.m., https://twitter.com/sleepingkook/status/1467685374512164866.

20   PrinceJimin♤♡LikeCrazy (@yexelyn2573), "THE MASCULINE MAN . . . #WithYou by #JIMIN #BTSJIMIN of #BTS (@BTS_twt) and Sungwoon,"

Twitter, June 5, 2022, 2:22 a.m., https://twitter.com/yexelyn2573/status /1533333423174979586. Thank you to my research assistant, Caroline Monaghan, for foundational research (such as this tweet) for this piece.

21   SOFT SUGA[7] | FESTA[10] ☽ (@SincerelySugaa), "This is no longer big dick energy it's on its own plane of fucking existence," Twitter, September 9, 2018, 6:15 p.m., https://twitter.com/SincerelySugaa/status /1038913802354479104.

22   Abad-Santos and Grady, "How Big Dick Energy Explains Modern Masculinity."

23   For robust discussions about Asian American masculinity and sexuality in popular culture, see R. Lee, "Orientals"; Nguyen, "Bruce Lee I Love You"; Shimizu, "A History of Race and (Hetero)Sexuality in the Movies"; and Lopez, "Asian American Gone Viral."

24   For robust discussions on how male *Hallyu* celebrities are filtered through racialized understandings of Asian masculinity in the West, see Joo, "Transnational Sport," and S. Lee, "The Politics and Promises of Gangnam Style."

25   According to Michelle Cho, the rise of KCON (2019) and CJ ENM's partnership with Netflix (2020) mark the shift to Hallyu 3.0, which was further solidified by the isolation and thus increased internet usage created by the COVID-19 global pandemic. Cho, "K-Crossover, or, Crying over Marbles."

26   Lemoring, "BTS—Boy In Luv (방탄소년단—상남자) [Color Coded Lyrics/ Han/Rom/Eng/가사]—YouTube," August 22, 2019, YouTube video, 3:52, https://www.youtube.com/watch?v=eKYd_sdo2LU; HYBE LABELS, "BTS (방탄소년단) '작은 것들을 위한 시 (Boy With Luv) (feat. Halsey)' Official MV," April 12, 2019, YouTube video, 4:12, https://www.youtube.com/watch ?v=XsX3ATc3FbA.

27   @lin.csa, "OLD JIMIN MEETS NEW JIMIN," posted by Chim_chim.95 to ARMY's community (Btsarmy) on Amino, October 24, 2018, https:// aminoapps.com/c/btsarmy/page/blog/old-jimin-meets-new-jimin /N45Q_l4JCMumN7K74m3dMgRz3kYdwLEaQ4.

28   While there is no definitive large-scale study surveying the demographics of North American K-Pop fans, given the visible constituencies at KCON and on online platforms such as Twitter, *Hallyu* scholars believe North American ARMY is mostly composed of LGBTQ+ youth of color. See Yim, "K-Pop Fans: A Diverse, Underestimated, and Powerful Force." The most comprehensive study on international fans to date was conducted by Crystal Anderson in her *Hallyu* Korean Music Survey, a five-year study of international fans. The study was conducted in the mid-2010s and outlines the K-Pop preferences of 282 respondents. See Anderson, "Like vs. Love: Research Reveals Degrees of Attachment among K-Pop Fans," CSAPHD *Crystal Anderson*, July 14, 2014, https://

csaphd.com/2014/07/14/like-vs-love-research-reveals-degrees-of
-attachment-among-k-pop-fans/.

29   Kim, "BTS, Alternative Masculinity and Its Discontents," 132, 139.

30   Crystal Bell, "For K-Pop Fans, Gender Envy Is Everywhere," November 3, 2022, https://headtopics.com/us/for-k-pop-fans-gender-envy-is
-everywhere-31304923.

31   isa⁷ 🎀💜 (@promiserendpty), Twitter, May 3, 2021, 12:35 a.m., https://
twitter.com/promiserendpty/status/1389076058083835904.

32   leo (@itboypop), Twitter, February 19, 2023, 1:15 p.m., https://twitter.com
/itboypop/status/1627371393003450368.

33   Bɾιαɳα Jihope⁷s military wife 💙 (@HopeBriMino213), "Gender Envy Is so
Real. The Way Jimin Is Thee Gender Envy for Everyone Regardless of
Their Gender! I LOVE How He Embodies Femininity, Masculinity and
Gender Fluidity so Well. He's so Fckin Perfect inside and out. He's Everything They Wish They Were 🏛️," Twitter, May 6, 2023, 3:43 p.m., https://
twitter.com/HopeBriMino213/status/1654934912061906946.

34   BIDI BIDI BIMBO (@princessa_jota), Twitter, May 2, 2021, 2:46 p.m.,
https://twitter.com/princessa_jota/status/1389018482537209857.

35   mez⁷ 🏳️ 🎀 FESTA💜LOCKDOWN (@enbyoonji), Twitter, March 24, 2023,
3:08 a.m., https://twitter.com/enbyoonji/status/1639162275008503808.

36   🌙✧ (@lovelybangta), Twitter, August 17, 2019, 1:56 p.m., https://twitter
.com/lovelybangta/status/1162785269755461634.

37   At the time of publication, I have not been able to determine if the
transcript was fan-subbed or officially generated.

38   k⁷ || INACTIVE (@taegiberry95), "jimin asking for the bigender symbol, jimin wearing a sweater that says radical feminism and gender
equality! yes we stan the right man!!💜," Twitter, May 14, 2020, 9:57 a.m.,
https://twitter.com/taegiberry95/status/1260932180651343877/photo/1.

39   misa-ndry, "A Clarifying Talk with BTS' Jimin about Radical Feminism,
His Gender Identity, Makeup Culture and Prostitution," Tumblr, accessed
June 1, 2023, https://misa-ndry.tumblr.com/post/655348131936059392/a
-clarifying-talk-with-bts-jimin-about-radical.

Works Cited

Abad-Santos, Alex, and Constance Grady. "How Big Dick Energy Explains Modern
      Masculinity." Vox, June 27, 2018. https://www.vox.com/culture/2018/6/27
      /17506898/big-dick-energy-explained.

Anderson, Crystal S. "That's My Man! Overlapping Masculinities in Korean Popular
      Music." In The Korean Wave: Korean Popular Culture in Global Context, edited
      by Yasue Kuwahara, 117–31. New York: Palgrave Macmillan, 2014.

Cho, Michelle. "K-Crossover, or, Crying over Marbles." *Post45* (blog), February 23, 2023. https://post45.org/2023/02/k-crossover-or-crying-over-marbles/.

Financial Times. "K-Pop: Idol Speculation." December 15, 2019. https://www.ft.com /content/8f96c583-e4ba-4e1e-bfad-1202c3a766a9.

Hong, Grace Kyungwon. "Speculative Surplus: Asian American Racialization and the Neoliberal Shift." *Social Text* 36, no. 2 (2018): 107–22.

Jin, Dal Yong. "New Perspectives on the Creative Industries in the Hallyu 2.0 Era: Global-Local Dialectics in Intellectual Properties." In *Hallyu 2.0: The Korean Wave in the Age of Social Media*, edited by Sangjoon Lee and Abé Mark Nornes, 53–70. Ann Arbor: University of Michigan Press, 2015.

Joo, Rachael Miyung. *Transnational Sport: Gender, Media and Global Korea*. Durham, NC: Duke University Press, 2012.

Jung, Sun. *Korean Masculinities and Transcultural Consumption: Yonsama, Rain, Oldboy, K-Pop Idols*. Hong Kong: Hong Kong University Press, 2011.

Jung, Sun. "The Shared Imagination of *Bishōnen*, Pan–East Asian Soft Masculinity: Reading DBSK, YouTube.com and Transcultural New Media Consumption." *Intersections: Gender and Sexuality in Asia and the Pacific* 20 (2009).

Kang-Nguyễn, Dredge Byung'chu. "Eastern Orientations: Thai Middle-Class Gay Desire for 'White Asians.'" *Culture, Theory and Critique* 58, no. 2 (2017): 182–208.

Kang-Nguyễn, Dredge Byung'chu. "The Softening of Butches: The Adoption of Korean 'Soft' Masculinity among Thai Toms." In *Pop Empires: Transnational and Diasporic Flows of India and Korea*, edited by S. Heijin Lee, Monika Mehta, and Robert Ji-Song Ku, 19–36. Honolulu: University of Hawai'i Press, 2019.

Kim, Gooyong. "BTS, Alternative Masculinity and Its Discontents." In *The Soft Power of the Korean Wave: "Parasite," BTS and Drama*, edited by Youna Kim, 129–41. London: Routledge, 2021.

Lee, Robert G. "The Third Sex." In *Orientals: Asian Americans in Popular Culture*, 83–105. Philadelphia: Temple University Press, 1999.

Lee, S. Heijin. "The Politics and Promises of Gangnam Style." In *Pop Empires: Transnational and Diasporic Flows of India and Korea*, edited by S. Heijin Lee, Monika Mehta, and Robert Ji-Song Ku, 97–120. Honolulu: University of Hawai'i Press, 2019.

Lim, In-Sook. "The Trend of Creating Atypical Male Images in Heterosexist Korean Society." *Korea Journal* 48, no. 4 (January 2008): 115–46.

Lopez, Lori Kido. "Asian American Gone Viral: A Genealogy of Asian American YouTubers and Memes." In *Routledge Companion to Asian American Media*, edited by Lori Kido Lopez and Vincent Pham, 157–69. New York: Routledge, 2017.

Nguyen, Mimi Thi. "Bruce Lee I Love You: Discourses of Race and Masculinity in the Queer Superstardom of JJ Chinois." In *Alien Encounters: Pop Culture in*

Asian America, edited by Mimi Thi Nguyen and Thuy Linh Tu, 271–304. Durham, NC: Duke University Press, 2007.

Shimizu, Celine Parreñas. "A History of Race and (Hetero)Sexuality in the Movies: James Shigeta's Asian American Male Stardom." In Global Asian American Popular Cultures, edited by Shilpa Davé, Leilani Nishime, and Tasha Oren, 46–60. New York: New York University Press, 2016.

Stutz, Colin. "Louis Vuitton to Invest $80 Million in K-Pop Culture Factory YG Entertainment." Billboard, August 20, 2014. https://www.billboard.com/pro/louis-vuitton-invest-80-million-k-pop-yg-entertainment-psy/.

Yi, David. "How K-Pop Empowered Men Everywhere to Embrace Make-Up." Esquire, June 21, 2021. https://www.esquire.com/style/grooming/a36743526/k-pop-influence-mens-makeup-bts/.

Yim, Hyunsu. "K-Pop Fans: A Diverse, Underestimated and Powerful Force." Korea Herald, June 12, 2020. https://www.koreaherald.com/view.php?ud=20200612000721.

23 · Permission to Desire

— Rani Neutill

In May 2021, I published an article on CNN titled "I'm 43 and a Proud BTS Fangirl. You Should Be Too." It's a love letter to BTS that asks a simple question: why would a forty-three-year-old woman fall so heavily in love with a boy band? Even though I am in my forties and part of what's known as "pandemic ARMY," BTS has gotten me through this time of isolation. The narrative of BTS's appeal often centers on mental health and their sincerity. People attribute their success to their talent, love, kindness, and positive messaging, which I do as well. But what I didn't mention in my article is that I also see the men of BTS as *sex symbols*. I was too embarrassed to articulate my attraction toward the members and felt ashamed at publicly declaring that I was attracted to men who are significantly younger than me. Older women aren't allowed to express sexual desires, let alone a desire for younger men. We aren't supposed to have "girlish" obsessions with a "boy band."

After the article was published, I found a few online groups for older ARMY. While the groups consist of mostly women from all over the world, the majority are located in the US. These women are *not* afraid to show how much they sexually desire the men of BTS. I was struck by some of the women's posts. Many of them were playful about their sexual attraction. For instance, one woman posted photos of Jung Kook with a guitar between his legs and wrote that she has wanted to be a lot of things in her life, but a guitar was a first.

Seeing declarations of sexual desire among a group of women my age and older felt liberating. Knowing the history of Asian American representation in film and television, I was also intrigued by how there are many Gen X women (loosely defined as people in the US who were born between 1965 and 1980) who were raised with the worst images about East Asian masculinity, yet express a deep sexual attraction to seven Korean men. The subjects of their and my newfound desires were nothing like those that we grew up watching.

Raised by a single Indian immigrant mother in the US, my childhood images of masculinity were wallpapered with brown and white bodies. Bollywood films my mother brought back from our long trips to India flickered across our TV screen all the time. My mother was enthralled with their song and dance, opulent sets, and gold-threaded saris. Many of the heroes like Salman Khan were muscular and wore tight button-down shirts that were unbuttoned *just* enough to accentuate their pectorals. The men always saved the women they loved, women who were never given as many lines as the male actors. Instead, the women were bejeweled ornaments that hung like Christmas lights on men in tight white sleeveless shirts, which in the US were called wife beaters, a telling descriptor for the culture of men we grew up with, a culture that still exists.

My mother never seemed to care what I watched. She was more concerned with making money, so like many kids in the 1980s, American popular culture was my babysitter. Television taught me that promiscuous men like rakish bartender Sam Malone from *Cheers* were the most attractive. Alongside elusive and noncommittal men were the macho men—much like in Bollywood—whose masculinity I was supposed to desire. Johnny Depp in *21 Jump Street* with his leather jacket and torn jeans with a gun in his hand, Brad Pitt in *Thelma and Louise*, ripped, shirtless, wearing a cowboy hat, and waving a hair dryer around, a symbol of what was inside his pants (and how big it was)—these were the images of what I was supposed to lust after. Strong and stoic, these men weren't invested in communicating with women; saving a woman was more manly than having a conversation with one. In turn, I learned to want a strong man too and the more inaccessible, the better. And so I fell for Amir and Salman Khan, New Kids on the Block, and the ultimate teenage heartthrob, Jake Ryan from John Hughes's *Sixteen Candles*, which also featured one of the most racist depictions of an Asian man in American film history—Long Duk Dong. An Asian foreign exchange student with a heavy accent who says things like "what's happening, hot stuff," Dong pursues and is pursued by a bigger, athletic white woman nicknamed "Lumberjack." Her name, size, and strength are a foil used to emphasize Dong's small stature, and Lumberjack's desire for him (and his for her) is seen as obscene and comical because of this difference. In the 1980s and 1990s then, East Asian men rarely appeared on American screens and when they did, it was for background noise, whether racial comedy or racial threat. The culmination of my exposure to cinema and television is simple as can be: who was represented and how they were represented shaped my libidinal life, and East Asian men were not a part of that landscape.

Given my visual erotic education and my age, I am not supposed to find seven Korean men hot. But I do, and others like me do too. Because of the contrast between my childhood instruction and my captivation with BTS, I decided to interview Gen X ARMY to better understand the contours of our desires. I wanted to know who they saw on screen while growing up, and if they thought those images shaped who they had dated and sexually desired. I wanted to know about the specific cultures of masculinity they grew up with, and how they carried the burdens of womanhood within those cultures. Finally, I wanted to understand how and why they fell in love with BTS, despite the representations they consumed as young girls.

What I heard were stories about their struggles, their depression, and how BTS alleviated the sorrows that came from living through the pandemic as stay-at-home moms, remote workers, being unemployed, and as women who feel as though they are no longer allowed to do things for themselves. What I found is that BTS has been a catalyst for a collective reckoning among Gen X women about how their desires have been shaped by the media. I sensed some melancholy about how their mediatized education on the life and men they were supposed to want may have turned out differently than expected, and I observed what I call a gleeful grieving of that past. In desiring BTS, I discovered a reencountering with our past selves through meeting new representations, which allows for a gleeful rewriting—as well as a grieving for what could have been—of our desires. What desires did I not get to have, that could have given me something more fulfilling or beautiful than what Jake Ryan, or Mark Wahlberg, offered?

In her book *Desire/Love*, Lauren Berlant describes desire as the "cloud of possibility" generated by the gap between an object (which can be something or someone) and "the needs and promises projected onto it." Desire is something that "visits you from the outside," but as it encounters "your affects" (the range of feelings that embody you), it "makes you feel as though it is coming from within you; this means that your objects are not objective"—that is, there isn't something essential in the object that provokes our desires the way we often believe. Berlant continues: "what seems objective and autonomous in them is partly what your desire has created and therefore is a mirage. . . . Your style of addressing those objects gives shape to the drama with which they allow you to reencounter yourself." In other words, we feel as if desires solely come from ourselves in response to what we find innate to the object, instead of something we project onto it. However, in actuality, desire is shaped from the outside. Because desire is an encounter between the outside world and the image we produce when we meet the object, the way we address the objects of desire can give shape to new stories (what Berlant has called dramas).[1]

In talking to the women I interviewed, I perceived Berlant's idea of "re-encountering" yourself. There was a recognition of how the objects of desire from these women's past were not objective but shaped by what they saw when they were young. In finding BTS, they forged new narratives spawned by the gap between the past and present of these women's psychic worlds, where BTS stood in opposition to the mediatized objects of their youth.

Almost all of the women, even those born and partially raised outside of the United States, unsurprisingly had the same story as I did about the images of men they recalled from childhood. In the Philippines, where a few of my interviewees were raised, American media flooded their homes as a result of US colonialism. The national movie stars were light-skinned and mestizo and stereotypically "strong." When I asked about what the women remembered about East Asian men on screen, they remembered Jackie Chan and Bruce Lee, nimble actors whose stardom stitched together the spectacle of agility and the orientalist fascination with martial arts. Despite their physical prowess—Bruce Lee was famous in the '70s for his cult films, often terribly dubbed, and Jackie Chan broke into the US market with the popular '90s franchise *Rush Hour* with comedian Chris Tucker—most of the women did not think of either of them as sex symbols. Some remembered East Asian men as nerds, like Long Duk Dong. About a third didn't remember seeing any Asian men at all.

Of the twenty-five women I interviewed, most were married and a few divorced. Two-thirds of the respondents' partners were cis white men. Out of those married, ten used the word *macho* to describe their husbands. They went into detail about how their husbands are unemotional, or that they have only seen them cry once in their lives. With the "macho" partners, the women told me that some were prejudiced against BTS. Some spouses criticized the fact that the members wear makeup and skirts, and one husband even called them homophobic and racist slurs. When one of the women brought back j-hope merchandise from a show, her husband said, "If I hear the name j-hope one more time, I am going to throw all this stuff out." I caught the melancholy in her voice as she narrated this threat that runs counter to how j-hope, the member famous for his cheery demeanor, behaves. Through j-hope, she encounters a different tenor of masculinity, one that is not threatening or narrow, and through this encounter imagines an alternative world of desirable men.

In interviewing all the women, there was a shared reason for their attraction to BTS, a reckoning with the masculine education of their childhood. The members gave a lot of the women what their husbands did not: displays of emotion and a sense of care. More than one noted that they loved and desired them because of their ability to cry in public, touch each other, and provide language of encouragement. They told me that they adore how the members talk to ARMY. When BTS speaks to ARMY, the women feel like they are speaking directly to them. In BTS, they discovered what they might not fully have in their life: a domestic experience of mutual care and demonstrative expressions of sensitivity and love, a new world with new dramas and new objects to encounter and reshape desire, the ability to gleefully grieve their past understanding of what is sexually and emotionally attractive.

Many of the women I interviewed were nurses, stay-at-home moms, or grade school teachers. Their lives are intimately (and exhaustively) connected to the field of care. The pandemic wore them down. Before finding BTS, the women told me they felt depressed and isolated and some were deeply worried about their mental health. During the pandemic, many women in the US lost their jobs. According to the National Women's Law Center, from 2020 to 2022, many American men regained the jobs they lost during the start of the pandemic. However, 1.1 million women in the United States lost or withdrew from their employment, making up 63 percent of jobs lost. Of that number, the majority of women were Black, Latinx, and lower income. The labor dynamics of the pandemic are fiercely classed, racialized, and gendered because women are made to take on the responsibility of the home, and only those who are privileged can work from home and keep their jobs. Like so many, some of the women became ARMY during the pandemic as they found BTS to be a source of comfort and joy. BTS made them feel less alone.

A Filipina nurse, Victoria, described how much the pandemic had exhausted her. She fell into a deep depression fueled by isolation and work and couldn't claw her way out. One day, she heard Jin's "Epiphany," a song about self-love and depression, and cried. Things changed as she sprinted down the BTS road to happiness. Once COVID measures were loosened, she went to see them in concert in Los Angeles and Las Vegas. She told me that not only was it the first time in ages she had felt alive but also (she admitted, embarrassed) that it was the happiest she had ever been in her life, even more than when she gave birth to her children or got married—conventional milestones in many women's lives. The word *alive* stuck out to me. If seeing BTS was the first time she had felt alive in a long time, it would seem that being a woman in our culture is a robotic experience of rituals like chores and housework. When I asked Victoria if she felt like she was allowed to feel that kind of euphoria at her age, she said, "No, women aren't allowed to have desires because people think we are past the desire age, even at this age, having sex is something that isn't supposed to happen anymore. That's the reason people mock us for being fangirls. We're not allowed to be cute and scream like a young girl and feel the joy that we felt as children." The joy she felt as a young girl was reawakened as she reencountered her younger self. Victoria told me that after the Las Vegas show, she went out dancing with fellow older ARMY. Her husband, who supports her love for BTS, watched her from afar and later said that she seemed out of control. She replied, "You've just never seen me so happy and not caring about the world." What her husband saw as madness ("out of control") was really her happily grieving the life she lived before she found BTS. With other older women, Victoria felt the freedom to express her glee through the parasocial phenomenon of being ARMY.

A lot of women said that their husbands thought their wives were too old to like a "boy band." They were not supposed to act like what a fangirl supposedly is: a teenager. In a repressive culture, which ours increasingly is, women of any age must be disciplined and forbidden to express passion, but aging women more so. Any hint of elation is a regression into puberty, and teenage girls are often the butt of jokes, seen as a wild, irrational bundle of drives. In rediscovering the fangirl-esque potential of their younger selves, these older women break the rules and tenaciously love a "boy band" regardless of societal notions of how they are supposed to act. They are women who have made altars out of BTS merchandise in their homes, defiantly challenging their surroundings, and making space for newfound versions of themselves.

Another interviewee, Nina, a Black woman, told me about her newfound understanding of her desires and the images of her youth. New Kids on the Block (NKOTB) was one of her favorite bands. She noted that even with a young band like NKOTB, the narrative of becoming a man was all around "hanging tough." She recalled the precise moment she fell for BTS. She was watching an episode of *Run BTS!*, their long-running reality show. Jimin and V were in a bunk bed together. They were cuddling and fell asleep. She realized: this is how men should be allowed to act. She believes the reason for shifting desires is because women our age are old enough to see through the bullshit, and we are being educated through social media to critique the schooling of our past. A few women noted how social media has sparked an awakening and has distributed a new world of possible masculinities. In Nina's recognition of "women our age," the use of "we" signals the collective experience of reckoning with the mediatized instruction of what life was supposed to be for us, for Gen X women, that is being shattered through new representation and discussions around the lingering racism of our past. In citing social media,

Nina was also pointing to the knowledge that a new type of screen is part of our edification. Desire has shifted to the image of a fantasmatic and better form of masculinity. But the mediatized methods by which that desire has been constructed remains the same. The whitewashed film screens of our youth are replaced with apps on our phones and websites on our computer. Many interviewees recognized that BTS's image could be a smokescreen, a performance, but Nina also noted, "if that's the case, give them all Oscars." She was happy to live with the mirage.

There were five women who said that they did not think of the men in BTS as sexual beings because some had sons their age, or they were uncomfortable due to the age difference, and they couldn't express sexual feelings given their age. That said, they all professed to thinking the men are gorgeous. When they admitted that they find the members attractive, it felt like they were telling me a secret, an admission they could only disclose anonymously. One person told me about a time when her daughter caught her watching videos of j-hope and said she was "too old to look that thirsty." I laughed. But in her daughter's statement of being "too old" is the foreclosure of sexual desire based on age and the woman's identity as a mother. Nevertheless, the interviewee indulged in the pleasure of watching j-hope.

There were women who were extremely blunt about their sexual attraction to the members. They described their desires as overwhelming. A woman in her fifties, born and raised in Vietnam, married to a white man, and now living in the United States, described an almost orgasmic moment of hearing Jimin's voice. She thought she heard a girl singing while she was watching the Grammy Awards broadcast, but when she opened her eyes, she saw Jimin, a man. She thought to herself, who is this angel on earth? A woman in her forties, when asked if she was attracted to them, firmly replied, "Oh yes. I am a hard stan," a hard stan being someone who views BTS in a sexual way. When I asked the same question to another white woman, she chuckled and replied, "I would trip them and beat them to the ground." She also told me that BTS allowed her to break free of the box of womanhood and said, "I am not just a homemaker. I work outside the home. I work inside. I am not a box. Let me open up." Another remarked, "Why is it ok for older men to dump their wives and marry younger women and bad for us to look at younger men?"

A few women admitted that they never found East Asian men attractive before BTS. A woman who was born and raised in Mexico, and now lives in the US, expressed her previous disinterest in East Asian men and said that after being introduced to the members, she finds *only* East Asian men good-looking. A white woman, Grace, who is in her forties and grew up in a diverse part of LA County, confessed that she had never thought of East Asian men as viable sexual partners. Grace considered herself to be liberal and politically aware. When she found BTS, she realized how racist she was in her thinking and felt shame. She also recognized the fetishistic aspect to her feelings. But her desires are deep. If there was a world in which one of the BTS members wanted to be with her, Grace said she would risk everything, her husband and child, to be with them.

They all discussed their ecstatic desires for BTS as stemming from the members' vulnerability and honesty about their foibles and limitations. Many described the members' "duality"—or ability to switch from feminine to masculine in a flash—made them even more attractive. Almost all said, "If you put them all together, they make the perfect man." Women used the word *permission* to define what BTS provided them. BTS has given some the permission to sexually desire. Some said that the men allowed them to be "curious" about new things, which made me wonder how much the attraction toward them is an awakening around different kinds of sexualities. In BTS, they reencountered the affects of their younger selves, but this time through a new object of desire that allowed them to happily expunge their history with masculinity in favor of a new one. In finding BTS, Gen X women rewrite their past. They meet new objects through new screens, a new mediatized education that provokes new fantasies, replacing the white men of their youth.

One woman shared a story that illustrates the experience of reencountering the younger self with new mediatized images and reveals what Berlant's idea of reencountering *looks* like. Carolina is forty-four, white, and Midwestern, and a member of the US Army. Like all of the other women, she didn't grow up seeing East Asian men on screen and she described her husband as being very macho. She is stationed in Kuwait one night after just returning from being deployed in Baghdad. I imagine her sitting on a narrow bunk bed. A cold metal frame edged with neon rust is pushed against a beige wall. Two gray lockers surround it, faux walls for a faux bedroom. A tattered sheet hangs between the lockers to provide the fantasy of seclusion, its edges are embroidered with dust. There are three other women in the room, each setting up their space in the exact same way, erecting an illusion of privacy. The internet is spotty and the time difference vast, so Carolina hasn't been able to get in touch with her family for days. Even though she is surrounded by people, she feels all alone.

The soldiers live in twenty-four-hour shifts, some in mandatory silence while others work the day away in the 120-degree weather. Carolina stretches herself onto the thin mattress, pulls out her phone and WiFi puck, and puts on her headphones, hoping that if she watches some videos they will coax her to sleep. She clicks on the red and white YouTube app to watch a new music video from her favorite childhood band, NKOTB. Afterward, a recommendation pops up on the screen: a fan-made compilation of BTS's choreography for "FIRE." Here, leaping into the BTS rabbit hole, the click of one video and then another, the Google search for names and birthdays, the endless swim through a river of content, she no longer feels the heat or humidity. She no longer feels so alone.

In this scene of isolation and discovery, steeped in the hypermasculinity of the US military, the mirror between Carolina's younger self and a new one meets. Sitting in the site of a war fueled by a history of American imperialism, she finds joy in seven men who preach peace and self-love. Men who run counter to many of the men she must be surrounded by, at work and at home. Men who don't look like the members of NKOTB. Men who will eventually have to join the military too. Is it her finger that touches play on the recommended video that forces the encounter between herself and a new object, an encounter that reorients her to the glee of Carolina's younger self and transitions from the white men of NKOTB to something that feels radically other from her youth? A new world of mediatized instruction and masculinity? The transition made by sentient-like algorithms that wonder: *if she likes this band she may like this other, different one, too. Maybe we can make her watch for just a little bit longer.*

Notes

A shorter draft of this chapter appeared in the *Los Angeles Review of Books* in February 2023, titled "BTS: Permission to Desire."

1   Berlant, *Desire/Love*, 6.

Works Cited

Berlant, Lauren. *Desire/Love*. New York: Punctum, 2012.
Neutill, Rani. "I'm 43 and a Proud BTS Fangirl. You Should Be Too." CNN, May 21, 2021. https://www.cnn.com/2021/05/21/opinions/bts-butter-bts-army -saved-me-neutill/index.html.

24 · Fifty Shades of Butter: Consensual Nonconsent in BTS Fan Fiction — Raymond San Diego

As someone who studies BDSM (bondage and discipline, domination and submission, and sadomasochism), kink, and other queer sexual cultures and practices—but is also an ARMY—my social media feeds oscillate from the newest BTS interview clips to upcoming leather pageants and workshops on explicit prior consent. One day, the YouTube algorithm directed me to a video titled "BTS IMAGINE: When he forces you to do it."[1] Curious about what "it" could be and who or what Y/N is, I decided to play the video. Roughly ninety seconds of seven GIFs portraying RM, Jin, SUGA, j-hope, V, Jimin, and Jung Kook as dominant and dismissive of Y/N's refusal to engage in a sexual activity filled the screen. The graininess of the images and basic font overlay of captions like "No is not an answer here!" and "Daddy doesn't like no baby!" highlighted the video's amateur aesthetic. The copious usage of exclamation marks accompanying each BTS member's defiance confounded me. Was I to be aroused by Jin's feral sexuality or bemused by Jung Kook referring to himself in the story as a daddy (an older, dominant sex partner) despite being the youngest member? The comments revealed high praise for the newest addition to this creator's oeuvre, with many expressing appreciation for "hard stans" who desired, created, and circulated sexually explicit BTS content. This approval is in contradistinction to the "soft stans," who find consensual nonconsent (CNC) scenes—where all parties involved agree to hold consent and indeterminate and eroticized force, resistance, and surprise as elements of a submission fantasy—to be antifeminist, anti-BTS, and pro-rape culture. I also learned Y/N stands for "Your Name"—a subgenre of self-insert fan fiction—and realized I had viewed a consensual nonconsent fantasy, a node within a more extensive network of ARMY-produced, kinky audiovisual BTS content.

Enabled by a transmedial landscape, where BTS exists across multiple new and old media platforms, some members of ARMY have sought new strategies and genres of participatory sexual fantasy. Despite almost a decade of global and multigenerational popularity, BTS—in mainstream news outlets, industry blogs, and even Wikipedia—are often categorized as a "boy band," even though the seven members are, as of this publication date, currently in their midtwenties to early thirties. Although not being used pejoratively, the designation of "boy band" simultaneously infantilizes their global fandom and limits expressions of sexual maturity from the group themselves (or, at a minimum, makes any allusion to the erotic exponentially shocking or newsworthy). Fans have amplified BTS's sporadic forays into sensuality by fantasizing, producing, and disseminating their erotic (re)imaginings of BTS. Appropriating photos, GIFs, and clips from interviews, concerts, or programs and repurposing them in fantasy scenarios, "BTS Imagine 'Y/N'" stories are a largely Anglophone genre of fan-fiction videos distributed on social media platforms like YouTube, Instagram, and TikTok. Removed from their original contexts, images and video clips of RM, Jin, SUGA, j-hope, V, Jimin, and Jung Kook become erotically charged through the author's writing and video editing. Hybridizing existing traditions of fan fiction, including long/short form text-based stories and visual media-based approaches like vidding, Y/N stories are a new iteration of fan-based content creation to flourish on convenient, accessible modes of technology.[2]

The final product of CNC storytelling typically places the viewer in scenarios where they can fantasize about a submissive sexual relationship with the members of BTS, who occupy various iterations of hegemonically masculine power. For example, a video of j-hope in black-tie attire catching his breath after a dance-heavy performance is slowed down in GIF format and transformed into a mafia boss's sighs of frustration at Y/N's coquetry. Another video cuts and pastes photographs of V and SUGA in bespoke suits at the United Nations into images of generic Zillow penthouse apartments, building a fantasy of the band members as suave corporate leaders à la Christian Grey. Both are examples of audiovisual Y/N stories. In this format, authors rework existing videos to provide sonic and visual elements to their stories and feature a Rorschach-like main character known as Y/N, whose perspective is the central experience for the viewer.

The BTS consensual nonconsent Y/N stories show the disentangling of consent, desire, and pleasure from the reductive, administrative boilerplate about consent (often circulating through educational institutions) that flatten these distinctions for legal liability and further mystify sexual relations.

As gender and sexuality studies scholar Joseph Fischel argues, consent does not always equate to good or pleasurable sex and, conversely, the absence of consent does not signify violation or displeasure.[3] Prior to initiating the CNC fantasy, the assessment of volition may be established and negotiated, beyond expressions of verbal agreement. Withholding consent within a CNC framework may bring into relief how pleasure and consent are not binary but intertwined across a spectrum. To be clear, rape and rape fantasies are not congruent, and these are distinctions beyond semantics. In the words of transgressive kink practitioner Mollena Williams, "Rape is in and of itself an act of *violence*. Not lust, not desire—violence."[4] Situating lust and desire within possible responses to CNC creates space to unpack the politics and potentialities of pleasure from an unexplored path. As these stories are user-generated, the author is always in control. Therefore, the CNC fantasy moves away from the eroticization of dominance, as well as the eroticization of egalitarians, in favor of a scenario in which submission is entertained as a site of unencumbered joy.

Across digital platforms, members of the BTS ARMY are crafting narratives foregrounding hardcore sex.[5] Within online forums like An Archive of Our Own, Wattpad, and Tumblr, fan-fiction studies have tracked various "insertion fantasies," where "the text envisions the author entering the story, usually to meet the stars and often to become romantically involved with them."[6] Allowing the viewer to participate more actively in the world being curated, Y/N stories demonstrate the diversity of the BTS readership/fandom.[7] Some Y/N stories take a softer approach to intimacy (e.g., "Imagine BTS holding 'Y/N's hand") or are about vulnerable moments when in the presence of BTS (e.g., "When You Get Your Period While You Are Stuck in a Room with Him"). However, the most popular Y/N stories are sexually explicit and accompanied by kinky overtones. In these stories, BTS might be portrayed as part of the mafia or involved in seedy plots. Scrolling through the permutations of "BTS/Imagines/'Y/N'/18+" search results on YouTube reveals a trove of stories where Y/N is touch-starved and suffering from a "cold husband," or sold by parents and forced to marry a member of BTS as part of a sex-trafficking ring, or kidnapped and "forced to do it." In addition to Y/N being a naive student, a pure and innocent daughter, or a child, another role frequently encountered is that of a lactating mother, who can turn even the coldest CEO or mafia boss into an obsessed, needy, or jealous partner.[8]

What does creating and sharing these fantasies through audiovisual storytelling methods do for this sector of the ARMY? The excesses of violence, at times oversimplified and overromanticized, carve out an image of BTS that overlaps with and transgresses the Svengali nature of the K-Pop industry, which places high value on image management and respectability under Korean standards—sentiments that are enforced by many sectors of the fandom as well. Y/N videos provide a glimpse of how global BTS fans are taking these standards into their own hands through what I identify as a form of erotic affective labor. BTS's management company, Big Hit Entertainment (now HYBE Corporation) can start the narrative, but they cannot control it. Even as data from consultants and months of strategic planning and marketing curate the perfectly calibrated PG-13 branding of BTS, audiences find ways to imagine otherwise—that is, to envision what sexual escapades could take place beyond the frame of a photo when the cameras stop rolling, or when the song ends. While anxiously awaiting new BTS content to enjoy alongside other ARMY, writers and consumers of erotic fan fiction are using smartphones and laptops to fill in the gaps. In doing so, we are reminded that audiences are not passive consumers. BTS fans inhabit, resist, and actively submit to various platforms of pleasure and power.

Cultural critics attribute the global success of BTS to Big Hit Entertainment's ability to facilitate digital intimacy across multisensory and transmedial networks. BTS's fans exhibit and extend this digital adeptness, contributing to the reach of BTS by translating tweets and captioning online content in multiple languages, as well as circulating fan-produced content that makes "the BTS sensation" what it is today.[9] Demonstrating their transmedial nature, as well as the ease with which these frameworks travel across networked fandoms, the brevity of short-format "imagine" videos makes it easier to visualize and share across multiple social media platforms.

The intersections of K-Pop fan fiction and the practice of fan cultures have been derided due to xenophobia and misogyny. Studies about non-Korean-speaking BTS fans detail how respondents are mocked for enjoying music in a language they do not understand or for obsessing over men who read as feminine or gay compared to normative masculinities lauded in the United States.[10] Even within fan-fiction communities, self-insert fan fiction is considered fringe, with self-insert RPF (real person fiction, where the main character exists in the same world as the author rather than someone fictional) ethically suspect as there exists the possibility of causing harm or distress to the story's muse. Yet these fan content creations proliferate around the world (including the United States, India, South Korea, the Netherlands, Bangladesh, and Japan) generated by ARMY of diverse backgrounds and in different stages of their lives.[11] In the video's description or within the diegetic space, disclaimers for the content appear alongside apologies for their lack of English fluency. It would not be a stretch to assume many of these stories are written by women, although I would also entertain the possibility these stories could be written *as* women, given the association of fan fiction as a "feminine hobby" and the silencing force of homophobia. Perhaps due to my queer sensibilities, like these fans, I find joy, and even value, in the aspects of life considered inconsequential, quotidian, or minor.

We Don't Need Permission To . . .

Writing fan fiction, stories using source material from real celebrities or fictional characters, is one aspect of fan labor, along with "creating fanart, learning or creating choreography, editing videos, covering songs, and cosplaying."[12] Fan-fiction writers do not have to start from scratch but integrate already existing characters, lore, settings, and situations with their internal machinations. It has allowed minoritarian bodies not reflected in mainstream media to seize their opportunity for representation. In particular, slash fan fiction—where queer and feminist writers imagine the gayness of supposedly heterosexual characters—has been celebrated as a way to subvert the patriarchy, articulate embodiments and practices of pleasure on their terms, resist studio and institutional norms, and build community with others who view a television program, film, or literature as a jumping-off point for further adventures.[13]

Since the summer of 2020, when everyone, including BTS, realized the COVID-19 pandemic was not going to resolve quickly, numerous YouTube channels hosting BTS Y/N videos emerged, with about a dozen consistently posting content.[14] The most active—and therefore most popular—accounts have collections of between 80 to 100 videos or more, with view counts well into the tens of thousands. These videos often run between thirty seconds to ten minutes, with the most popular videos (over 100,000 views) clocking in at under two minutes. Common tags on these videos include "Hard Stan"—someone who lusts after and sexualizes idols while enjoying darker or more controversial topics, such as mpreg (male pregnancy), incest (including step-siblings), dubcon (dubious consent), and non-con (nonconsensual) encounters.[15] Despite the occasional use of gendered language (wife), Y/N is typically nondescript. Numerous BTS hard stan videos eroticize power differentials. Y/N is often an average person who lacks the same influence, status, and resources as the seven men. The domination fantasies transport the consumer into a different world where, instead of glamorous K-Pop idols, the BTS members are white-collar criminals or mafiosos. The ruthless traits that allowed their ascension among organizational ranks are simultaneously dangerous and alluring—a masochistic bottom's dream where the public persona extends into the private.

The video I cite at the beginning of this chapter premiered in February 2022. Nine months later, it was the most viewed and commented-on video across all the accounts I looked into, with over half a million views and six hundred comments. Not unlike a recent BDSM-inflected fan-fiction-turned-book-trilogy-turned-movie franchise, this kinky genre of self-insert BTS fan fiction serves to highlight the parallels with the mainstreaming of BDSM popular texts, a *Fifty Shades of Butter* if you will. While the stories I have encountered do not explicitly acknowledge queer subjectivities, the clean slate of Y/N grants a more expansive interpretation for the audience, such as in this CNC story. The ninety-two-second video begins with a flashing warning reminding the viewer/reader that "This is just a work of imagination/do not take it seriously/do not hate or spam!" As a staccato beat of "Long Night (pt. II)," by JPB featuring M.I.M.E & Drama B, amps up, the caption "BTS Imagine: When he forces you to do it!" is superimposed on an image of what appears to be a gothic Lolita fantasy of two Asian vampires embracing in front of billowing curtains. A rapid drumbeat accompanies a block of white text exploding and expanding within the black screen: "Y/N: Get away from me! I really don't want to do it!" When the beat drops, a succession of slow-motion GIFs appears featuring a close-up of each member reacting to Y/N's plea. The sequence in which the members appear in the story is the same as the main fanchant for BTS: each member appears solo in a GIF with their dialogue written over the repeating clip until a quick cut jumps to the next member. While the images, and even parts of their dialogue, are repurposed from already circulating content, recordings of their voice are not used to save time and to avoid copyright issues. Occasionally, the asterisked text is present, describing the movements and actions someone from BTS is making, like stage directions in a script.

In the brief clip, the first member to respond to Y/N is RM, who appears in a close-up shot wearing a black bomber jacket, his Adam's apple bulging while red lights flash behind him (see figure 24.1). His stoic expression is unfazed by Y/N's pleas as he replies, "No is not an answer here!" The asterisked text above RM implies he is "thrust[ing] in," getting the video started by simultaneously layering feelings of physical and psychological domination. Next is an extreme close-up of Jin's handsome face. Clad in white, his sweaty hair is swept off his forehead. He looks the viewer right in the eyes, licking his lips, while responding in the captioned dialogue, "Too late baby! Its [*sic*] already out of control." Jin's scene ends with a hard cut to a three-quarter pro-file of SUGA, his pale skin starkly contrasting against the saturated, deep blue lighting matching his shirt. A GIF of him panting and moistening his lips with his undulating tongue repeats three times. SUGA's clip is accompanied by asterisked text, indicating that he is putting his hand over your mouth while saying, "Shhhh night is going to be long for you!" j-hope follows, wearing a col-larless black suit. Turning his shoulders away in front of large wooden doors, he counters Y/N's refusal with "Don't spoil my mood babe! Won't be good for you!" A blonde Jimin is next, and his remark, "Fine, I won't touch you," indicates that he is unworried about Y/N's refusal. He huffs and manspreads on a metal chair as he commands, "Touch yourself right now in front of me!" V lounges on a white couch, and mockingly declares, "I can't hear you sweetie! Louder! Louder!" His refusal to heed Y/N is compounded by text about how he "in-creases his speed" while commanding Y/N to be more vocal. Last is Jung Kook, wearing a white suit with his mouth agape, the outline of his tongue bulging out the side of his cheek. His frustration is narrated by text describing throw-ing Y/N on the bed while exclaiming, "Daddy doesn't like no baby!" There is no resolution or formal conclusion to the story after Jung Kook's response, and the video ends without a clear response from Y/N. This video—typical fare for the CNC genre—makes clear that the fantasy of BTS members not needing permission to have their way with Y/N holds value for a subsection of ARMY. Depicting BTS members using threatening and demanding speech and de-scriptions of sexually aggressive action that are immediately legible as violent in other contexts, the creators of CNC stories redirect heightened emotional and physical responses to fear and violation through curated facsimiles of risk.

The integration of hardcore and kinky sexual practices into fan fiction is nothing new, and the past decade has shown the mainstreaming of these stories by Hollywood. The most notable example is the *Fifty Shades of Grey* trilogy by E. L. James, which started as BDSM-infused *Twilight* fan fiction in the late 2000s. More recently, Esther Yi's K-Pop-inspired *Y/N: A Novel* has met with critical success.[16] This genre is reminiscent of the "ravishment fantasy," a misogynistic trope where a "proper woman" does not express her desire for sex. The CNC fantasy allows for her claims to innocence to remain intact because she lacks agency in the encounter and cannot take responsibility for any pleasure experienced.[17] For an industry like K-Pop, where scandals of any kind—but mainly dating—can negatively impact the idol's career (and by ex-tension, their company and shareholders), and for a fandom that is disciplined both horizontally (by fans who frown upon *sasaeng*—obsessed fans who do not respect an idol's boundaries) and vertically (by HYBE threatening legal

thrust in

Namjoon - no is not an answer here!

24.1 · Still from Bangtanyn2397, "BTS IMAGINE: When he forces you to do it," YouTube.

action), these videos become a site where sexual perversity in, through, and with BTS become possible. The CNC videos also signal a level of comfort—as a point of openness and familiarity, but not necessarily expertise—with one's sexuality that is sparked or amplified through BTS. With their assumed levels of higher education and appearance of social and cultural capital, white-collar professions add to the aura of authority of BTS within the realms of fan fiction. This fantasy translates BTS's hard work ethic, cloaked in the guise of well-groomed K-Pop idols, to a performance of an elitist masculinity. It also cannot ignore the trust fans have in BTS, as many have remarked that they seem more "real" and have "been there" for them in difficult times. This trust creates safety in imagining a more extreme fantasy with someone from BTS who mediates one's pain and pleasure.[18]

As with any internet platform, the YouTube comments vary in reaction, tone, and affective response. The comments under the aforementioned video, for example, range from an overwhelming amount of praise, support, and glee, to expressions of anger and disdain, taking issue with the perceived lack of consent. One user appreciates the pedagogical aspects of the video and states, "I never knew the meaning [of] thrust until I joined this fandom." Possibly typed with a wink and a nod, this comment plays coy with sexual pretense while also receiving the acknowledgment of eight hundred similarly thirsty fans who liked the comment. Some echo the kink education gained from watching the video and being part of the hard stan fandom, while also noting they are no longer "innocent." Others make observations about how the personalities of each member emerge through the choice of GIF or text, especially when Jung Kook refers to himself as "daddy." Out of over six hundred comments, only a few are critical of its contribution to CNC fantasies (which is likely also a reflection of the audience's self-selection). For example, one user expresses disgust by the "toxic ARMY" who romanticize assault with a comment stating, "when he forces you to do 'it' it's considered rape because 'y/n' didn't give permission for them to move or do anything." Another user reminds everyone that this is a work of fantasy, exclaiming that "we all know they would never do this to ANYONE EVER," and they hope that "Y/N has a CNC kink." Examining the comments section allows for a more nuanced look at the divergent viewpoints about sex(uality) education, consent, and CNC and other kink practices, with praise often motivating the creator to produce more stories. As there are no editors to provide feedback about the stories prior to their publishing and limited formal opportunities for analyzing their content, the comments—which range from informal to flippant to pedagogical—are part of how like-minded ARMY process what they are watching and learn to exist in these spaces where kink and BTS overlap.

BTS Y/N videos are a space where writers explore their bodies, refer to sexual likes and dislikes, and build community with others through a form of non-alienating labor. While other instantiations of fan labor emphasize queer and feminist reception and production practices, these videos are more similar to kink meme communities, or what Silja Kukka identifies as "fandom's pornographic subset," a "collage of selectively picked parts of the source material, eroticized body parts of the actors or characters, and fetishized fan fiction tropes."[19] Despite the hours of time crafting stories, curating images, and editing videos, and the hundreds of comments and millions of views kinky Y/N videos receive, this fan labor is not remunerated. Per the YouTube Help Page, "adult content" with "highly sexual themes" (including visual depictions and textual descriptions of fetishes) are not eligible for monetization, as they violate YouTube "community guidelines" for their "sexually gratifying" content. An example (or is it a warning?) of a titillating title to avoid if you want to turn a profit is "a hot make-out session," which seems more a sanction against adjectives than the act of intimacy. In other words, content perceived as providing erotic pleasure is barred from monetization through stream counts or in-video advertisements, a standard unevenly applied to sex educators, artists, fat bodies, and fan fiction. For now, creators cannot capitalize on BTS Y/N fan fiction because of the strict standards of YouTube and because, unlike *Fifty Shades of Grey*, there is not already a coded contemporary figuration where Christian Gray equals Edward Cullen, so the likelihood of HYBE co-opting these stories is negligible. Therefore, the continued production of CNC YouTube videos is encouraged through the feelings of curiosity, joy, and pleasure that connect this sector of ARMY through risqué BTS fantasies.

Rather than foreclosing sexual potentialities, Y/N videos facilitate individual and collective (re)assessments of both BTS and ARMY's bodies, politics, and pleasure. This matters because they invite proactive conceptualizations of sexuality that wink at but are not overdetermined by shame; CNC content creators give themselves and their viewers permission to explore. In 2022, before performing their single "Permission to Dance," BTS gave a speech to the UN General Assembly about how young people survived during the COVID-19 pandemic. When addressing concerns of parents about youth who were attending and graduating from school online and all that was lost, RM counters with, "I think it's a stretch to say they're lost just because the paths they tread can't be seen by grown-up eyes." Further acknowledging that what is productive may not always be material, Jimin adds there are many ARMY "who are trying hard to continue their friendships online in new ways. . . . These kids are trying to learn new things and trying to figure new things out. But they don't look lost. They look like they are finding new courage and taking on new challenges." Following the spirit of the fan-fiction authors, I want to rework and expand the focus of RM and Jimin's convocation, from an emphasis on labor to one of intimacy and titillation, as many of these Y/N-based YouTube channels first emerged during the pandemic. A segment of ARMY found themselves online with new friends who wanted to delve into less conventional paths for exploring their carnal cravings. If BTS has taught us anything, it is that the conventional, prescribed path is not always the best and certainly not the only path. Arbitrary quests for etiology only serve to hold up dichotomized thinking where one position is viewed as normal, natural, or good even if the supposed "other side" feels safe, satisfied, and happy. For many producers and consumers of BTS CNC fantasies, pleasure is attained via the suspension of consent—an illusion where surprise, ravishment, and even force can lead to pleasure. Following this line of thought, this means consent can be an illusory, and just as risky, means toward pleasure. All that is guaranteed with consent is the temporary permission to specific acts with another's body parts, not the achievement of satisfaction or enjoyment. The CNC fantasy is not intended for everyone, even if everyone on the internet feels as though they have a say, which makes me wonder, do we need permission to fantasize? No. What we need are more stories to tell, more dialogues to be held, and more paths to be forged. In so many words, we need more ways to love all parts of ourselves.

Notes

Special thanks to Jonathan Magat, Elaine Andres, Erica Cheung, and Erin Ninh for their provocative questions and incisive feedback.

1   BANGTAN YN, "BTS IMAGINE: When he forces you to do it," February 9, 2022, YouTube video, 1:32, www.youtube.com/watch?v=TL7_NizvWzs. As of October 1, 2022, this video was still available on YouTube and had almost 515,000 views.

2   Audience-produced fictional narratives have a long history of cele-bration, critique, and controversy for their ability to reimagine, trans-gress, and expand existing canon with queer and feminist approaches to (the lack of) race, gender variation, and sexuality. Once printed and distributed at fan conventions, digital platforms like An Archive of Our Own, Wattpad, and FanFiction.net now host millions of stories in multiple languages from across the globe that often reiterate different versions of queer sexuality, including slash, "shipping," and the Omega-verse. For more on the practice of vidding, fan-produced videos that juxtapose mainstream media with dissonant soundtracks to produce alternate meaning, see Russo, "User-Penetrated Content," and Busse and Lothian, "Scholarly Critiques and Critiques of Scholarship."

3   Fischel, *Screw Consent*.

4   Williams, *The Toybag Guide*.

5   For example, as of July 2023, An Archive of Our Own has over 190,000 works on BTS covering a wide variety of topics (mental health, sexuality), relationships (polyamory, queer, straight, friends with benefits), and cross-overs (with *Harry Potter*, *Twilight*, *The Avengers*, and other K-Pop groups).

6   See Busse, *Framing Fan Fiction*.

7   This is not always the case. Despite the openness of Y/N, other details in the story might indicate particular forms of gendered, racialized, and sized embodiment. For more, see Stitch, "On 'Y/N.'"

8   Although outside the scope of this chapter, the milk-based fantasies are a site from which Y/N gains power over a member of BTS through differential forms of embodiment. BTS submits to Y/N, who has some-thing the men (supposedly) have no access to otherwise.

9   Kim, "BTS as Method."

10   Lee, Lee, and Park, "Unpacking K-Pop in America," 5908.

11   My understanding of the content creator's location is based upon the self-reported information provided to each YouTube account's "About" section. Age, when provided, spans from the midteens to early forties.

12   Kuo et al., "Performance, Fantasy, or Narrative."

13   For a genealogy of Boys Love (BL), a homoerotic media genre, which started in Japan but has since spread—through both mainstream content publishers and fan-fiction networks—and the influence of the Anglophone Omegaverse, see Welker's introduction to *Queer Figurations*.

14   To be clear, Y/N videos (that are still available on YouTube) can be found as early as February 2016. For the next four years, the genre slowly grew, with common themes drawing from conventional romance tropes like a member of BTS confessing their feelings for Y/N or crying dramatically after Y/N dies in a car crash.

15   Spacey, introduction to *The Darker Side of Slash Fan Fiction*, 5. According to Milena Popova's *Dubcon: Fanfiction, Power, and Sexual Consent*, what distinguishes dubcon from non-con is how dubcon stories focus on the gray areas of consent, where permission is given but under duress, while in non-con, sex is unwanted.

16   Yi, *Y/N*.

17   Spacey, "Dubious Consent," 206–7.

18   Many ARMY find solace in BTS's lyrics, interviews, and speeches, particularly with their "Love Myself" campaign. This chapter extends this feeling of "solace" into kinkier realms. For more stories, including those who left toxic relationships or came to terms with their mental health, see McLaren and Jin, "You Can't Help but Love Them.'"

19   Kukka, "'Fandom's Pornographic Subset.'"

Works Cited

Busse, Kristina. *Framing Fan Fiction: Literary and Social Practices in Fan Fiction Communities*. Iowa City: University of Iowa Press, 2017.

Busse, Kristina, and Alexis Lothian. "Scholarly Critiques and Critiques of Scholarship: The Uses of Remix Video." *Camera Obscura: Feminism, Culture, and Media Studies* 26, no. 2 (2011): 139–46.

Fischel, Joseph J. *Screw Consent: A Better Politics of Sexual Justice*. Berkeley: University of California Press, 2019.

Kim, Ju Oak. "BTS as Method: A Counter-hegemonic Culture in the Network Society." *Media, Culture and Society* 43, no. 6 (2021): 1061–77.

Kukka, Silja. "'Fandom's Pornographic Subset': Kink Meme Communities as Queer Female Practices." *lambda nordica* 26, no. 1 (2021): 53–79.

Kuo, Linda, Simone Perez-Garcia, Lindsey Burke, Vic Yamasaki, and Thomas Le. "Performance, Fantasy, or Narrative: LGBTQ+ Asian American Identity through Kpop Media and Fandom." *Journal of Homosexuality* 69, no. 1 (2022): 145–68.

Lee, Jeehyun Jenny, Rachel Kar Yee Lee, and Ji Hoon Park. "Unpacking K-Pop in America: The Subversive Potential of Male K-Pop Idols' Soft Masculinity." *International Journal of Communication* 14 (2020): 5900–19.

McLaren, Courtney, and Dal Yong Jin. "'You Can't Help but Love Them': BTS, Transcultural Fandom, and Affective Identities." *Korea Journal* 60, no. 1 (2020): 100–127.

Popova, Milena. *Dubcon: Fanfiction, Power, and Sexual Consent*. Cambridge, MA: MIT Press, 2021.

Russo, Julie Levin. "User-Penetrated Content: Fan Video in the Age of Convergence." *Cinema Journal* 48, no. 4 (2009): 125–30.

Spacey, Ashton. "Dubious Consent: The Revival of Ravishment." In *The Darker Side of Slash Fan Fiction: Essays on Power, Consent and the Body*, 200–223. Jefferson, NC: McFarland, 2018.

Spacey, Ashton. Introduction to *The Darker Side of Slash Fan Fiction: Essays on Power, Consent and the Body*, 5–24. Jefferson, NC: McFarland, 2018.

Stitch. "On 'Y/N,' Reader-Insert Fanfiction and Writing Yourself into the Story." *Teen Vogue*, November 10, 2021.

Welker, James. "Introduction: Boys Love (BL) Media and Its Asian Transfigurations." In *Queer Transfigurations: Boys Love Media in Asia*, 1–16. University of Hawai'i Press, 2022.

Williams, Mollena. *The Toybag Guide to Playing with Taboo*. Emeryville, CA: Greenery, 2010.

Yi, Esther. *Y/N: A Novel*. New York: Astra House, 2023.

25 · Bangtan Scholars and the Ethics of Care — Courtney Lazore

It all started with a single tweet. That might be a one-line horror story in our world permeated by social media and virality but, for us, it was the beginning. "Can someone please make a BTS fan account for those working in Academia/ Research?" The tweet sparked interest from several ARMY, and a few volunteered to make it happen.

Our fandom project—Bangtan Scholars—has since grown over the last few years into a complex effort to create a community of ARMY researchers. As ARMY is perhaps the most visible online fandom, our group is just one in a sea of fan endeavors ranging from voting projects to charity campaigns. Accounts maintained by ARMY provide many services: assisting students with subject tutoring, teaching Korean language, providing instructions for streaming, offering mental health support, and educating others on medicine, law, and art.[1] Despite the diversity of these groups, many ARMY-run organizations share a common thread beyond their devotion to BTS: helping others. It's an observation that communicates something important about the core culture of ARMY fandom. Though there is much to be explored in the cultures and complexities of ARMY groups, this chapter focuses on the development of Bangtan Scholars, what drives our activities, and how we, as fans and researchers, intersect with the ethics of care.

Creating Bangtan Scholars

When Cecilia Perez was working on her MBA in branding in 2017, she wanted to write her thesis on how ARMY functions as influencers for BTS. However, English-language academic resources on BTS were scant, and her supervisor was not convinced her topic was viable. Though Cecilia later succeeded in writing her thesis on BTS and ARMY, the experience was still discouraging.

Just a few years later, in April 2020, Cecilia posted the tweet that pulled our disparate community together. Moving into group chats with the volunteers, the earliest vision for what Bangtan Scholars would become emerged: a platform for ARMY researchers to connect with one another, share resources with each other and the rest of ARMY, and promote their work. A major motivating factor for creating this group was Cecilia's memory of how helpful a support group would have been to her during her MBA program. She recalled how the "memory made me think ARMYs who've encountered this get disheartened whether they can actually do valuable research on BTS and ARMY. I wanted to spread knowledge and encourage ARMYs that you can infuse your passion for BTS into education."[2] Now, with like-minded friends, she was able to start such a community.

Work on Bangtan Scholars began as Cecilia decided our first steps and figured out what roles we needed to fill. Nicole Santero, whom Cecilia had met at a conference, volunteered to work on our email list, social media content, and our directory. Rebecca Wright, who joined after responding to Cecilia's tweet, offered her expertise in running a Discord server, a platform where communities can participate in text, voice, and video discussions. After Cecilia brought the project up with me, I signed on to help with newsletters, the website, and other content curation. Initially, additional ARMY expressed interest in helping, but they were unable to commit due to their careers. Thus, Bangtan Scholars proceeded with four founders.

As a fandom for a musical act, ARMY is often a source of joy, entertainment, or escapism for fellow fans, so Cecilia's desire for an academic community for ARMY may seem surprising. But her call for community-building among ARMY researchers was a well-timed crystallization of desires, ideas, and goals that had been percolating for some time, thanks to burgeoning interest in BTS research. Just three months earlier, in January 2020, the first BTS Global Interdisciplinary Conference was held at Kingston University in the United Kingdom. The conference, which was followed by three more in 2021, 2022, and 2023, served as one of the first efforts to formalize BTS studies as a field. But this conference was unusual in that it wasn't just targeting academics and researchers—it was aimed at fans too. Conference organizer Colette Balmain emphasized the importance of a nonhierarchical space, creating an open environment for both ARMY and researchers.

Unsurprisingly, Bangtan Scholars emerged as a natural offshoot of the conference. Each founding member attended, and our experiences there were formative. We drew motivation from the kinship we felt with other ARMY, as we went from research presentations and discussions of BTS's impact to collectively watching live performances during lunch breaks. The conference's ethos inspired the root of our mission "to create a collaborative network that empowers those engaging in or interested in BTS scholarship to promote their work, exchange ideas, and expand knowledge across different disciplines and around the world." We envisioned Bangtan Scholars as a place for ARMY interested in research on BTS to "connect, inspire, and grow together."

To achieve these goals, we decided on three main initiatives: maintaining a Twitter account, creating a resource database, and collating ARMY researcher profiles. On Twitter, we share research and analysis-based materials on BTS and ARMY and promote academic events. Building our website proved to be a larger endeavor, but we set to work archiving much of the available academic (or otherwise pertinent) content published about BTS and ARMY into a resource library.[3] We further built out our library by cross-checking our resource list with another ARMY-led project called "#BTSSyllabus," a crowdsourcing initiative that endeavors to "make research, teaching, and writing about BTS more accessible," by cataloging content including blogs, videos, magazine articles, and academic pieces.[4] Researcher profiles were the other major component of the website. Hoping to help ARMY researchers find each other, we posted profiles submitted to us that included names, contact details, specializations, and publications. It was important to us that we framed the idea of "researcher" or "scholar" with more flexibility than traditional academic definitions. While there may not be much space in academia for independent researchers, we hoped to offer such a space to anyone seriously engaged in research, including fans, students, and professionals working outside of universities.

Overall, our initiatives have been successful. Our Twitter account has seen steady growth since we opened it in 2020 and, as of mid-2023, has 47,000 followers. We collected over 400 resource citations in our online library, and after receiving 687 respondents to our call for researcher profiles, we posted a directory of 273 ARMY researchers on the initial version of our website.

As with any new endeavor, there were bumps along the way. While we succeeded in a few key areas, we also had to abandon other initiatives. For example, part of our original planning involved a newsletter and a Discord server. But it's difficult to bring multiple goals to fruition with only a team of four, especially when we have our own obligations like work and school. Though the newsletter and Discord would offer value to our community, we didn't have the capacity in our early stages. Thankfully, in 2023, we were able to revisit old initiatives. We completed a website relaunch and soft launched our Discord server. Additionally, we took a major step forward by announcing our first event, a virtual symposium.

Perhaps a more arduous challenge has been positioning ourselves in that somewhat contentious, liminal space between academics and fans. We'd like to be a bridge between these subsets, but how do we navigate this space? How will we define what a "Bangtan Scholar" is, or what valuable scholarship is? Bangtan Scholars may be seen as an "aca-fan" group. The term *aca-fan* (academic fan) has become popular among career academics who also identify as fans, often studying their fandoms as part of their ongoing research. But what best fits our definition of a Bangtan Scholar is more in line with two terms offered by Matt Hills: scholar-fan (identical to aca-fan) and fan-scholar, where the first word indicates the person's primary identity.[5] Expanding our definition to include fan-scholars gives us more flexibility, as one doesn't need to be a professor or career academic to be a fan-scholar.

Similarly, we have a broader understanding of not only who "counts" in aca-fandom, but what "counts" as research. While formal, rigorous research is necessary, we don't limit what we share as published research. Instead, we recognize the significance of informal fan-created analyses, such as blog posts or video essays that critically examine BTS and ARMY topics. Our freedom to broaden what "counts" is due to our independence from academic institutions. Bangtan Scholars can set its own goals and rules, without interference from other academic structures. We're accountable only to ourselves and our ARMY community. This freedom to operate independently allows Bangtan Scholars to democratize its corner of the academic world, providing an alternative perspective to that of traditional academia that we hope is open and inclusive.

Our position as a group focused on research within our larger fandom presents us with another challenge. Disagreements between fandoms and those who research them are not uncommon, and when tensions do inevitably arise, we will by definition be caught in the middle. No matter what action we take, we may displease people on either side. For example, some fans may feel that researchers are outsiders who are invading their safe spaces; they may feel watched, or like their privacy is being invaded (e.g., when researchers quote social media posts or use screenshots without permission). Or, fans may take issue with how researchers speak about BTS or ARMY, such as criticizing ARMY's streaming strategy as hyperconsumption, or characterizing the entire fandom as a monolith. Sometimes the problem is guilt by association. When Bangtan Scholars posted information about a BTS-related conference that included work by a researcher some fans disapproved of, we were perceived by some fans as "disloyal." Promoting research activities in general can result in comments like "fans are not lab rats," regardless of whether Bangtan Scholars itself is involved with the activity. Conversely, not sharing information about conferences or projects that also involve the work of many ARMY would be a disservice to the fan-scholars we have. Fan-scholars and their unique experiences can further enrich the research landscape while also respecting the customs of fandom, and we must do what we can to support their work too. The best Bangtan Scholars can do is to try to mediate by offering information to both sides. We can help researchers understand that studying fandoms requires additional ethical considerations. We can advocate for more ethical research by emphasizing the importance of robust informed consent, identifying oneself as a researcher, or being receptive to fan feedback. For ARMY, we can offer information about participating in research studies and how to identify a good informed-consent document, to help them make their own decisions. Or, we can try to answer questions they may have about a published study or the research process itself. It's often a lose-lose situation, but learning how to honor both sides of our identity and be a stronger bridge between them is something we negotiate on a regular basis.

For the sustainability of our project, Cecilia and I have spent hours contemplating, writing, and revising internal policies for ourselves as a collective. Policies and processes are necessary for any group to function well, especially one that values consideration of platform, fandom, and community. What do we do when there's mis/disinformation about BTS, ARMY, or fandom research circulating on social media? What events, articles, blogs, or books do we promote? What topics can we comment on as a collective, as opposed to individuals? How will we manage our Discord community so that it's a comfortable space for everyone? What can we do to bolster ethical consideration among ARMY researchers and others who research from the outside? How will we operate as fans? As researchers? There are multiple aspects that require careful consideration, which we did not anticipate at the start. What has become clear throughout our work, however, is how we grew out of, and continue to negotiate, care.

Bangtan Scholars and Care

The ethics of care (or care ethics) is a moral theory that places personal relationships and human interconnection at the heart of ethical decision-making. At its core, the concept of "care" values meeting needs in our interrelated existences, whether it's the needs of others, ourselves, or the world. The history of care ethics is complex; there is no singular definition of "care." Perhaps the most relevant definition for us was offered by political theorist and care ethicist Joan Tronto and feminist scholar Berenice Fisher, who suggested that caring is an "activity that includes everything that we do to maintain, continue, and repair our 'world' so that we can live in it as well as possible. That world includes our bodies, our selves, and our environment."[6] With this definition in mind, we can identify care in the nature and activity of many ARMY communities, including Bangtan Scholars.

Tronto illuminates four phases of care that can elucidate how Bangtan Scholars centers this concept. In doing so, Tronto suggests thinking of care as a practice, rather than "conceiving of care as a principle or as an emotion."[7] If care is a practice, then it "involves both thought and action," which are "interrelated" and "directed toward some end."[8] This course of thought translated into action is illustrated by her four phases of care: caring about, taking care of, care-giving, and care-receiving. The first phase, caring about, simply requires that one realizes there are needs that should be met. Bangtan Scholars was born out of one tweet that recognized the need for a space that connects ARMY who do research. Though articulated as the need of one person, voicing this need brought together others who felt similarly. When setting up Bangtan Scholars, we believed ARMY researchers needed a supportive place to go for academic resources, information, or advice. As a second charge, we placed importance on the need for both ARMY researchers and ARMY in general to be more aware of the research that takes place within our community.

The second phase of care is taking care of; as in, someone decides to take responsibility for the identified need and figures out what to do about it. When Cecilia decided to formally create Bangtan Scholars, she made the first attempt at taking care of the needs she perceived within ARMY research. As our project continues, we reevaluate what needs we can fulfill, such as when we recently shifted our focus back to developing better internal policies for our group, as well as a Discord server for our community.

The third phase of care is the action phase of care-giving, or performing the actions that will fulfill the need. Providing information on Twitter, populating a library of research, and creating our directory were all actions we took to provide for our community's needs. As mentioned, care sometimes needs reassessment. While one of our biggest goals was to create an ARMY researcher directory, we deleted it in 2021. This decision was also made through the care process of identifying how to best serve the needs of our community—when we received negative messages from fans upset that research was being conducted in their spaces, we felt our community members' right to privacy outweighed our goal of encouraging collaborations. We went back to brainstorming. We searched for an alternative that would support ARMY researchers and their need for a network while also trying to offer privacy, especially since we collected contact details. Balancing the need for community-building and the right to keep one's information private is one reason we began development on older initiatives, such as a Discord server. Weighing our options was necessary for this decision-making process to be ethical, and also allowed us to better preserve our relationship to our community, even when that required change.

Finally, the fourth phase of care is care-receiving, or when those who received care respond, letting the caregiver know if their needs have been met. We observe how our efforts are taken, but we are not the ultimate decision-makers when it comes to whether our attempts to provide care are satisfactory. It is, however, up to us what we do with the feedback, and how we choose to change (or not) moving forward. Given our place as a bridge between ARMY and researchers, the feedback loop of these phases of care greatly factors into what course we chart next.

While Tronto's phases of care are useful when applied to Bangtan Scholars, there is an important difference. Care is most often thought of as an in-person practice; there's very little written about care in digital spaces. Most of what Bangtan Scholars and other ARMY groups do is perform digital community care, often for people we will never meet offline or develop a deeper relationship with beyond our shared identity as ARMY. Our shared identity is a crux for motivating these care practices. While care may be found in other online communities, it's generally focused on supporting others in relation to the subject of that community. An online gaming community may share content updates about their game of choice, or create resources to help other players improve their skills or better understand the in-game lore. But, unlike ARMY groups, they aren't helping their community members with needs that lie outside of the game. Many ARMY groups, including Bangtan Scholars, meet needs that aren't absolutely necessary for supporting BTS's career or ARMY's fandom participation. We don't teach others how to buy BTS's music or stream and vote, and one can participate in ARMY without interacting with Bangtan Scholars' resources. But ARMY constructs essentially a digital village or microcosm, where different groups can have specializations that account for needs outside of directly supporting BTS's music. By leveraging our online world, Bangtan Scholars can provide care for BTS and ARMY's extraneous needs.

The digital care offered by Bangtan Scholars occurs in several classifications: care toward BTS, toward ARMY, and toward ARMY researchers. We demonstrate our care toward BTS by amplifying work that considers how BTS and ARMY impact culture, industry, and fans themselves, and by trying to counteract harmful, stereotypical narratives that exist about boy bands and fandoms. Our group aims to help preserve an accurate account of BTS and their fandom, because otherwise, we are at the mercy of the narratives presented by mass media and published research. Not all media and research treat BTS or ARMY unfairly, but it's imperative that groups like ours make an effort to promote accurate information and fans' lived experiences. ARMY should have a voice in our own story.

We also demonstrate care toward ARMY by expanding awareness of and access to research. Fans should be aware of the research being conducted in their fandoms, because researchers rely on data generated by fans. It's crucial for the community to know what their data, even publicly available data, are being used for. We hope to help more ARMY learn of the research that's available as well as opportunities to participate, which results in more accurate data. Helping more fans become aware of research outputs also creates opportunities for fan commentary on published research. Community concerns about research results are valuable and should help inform future projects. Likewise, fans deserve easy access to the papers published about them; it's our space, after all. But academic papers are often not widely circulated, hard to find, or exist behind paywalls. By expanding access to research on BTS and ARMY, Bangtan Scholars can further democratize its part of the academic community.

Determining what we share across our platforms also requires some ethical assessment, where we strive to make choices based on the objectivity required of research tempered with the lens of fandom. For example, we may choose not to promote research published by someone who has been disrespectful or prejudiced toward the fandom (stereotypes of toxicity, "screaming teenage girls," and so forth), or who has invaded fans' privacy by sharing screenshots of social media posts without permission. We may share a response to such research that calls into question its conclusions and ethical underpinning. And we decline requests to promote calls for research participants if those documents don't have proper informed consent details. Learning how we can best care for the broader ARMY community is a process, and Bangtan Scholars intends to pivot to meet needs as best as we can.

We also demonstrate care toward our fellow ARMY researchers, as we try to provide them with community, support, and education. Sometimes that care comes in unexpected forms, like deleting our directory to protect privacy. But we have future plans for better resources for ARMY researchers, including the Discord and resources on conducting ethical research and informed consent. Having more ARMY involved in research is desirable, because we can bring expertise to the field that may otherwise not exist. Bangtan Scholars can help budding ARMY researchers on their journey, and we hope to nurture great relationships among our community by focusing on care.

All of this sounds like an awful lot of work, and that's because it is. Why put in so much effort into something that some might see as a hobby? Because we *care*. We care about BTS and ARMY. We care about preserving BTS's legacy and sharing available research as widely as possible. We care about supporting ARMY who want to get involved in research. Our care makes it worth the effort. I believe identifying and applying the ethics of care framework to our operations as Bangtan Scholars helps us better understand our own motivations and actions, as well as how we might continue down our path with this philosophy in mind.

On the Caring Path

As we move forward with our work, we keep the focus on care. How can we infuse care into our policies? How can we create a supportive environment for ARMY researchers to grow and thrive? What can we do to better care for our community through our projects? These are the questions we continue to meditate upon. There's so much more we'd like to do as Bangtan Scholars, should the opportunity arise. Plenty of our aspirations would allow us to care for other needs. But the core of Bangtan Scholars for us will always be a sustainable online (and sometimes offline) community that encourages ARMY researchers from all backgrounds and experience levels while also liaising with the ARMY community. If we can achieve that while also championing caring relationships, I think that's all we could ask for.

Ultimately, whether spreading how-tos on fandom activities, organizing campaigns, sharing mental health resources, or creating communities to support a subset of ARMY, so many ARMY-created groups exhibit an ethic of care. Operating within care helps provide a roadmap for our group, and this model opens many possibilities for ARMY organizations. Ethics of care can also have wider implications for online fandoms, especially where there is a population of aca-fans and fan-scholars. Academia is hierarchical and sometimes closed-minded regarding what subjects or populations matter and who should be allowed to participate in research; care ethics shows us one way to think beyond traditional academic structures and foster more supportive, more inclusive spaces for both researchers and fans. When we shift the focus to caring relationships, we can help those relationships thrive, help others feel more respected, and build better communities for fostering connections. Care ethics can also help smooth over some of the tensions that exist between fans, aca-fans, and fan-scholars, breaking down borders instead of constructing more. Perhaps Bangtan Scholars can serve as a model for how to do better in academia, as well as in the world we all share.

Notes

1   One major method ARMY uses to support BTS is streaming the group's songs on services like Spotify and Apple Music. Music streams contribute to how well songs perform on charts, and each streaming service and chart has its own rules. Some ARMY work together to create how-to guides for each platform that educate other fans on best practices for making the most of their streaming habits.

2   Cecilia Perez, in discussion with the author, 2022.

3   "Resources," Bangtan Scholars, last modified March 2023, https://www .bangtanscholars.com/resources.

4   Candace Epps-Robertson, Jin Ha Lee, and Cassie Nguyen, eds., "#BTSSyllabus," last modified March 23, 2023, https://bit.ly/BTSSyllabusProject.

5   Hills, *Fan Cultures*, 11–15.

6   Tronto and Fisher, "Toward a Feminist Theory of Caring," 40.

7   Tronto, *Moral Boundaries*, 108.

8   Tronto, *Moral Boundaries*, 108.

Works Cited

Hills, Matthew. *Fan Cultures*. London: Routledge, 2002.

Tronto, Joan. *Moral Boundaries: A Political Argument for an Ethic of Care*. New York: Routledge, 1993.

Tronto, Joan C., and Berenice Fisher. "Toward a Feminist Theory of Caring." In *Circles of Care: Work and Identity in Women's Lives*, edited by Emily K. Abel and Margaret K. Nelson, 36–54. Albany: State University of New York Press, 1990.

26 · *Sincerely Yours, ARMY*: Exploring Fandom as Curatorial Methodology

— Sophia Cai

The word *curator* derives from the Latin verb *curare*, which means care, or to take care of. A traditional curator working at an art gallery or museum would typically be responsible for a collection of objects, as well as their acquisition, preservation, interpretation, and display. Contemporary curatorial practice today expands beyond the four walls of the institution and can take many forms of presentation (from exhibitions to publications and more), but what remains is a specialized knowledge and responsibility for artists and artworks. This legacy of artistic selection and interpretation is not one without ingrained biases, however, due to the persistence of "entrenched patriarchal and Eurocentric structures" in the institutions of art.[1] As individuals with the power to select and determine what is collected and displayed, curators wield immense power as cultural gatekeepers.

This chapter will use the cultural phenomenon of BTS and ARMY as a case study to consider how fandom can be applied as an expanded curatorial methodology, with potential to activate more inclusive means of engagement with contemporary art audiences and practitioners. By reflecting on two curatorial projects, I consider how my work as an independent curator is informed and influenced by my participation as a BTS fan or ARMY. The two case studies are *Zero O'Clock*, an online exhibition hosted by the Feminism and Intersectionality Research Group at the Centre of Visual Art, University of Melbourne (2020), and *Sincerely Yours*, a group exhibition curated on the topic of love, devotion, and fandom held at West Space and Arts Project Australia (2022). Through an analysis of curatorial motivations, methodologies, and outcomes, this chapter proposes that participation in fandom and fan culture might offer a novel creative and critical lens through which to rethink intersections of art and identity from an autotheoretical position—combining the subjective with the theoretical as a mode of practice.[2]

I locate my personal engagement with BTS's fandom as a curatorial methodology in a broader context of activist curating and care, concerns that have taken on additional urgency following the disruptions caused by the COVID-19 global pandemic and the context from which these exhibitions arose. In the field of contemporary art, questions persist about the ethical responsibilities of curators and art institutions to employ "counter-hegemonic strategies" to ensure the meaningful inclusion of feminist, queer, working-class, racialized, and Indigenous voices.[3] This in part requires a reimagination of the possibilities, role, and agency of curating as not just a mode of cultural and aesthetic production, but as a living practice embedded in care and caretaking for artists and communities. While historic curating was bound to a duty of care for the preservation and display of static objects, contemporary curating, which deals with living artists, locates care as a methodology in a much "broader cultural, social, corporeal, emotional, affective and intellectual sense."[4] Care in this context can look like advocating for artists' rights, including protecting their cultural safety and creative expression, as well as providing accessible conditions for the viewing of art. At a time during which global art institutions grapple with long-entrenched structures of racism, sexism, and classism, I propose that the political and oppositional possibilities of fandom offer an opportunity to challenge the long-dominant patriarchal Eurocentric discourses of art history and to imagine new art futures.[5]

Fandom and Curation as Care Practices

As practices borne from similar displays of devotion and care (whether for a chosen object and/or subject), fandom and curation share similar motivations and goals that invite further consideration. In his essay "The Labor of Curating," Philipp Dominik Keidl argues that "fan and museum culture are inextricably linked."[6] This connection is established not only through the manner in which fan collections sometimes become part of museum archives, but also through the curation of exhibitions that address the topics of fandom.[7] While Keidl was writing specifically about a fan-run museum in

Germany, Stars of the Galaxy (SOTG), this similarity between fan culture and museology has longer historical precedents in the development of *Wunderkammers* (or "Cabinet of Curiosities") in sixteenth-century Europe. These private collections of objects and artifacts, which reflected the taste and interests of individual collectors, were popular in aristocratic and royal courts as a way to display wealth and cultural power. Importantly, *Wunderkammers* are not only historical precursors to today's museums, but may also be regarded as a historical example of fandom. After all, what is it that separates a twenty-first-century science-fiction lover's collection of film memorabilia at the SOTG from a mid-eighteenth-century curio of botanical and geological specimens housed in a home library? Arguably, the process of selection imbues both collections with similar sentiments of subjective interest, caretaking, and preservation.

Despite these similarities, expressions of fan culture remain sidelined in art history, contemporary art, and curatorial studies. This is in part because fandom is not taken seriously as a field of study in these areas, and because the art world has historically maintained a contentious relationship to popular culture and mass media. In the recently published contemporary art anthology, *Fandom as Methodology*, editors Catherine Grant and Kate Random Love write that "within art history, fandom is often used as a throwaway term, a casual aside, unworthy of serious consideration."[8] That is, while fan culture shares much in common with the making and showing of art in that they both operate as aestheticized forms of cultural consumption and production, the "palpable fandom in artworks and of artists is explicitly denied and derided, due to its troublesome alignment with taste, embodiment and the locatedness of subjectivity."[9] It is of course important to acknowledge the gendered and racialized biases that inform what artistic practice is considered "subjective" and what is considered "universal," and how the denial of fandom expressed in artworks reveals entrenched patriarchal and Eurocentric values imposed on the artistic canon. While Grant and Love's anthology focuses on artists and writers who engage with fan culture or fandom as artistic themes, I go further to argue that fandom *as a methodology* applied to contemporary curatorial practice and exhibition-making enables a space of inclusivity, connection with personal joy, and empowerment during times of crisis. Given that the scholarship, study, and viewing of art has historically been occupied by white men (and a small fraction of women and/or people of color), to recognize alternate subjectivities or lived experiences as worthy of artistic recognition is a radical act of expressing difference and identity.

Case Study 1: *Zero O'Clock*

My exploration of fandom as curatorial methodology was first demonstrated in the online exhibition *Zero O'Clock*, which was born during the middle of one of Melbourne's many lockdowns as I was contending with questions of art's purpose (see figure 26.1).[10] This was the third in a series of online, guest-curated exhibitions hosted by the Feminism and Intersectionality research group at the University of Melbourne's Centre of Visual Art (CoVA). This research group was designed to "propose new frameworks through which to continue making and legitimising forms of knowledge and cultural production that are otherwise rendered invisible and deemed untenable."[11] Each previous iteration of the project was curated through an open call process to current fine arts students at the university, bringing together both undergraduate honors and masters level students across different artforms and disciplines whose works address feminist discourse and methodology.

Recognizing the symptoms of burnout and emotional fatigue following extended lockdowns (at that stage, Melbourne was three months into what would become a six-month hard lockdown of stay-at-home orders, movement restrictions, and curfews), I pivoted my curatorial premise to reflect on how this exhibition could perhaps offer an opportunity to consider rest and care for ourselves and each other. This was also driven by my recognition of the stress of online teaching and learning on the students and university staff, and a desire to extend care through a relatable exhibition theme that could provide some comfort.

Taking inspiration from the BTS track "Zero O'Clock," a song of hope for a better tomorrow from the 2020 full-length album *MAP OF THE SOUL: 7*, I proposed an exhibition that centered on experiences of time and timelessness during lockdown. For the open call process, I posed a question to the artists based on the song's lyrics and temporal themes: "At 00:00 when the clock resets, can we find comfort in the promise of a new day?" This open call was accompanied by a link to the song. Significantly, I emphasized in the open call that I did not want new artistic works, recognizing the labor that goes into artistic output and delivery of outcomes, but rather wanted to exhibit existing works that were well suited to adaptation to a digital exhibition context. The curatorial decision to seek existing artworks, rather than new artworks, was also driven by this desire to minimize creative burnout and embody the ideas of "resetting" as suggested by the song.

The artworks in *Zero O'Clock* demonstrated a range of artistic responses to the theme of time and its passage. Rebecca Diele, Astrid Mulder, and

26.1 · Screenshot of *Zero O'Clock*, online exhibition curated by Sophia Cai.

Christina Darras exhibited works that were made as a direct personal response to the experience of lockdown and its impact on creative expression. For Rebecca Diele, this took the form of a series of large-scale grid drawings that visually signified the monotony and repetitiveness of daily life in isolation. Christina Darras's mix-collage drawings, titled *right now, right now*, playfully merge different mediums and objects to capture the fleeting feelings of the artist during lockdown.

Notably, it should be made clear that the ten artists who participated in the exhibition were not ARMY, and no one explicitly made work about BTS. In fact, most of the artists did not know about BTS prior to the exhibition, except for passing pop-culture knowledge gleaned from media coverage and social media content. This, however, was not a deterrent to my curatorial aims or the cohesiveness of the show and the way the artworks were presented together. This cohesion was also evident in the exhibition design choices, such as the use of a pale pink background on the webpage, and the presence of soft purples in the introductory icon for the exhibition—at visual odds with the usual "white cube" expectations of contemporary art spaces. Purple is also a signature color for the parasocial relationship between BTS and ARMY, popularized by the phrase *borahae* ("I purple you"), first coined by BTS member V. It was not the artists or their works that were reflective of a fandom methodology, but rather my curatorial practice and exhibition design that was informed by my personal connection to BTS's music and message. The exhibition provided a means to translate some of the themes of comfort from the song "Zero O'Clock" to a more emotionally charged engagement with contemporary art practice.

This connection to BTS was also expressed through the inclusion of an exhibition playlist, where I matched *Zero O'Clock* artists and their works with songs and performances by BTS.[12] The full playlist was developed in consultation with each artist, who were asked to provide feedback on the musical selection and performances. This inclusion provided an additional layer of interpretation to the exhibition and also further demonstrated the application of fandom knowledge as curatorial methodology. For instance, BTS's hit single "Dynamite" was paired with Chelle Destefano's work *Imagine through Auslan*, a video work that sees the artist signing along to John Lennon's song "Imagine," using Auslan (Australian Sign Language). In the accompanying caption, I wrote, "BTS is often compared to the Beatles in terms of their social and cultural impact, and I like to think ['Dynamite'] might be the 'Imagine' of our era." Other pairings include matching the empowering self-love track "Answer: Love Myself" with the writing and photography of artist Lia Dewey Morgan, whose works are an expression of queer affirmation and love. The solitary photographic series by Astrid Mulder was matched with the song "Whalien 52," a lament for the world's loneliest whale whose calls cannot be heard by any other creature.

Presenting a fan-driven curatorial premise provided a chance for me to honor and recognize the impact that BTS has had on my personal and professional life, and to acknowledge the gendered double standards of what it means to love or "stan" something.[13] In my dedication page for the show I wrote, "This project is dedicated to BTS and to ARMY worldwide. I hope this project can bring you some comfort, just like BTS brings to me." Working on *Zero O'Clock* provided an opportunity to fulfill two of my roles as a "curator-fan": as a curator, my job is to connect artists with audiences, but as a fan of BTS, my "job" is to support the group and share their positive message with others. This purpose of embodying BTS's message and values through fan-led action has been theorized as a form of "transnational cyber-nationalism" of shared interests and values but one that is organized around a nonstate affinity.[14] Significantly, this mode of culture-making and curating offers a chance to rethink the usual relationships that connect contemporary art and its audiences and provides an opportunity to challenge these established hierarchical networks. In many respects, traditional curatorial practice is vertically structured, with the role of the curator operating as a form of power and gate-keeping. Through working on *Zero O'Clock*, I started to think about how fandom might provide an alternative curatorial methodology to this top-down structure and reach audiences and artists in a more inclusive manner.

Case Study 2: *Sincerely Yours*

Curating *Zero O'Clock* laid the groundwork for considering a more expansive approach to fandom in my next curatorial project. While the connections to fandom in *Zero O'Clock* were more covert (contained mostly within the playlist and the exhibition dedication page and design), the topic of fandom was integral to *Sincerely Yours*, a group exhibition held across the neighboring art spaces of West Space and Arts Projects Australia (APA) in Melbourne in 2022. As a collaboration between two contemporary art spaces, *Sincerely Yours* brought together six studio artists from APA—a social enterprise, studio, and gallery that supports artists with intellectual disabilities—as well as six invited contemporary artists from around Australia. Like *Zero O'Clock*, *Sincerely Yours* was developed during and following a period of extended lockdown and social isolation in Melbourne, which in turn influenced the development of the curatorial theme and methodologies of care that shaped the working relationship between curator and artists.

The topic of fandom provided a rich context to consider the varied practices of APA artists and the invited artists, whose works each explored a range of objects or subjects that inspired fannish love and devotion. This was a theme that found particular resonance with APA artists, given the visible presence of overlapping interests and hobbies in their shared working studio space. On one of my first research visits to the studio, I noted immediately a "footy tipping competition" on the common notice board, and the prevalence of common themes of sports, music, and pop culture in the artists' works. Speaking with APA curator Sim Luttin about these shared interests, Luttin shared how the studio artists would often be given similar source material from which to take inspiration.[15] This provided a rich, shared visual language and methodology for the artists at the studio, while also highlighting the personal interests, taste, and voice of each individual artist. In my time spent working through the extensive artist archives kept on site, which includes works on paper, ceramics, soft sculpture, paintings, and artist books, I noted that this clear and strong point of connection in the works to fan interests and fandoms was worth pursuing more.

At the heart of *Sincerely Yours* was a celebratory recognition of the power of fandom to bring joy and comfort to people during trying times (see figure 26.2). This truth, which I already personally knew through my affiliation with BTS and ARMY, was further exacerbated during the years of 2020 and 2021 as people experienced mass isolation and lockdowns around the world. During this time, many people turned to indoor activities, including creative pursuits and collecting hobbies, to seek comfort and distraction. As a result, while I wanted to acknowledge my own positionality as an ARMY that I brought to this project, I most of all wanted to work with artists from a range of diverse backgrounds and who encompassed a range of fandoms and creative approaches and to be guided by their individual needs. This, for me, was central in recognizing that fandom held the potential to activate personal joy and empowerment regardless of age, ethnicity, or gender, through reflecting the desires and interests of the artist as fan.

The artists I worked with covered a broad range of fandoms, including Nintendo (Jenny Ngo), *Star Wars* (Nick Capaldo), Frank Sinatra (Raquel Caballero), Australian Rules football (Alanna Dodd and Miles Howard-Wilks), *The Simpsons* (Carly Snoswell), and Disney (Daniel Pace). The work of artist Mel Dixon, whose self-confessed subject of fandom was writer and ceramicist Edmund de Waal, also demonstrated the reach of fandom practices beyond pop culture. Dixon's video work, which showed the artist receiving a customized tattoo based on de Waal's work, perhaps most clearly communicated the underlying earnestness of the exhibition—as she literally inscribes the work of her favorite artist close to her heart for eternity. The influence of K-Pop was also well represented in the exhibition by Dylan Goh and Ari Tampubolon, whose works responded to the musical influences of BTS and TWICE, respectively. Goh's video installation was a queer fantasy depicting an imagined encounter between the artist and V of BTS, while Tampubolon's work used the dance choreography of TWICE to challenge the white cube model of art exhibition spaces.

In recognition of the importance of fan-writing practices, an exhibition zine was specially produced and designed for *Sincerely Yours*, featuring four newly commissioned texts by invited writers. These contributions included a lyrical dedication to Britney Spears (Sunanda Sachatrakul), a work of fan fiction on the relationship between Jimin and Jung Kook of BTS (Natasha Hertanto), and stories about Olympic weightlifters (Jinghua Qian) and vampires (Diego Ramírez). My own contribution was a curatorial essay taking the form of a fan letter to my "bias," Min Yoongi, where I try to unpack why I write to him knowing he will never read it:

26.2 · Installation view, *Sincerely Yours*, curated by Sophia Cai, Arts Project Australia and West Space, Melbourne, 2022. Photo by Janelle Low.

> Mostly, what I love about loving you is that it does motivate me to be a better version of myself. I don't need you to know me, to know that this made an indelible impact on my life. Being a fan, opening myself to the joy and pain that this has brought me, makes me a better person and curator.[16]

Putting these words to paper felt like a way of recognizing and also valuing the importance of BTS to the development of my own personal identity and my curatorial practice. For me, this came down to a recognition that fandom, like artistic expression, is built on imagination and fantasy as a form of world-building: to create something based on an expression of love.

Recognizing the Possibilities of Fandom

One of the critiques often leveled against fandom is a lack of criticality; that by virtue of one's devotion and love to the subjects, this devotion and love somehow makes fandom less credible or less likely to be taken seriously as a theoretical proposition. This disparagement of subjective or self-reflective work, particularly when presented by women or people of color, is at the center of Lauren Fournier's book *Autotheory as Feminist Practice in Art, Writing and Criticism*. For Fournier, the denigration of autotheory (or work that merges the autobiographical with the theoretical) as "narcissistic" or lacking in criticality is a symptom of the "Euro-American, male-centric academic culture of scholarship."[17] This is, at its core, a question of value, and what forms of knowledge are regarded as legitimate.

Given that art institutions are in large part built on similar patriarchal and colonial legacies, this question of legitimacy, credibility, and subjectivity is also relevant to my work as a curator. Recent efforts by artists and activists to "decolonize" museum spaces demonstrate the ongoing work in challenging assumptions of neutrality in museum spaces.[18] Working as a contemporary art curator—especially an independent, feminist, queer, Asian, first-generation migrant curator—I have grappled with these questions of purpose and identity for much of my career. My concurrent journey as an ARMY since 2019 has also informed the development of my curatorial values, allowing me to recognize the importance of prioritizing self-love, sincerity, and the pursuit of justice (as well as an unabashed appreciation for joy).[19] Within the at times constrictive expectations of an extractive art world where people who looked like me were more often the topic rather than author, to express my work and identity through the framework of fandom provided me a way to center lived experience and subjecthood that was empowering. This, I came to recognize, situated my work in a long line of feminist, postcolonial, and queer artists and theorists since the 1960s who sought to challenge cultural hegemony through exhibition-making.[20]

Instead of disparaging the subjective in exhibition-making, I propose we recognize how curatorial methodology, like other forms of creative labor, is a deeply personal pursuit and, in this way, has more in common with fandom than we might realize. To maintain a firm distinction between the two misses the radical opportunities afforded by this intersection as a place of creative potential and embodied knowledge. Fandom can offer curators and artists an opportunity to challenge entrenched biases and vertical structures of power by acknowledging the role of subjective identification and connection in art. There is also an opportunity for fan-led curatorial projects to challenge established art circuits, through a process of self-identification by audiences and creative practitioners. Accepting this possibility presents an opportunity for a radical reimagination of art, artists, and audiences.

Notes

1   Micossé-Aikins and Sharifi, "Curating Resistance," 126.
2   Fournier, *Autotheory as Feminist Practice*.
3   Reilly, *Curatorial Activism*, 23.
4   Krasny et al., *Radicalising Care*, 12.

5   See @changethemuseum and @changethemuseum_aunz on Instagram.

The connection between fandom and oppositional practice has been recognized and discussed within fan studies. See Jenkins, *Textual Poachers*. The term *oppositional practice* comes from the work and writing of Michel de Certeau.

6   Keidl, "The Labor of Curating," 410.

7   Keidl, "The Labor of Curating," 410.

8   Grant and Love, *Fandom as Methodology*, 1.

9   Grant and Love, *Fandom as Methodology*, 1.

10   Sophia Cai, curator, *Zero O'Clock*, Assembly Point / ReAssemble, Centre of Visual Art, University of Melbourne, Victoria, September 10, 2020, https://sites.research.unimelb.edu.au/cova/research/feminism-and -intersectionality/assembly-point/zero-oclock.

11   Just, Martinis Roe, and McInnes, "Feminism and Intersectionality."

12   See Sophia Cai, curator, *Zero O'Clock* exhibition playlist, September 10, 2020, https://sites.research.unimelb.edu.au/cova/research/feminism -and-intersectionality/assembly-point/zero-oclock/0000-playlist.

13   Lucy Blakiston, "It's Time to Stop Shitting on Stans," *Shit You Should Care About*, May 18, 2021, https://shows.acast.com/the-shit-show/episodes /itstimetostopshittingonstans.

14   Jin, "The BTS Sphere."

15   From a conversation with Sim Luttin conducted in late 2020.

16   Read the curatorial essay as fan letter to Min Yoongi in full: Sophia Cai, "#CASUALFAN," for *Sincerely Yours*, January 22, 2022, https://offsite .westspace.org.au/work/casualfan/.

17   Fournier, *Autotheory as Feminist Practice*, 12.

18   See, for example, the Museums Are Not Neutral website, archived December 20, 2022, at Archive.org, https://web.archive.org/web /20221220081916/http://www.museumsarenotneutral.com/.

19   While I acknowledge the fraught connotations of "self-love" within a neoliberal system to apply individual solutions to systemic issues, my use of the word also draws on the BTS and UNICEF "Love Myself" campaign against violence. See https://www.love-myself.org/eng/home/.

20   See *Curatorial Activism*, by Maura Reilly, which documents some of this legacy in exhibition history since the 1970s.

Works Cited

Fournier, Lauren. *Autotheory as Feminist Practice in Art, Writing, and Criticism*. Cambridge, MA: MIT Press, 2021.

Grant, Catherine, and Kate Random Love, eds. *Fandom as Methodology: A Sourcebook for Artists and Writers*. London: Goldsmiths, 2019.

Jenkins, Henry. *Textual Poachers: Television Fans and Participatory Culture*. New York: Routledge, 1992.

Jin, Dal Yong. "The BTS Sphere: Adorable Representative M.C. for Youth's Transnational Cyber-nationalism on Social Media." *Communication and the Public* 6, nos. 1–4 (2021): 33–47. https://doi.org/10.1177/20570473211046733.

Just, Kate, Alex Martinis Roe, and Vikki McInnes, coordinators. "Feminism and Intersectionality." Centre of Visual Art, Research, University of Melbourne. Accessed February 8, 2024. https://sites.research.unimelb.edu.au/cova /research/feminism-and-intersectionality.

Keidl, Philipp Dominik. "The Labor of Curating: Fandom, Museums, and the Value of Fan Heritage." *Journal of Popular Culture* 54, no. 2 (2021): 407–31. https://doi.org/10.1111/jpcu.13014.

Krasny, Elke, Sophie Lingg, Lena Fritsch, Birgit Bosold, and Vera Hofmann, eds. *Radicalising Care: Feminist and Queer Activism in Curating*. London: Sternberg, 2022.

Micossé-Aikins, Sandrine, and Bahareh Sharifi. "Curating Resistance: Political Interventions into an Elitist, Hegemonic Cultural Landscape." In *Curating as Anti-racist Practice*, edited by Natalie Bayer, Belinda Kazeem-Kamiński, and Nora Sternfeld, 125–42. Espoo, Finland: Aalto University, 2018.

Reilly, Maura. *Curatorial Activism: Towards an Ethics of Curating*. London: Thames and Hudson, 2018.

27 · The Digital ARMY-
Ummah: Faith and
Community among
Muslim BTS Fans __ Mariam Elba

Before achieving the level of global fame they are currently known for, BTS members gave a twenty-minute interview with KBS World Arabic that aired on July 15, 2015.[1] Conducted in Arabic, for Arabic-speaking BTS fans, the interview took place at the close of Ramadan, the holy month of fasting in the Islamic calendar. During the interview, BTS members discussed the meaning behind the band's name, themes in their music, and the group's reactions to the reactions from their Arab fans. BTS began their interview by substituting their usual Korean group greeting, "*Annyeong haseyo, Bangtan Sonyeondan imnida!*" (Hello, we are BTS!) with "*Assalamu Aleikum*, we are BTS!" (Peace be upon you), which is the common greeting Muslims use throughout the world. The greeting was shared, retweeted, and liked across the world by Muslim and Arabic-speaking fans. Muslims beyond the Arab world were enamored by BTS's interview. j-hope introduced himself in Arabic as "*ismi* j-hope" (my name is j-hope), while other members described the hijab (head covering worn by many practicing Muslim women as a show of modesty) as "beautiful." BTS ended the interview with the holiday greeting "*Ramadan Kareem*" (May Ramadan be generous to you).

As BTS's popularity grew among their Muslim fanbase around the world, Muslim fans had consistently remarked on the band's sensitivity toward Islamic norms. Ahead of BTS's 2019 concert in Riyadh, Saudi Arabia, Big Hit Entertainment posted Ramadan greetings during the group's appearance on VLIVE for a livestream with fans.[2] Fans who attended the concert noted that sexually suggestive choreography was toned down and called the absence of j-hope's signature hip thrusts during "Baepsae" as *halal baepsae*—a permissible version of the choreography.[3] BTS also refrained from taking their customary bows at the end of the concert, which Muslim ARMY interpreted as deference to the Muslim practice of only bowing for prayer. Fans who went to the stadium during rehearsal time reported that the members paused when the *athan* (call to prayer) began and resumed rehearsal after it ended. These acts were interpreted as a show of respect to the majority-Muslim audience.[4]

How fans across the diverse Muslim-majority world engage with BTS's media appearances geared toward Muslims and the Arabic-speaking world is telling of how a significant segment of the BTS fandom connect their love of BTS to the band's public acknowledgment of Muslim ARMY. The online interactions of Muslim ARMY create a subcommunity of the BTS fandom, which I call a digital *ummah*, or a global Muslim community on social media platforms. Muslim ARMY form the most significant discursive and digital *ummah* centered on a music group. Muslim BTS fans are a diverse group in terms of age and nationality. They use consumption of BTS's content to connect with other Muslims across the world.

For this case study, I interacted online, conducted interviews, and administered surveys with twenty-eight Muslim fans between the ages of thirteen and forty-eight, from Indonesia, Pakistan, Egypt, the United States, and the United Kingdom. Many of the people I interviewed and surveyed engaged regularly with BTS's music and visual material as both consumers and makers of fan-produced content. How individuals use their fandom to engage with their Muslim identity varies. In some cases, Muslim fans view and interpret Islam through the wide range of BTS content that includes music, song lyrics, music videos, and performances, as well as the band's appearances in media interviews and variety shows. Other Muslim ARMY engage with BTS material creatively by producing fan-made content designed to combat Islamophobia by correcting misconceptions about Islam and connecting with non-Muslim ARMY.

Faith and Fandom

Attending to the online activities of Muslim ARMY offers a more complex understanding of the intersection between religion and fandom. At first glance, stanning BTS could be perceived as antithetical to Islam. The cultivation of a devoted fandom is an important part of the K-Pop industry and devotion to an idol group could be interpreted by doctrinaire interpretations of Islam as representing a competing figure of worship. Some conservative preachers have denounced the practice of fandom itself—and particularly BTS fandom—as *haram*, or Islamically forbidden. Andrew Crome, a scholar of religion and popular culture, notes, "the idea that fandom is a form of pseudo religion," a notion that "aims to 'other' both religion and fandom," is far less interesting than observing how faith and fandom work together.[5] Following Crome, this chapter examines how Muslim ARMY navigate fandom alongside their faith and identities as Muslims in online communities around the world. Muslim fans actively engage their Muslim faith and identity *with* their fan identity by using secular BTS-centered music, art, and content to practice faith and develop community.

Given how global Islamophobia is reinforced by widespread circulation of Muslim stereotypes, BTS's acknowledgment of Muslim customs in their media appearances is viewed by Muslim ARMY as affirmations of faith and identity. During a 2017 appearance on *Music Bank* Singapore, the members of BTS greeted a female fan wearing the hijab while maintaining their distance (see figure 27.1).[6] Since Muslim women who wear the hijab refrain from physical contact with men who are not their spouses or blood relatives, Muslim fans around the world perceived j-hope's act of reminding the members to keep their distance from the woman as a meaningful gesture. Online, Muslim ARMY cited this particular exchange as evidence of BTS's awareness, respect, and acceptance of Muslims.

The hijab has been a contentious and fraught site of political and ideological contestation. During the KBS interview, RM commented on how often they see hijab-wearing fans at their concerts and noticed how frequently hijab-wearing fans may need to adjust their hijabs during concerts, while SUGA talked about the hijab in terms of beauty. "I believe they have to wear the hijab because of their extreme beauty. Their beauty would surpass Korean beauty!" One fan on YouTube commented that hearing hijab-wearing fans being called beautiful "made me cry happy tears." Another fan posted on Twitter that V referred to hijab-wearing fans as having eyes that sparkle. Respondents to my survey noted that hearing BTS talk about the hijab in an endearing manner without reference to politics or institutionalized religious discourse made them (fans) feel happy, "respected, and acknowledged."

Not only did Muslim fans feel seen and appreciated as Muslims, they cite BTS's specific acknowledgment of them as "permission to pray." In response to a survey I conducted in 2019, Kawthar, a fan from Palestine, singled out the early 2015 KBS interview as a pivotal moment, saying, "I felt accepted. Sadly, as a Muslim you kind of feel pushed aside in the media. But in BTS,

nurul h.
@owlnuna

THANK YOU FOR CALLING ME. SELCA WITH THEM!
고마워요. 그리고 사랑해요! 👤 #MUSICBANKinSG

Translate Tweet

👤 방탄소년단

10:39 AM · Aug 4, 2017 · Twitter for iPhone

27.1 · *Music Bank* Singapore Fanmeet.

through their music and through their actions, I felt appreciated to have an opinion and be different. I felt like it was okay to be who I wanted."[7] Other fans I spoke to told me that the KBS interview not only made them passionate fans of BTS, but they felt their faith as Muslims grow as a result. A young Muslim fan in Palestine told me that when she saw BTS give their *salam* greeting at the beginning of the interview, "My heart soared and my *iman* [faith] flared." On Twitter, fans posted excerpts of the interview that featured BTS speaking Arabic and offering a Ramadan greeting. The fan edits not only appeal to Arabic-speaking fans but fans in the broader Muslim-majority world. The circulation of fan edits created a virtual community of Muslim fans to feel connected to each other.

While Muslim fans engage with BTS for affirmation and recognition, they also see BTS members as role models who embody behaviors considered characteristics of being a "good Muslim." Norah, a Muslim ARMY from Indonesia, said that she views BTS members in their different media appearances as living examples of how Muslims should carry themselves in accordance with the Quran. In our interview, Norah cited Quranic verses that she directly connects with BTS members' actions. For example, she referred to verse 49:11:

O you who have believed, let not a people ridicule [another] people; perhaps they may be better than them; nor let women ridicule [other] women; perhaps they may be better than them. And do not insult one another and do not call each other by [offensive] nicknames. Wretched is the name of disobedience after [one's] faith. And whoever does not repent— then it is those who are the wrongdoers.[8]

And she recounted reading the verse for the first time. She said, "I remember when the first time I read [this verse], it reminded me of Bangtan, [and] how people in Korea . . . called Namjoon ugly, how there was an ARMY that skipped Taehyung at a fansign, and how b.free insulted them. The verse [says] 'Ya ayyuhallazina ammanu' which in English is 'O you who believe,' or 'O you who have faith,' but it doesn't mean the result should be applied only to Muslims." Norah viewed BTS members' manner of handling difficult situations in their early days reflected Quranic values. "I don't know why but it seems like Allah taught me the virtue of the Quran through them," she told me. "We know as Muslims, Allah doesn't see us through religion, race, skin color, etc., but Allah sees us from our *taqwa* [God-consciousness] and Allah's promises are applicable for us, even for BTS."

BTS fandom, for Norah, is a means through which she practices, interprets, and understands her faith. On her personal Twitter account, she frequently posted threads connecting BTS's actions with the Quran. In an interview conducted over chat she wrote, "In the near future, I hope I'll be able to build a foundation for Muslim ARMYs to be able to do good for the sake of God with BTS as the motivation." Her posts act as a public document of how her fandom is not antithetical to being a practicing Muslim.

While religious leaders have criticized devotion to BTS as being in competition with devotion to Allah, Muslim ARMY have pushed back by pointing out how BTS's music and message align with their religious beliefs. I spoke to Khadija, who talked about how she found lyrics in BTS songs as having a distinctly Islamic character:

Idol worship is a huge sin in Islam, and K-pop idols are you know, called "idols." And although fan fervor around me can reach the point of intensity that it does feel like ARMY does worship them to an extent, I like that BTS are self-aware in the sense that they know the dangers of fans putting the group on a pedestal. It was their song "Pied Piper" that addressed that. I found their candidness in the lyrics about how overly passionate fans get and how it's better to take several steps back from complete obsession to be refreshing.[9]

Referencing "Pied Piper," a song that uses gentle humor to warn their fans about the intensity of fandom love, this fan took seriously the lyrics asking listeners to "now stop and study for your exam."[10] In contrast to the way religious leaders warn against idol worship, Khadija views the message of "Pied Piper" as a caution against overzealous behavior in the fandom. She adds, "Although I didn't choose to stan from a faith-based perspective, there were things that did overlap with Muslim values." Pointing to their kindness, manners, and propensity for charitable giving, she states, "It was those personal qualities that really made me a fan of them as people."

Connection with the Digital Fan-*Ummah*

The digital fan-*ummah* connects Muslim fans located in different countries around the world. On platforms such as Twitter, Curious Cat, and Discord, Muslim fans share memes with fellow Muslim fans to consolidate their place in the broader fandom and affirm their identity as Muslim ARMY. For example, Muslim fans had their own take on ARMY Selca Day on Twitter, a designated day during which fans post a selfie where they are re-creating a photo of a BTS member, or wearing similar clothing next to the member's photograph they are imitating. Muslim ARMY created a distinctly Muslim space aside from ARMY Selca Day by using #MuslimARSD and posting jokes about the "halal gap" between ARMY and the members of BTS alongside their selfie. Shortly after BTS released their 2019 album, MAP OF THE SOUL: PERSONA, which coincided with Ramadan, fans used hashtags such as #RamadanWithLuv (referencing one of BTS's releases at that time, "Boy with Luv") to post *dua* (prayers) to recite during Ramadan. In 2020, Muslim ARMY caught the attention of online news outlets, after using the hashtag #IftarWithARMY on Twitter to share photos of their *iftar* meals on social media. In early June when Eid al-Fitr (the feast day after Ramadan) approached, Muslim ARMY used the hashtag

#EidWithLuv to post photos of the new outfits and formal wear worn to the mosque in celebration of the holiday.[11] Fans also shared information about charities to donate to for *zakat* and *sadaqah* (almsgiving).[12]

An important element of ARMY culture is participation in giving campaigns. Groups such as One In An ARMY (OIAA) organize ongoing charitable drives in the name of BTS members. Muslim fans tie their charitable campaigns directly to the Islamic practice of giving alms. In Muslim ARMY spaces, the act of giving takes on special meaning when done in conjunction with major Muslim holidays like Ramadan, Eid al-Fitr, or Eid al-Adha. Fans make the extra effort to contribute to campaigns affecting Muslim-majority communities. During Ramadan 2021, ARMY in Pakistan rallied to donate money to a local organization in their country working to provide orphans and low-income families with basic necessities such as food, clean water, educational support, and support in their everyday lives.[13] The same year, in response to the ongoing strife in Yemen that saw the destruction of important infrastructure, Muslim ARMY organized donations to build wells to provide Yemenis access to clean water.[14]

The congruence between ARMY giving practices and Muslim almsgiving has allowed Muslim ARMY to diversify the campaigns of ARMY in general. In 2019, One In An ARMY launched #ARMYxRamadanChallenge, in which ARMY collaborated with a UN program called Share the Meal, to provide meals for people in Yemen, Venezuela, and other countries.[15] As an example of cross-cultural collaboration within ARMY spaces, the administrators of One In An ARMY revealed that non-Muslim fans spearheaded a Ramadan charity and consulted with Muslim fans within OIAA about the project. Erika told me in a Twitter chat in November 2019, "From our team's perspective, it is not so much about the faith itself as it gives people another avenue to help others, makes people know that they are included and respected, that we can celebrate with them as they practice their faiths and beliefs and remember that ARMY is made up of all of us."

Digital Da'wah: Educating ARMY

Most studies of online Muslim communities focus on intracommunal relations, and there is little exploration of the intersection between Muslim and online fan spaces. Muslim ARMY spaces, like much of the internet, are neither static nor homogenous. These spaces are active sites of encounter, where Muslim ARMY and non-Muslim ARMY can build on their shared fandom to foster dialogue, educate each other, and hold discussions about political issues and current events affecting Muslim-majority countries.

The now-defunct "BTS Global Muslim" Twitter and Curious Cat pages and the BTS Muslim Base Twitter page served not only as focal points for Muslim ARMY but also as educational platforms for their non-Muslim ARMY counterparts. For example, non-Muslim fans have asked the Muslim fans running the BTS Global Muslim Curious Cat page questions ranging from whether it is acceptable to compliment a Muslim girl's hijab to what is appropriate in wishing Muslim "mutuals" a happy holiday. In the lead-up to Ramadan, a non-Muslim fan used the acronym NSFR (not safe for Ramadan) to ask for advice on what kind of content to avoid posting in consideration of their Muslim followers. Since NSFR is primarily used by Muslim ARMY to tag content considered inappropriate during the holy month of Ramadan, it is noteworthy that a non-Muslim poster used the term out of respect for Muslim fans.[16] Another asked what *dua*, or supplications, one could recite to aid in SUGA's recovery when he underwent surgery in 2020. In 2021, the fans who ran the BTS Muslim base page posted a guide for their fellow non-Muslim fans on what they can or cannot engage in during Ramadan.[17] Some have even sought advice on converting to Islam.

The BTS Global Muslim group, a Twitter account that has since been suspended, created safe online spaces for non-Muslim fans to learn more about everyday Muslim practices from nonclerical voices. While the fans running the BTS Global Muslim Curious Cat answered many questions about commonplace routines for Muslims around the world, the BTS Global Muslims referred their inquirers to Islamic scholars for consultation on more complicated questions that they could not answer. This is arguably a prime example of one of the "intellectual technologies" or mediums, in which religious pedagogy is employed in the age of mass media and widespread use of the internet.[18] As opposed to simply learning about Islam in school, television broadcast media, or questionable internet sources, non-Muslim BTS fans are asking their fellow Muslim BTS fans about Islam.

In being openly Muslim online, Muslim ARMY fill an important gap in fandom spaces by directly and indirectly teaching non-Muslim fans how Islam is practiced and who Muslims are around the world. The BTS fandom has become a site in which Muslim fans can conduct *da'wah*, the practice of educating others about Islam (sometimes, but not necessarily, with an intent to invite people to convert). The emergence of the digital fan *ummah* is significant in the context of Islamophobia and operates as a much-needed space for non-Muslim fans to learn about issues in Muslim-majority communities. Facilitated by a common love of BTS, Muslim ARMY can foster dialogue where harmful religious/ethnic stereotypes are broken down.

Muslim populations around the world face unprecedented discrimination and repression. The digital fan *ummah* has the potential to host dialogues on complex and contentious topics. For example, some fans have used BTS to draw attention to atrocities like the continuing ethnic cleansing of Uyghurs in China,[19] the assault on Palestinians in Gaza, and those at risk of losing their homes in the Sheikh Jarrah neighborhood of east Jerusalem, by directing other fans to educational materials on their Twitter accounts.[20] Western media covering events in the Muslim world often do so in a biased manner that equates Islam with terrorism. In the context of this mediascape, the Muslim BTS fandom can be a place where fans with little or no connection to Muslim-majority countries can put human faces with news events and learn more about the issues.

Even though Muslim ARMY are only a subsection of BTS fandom, they are as heterogeneous as the broader fandom in terms of how fans engage their faith with fandom or bring politics into fan communities. For example, Muslim fans had mixed reactions to BTS's 2019 concert in Riyadh and the concert itself was a source of contention among the broader fandom. There were many fans, both Muslim and non-Muslim, who were overjoyed that BTS was performing in a Muslim, Arabic-speaking country; however, both Muslim and non-Muslim fans also pointed out how the state-organized concert would whitewash violations against Saudi citizens. Some recalled how one year prior to the BTS concert, Saudi journalist Jamal Khashoggi was murdered inside the Saudi embassy and that women's rights activists were being imprisoned by the Saudi regime.

The *ummah* is populated with the diversity of humans who make up the Muslim world and can also host fans who just want to make human connections that are not necessarily motivated by politics. One fan from India traveled to Muslim-majority Kashmir, a territory that was under martial law for nearly two years after it was stripped of its special autonomous status in 2019 by India.[21] The region endured an eighteen-month communications blackout, but the fan's vlog made no reference to the situation in Kashmir and focused solely on meeting fellow BTS fans and discussing one another's biases. Even in these seemingly apolitical moments, a space is opened up to imagine Muslims as fans and as humans with the same passions as everyone else. In these small ways, encounters with the Muslim BTS fandom opens up possibilities of deeper understanding to push back against Muslim stereotypes. By using fandom to "speak themselves," Muslim fans are not only building community, but also countering Islamophobic narratives across the globe.

Notes

1   "[Star Interview] BTS (방탄소년단)," March 15, 2018, YouTube video, 17:12, https://youtu.be/znT99VidLno.

2   @ygpluto, "SHUT UP I GOT AN AD FOR VLIVE ON YOUTUBE AND ITS JUST ABOUT BTS KEEPING US COMPANY DURING RAMADAN EYEM," Twitter, May 14, 2019, 2:30 p.m., https://twitter.com/ygpluto/status /1128366990861721605.

3   @btsmashallah, "When we got halal baepsae," Twitter, December 25, 2020, 5:53 p.m., https://twitter.com/btsmashallah/status/1342604470564360192.

4   SBS News, "BTS Reportedly Stopped Rehearsal out of Respect for Muslim Culture," October 11, 2019, https://news.sbs.co.kr/news/endPage.do?news _id=N1005474488.

5   Crome, "Religion and the Pathologization of Fandom," 130.

6   nurul h. (@owlnuna), Twitter, August 4, 2017, 7:39 a.m., archived February 9, 2020, at Archive.org, https://web.archive.org/web/20200209030938 /https://twitter.com/owlnuna/status/893481592764547073.

7   Kawthar Barakat, interview by author, online, October 15, 2019.

8   The Qur'ān: English Meanings, rev. and ed. Saheeh International (London: Al-Muntada Al-Islami 2004), 519. Brackets in original.

9   Khadija (pseudonym), interview by author, online, October 13, 2019.

10   Anonymous, "Pied Piper," Doolset Lyrics, June 17, 2018, https:// doolsetbangtan.wordpress.com/2018/06/17/pied-piper/.

11   Dahir, "BTS Fans Are Sharing the Ways They Celebrate Eid Using #Eid-WithLove and It's so Cute."

12   BORAHAE BD ARMY, "Hello BD ARMYs," Twitter, March 20, 2021, 10:36 a.m., https://twitter.com/BorahaeBD_ARMY/status/1373282317884563459.

13   BTS PAKISTAN WEVERSE & VOTING⁷, "Ramadan Project 2 Done," Twitter, May 10, 2021, 8:36 a.m., https://twitter.com/BTS_pk_weverse/status /1391733873520873472.

14   @rmsternocleid, "CALLING ALL MY BORAPEOPLE," Twitter, April 20, 2022, 1:39 p.m., https://twitter.com/rmsternocleid/status /1516833904296144896.

15   @OneInAnARMY, "ARMYs donated 7k+ meals for hungry children in Yemen, Venezuela, and more in the #ARMYxRamadanChallenge," Twitter, June 14, 2019, 2:02 a.m., https://twitter.com/OneInAnARMY/status /1139412875351511040.

16   BTSGlobalMuslim, CuriousCat.live, reply to "Anonymous," May 13 and 19, 2019, https://curiouscat.live/BTSGlobalMuslim/post/867885979.

17   BTS Muslim Base, "[Ramadan Guide,]" Twitter, April 12, 2021, 11:00 p.m., https://twitter.com/BTSMuslimBase/status/1381804498595667969.

18   Kassam, review of *Muslim Networks from Hajj to Hip Hop*.

19   @MY_btsarmy, "bts Malaysia army⁷ | golden," Twitter, December 21, 2019, 8:11 a.m., https://twitter.com/MY_btsarmy/status/1208374331400523776.

20   @noorfromwithin, "Muslims/non-Muslims, please educate yourself," Twitter, May 10, 2021, 2:46 p.m., https://twitter.com/noorfromwithin/status/1391827010603864067.

21   Zoha, "Met BTS ARMY near the Border in Uri, Kashmir | Kashmir Vlog 3 | URI VLOG | Indo-Pak Border in Kashmir," January 16, 2021, YouTube video, 5:27, https://www.youtube.com/watch?v=6cg3l6Uk1LU.

Works Cited

Crome, Andrew. "Religion and the Pathologization of Fandom: Religion, Reason, and Controversy in My Little Pony Fandom." *Journal of Religion and Popular Culture* 27, no. 2 (2015): 130–47.

Dahir, Ikran. "BTS Fans Are Sharing the Ways They Celebrate Eid Using #EidWithLove and It's so Cute." *BuzzFeed*, June 6, 2019. https://www.buzzfeed.com/ikrd/muslim-teens-wanted-to-celebrate-eid-with-bts-and-fellow.

Kassam, Zayn. Review of *Muslim Networks from Hajj to Hip Hop*, edited by Mariam Cooke and Bruce B. Lawrence. *Journal of the American Academy of Religion* 76, no. 4 (2008): 1013–18. https://doi.org/10.1093/jaarel/lfn068.

28 · "Let Us Light Up the Night": BTS and Abolitionist Possibilities at the End of the World — UyenThi Tran Myhre

On a spring day in April 1975, as the last US troops pulled away and North Vietnamese troops drew close to Saigon, my family fled Vietnam. This is a story that is as familiar to me as a fairy tale, with details I can vividly imagine but never fully know. My mom would share these memories with me on long car rides or before I fell asleep at night, tucked into bed at home in a quiet suburb outside Minneapolis. She told me that those who fled, who resettled in places like Minnesota or California, look back on that month and call it Black April. In Vietnam, I recently learned, April 30 is Reunification Day, a national holiday commemorating liberation from the imperial United States. For families in the diaspora like mine, that spring day marks the abandonment of the US government and the fall of Saigon. My parents have never returned to their homeland.

"봄날 (Spring Day)" happens to be the BTS song that marks the beginning of my ARMY origin story. When I first found the video, I watched it on repeat, hitting pause here and there as I tried to identify which member was walking along the snowy train tracks or which members were standing in front of the neon sign reading "Omelas.'" As I read up on the song and the video, I learned that the neon sign was a reference to "The Ones Who Walk Away from Omelas," a short story by Ursula K. Le Guin about a city where the residents' sublime happiness is knowingly facilitated by a single child's endless suffering.

Coincidentally, at the same time I was becoming ARMY, I was reading another story by Le Guin, *The Dispossessed*, a novel about a police-free, anarchist utopia founded by a historical figure called "Odo." A prolific author, Le Guin set some of her works in a shared universe. For example, Odo also appears as a character called Laia Asieo Odo in "The Day before the Revolution," a short story set some time before the events in *The Dispossessed*. In Le Guin's discussion of this story, she refers to Laia as one who walked away from Omelas after learning the ugly truth behind her city's prosperity.[2] In the introduction to the Library of America set collecting these novels and stories, published a year before her death in 2018, Le Guin wrote:

> *The Dispossessed* started as a very bad short story, which I didn't try to finish but couldn't quite let go. There was a book in it, and I knew it, but the book had to wait for me to learn what I was writing about and how to write about it. I needed to understand my own passionate opposition to the war that we were, endlessly it seemed, waging in Vietnam, and endlessly protesting at home. If I had known then that my country would continue making aggressive wars for the rest of my life, I might have had less energy for protesting that one. But, knowing only that I didn't want to study war no more, I studied peace.[3]

As a storyteller, Le Guin helps us imagine what else is possible when we begin to question and refuse the status quo. Thinking about the stories my mom told me as a child, I know my parents didn't get to choose between studying peace and war; they just had to survive. As a storyteller myself, but also as a daughter of refugees, I recognize what a luxury it is to be *writing* about this. I have the spaciousness to dream about a more just world, to do more than just survive.

Recently, I visited my parents at their house in the suburbs, the same house where I grew up. It was mid-May, but spring came late this year, and the bright pink peonies in the front yard were just beginning to bloom. As my dad watched soccer on the TV in the corner of the dining room, mom opened the YouTube app on her iPad to show me an *America's Test Kitchen* video for perfectly crispy roast chicken, and, in turn, I showed her a performance of "Spring Day" with Vietnamese subtitles.

Peering at the screen through her readers, she asked in Vietnamese: *You went to Vegas to see them? How many of them are there? They look so young. How old are they? Which one is the oldest, and which one is the youngest? You like them even when you can't understand what they're singing?* I answered her questions and explained about English subtitles as she read the Viet subs aloud and explained them to me in her own words. My vocabulary and reading comprehension of my mother tongue is embarrassing, and as we watched the members sing around a campfire, I caught just a few Vietnamese words in the captions: *winter, August, snow*. Listening to the lyrics, I recognized the line *I miss you* in Korean. Reading the Viet subs, I thought about how, depending on context, *tớ nhớ cậu* could mean *I miss you*, or *I remember you*.

In one tab on my browser, I have the performance of "Spring Day" with the Viet subs, paused on RM's verse. In another, I have Bangtan Subs' page with Korean to English lyric translations. In another, an English to Viet dictionary. It takes me ten minutes to remember how to turn on the Viet keyboard on my Mac, but once I figure it out, I remember how to type the tone marks in an instant: *Trái tim này cũng chạy đua với thời gian*.[4] It occurs to me to locate this part in the official music video, where the English subtitles read "It's all winter here even in August / My heart is running on the time alone," as RM runs toward the neon "Omelas" sign. After playing telephone with the translations, I can finally read the Vietnamese ARMY's subs effortlessly: *My heart is racing against time*.

* * *

The day before the abandonment/fall/liberation, on the evening of April 29, 1975, my family secured passage on an oil rig leaving the Saigon harbor. Staying meant forced labor/incarceration/reeducation camps for my father and my uncles. Escaping, because they had the right connections, meant a future together was possible. It was almost August when they arrived in Minnesota, by way of a refugee camp in US-occupied Guam and then another at an army base in Florida. The volunteers in Florida warned them of the cold northern winters and made sure to equip everyone with warm coats and hats. Taking weather precautions seriously, the family wore the puffy winter jackets on the flight to Minneapolis. Every time mom shares this part of the story with me, she laughs when she remembers how ridiculous she felt stepping off the plane into the summer heat.

Three days before my family left home, on April 26, 1975, at the Nebula Awards for science fiction and fantasy writing, Ursula K. Le Guin won Best Novel for *The Dispossessed* and Best Short Story for "The Day before the Revolution."[5] The fall before that, in September 1974, ten years before I was born and some forty years before Omelas would find its way into Bangtan's music video (MV) for "Spring Day," Le Guin won the Hugo Award for Best Short Story for "The Ones Who Walk Away from Omelas."[6] A few weeks ago, I found a copy of *The Dispossessed* in a Little Free Library in my neighborhood. The copyright page shows it's a first edition paperback, published the same month my family arrived in Minneapolis: July 1975. Even though I know human beings look for patterns as a survival mechanism, as a way to make sense of the chaos around us, it's still comforting to imagine that "all this is not a coincidence."[7]

* * *

There's a sentimental saying among ARMY that we find BTS when we need them the most. In 2021, the summer I began to obsess over the "Spring Day" music video, and the summer I was reading Le Guin for the first time, I had just left my nonprofit job doing diversity, equity, and inclusion work. Even though I know my parents understand that leaving something behind is a chance to go toward something else, to this day, knowing it would cause them unnecessary worry, I haven't told them that I quit without another job lined up.

I had started working there in March 2020, just a week before COVID-19 shut everything down. Between orientation and attending a conference my first week, I was in our downtown Minneapolis office for only one day before we were all sent home to work remotely for the rest of my time in that position. The team pivoted from facilitating in-person sessions on implicit bias and "transforming workplace culture" to delivering virtual workshops. Less than three months later, Minneapolis police murdered George Floyd.

Today, when you search online for "Minneapolis uprisings," the image results are primarily photos from the night of May 28, 2020. Scroll and you'll see photo after photo of protesters silhouetted against the giant flames that engulf the Third Police Precinct, located just a couple of miles away from the convenience store at 38th and Chicago where MPD killed George Floyd three days earlier. When I think back to that week and that summer, I remember moments more than an exact timeline: texts and tweets warning of fires spreading on the North and South sides; friends creating a Discord to organize a nightly neighborhood defense against the roving groups of white supremacists who were using the protests as cover to create chaos; the massive deployment of police and National Guard who were creating their own chaos; my cousin fulfilling mutual aid requests by bicycle since so many streets were shut down. I remember people sharing screen shots of a Yelp review of the Third Precinct: *One star. It burn down.*

The uprisings continued that summer across Minneapolis, the US, and the world. I wasn't ARMY yet, but I remember seeing tweets about K-Pop fans who contributed to the protests by jamming police surveillance websites with fan cams. Later, I learned that BTS donated $1 million to Black Lives Matter (an amount quickly matched and exceeded by ARMYs). My own work received a $5 million donation in memory of George Floyd. The press release announcing this donation noted the need to address the larger societal issues at the root of George Floyd's death.

Outside of work, it felt so clear that there was a shift in how people were understanding police violence; that people were beginning to see that the societal issue at the root of George Floyd's death was policing itself. For years, a common chant at protests and marches was "No justice, no peace; prosecute the police." But with the murder of George Floyd, that chant had shifted to "No justice, no peace; abolish the police." That shift in language was, and is, more than simply a matter of activists coming up with a catchier slogan. The call to divest from policing and prisons while simultaneously investing in life-affirming institutions (to paraphrase abolitionist scholar Ruth Wilson Gilmore) has deep roots in the Black radical tradition.[8] In their book *No More Police*, Andrea Ritchie and Mariame Kaba write that, "[Prison industrial complex] abolition is a vision of a restructured society where we have everything we need to be safe, to not only survive but thrive: food, shelter, education, health, art, beauty, clean water, and more."[9]

Here in Minneapolis, political education and organizing around police violence and community safety, led by Black community members, had been underway long before the city became the center of the global uprisings in 2020. More of us were realizing that no amount of reform would prevent police violence because that violence is a *feature* of the system, not a bug. The system is functioning exactly as intended—and it can't create safety because it was never meant to protect us in the first place.

At work, these shifts were less apparent. I felt some hope when I was given ten minutes to give a presentation (at my own request) to my team on the nuances of reform versus defund. Everyone listened thoughtfully, brows furrowed. My supervisor, a senior leader herself, suggested I share my presentation with our CEO. That never happened, but soon after, with the receipt of the $5 million grant, my office began to expand our team and our work to include DEI workshops for cops. I continued working with K–12 educators and higher-education faculty as usual but requested that I not be assigned to any of the new work that the rest of the team was doing with police. Over the next year, in heartfelt conversations with my supervisor, I tried my best to explain why I didn't believe training police on implicit bias or workplace culture would keep us safe. I think she tried her best to understand, but in the end, it was clear that neither of us was going to change the other's mind. I turned in my resignation.

* * *

Being between jobs was an ideal time to become ARMY. I had no responsibilities, just a lot of depression and a world of time. After stumbling across the "Black Swan" MV on YouTube one night, then their *Saturday Night Live* performance and the "Spring Day" MV, social media algorithms zeroed in on my new obsession and kept serving me more BTS content. It seems fitting that nearly a year after having found BTS while on a break myself, everything has come full circle, with the members' recent statement about their own break. After their FESTA dinner announcing their hiatus to focus on solo work, Jung Kook came on VLIVE one morning to reassure ARMY and sing to us. On my Twitter timeline that day, in between ARMY accounts translating Jung Kook's live and tweets about the impending fall of Roe, there was a *Teen Vogue* interview with Ruth Wilson Gilmore, who talked about how different struggles can have "abolitionist characteristics," how it's important to use our curiosity to see *patterns*, to study what's in front of us.[10]

What's often in front of me, unsurprisingly, is BTS—and even in their content (music, variety shows, interviews, and beyond), patterns emerge. Take, for instance, their visit to Washington, DC, in spring 2022. In a video released on the White House YouTube channel, the members speak with President Biden about the importance of Asian diversity and inclusion, and RM thanks him for signing the COVID-19 Hate Crimes Act into law. Biden tells the members that he got involved in public life because of the civil rights movement, and how "even back then, famous artists helped move people."[11] With so much debate in Asian American communities about whether hate crime legislation protects us, or just gives more power and resources to the carceral system, the abolitionist question emerges: *what are we moving people toward?*

Biden's meeting with BTS was attempting to signal that he cares about the same things that I do, that we share an agreement about social movements and what needs to change. But I know that the president is vehemently against abolition. In March 2022, he received a bipartisan standing ovation when he said, "We should all agree the answer is not to defund the police, it's to fund the police."[12]

As for BTS, while I know they aren't explicitly trying to "move people" toward abolition, I can't help but see glimmers of another world in their work. As bell hooks said, "Whether we're talking about race or gender or class, popular culture is where the pedagogy is, it's where the learning is."[13] Throughout BTS's work, there are hints at what we want to turn away from: In 2013, the members are fighting futuristic authorities in an all-white classroom in the "N.O (엔.오)" music video.[14] In 2015, cops slam V into the side of a patrol car in the "RUN" music video.[15] In 2021, the group's *PERMISSION TO DANCE ON STAGE* setlist opens with a graffiti sign declaring "We don't need permission," as the members break out of prison.[16] Even the animated Tannies, running alone through the MV for "We are Bulletproof: the Eternal," encounter burning streets and riot cops before they pass the edge of winter to find each other and their ARMY.[17] And, in perhaps the most powerful metaphor for abolition in their work, there's a scene near the end of the "Spring Day" music video, where the members find each other, leave the literal darkness of Omelas behind, and run together toward a brighter world.[18]

In a BTS interview with *Variety* in 2020, SUGA said, "Everyone wants to live in a better world and try to make this a better world."[19] Writing about artists in social change movements, Ray Levy Uyeda argues, "It's artists who help us envision most literally the alternate possibilities of relating to one another, understanding ourselves, and building a future that values differences rather than tries to smooth them over."[20] Although Uyeda was writing specifically about visual artists and movement art, I think these points of entry can also be found within BTS, in how their music opens possibilities to imagine an alternate future—a better world, for everyone.

From abolitionist organizers in Minneapolis to BTS themselves, we express this desire to build another world, one with more justice and more peace. Moving people—organizing people—to join this work requires us to know where we've come from, what we want to leave behind, and what we want to focus on growing instead. To paraphrase Le Guin, if we're not studying war, how might we study peace? As a writer and artist, Le Guin doesn't tell us exactly *how* the people of Anarres created a world where police and prisons are obsolete, how they found ways to respond to harm without locking each other away. And even while we dream about the world we deserve, even as we try to manifest it into being, we face our own (and others') doubts, uncertainties, and fears. So, again, we look for patterns. For me, I notice how pieces of this unknown future can be seen in the present. My existence is proof of it. My family survived and endured not just because we had no other choice but because community held us up. We got access to the support we needed, which allowed us to stay together, to be safe, to create a new life. And because of all of this, I get to be here, weaving together an existence as a daughter of refugees, a feminist, an abolitionist, and ARMY.

Looking back on my own journey into the fandom, finding BTS during a depressive low after resigning from my job, I think about how ARMY often joke that loving Bangtan is easier than going to therapy. As tempting as it was (and is) to escape from the world and stay cocooned in a literal BTS blanket forever, the more time I spend with them, the more reminders I find to stay grounded in these wild times, to keep fighting and contribute in a meaningful way.

In 2020, when the members were asked whether they see themselves as political, RM replied: "We are not political figures, but as they say, everything is political eventually."[21] He understands that BTS, like all pop culture, doesn't exist in a vacuum. There is the concept of Bangtan Sonyeondan acting as a shield for youth, the lyrics of "Anpanman" on the superpower of offering support and help to anyone who needs it.[22] There is the hopefulness of seven billion lights on the darkest of nights in "소우주 (Mikrokosmos)."[23] There is the reminder to generate joy and love where we can in "작은 것들을 위한 시 (Boy With Luv)"—a song that is "A Poem for Small Things."[24] Everything does become political eventually, because there is power in the stories we tell and the communities that share them.

The afternoon I showed my mom the performance of "Spring Day," in between her making me lunch and me giving her a crash course on BTS, I asked her to help me translate an Instagram story saved to my phone. The post was musing about the meaning of the word *thương*, the only Viet word I have in my vocabulary for love. The person was saying how *thương* was close to the word *yêu*, and perhaps similar to love, but not quite the same thing. So, when do you use *yêu* then? I asked my parents. *Mình xài chữ yêu cho* (boyfriend/girlfriend), they said. We use the word *yêu* for the love between boyfriend/girlfriend. She translated the rest for me: how the emotions (a word I didn't know) we associate with *thương* are difficulty and suffering (words I do know).[25]

When I let my heart leap through time, I see the choices and sacrifices my parents made so there could be a future for our family. *Khó khăn, khổ đau* are undoubtedly present, but *thương* is the main thread woven throughout the stories I've heard since I was a child: Bà Nội and Cô Ba, who cared for my cousins and me while our parents worked long shifts; sponsors who became family friends over the decades, who drove my parents to English classes and job interviews, who took my siblings and cousins along with their own kids to Buck Hill that first winter for a sledding party, who taught my mom how to make banana bread. I've seen that recipe: faded ballpoint pen on a fragile slip of paper that is older than I am, tucked into a small red notebook on the kitchen shelf, in between pages that contain my mom's own handwritten recipes for everything from *bánh choux* to *bánh bò*.

It occurs to me that while I didn't know the Vietnamese word for romantic love, I still don't have the English words to fully describe *thương*, except that maybe it's about love in action, that it means showing up for each other. At their White House visit, RM emphasized that the members "just want to give back all the love that we got," a sentiment we've heard BTS express time and again.[26] Each time they say this, I know they aren't speaking about abolition as a guiding principle. Yet, again, I can't help but see the patterns, the connections with abolition: this idea of giving back, of redistributing love, of showing up and doing the difficult work of building relationships and communities that don't leave anyone behind. I'm imagining how we can light up the night as we're working our way toward a different future, where love means justice and liberation, and justice and liberation aren't policing or prisons or forced labor camps, but a commitment to making sure everyone has more than enough.

I don't know if we're at the end of the world, but I do know that my family has already survived the end of a world, survived war, and endured—with the support of beloved community. In the face of that legacy, knowing that so much had to fall perfectly into place for me to exist, is a reminder that indulging in despair and fatalism is selfish. As V said, "There are still many pages left in the story about us . . . we shouldn't talk like the ending has already been written."[27]

Choosing to believe another world is possible, to find joy in the small things, to keep showing up for myself and the people I care about—these are all acts of defiance. I see more and more of us refusing despair by turning hope into practice, love into action. I hear thousands upon thousands of voices whispering "dream, hope, forward, forward."[28] All we have is each other, and we're paving the way to another world. We believe the best is yet to come.

Notes

1   HYBE LABELS, "BTS (방탄소년단) '봄날 (Spring Day)' Official MV," February 12, 2017, YouTube video, 5:28, https://www.youtube.com/watch?v=xEeFrLSkMm8.

2   Le Guin, "The Day before the Revolution," 285.

3   Le Guin, "'Introduction.'"

4   MYNIE BANGTAN, "[VIETSUB] BTS (방탄소년단) 'Spring Day'(봄날)—A Butterful Getaway," July 18, 2021, YouTube video, 4:38, https://youtu.be/8155vL1od5o.

5   "1974 Nebula Awards," accessed June 20, 2022, https://nebulas.sfwa.org/award-year/1974/.

6   "1974 Hugo Awards," accessed June 20, 2022, https://www.thehugoawards.org/hugo-history/1974-hugo-awards/.

7   "Serendipity," lyrics translated by *Doolset Lyrics*, August 24, 2018, https://doolsetbangtan.wordpress.com/2018/08/24/serendipity/.

8   Kaba and Ritchie, *No More Police*, 16.

9   Kaba and Ritchie, *No More Police*, 16.

10   McMenamin, "Ruth Wilson Gilmore Talks Abolition Geography and Liberation."

11   White House, "President Biden and Vice President Harris Welcome BTS to the White House."

12   Harris-Perry, "Deep Dive: Police Abolition."

13   hooks, *Cultural Criticism and Transformation*.

14   1theK (원더케이), "[MV] BTS (방탄소년단) _ N.O(엔.오)," September 10, 2013, YouTube video, 4:02, https://www.youtube.com/watch?v=mmgxPLLLyVo.

15   HYBE LABELS, "BTS (방탄소년단) 'RUN' Official MV," November 29, 2015, YouTube video, 7:30, https://www.youtube.com/watch?v=wKysONrSmew.

16   BTS LIVE 2, "BTS/방탄소년단 'ON' Live PTD On Stage Las Vegas D-4," September 28, 2022, YouTube video, 5:10, https://www.youtube.com/watch?v=hr3SdEh2bTU.

17   BANGTANTV, "[2020 FESTA] BTS (방탄소년단) 'We are Bulletproof: the Eternal' MV #2020BTSFESTA," June 11, 2020, YouTube video, 4:32, https://www.youtube.com/watch?v=7UWBYJjuILo.

18   HYBE LABELS, "BTS (방탄소년단) '봄날 (Spring Day)' Official MV."

19   Davis, "BTS on the Decision to Donate to Black Lives Matter: 'Prejudice Should Not Be Tolerated.'"

20   Uyeda, "How Artists Help Us Believe in a More Just Future."

21   Davis, "BTS on the Decision to Donate to Black Lives Matter: 'Prejudice Should Not Be Tolerated.'"

22   "Anpanman," lyrics translated by *Doolset Lyrics*, June 1, 2018, https://doolsetbangtan.wordpress.com/2018/06/01/anpanman/.

23   "소우주 (Mikrokosmos)," lyrics translated by *Doolset Lyrics*, April 13, 2019, https://doolsetbangtan.wordpress.com/2019/04/13/mikrokosmos/.

24   "작은 것들을 위한 시 (Boy with Luv)," lyrics translated by *Doolset Lyrics*, April 13, 2019, https://doolsetbangtan.wordpress.com/2019/04/13/boy-with-luv/.

25   Soulvenir.co, "Fun fact about chữ 'Thương,'" Instagram, February 19, 2022, https://instagram.com/soulvenir.co.

26   White House, "President Biden and Vice President Harris Welcome BTS to the White House."

27   United Nations, "President Moon Jae-in and BTS at the Sustainable Development Goals Moment."

28   "Epilogue: Young Forever," lyrics translated by *Doolset Lyrics*, June 1, 2018, https://doolsetbangtan.wordpress.com/2018/06/01/epilogue-young-forever/.

Works Cited

Davis, Rebecca. "BTS on the Decision to Donate to Black Lives Matter: 'Prejudice Should Not Be Tolerated.'" *Variety*, October 2, 2020. https://variety.com /2020/music/news/bts-black-lives-matter-donation-1234789434/.

Harris-Perry, Melissa. "Deep Dive: Police Abolition." *Takeaway*, September 9, 2022. https://www.wnycstudios.org/podcasts/takeaway/segments/deep-dive -police-abolition.

hooks, bell. *Cultural Criticism and Transformation*. Film transcript. Media Education Foundation, 1997. https://www.mediaed.org/transcripts/Bell-Hooks -Transcript.pdf?_ga=2.34114657.1981692155.1662385794-1857741072 .1662385794.

Kaba, Mariame, and Andrea J. Ritchie. *No More Police: A Case for Abolition*. New York: New Press, 2022.

Le Guin, Ursula K. "The Day before the Revolution." In *The Wind's Twelve Quarters*, 285–303. New York: Harper and Row, 1975.

Le Guin, Ursula K. *The Dispossessed*. New York: Avon, 1975.

Le Guin, Ursula K. "'Introduction' from Ursula K. Le Guin: *The Hainish Novels and Stories, Volume One*." August 30, 2017. https://www.tor.com/2017/08/30 /introduction-from-ursula-k-le-guin-the-hainish-novels-stories-volume -one/.

McMenamin, Lexi. "Ruth Wilson Gilmore Talks Abolition Geography and Libera- tion." *Teen Vogue*, June 15, 2022. https://www.teenvogue.com/story/ruth -wilson-gilmore-qa.

United Nations. "President Moon Jae-in and BTS at the Sustainable Development Goals Moment | United Nations (English)." September 20, 2021. YouTube video, 18:20. https://www.youtube.com/watch?v=jzptPcPLCnA.

Uyeda, Ray Levy. "How Artists Help Us Believe in a More Just Future." *Mic*, March 15, 2022. https://www.mic.com/impact/movement-protest-art-artists -broobs.

White House. "President Biden and Vice President Harris Welcome BTS to the White House." June 4, 2022. YouTube video, 4:50. https://youtu.be /fHFgJux7MzM.

OUTRO · For Youth — Patty Ahn, Michelle Cho, Vernadette Vicuña Gonzalez, Rani Neutill, Mimi Thi Nguyen, and Yutian Wong

June 13, 2022, marked the nine-year anniversary of BTS's debut. Each year, the group has commemorated their birthday with an annual "FESTA" celebration, a weeklong (sometimes longer) deluge of special content, live performances, and group meeting in which members reflect upon their accomplishments and thank ARMY for their unwavering support. Usually jovial and celebratory in tone, BTS's FESTA dinner unexpectedly took a somber turn in 2022 as members announced that they would be taking a hiatus from all group activities in order to work on themselves individually and pursue solo projects. While the news devastated fans, it also confirmed what many had already suspected. Just days prior, BTS released a three-disc anthology album called *Proof*, which compiled the most iconic and personally meaningful singles for members throughout the years. A departure from their usual Comebacks, which usually come replete with a new slate of music, *Proof* contained only three new songs alongside several previously unreleased demo tracks. Although the lead single, "Yet to Come," signaled that BTS's best years still lay ahead of them, the album felt more like the closing of a chapter in their career than a future-facing pronouncement. Even the music video (MV) for "Yet to Come" paid homage to iconic scenes and backdrops from past music videos rather than offering a fresh visual concept as they normally have done.

Indeed, *Proof* marked a major transition in BTS's musical and personal evolution, ushering in what the group calls "Chapter 2" of the BTS chronicle. Since their 2022 FESTA, members have produced an avalanche of solo content, including j-hope's raucous album *Jack In The Box* (March 2022), featuring a new alter ego ("Jay" with a mullet), whose growling rock god persona closed out the Lollapalooza music festival's main stage (August 2022); Jin's preenlistment ode to ARMY, "The Astronaut," in collaboration with Coldplay (October 2022); RM's genre-bending solo album *Indigo* and multiple collaborations with indie artists (December 2022); Jimin's synth-pop EP *FACE* (March 2023), with its Billboard #1-charting dance track "Like Crazy"; SUGA's studio album *D-Day* (April 2023), released under his hip-hop moniker Agust D, which launched a sold-out US and Asia tour; V's moody R&B and soul-inspired album *Layover* (September 2023), heavily featuring Yeontan and Yeontan's canine stunt double, Rocky; Jung Kook's English-language pop debut, *Golden* (November 2023), delivering radio-friendly, chart-topping hits apropos of a pop prince. The list goes on and on. As typical of their mix of career-defining albums and large-scale events intertwined with intimate moments of humor and companionship, the months after their announcement also saw band members hanging upside down like bats for an aerial yoga class filmed for their variety show *Run BTS!*, growing out their hair, getting matching tattoos, and promoting their solo endeavors on social media and other venues. In other words, despite "taking a break" from being BTS, the members have continued to produce content at a breathless pace, albeit in much more distinct individual styles.

The atomization of BTS's collective identity as a seven-member unit has undeniably changed the shape of ARMY as well. Following BTS's hiatus announcement, fans took to Twitter and Instagram to express melancholy, grief, and even enthusiasm about the members' emancipation from performing as an idol group. While many continue to show their love for the group by way of supporting members' solo careers, others have opted to take a break or move on entirely from the fandom, evidenced in part by the growing number of social media fan accounts indicating that they too have gone "on hiatus." Rather than giving in to declarations that BTS is "over," we see their transition as an invitation into a next phase of reflection on what we have learned, gained, and, in some sense, lost at the so-called end of this historic era of their career.

BTS undertook what would be their last live performance as a group after the announcement of their break. They held a free concert in Busan on October 15, 2022, as part of the city's bid to host the World Expo in 2030. Uncertain of when all seven members might take the stage together again, tens of thousands of ARMY members flocked to South Korea's largest port city to witness the event in person, while millions more logged on to Weverse at odd hours to watch the livestream, crashing the platform's server for most of the show. In addition to performing the three new tracks from *Proof*, including jaw-dropping, never-before-seen choreography for *Run BTS!*, the group treated audiences to a stunning retrospective of some of their most beloved songs— some of which they had not played live in years. Two days later, BTS's oldest member, Jin, formally announced his plan to withdraw his enlistment deferral request, and HYBE made their first unequivocal statement on the certainty that the members would serve. The specter of South Korea's military service requirement has loomed heavily over the fate of BTS's career. Mandatory enlistment has long halted the activities of male entertainers in the country, and BTS had been awaiting a decision by the Military Manpower Administration, at the urging of some members of the National Assembly, on whether they would receive special exemption from military service. However, this announcement put to rest months of debate.[1]

Months later, the BTS: *Yet To Come in Cinemas* concert film released in February 2023 made possible a collective and uneven mourning and celebration of what BTS describes as Chapter 1: Reflection of Youth.[2] The film reprises the Busan concert, edited and remixed for the big screen, with added close-ups and panoramic shots. BTS: *Yet to Come in Cinemas* provided fans not only with an interactive way of experiencing BTS's monumentally significant performance in Busan but a communal space in which to commemorate the end of this important chapter, since, by the time the film entered theaters, Jin was already two months into his service. As with all BTS concerts, some ARMY handed out lovingly assembled gift bags filled with buttons, candies, stickers, photocards, and beaded bracelets. In the dark of the theaters, fans sang along, waved ARMY Bombs, shouted members' names and inside jokes, while some even stood up to dance from their seats. For fans, experiencing the film in the theater was not necessarily about the novelty of seeing the concert on the big screen, but revisiting the joyous rituals that have made being a fan of BTS a hugely meaningful event in our own lives. As we relived the rapture of seeing them perform as "One True 7," a sense of catharsis cut across the theater. The film's temporal distance from the hiatus announcement offered a therapeutic opportunity for fans who were unable to attend the Busan concert, or to see its livestream with other fans. Almost ceremonial in nature, and immersive as an experience, the screening gave us permission to grieve (even if, hopefully, temporarily) a fandom and group formation that we have loved.

Nowhere does the concert film elicit this sense of mourning from the audience more than in BTS's back-to-back performance of "EPILOGUE: YOUNG FOREVER" and "For Youth," a duo of introspective ballads dedicated to ARMY that lead us into the final act of the show. While BTS performed both numbers in their entirety at the Busan concert, BTS: *Yet to Come in Cinemas* takes significant editorial liberties to emotionally reinterpret the songs and guide fans through a nostalgic filter. Released in 2016, "YOUNG FOREVER" has served as an unofficial anthem for ARMY who always sings the chorus in unison with BTS when they perform it live. The song captures the sense of mourning that members felt, even then, for the inevitable end of their careers and relationship with fans, and the accompanying tension between their desire to pursue their dreams and remain frozen in the feeling of youth forever.

> The thundering applause, I can't own it forever
> I tell myself, so shamelessly
> Raise your voice higher
> Even if the attention isn't forever, I'll keep singing
> As today's me, I want eternity
> Forever, I want to be young . . .[3]

The song's lyrics captured many spectators' sentiments, wanting to forestall the end of the group and extend the concert experience's utopian nowness, while plucking it out of time. BTS: Yet to Come in Cinemas accommodates this overwhelming yet paradoxical desire with the well-worn technological tricks of cinema, especially editing and slow motion. The film version of "YOUNG FOREVER" offers a highly truncated remix of the concert version. The members' first verse delivery fades into an instrumental arrangement of the song playing as background music as the members take turns delivering their "Ments"—their reflections on the performance and gratitude to fans. After Jimin wraps up the members' comments, the sounds of ARMY singing the chorus, "Forever, we are young," overtake the soundtrack, as the film transitions into the group's performance of "For Youth," one of three new tracks released on *Proof*. The song opens with a sample of ARMY's surprise performance of "YOUNG FOREVER" for BTS at their 2019 concert at Wembley Stadium. As slow-motion shots of ARMY Bombs from close-up and afar send waves of purple orbs glittering across the screen, the voices of ARMY in Busan blend with the voices of ARMY at Wembley and those of ARMY spectators at the film screening, in a brilliant and purposeful use of sound design to connect past and present moments in BTS and ARMY's symbiotic journey together.

In this moment, it is clear that ARMY's ability to witness itself is just as central to the film as celebrating a beloved spectacle. The film positions ARMY at the emotional climax of the concert as mourning ritual, and the shift changes the object of loss or grief from not only BTS's parasocial relationship with fans, but also the sense of belonging and mass intimacy among ARMY around the globe. This collectivity is conjured by the lyrics of "For Youth," which characterize the BTS-ARMY relationship as a best friendship that stretches eternally into the future: "You're my best friend / For the rest of my life / I wish I could turn back time."[4] The film's deviation from the original concert and livestream (which was viewed by millions of fans who would register the differences) does little to diminish its emotional resonance, because each screening stages a new ritual for a different set of participants. Instead, its privileging of cathartic ritual reinforces the point that BTS members are multiple—as performers, artists, workers, characters, avatars, and more. As the group transforms, so too will ARMY's irreducibly varied investments in BTS, which, like the film's re-created experience, are no less significant for being imaginatively produced. The moments of relief in the midst of tumult—whether experienced in the warm embrace of a theater, as part of the universe of stars in a stadium and its chorus of voices, or through the bonding of fans through social media—offer respites as we continue to struggle for our collective futures.

Notes

1   "BIGHIT Music Confirms BTS to Fulfill Mandatory Military Service (+Kor/ Jpn/Chn)," Weverse, October 17, 2022, https://weverse.io/bts/notice/9371.
2   "Chapter 1" refers to the period from BTS's debut to their 2022 FESTA announcement.
3   BTS, "Epilogue: Young Forever," lyrics translated by Genius, April 19, 2016, https://genius.com/Genius-english-translations-bts-epi-logue-young-forever-english-translation-lyrics.
4   BTS, "For Youth," lyrics translated by Genius, June 10, 2022, https://genius .com/Genius-english-translations-bts-for-youth-english-translation-lyrics.

BANGTAN GLOSSARY

Bangtan Sonyeondan / Bulletproof Boy Scouts (BTS members, stage names, and roles)

RM / KIM NAMJOON: leader, rapper, and lyricist

JIN / KIM SEOKJIN: visual and vocal

SUGA / AGUST D / MIN YOONGI: rapper, producer

J-HOPE / JUNG HOSEOK: rapper, dancer, and dance captain

JIMIN / PARK JIMIN: vocal, dancer

V / KIM TAEHYUNG: vocal, dancer

JUNG KOOK / JEON JUNGKOOK: center, main vocal, dancer, and sub-rapper

K-Pop Fan and Industry Terms

ARMY BOMB: the name of BTS's official light stick

ADORABLE REPRESENTATIVE M.C. FOR YOUTH / A.R.M.Y / ARMY: the official name of BTS's fandom

BANGTAN BOMB: a series of behind-the-scenes videos posted on BTS's YouTube channel, BANGTANTV, of BTS members backstage, rehearsing, preparing for interviews, or engaging in other activities

BANGTANTV: BTS's official YouTube channel

BANGTAN UNIVERSE / BU: an open-ended storyline told across multiple media (music videos, webtoons, liner notes, films, songs, Twitter posts, etc.) featuring BTS members as characters in a time-traveling alternate universe

BIAS: a term referring to one's favorite member of a specific idol group. A "bias wrecker" is the second favorite or refers to the member who makes a fan question who their bias really is. A fan of multiple idol groups may have an "ultimate bias"—that is, a favorite member out of all K-Pop groups.

BIG HIT ENTERTAINMENT: the music label and management company that signed and produced BTS, originally founded by Bang Si-Hyuk; now renamed the HYBE Corporation

BIGHIT MUSIC / BIGHIT: the specific record label that is a subsidiary of HYBE; it currently manages only BTS and Tomorrow X Together, as well as a few solo artists

BORAHAE: a portmanteau coined by BTS member V at a 2016 concert, which merges the Korean words for "violet" (*bora*) and "I love you" (*saranghae*). V explained that the term means "I'll love you until the end of days," since violet is the last color of the rainbow.

COMEBACK: an official release of a new album or song

CONCEPT: the main theme or driving idea of an album that shapes the album's songs, music videos, and photoshoot aesthetics, as well as the costume, hairstyles, and makeup for the group

DEBUT: when a K-Pop artist or group transitions from being a trainee to an idol by releasing an official single or EP

FANCHANT: creations by music labels for songs so fans can sing or chant words and phrases at designated moments during live performances. There are also chants in which fans shout the names of members in a group. The official BTS fanchant consists of the members' birth names: "Kim Namjoon, Kim Seokjin, Min Yoongi, Jung Hoseok, Park Jimin, Kim Taehyung, Jeon Jungkook, BTS!"

FESTA: a virtual event celebrating the anniversary of the group's debut, on June 13, 2013. FESTA begins on June 1 and lasts two weeks. The group releases songs, photos (referred to as "family portraits"), and videos created specifically for the event. Part of the FESTA is an annual birthday party, in which the group reflects on the past year.

HALLYU / KOREAN WAVE: the cultural phenomenon that describes the increased export and rising popularity of South Korean popular culture abroad, beginning in the 1990s, primarily through Korean dramas and K-Pop

HANGEUL: the written alphabet of the Korean language

HYBE CORPORATION / HYBE: the new umbrella corporation that resulted from the restructuring of Big Hit Entertainment in 2021

LIGHT STICK: a handheld electronic device that lights up and is uniquely designed by a K-Pop group for its fandom. Light sticks are often used in concerts to enhance the unity and participation of fans with the onstage act.

MV: an official term for music video. For example, the music video for "Butter" is referred to as "'Butter' Official MV."

OT7: an abbreviation that stands for "One True 7" and refers to all seven members of BTS together. A fan might declare that they do not have a bias and are "OT7," meaning they love all the members equally. Or the term might refer to an image that features all seven members.

RAP LINE: the members of an idol group who take on the primary role of rappers. BTS's Rap Line, consisting of RM, SUGA, and j-hope, is understood to be the best in K-Pop.

ROLES/POSITIONS: official roles or positions—such as leader, center, main (rapper, vocalist, or dancer), lead, or visual—often assigned to members of idol groups

TRAINEE: an aspiring K-Pop artist who undergoes years of grueling dance, vocal, and media training in the hope of being placed in a group and eventually debuting as a K-Pop idol

VISUAL: the designated member of an idol group whose appealing appearance is meant to draw fans and most closely fits the South Korean beauty standard. Jin was recruited specifically as the visual member of BTS.

VOCAL / VOCAL LINE: the members of a K-Pop idol group who take on the main singing roles. In BTS, the Vocal Line consists of Jin, Jimin, V, and Jung Kook.

VLIVE: a South Korean streaming service developed by telecom corporation NAVER that merged with Weverse

WEVERSE: an online platform created by HYBE that enables interaction between artists and fans. Weverse allows artists and fans to post messages, images, and videos and includes subscription services and paid content.

CONTRIBUTORS

ANDREA L. ACOSTA is an assistant professor of media studies at Pitzer College. She works at the intersection of digital media and critical race studies, and her research explores online subcultures—including media fandoms, amateur content producers, and creative communities—as contemporary sites of racial and political work.

PATTY AHN is an associate teaching professor in the Communication Department at the University of California, San Diego. They have published in *Discourse*, *Cinema Journal*, *FlowTV*, and *Periscope* on K-Pop, transnational Asian and Asian American media, television, and popular music. They also have a background in music documentary production and worked at Mnet as a story producer. They are concurrently working on a documentary feature titled *Black Korea*, which examines K-Pop's relationship to Black American music through the historical lens of US militarism and empire in the Korean peninsula, and codirecting a second documentary feature on the culture and history of BTS ARMY with Grace Lee.

CAROLINA ALVES is a digital artist and advertising professional from Brazil. She brings her passion for creativity to the digital world. Throughout her journey, she strives to create captivating and colorful visual experiences by combining art with her love for pop culture. Instagram: @carolfcrart.

INEZ AMIHAN ANDERSON is a student at the UCLA School of Theater, Film, and Television. In their work as a filmmaker, they center marginalized voices in order to explore topics such as gun violence, land injustice in Hawai'i, and the experiences of LGBTQ+ youth. Their bias is Min Yoongi.

ALLISON ANNE GRAY ATIS is a graduate student in broadcast media studies at the University of the Philippines Diliman, specializing in media and gender studies, media culture and practice, postmodernism, and popular culture. Her current research projects are on myths about women in the Filipino female superhero Darna texts (an MA thesis), "queering" Darna, and critical analyses of BTS and ARMY texts and contexts. She works with coaches and consultants in the United States on queer leadership and justice, equity, diversity, and inclusion—leading the efforts on media and communications, creatives, research, and project management—while pursuing scholarly work.

KAINA "KAI" BERNAL is a K-Pop historian focusing on the Latino K-Pop fan experience in the diaspora. Along with her research, she created her K-Pop shop Micheljingelo Archivo, which challenges what Latino representation within K-Pop fandom merch can look like, combining her Mexican heritage with Korean culture.

MUTLU BINARK is a professor in the Department of Radio-Television and Cinema and chair of the division of Informatics and Information Technologies at the Faculty of Communication at Hacettepe University since 2014. She teaches media theories, media sociology, media literacy, and new media culture. Her research interests are digital inclusion and aging and creative content industries and cultural policy. Since 2017, she has been working on cultural policies and the political economy of the creative industries in Asia. She is author of *Cultural Diplomacy and Korean Wave "Hallyu": K-Movies, K-Dramas and K-Pop* (2019). She is a founding member of Alternative Informatics Association in Turkey.

JHEANELLE BROWN is a film curator/programmer, educator, and arts administrator based in Los Angeles whose curatorial practice creates frameworks to explore the boundlessness of Black life in experimental and nonfiction film and video. She is currently special faculty at California Institute of the Arts and curator of film at REDCAT. Her exhibitions and programs have been presented at Art + Practice, Museum of Contemporary Art Los Angeles, the National Museum for African American History and Culture, articule gallery, 18th Street Arts Center, and Project Row Houses, among others. At this moment, she is dreaming about cosmic marronage while trying to remember her terrestrial obligations.

SOPHIA CAI is a curator, arts writer, and lecturer based in Narrm/Melbourne, Australia. Sophia's research interests include Asian art histories, the intersections between contemporary art and craft, and feminist curatorial methodologies and community building as forms of political resistance. Since 2020, Sophia has been researching the connection between fandom and curating as dual practices rooted in care. Instagram: @sophiatron.

MICHELLE CHO is an assistant professor of Korean media and East Asian popular cultures at the University of Toronto. Her published work explores contemporary South Korean genre cinemas, self-reflexivity in South Korean television, digital platforms and K-Pop's politicization, and media histories of race and racialization in K-Pop and its fandoms. She's a frequent commentator on Asian media in outlets ranging from NPR to the CBC, the *LA Times*, the BBC, Al Jazeera, and the *Washington Post*, and she once hosted a public conversation between *Hallyu* stars and BFFs Lee Jung Jae and Jung Woo Sung at the Toronto International Film Festival.

MARIAM ELBA is a research-reporter at ProPublica and teaches news research at the Newmark Graduate School for Journalism at the City University of New York. In her spare time, she is a K-Pop "fanthropologist," looking at how K-Pop fandoms around the world exercise and express identity through fan practices. She has been a BTS ARMY since 2018.

AMEENA FAREEDA is a freelance illustrator and designer, living in Silver Spring, Maryland. She creates work that sheds light on cultural and social experiences of the Asian diaspora. As an Indian–Asian American woman, Ameena believes it is important to create work that enhances voices of the Asian American community. Creating work that sparks a sense of joy and curiosity through everyday nuances is her ultimate goal in illustrating.

VERNADETTE VICUÑA GONZALEZ is a professor of ethnic studies at the University of California, Berkeley. She is the author of *Securing Paradise: Tourism and Militarism in Hawai'i and the Philippines* (Duke University Press, 2013) and *Empire's Mistress, Starring Isabel Rosario Cooper* (Duke University Press, 2021) and coeditor of *Detours: A Decolonial Guide to Hawai'i* (Duke University Press, 2019). She is currently at work on a book about hospitality and its discontents while serving as coeditor of the *Detours* decolonial guide series. Her bias is Jimin, and her bias wrecker is SUGA.

ROSANNA HALL lives in the UK in the fairly historic city of Cambridge. Employee of a software company by day, artist by night, she spends almost all her time outside of work invested in learning about and working to overcome social justice issues. Her bias is Min Yoongi.

DAL YONG JIN is a Distinguished Simon Fraser University Professor. Jin's major research and teaching interests are digital platforms and digital games, globalization and media, transnational cultural studies, and the political economy of media and culture. His books include *Korea's Online Gaming Empire*

(2010), *Digital Platforms, Imperialism and Political Culture* (2015), *New Korean Wave: Transnational Cultural Power in the Age of Social Media* (2016), *Artificial Intelligence in Cultural Production: Critical Perspectives on Digital Platform* (2021), and *Understanding the Korean Wave: Transnational Pop Culture and Digital Technologies* (2023). Jin has been an International Communication Association fellow since May 2022.

JIN YOUNGSUN studied painting at Seoul National University and Pratt Institute Graduate School of Fine Arts in New York and later at Royal College of Art. JIN attained her PhD from Central Saint Martins College of Art and Design, London. She was trained as a fresco mural artist at the École Nationale Supérieure des Beaux-Arts in Paris and at ICCROM Roma, which enabled her to reproduce a Goguryeo tumulus fresco mural for the National Museum of Korea in 1996.

DESPINA KAKOUDAKI is an associate professor of literature at American University and director of the Humanities Lab, an interdisciplinary research center in Washington, DC. She works on film and media studies, cultural studies, literature, and the history of technology. Her book *Anatomy of a Robot: Literature, Cinema, and the Cultural Work of Artificial People* (2014) traces the history and cultural function of the mechanical or constructed person in both premodern and modern cultural contexts. Her work on BTS is part of a new research project on contemporary technologies and global culture.

YUNI KARTIKA is from Malaysia. She is @kartika.co_ on Instagram and has been a freelance embroidery artist since 2019. Her embroidery is based on thread painting, and it is often inspired by recognizable images of BTS.

ALPTEKIN KESKIN received his PhD from Istanbul S. Zaim University, Department of Sociology. His doctoral thesis is titled "K-Pop and Its Reflections in Turkey: A Sociological Analysis of ARMY-BTS Fandomship." His research areas are in cultural studies, music sociology, Korean Wave, fandom, and K-Pop fandom. His dissertation was published in 2022, and he has written several articles on the Korean Wave. He works as an independent researcher.

RACHEL KUO studies race, social movements, media, and technology. She is currently an assistant professor at the University of Illinois, Urbana-Champaign. She is a founding member of the Center for Critical Race and Digital Studies and a cofounder of the Asian American Feminist Collective. Her bias is Jimin.

MARCI KWON is an assistant professor of art and art history at Stanford and codirector of the university's Asian American Art Initiative. Her bias is Yoongi, and her bias wrecker is Taehyung.

COURTNEY LAZORE is a writer, editor, and independent researcher interested in BTS studies, fan studies, media studies, and ethics. She runs her own website at TheBTSEffect.com and is one of the founding members of Bangtan Scholars. Courtney became a K-Pop fan in 2007 and fully joined the ARMY fandom in early 2015. She has a BA in history (East Asia) and an MA in English. She now participates regularly in the BTS research space.

REGINA YUNG LEE is an associate teaching professor with gender, women, and sexuality studies at the University of Washington, Seattle, where she teaches and writes on transnational fan studies, critical feminist data studies, science studies and science fiction, and feminist pedagogies. She is on the editorial team at *Transformative Works and Cultures*.

S. HEIJIN LEE is an assistant professor of women, gender, and sexuality studies at the University of Hawai'i at Mānoa whose research explores the imperial routes of culture and media. In addition to her forthcoming book, *The Geopolitics of Beauty: Transnational Circulations of Plastic Surgery, Pop, and Pleasure*, which maps the convergence of pop culture and plastic surgery coming from South Korea, Lee is coeditor of *Fashion and Beauty in the Time of Asia* (2019) and *Pop Empires: Transnational and Diasporic Flows of India and Korea* (2019). Lee has been featured on National Public Radio's *Code Switch* and *Throughline*, on Korea Society's "K-Pop 101" series, at KCON, and in the *New York Times* discussing beauty, pop, and power.

WONSEOK LEE is a lecturer in Korean studies at Washington University in Saint Louis, where he teaches contemporary Korean popular culture. He earned his doctorate in musicology (emphasis on ethnomusicology) from the Ohio State University in 2023. In his dissertation, titled "K-Pop Resounding: Korean Popular Music beyond Koreanness," Lee examines how the meaning of "K" in "K-Pop" is (re)interpreted by individuals, how K-Pop resounds beyond Koreanness, and eventually what elements constitute the K-Pop phenomenon today.

AMANDA LOVELY (@Maerlyn8_BTS7) is a self-taught digital designer and an avid lover of art. After becoming ARMY in 2020, Amanda found a way to combine her interests through the merging of BTS and famous art from various time periods, movements, mediums, and cultures. In the last three years,

Amanda has created over seven hundred unique art edits, honing her editing skills and expanding her artistic horizons along the way. She loves sharing the edits she makes and the art she uses with ARMY around the world. She currently resides in Pittsburgh, Pennsylvania.

MELODY LYNCH-KIMERY is a doctoral student in literacy, culture, and language education at Indiana University Bloomington. Her research is focused on language policy and planning and how language creates, maintains, and transfers power through politics, social practice, and popular culture. Her current research focuses on K-Pop fans and language use in online spaces and English-language policy in Japanese elementary schools.

MARIA MISON (she/they) is an interdisciplinary artist and queer piece of sunshine from the Philippines. They love playing with play, enabling transformative work through narrative game design, ritual, dance, and embodied healing practices. They collaborated with Mara Andres to create the *Diary of Youth* BTS tarot deck. Mison is yoonjinjoon biased.

NOEL SAJID I. MURAD is an assistant professor in the Ramon V. del Rosario College of Business at De La Salle University (DLSU). He is a holder of the J. Romero and Associates Academic Chair in Advertising and is the thesis coordinator of the Department of Marketing and Advertising. He is completing a PhD in communication at the University of the Philippines Diliman. He earned his master's degree in marketing communications from DLSU and his bachelor's degree in communication arts from the University of Santo Tomas. His research interests include queer studies, popular culture, fandom-based activism, media representations, and marginalized identities.

SARA MURPHY is a freelance writer based in western North Carolina. Her work has appeared in the *New York Times*, Fast Company, Shondaland, and Gastro Obscura, among other publications. She has a PhD in English literature from Columbia University. Her bias is SUGA. She is also STAY (bias: Lee Know), MOA (bias: Beomgyu), and ATINY (bias: Yeosang). Her website is at www.saramurphyphd.com.

RANI NEUTILL is a recipient of a 2022 artist fellowship from the Massachusetts Cultural Council and has taught ethnic American and postcolonial literature at Harvard, Yale, Johns Hopkins, and other institutions. She teaches creative writing and Asian American literature at Tufts University and Emerson College. Her work has appeared in the *New York Times Book Review*, Al Jazeera English, CNN, the *Washington Post*, and the *Los Angeles Review of Books*, among other publications. She is working on a memoir about fractured identity, the nature of care, and her relationship with her mentally ill Bengali immigrant mother.

JOHNNY HUY NGUYỄN is a multidisciplinary dance artist based in unceded Ramaytush Ohlone territory (San Francisco) and is a second-generation Vietnamese American. His physical and often autobiographical works incorporate movement, theater, text, ritual, installation, and humor to interrogate the social, political, and cultural forces that shape us. His vision is to activate dialogue, action, and collective healing through expressions of the body that are raw, vulnerable, and honest. Instagram: johnny.huy.nguyen.

MIMI THI NGUYEN is an associate professor of gender and women's studies at the University of Illinois, Urbana-Champaign. Her first book is *The Gift of Freedom: War, Debt, and Other Refugee Passages* (Duke University Press, 2012), and her second is *The Promise of Beauty* (Duke University Press, 2024). She has also published in *Signs, Camera Obscura, Women and Performance, positions: asia critique, Radical History Review, Funambulist,* and *ArtForum.* Nguyen has made zines since 1991, including *Slander* and the compilation zine *Race Riot.* She is a former *Punk Planet* columnist and *Maximumrocknroll* volunteer.

KARLINA OCTAVIANY is a digital anthropologist and digital communication strategist with experience in the areas of journalism, digital media, knowledge management, and community-driven development. She works as a digital development adviser in Indonesia to support inclusive technology, ethical artificial intelligence, and safe digital access for marginalized communities. Octaviany holds a master of science degree in digital anthropology from University College London and is the founder of Indonesia Voice of Women, which empowers women by providing training in digital literacy to low-income women. She is a hyung line bias and an ultimate SUGA stan.

NYKEAH PARHAM is an AfroAsian researcher and historian based in Los Angeles and Seoul. She is a member of HWAITING! K-Pop Music Research Accelerator through KPK: Kpop Kollective (kpopkollective.com). Currently, she shares her research and opinions on her blog my2baek1.com, Instagram @my2baek1, and podcast, *It Ain't New* (@itaintnewpodcast), educating the masses on AfroAsian history, solidarity, identity, and culture through pop culture and the arts.

STEFANIA PICCIALLI is an independent researcher in media and gender studies. She has written on feminism, social justice, lesbian cinema, literature, and pop culture. Her interest in BTS led her to present her paper "Connect, BTS:

An Example of Innovative Transmedia Branding to Rethink Spatiality and Meaning-Making" at the 2020 ICAMA-KAS International Conference, later published in the *Asia Marketing Journal*. She works as an events officer for a feminist organization and is passionate about enjoying BTS's music, playing the violin, or having a blast in the mosh pit at metal concerts.

RAYMOND SAN DIEGO is an assistant professor of instruction in the Asian American Studies program at Northwestern University. Currently, he is working on *Touchy Subjects*, a book project about Asian Americans, BDSM, and qink of color critique. Published and forthcoming writings can be found in the *Journal of Asian American Studies* and *Love, Knowledge, and Revolution: Decolonizing Directions in Comparative Ethnic Studies*. His bias is Jin.

HANNAH RUTH L. SISON is an assistant professor teaching various media, communication, and production classes at several universities. She is currently pursuing her PhD in media studies at University of the Philippines Diliman. She earned her master's in communication in applied media studies at De La Salle University and graduated with a degree in multimedia arts at College of Saint Benilde. Her research interests include gaming, music, media, and pop culture. She has been a project-based multimedia artist specializing in graphic design, photography, videography, and illustration.

PRERNA SUBRAMANIAN (they/them, she/her) holds a PhD from Queen's University, Canada, and is a graduate educator specializing in cultural studies. Their research is focused on understanding the political-economic geographies of Indian cultural production and narrative logics of mobility with respect to antinormative, marginalized communities. Prerna loves Indian cinema, K-Pop, and trash TV and often uses them as icebreakers for initiating anti-oppressive conversations inside and outside classrooms.

UYENTHI TRAN MYHRE is interested in storytelling and narrative-shifting as strategies for movement and culture work. As a daughter of refugees, she is also a writer and facilitator, and her work explores the intersections of family, feminism, abolition, and beyond. UyenThi lives in Minneapolis, Minnesota, with her partner and their calico cat.

HAVANNAH TRAN is a designer, illustrator, and zine maker based in the greater Los Angeles area of California. She is a member of the Asian Prisoner Support Committee, where she helps run a literature correspondence program in women's prisons in California.

ANDREW TY teaches film and media studies at Ateneo de Manila University and is a PhD candidate in screen studies at La Trobe University. His thesis explores audiovisual musicality and intermedial performance in the music of BTS, focusing on how the delivery of BTS songs in modes other than the purely auditory may be studied as performances of popular aesthetic cosmopolitanisms.

GRACELYNNE WEST is a writer, media maker, and a former educator turned journalist. She is biracial, Black and Filipino, queer and neurodivergent, and finds her home in the Bay Area. She became part of ARMY during the 2020 BE era and has immersed herself in the abolitionist ARMY community. She runs a BTS stan account named "glynnesdrop" on Instagram and frequently writes critically about the K-Pop industry, the fandom, and the commodification of idols. She graduated from UC Berkeley's Graduate School of Journalism in 2022 and hopes to continue writing about stories that matter to the community she serves. She is Yoonminimoni (SUGA, RM, and Jimin) biased but loves all of the members wholeheartedly.

YUTIAN WONG is a professor in the School of Theatre and Dance at San Francisco State University. She is the author of *Choreographing Asian America* (2010), editor of *Contemporary Directions in Asian American Dance* (2016), coeditor of *The Routledge Dance Studies Reader*, 3rd edition (2018), and coeditor of "Dancing in the Aftermath of Anti-Asian Violence" (2023) for the journal *Conversations across the Field of Dance Studies*.

JACLYN ZHOU is a PhD candidate at the University of California, Berkeley, in the Department of Theater, Dance, and Performance Studies and the Berkeley Center for New Media. Her research interests include digital technology, Asian and Asian American pop culture, and fan studies. She is also a member of the Media Education Research Lab, a San Francisco–based art research collective developing quantitative and qualitative methods for measuring and representing diversity in media.

INDEX

James, E. L., 328–29
James, William, 268–69, 276n15
Japan: colonization of Korea by, 266, 300–301; idol industry in, 8–10; J-Pop in, 135; K-Pop and influence of, 8–14; postwar reorganization of, 23n17, 24n25; skinship in, 290; soft masculinity and, 307n5; US relations with, 211–13, 217n29
Jenkins, Henry, 146
j-hope (Jung Hoseok): Bangtan Universe productions and, 123; BE album and, 60; "Black Swan" performance by, 85–86; "Blood Sweat & Tears" and, 68; as BTS member, 1; in Hawai'i, 197; on Hawai'i, 197–98; in HYYH Trilogy, 144, 148–53; "IDOL" (BTS song) and, 37–41; Lollapaloozza performance by, 165–66; masculinity aesthetic and, 316–17; mixtapes by, 50–52; Muslim fans and, 357–59; Rap Line and, 30, 44–54, 164; rap music and, 82; in SAVE ME Graphic Lyrics book, 126–28; skinship and, 290, 295; solo tracks by, 50–51; as street dancer, 2
Jia Zhangke, 155n13
jihwaja jota (Korean expression), 33
Jimin (Park Jimin): Bangtan Universe productions and, 123; BE album and, 60; "Black Swan" performance by, 85–87; "Blood Sweat & Tears" and, 68–69, 73–76; as BTS singer, 1; dancing skills of, 182–83; in fanart, 280; in fan fiction, 352; fashion and luxury branding and, 302, 306–7; gender identity and, 286, 299, 302–7, 318–19; on Hawai'i, 196–98; in HYYH Trilogy, 144, 148–53; "IDOL" (BTS song) and, 37–41; in "I NEED U" (BTS music video), 122–23; on online concerts, 107–8; in SAVE ME Graphic Lyrics book, 126–28; skinship and, 290, 295–96; solo work by, 380; in "Spring Day" music video, 269–71; T-shirt incident, 101; in Vocal Line, 2; Y/N videos and, 328
JIMIN GENDER, 299, 302–7
jimseungdol, 13–14, 301. See also beast idol image
jimusho (Japanese performer management companies), 9, 11

Jin (Kim Seokjin): anti-Asian violence activism and, 210; BE album and, 60, 63; "Blood Sweat & Tears" and, 68, 75–76; as BTS member, 1; in Butterfly Graphic Lyrics book, 129–30; on Hawai'i, 198; HYYH Trilogy and, 144–53; idol status of, 182; military enlistment by, 215, 379–80; on performance, 22n5; sexuality of, 322; skinship and, 290, 295; in "Spring Day" music video, 271–72; as visual idol, 182; in Vocal Line, 2; Y/N videos and, 327–28
Jin, Dal Yong, 10, 92, 95–103
JIN Youngsun, 280
jing (gong), 38
J-Pop, 135, 173
Jung, Carl, 23n10
Jung Kook (Jeon Jungkook): anti-Asian violence and, 213; "Black Swan" performance by, 85–86; "Blood Sweat & Tears" and, 68, 72–73; as BTS member, 1; BTS Universe Story video and, 175; button GIF incident and, 93, 180–88; in fan fiction, 352; FESTA dinner and, 373; as Golden Maknae, 2; in Hawai'i, 198; in HYYH Trilogy, 144, 148–53; "IDOL" (BTS song) and, 37–41; on online concerts, 108; sexuality of, 322; skinship and, 289–90, 294–97; solo work by, 380; in "Spring Day" music video, 272–74
Jung's Map of the Soul (Stein), 19
Justice and Development Party (JDP, Turkey), 255–62
JYP Entertainment (JYPE), 10–11, 22n4, 96

Kaba, Mariame, 372
Kakampinks, 241–51
Kakoudaki, Despina, 92–93, 107–18
Kang, Dredge Byung'chu, 25n36, 301
Kartika, Yuni, 280–81, plate 4
Kartoğlu, Mustafa, 258
"Kay Leni Tayo" ["Let's go for Leni"] (Robredo campaign song), 248–49
KBS World Arabic, 357
"K-Community Challenge," 36
K-Community Festival, 36
K/DA (virtual K-Pop idol group), 23n23, 97, 98

6–8; expansion in Asia by, 211–13; Hawai'i occupation by, 197–98; K-Pop and influence of, 8–14; masculinity in popular culture of, 314–21; McDonald's BTS Meal promotion in, 136–42; South Korean relations with, 79–88, 192–93

United States Information Agency (USIA), 80

untact campaign, BTS and, 17–18

US BTS ARMY (fansite), 109–12

US Indo-Pacific Command, 197–98

US-ROK (Republic of Korea) Joint Security Alliance, 6–7

US service members, K-Pop performances for, 6–7

Uvalde, Texas, school shooting, 277n23

Uyeda, Ray Levy, 374

Uyghur population, Chinese persecution of, 255–56, 365

V (Kim Taehyung): "Black Swan" performance by, 85–86; "Blood Sweat & Tears" and, 68, 73–74; *borahae* (I purple you) coined by, 134, 244, 259–60, 285, 349–50; as BTS member, 1; Filipino ARMY activism and, 246–47; on Hawai'i, 196–98; hip hop and, 46; in HYYH Trilogy, 144–45, 148–53; masculinity and, 318; Muslim fans and, 359; in *RUN* Graphic Lyrics book, 124–25; skinship and, 289–90, 294–96; solo work by, 380; in "Spring Day" music video, 267–71; in Vocal Line, 2

Velveteen Rabbit, The, 296–97

vernacular genres, 174

Vernallis, Carol, 145

Versailles, 87

vidding, 171, 177n4

Vietnam War, 7, 211, 217n26, 268, 276n17, 368–71

Viki platform, 95

virtual idols, 23n23

virtual private networks (VPNs), Indonesian ARMY use of, 234

visual aesthetics: BTS music and, 31; idol body images and, 183–84; K-Pop idols and, 181–88

visual novels, Bangtan Universe production of, 169, 172–78

VIXX (K-Pop idol group), 51

VLIVE app, 24n32, 59, 62, 65n9, 357–58

Vocal Line, 2

Vogue Korea, 280

Vuoskoskui, Joanna K., 58

Wanderer above a Sea of Clouds (Friedrich), 68, 70

Wang, Jackson (Chinese K-Pop idol), 183

Warren G (American rap artist), 46–47

"Warrior's Descendant" (H.O.T. song), 5

Wattpad, 324, 332n2

"We Are Bulletproof, Part 2" (BTS music video), 182

"We are Bulletproof: the Eternal" (BTS music video), 374

Wedance (Korean indie duo), 36

WEi (K-Pop idol group), 36

Weki Meki (K-Pop idol group), 36

West, Gracelynne, 283, plate 12

West, Kanye (American rap artist), 161

Western culture: appropriation of Asian dance by, 81–82; perceptions of K-Pop in, 70–72

West Space and Arts Project Australia, 345, 351–53

Weverse chat platform, 24n32, 65n9, 95, 107, 114–16

"Whalien 52" (BTS song), 350

"What you STILL DON'T KNOW about BTS SPRING DAY MV" (Italian ARMY video), 265, 271–74

White Night Riots, 283

Williams, Linda, 180

Williams, Mollena, 324

Wilson, Anna, 175–76

WINGS (BTS album), 5, 69, 285

women: anti-Asian violence and targeting of, 199–201, 215n2; as BTS fans, 286; Turkish repression of, 254–62; violence against, Turkish protests on, 255–62

Wong, Yutian, 1–22, 79–88, 283–84, 379–83, plate 15